# JEFFERSON DAVIS

*Other Works by*

ROBERT McELROY

•

KENTUCKY IN THE NATION'S HISTORY

THE WINNING OF THE FAR WEST

GROVER CLEVELAND, THE MAN AND THE STATESMAN

LEVI PARSONS MORTON, BANKER, DIPLOMAT AND STATESMAN

THE PATHWAY OF PEACE
(The Sir George Watson Lectures for 1926)

IN THE NAME OF LIBERTY
(An Edition of the Speeches of William Bourke Cockran)

THE REPRESENTATIVE IDEA IN HISTORY
(Tsing Hua Lectures for 1916-1917, in China)

THE UNITED STATES OF AMERICA
(In Benn's Six Penny Series, London)

•

Jefferson Davis

From a Welch portrait painted for the contemplated Confederate Legation in Paris. The portrait was purchased by John Barton Payne, for Professor Hancock of the University of Cincinnati, and has hung on his wall since Reconstruction days. It has not been before reproduced.

# Jefferson Davis

## *The Unreal and the Real*


BY

ROBERT McELROY

Ph.D., LL.D., M.A. and D.Litt. (Oxon), F.R.Hist.S.

*Harold Vyvyan Harmsworth Professor of American History in Oxford University; Fellow of the Queen's College; Sometime Edwards Professor of American History in Princeton University*


VOLUME II


HARPER & BROTHERS PUBLISHERS

*New York and London*

1937

JEFFERSON DAVIS



10/7

FIRST EDITION

I-M

# CONTENTS

VOLUME II

# ILLUSTRATIONS

VOLUME II

JEFFERSON DAVIS

# CHAPTER XIX

## VICKSBURG AND GETTYSBURG

IN THE *Atlantic Monthly* of January, 1863, Mrs. Harriet Beecher Stowe quoted Alexander H. Stephens' address of March 21, 1861, as proof that the Confederacy had been from the beginning an instrument designed to ensure the perpetuation of slavery, and had she known of the forged address of January 5th she would doubtless have used it to strengthen her argument. She also attempted to prove that Lincoln's aim, to maintain the Union, meant "the Union in the sense contemplated by the original framers of it who . . . were from principle opposed to slavery." Both arguments were examples of special pleading, which utterly disregarded the facts. Certainly a Vice-President's impromptu utterance, later repudiated, did not prove her first contention, and as certainly the "original framers" of the Constitution did not attempt to form a Union upon the basis of opposition to slavery. Many of the most influential among them, including Washington himself, owned slaves, and with clear consciences; and one seeks in vain for any considerable body of abolitionists among them. She also declared, in apparent ignorance of the facts, that "the party which makes slavery the chief corner-stone of its edifice finds in England its strongest defenders. The voices that have spoken for us, who contend for liberty, have been few and scattered."

It is interesting to place beside this opinion of "the little woman who made the big war," as Lincoln called Mrs. Stowe, that of Herbert Spencer, who, in a brief essay entitled "Perverted History," wrote: "The vast majority of British subjects were, from the first, Northern sympathizers, although the South was supported by many of the 'ruling class.' I sent my secretary to the British Museum," he added, "to look up the evidence contained in the London daily and weekly press, immediately before the outbreak of the war and immediately after. My remembrance was absolutely verified. Extracts proved that with one accord our journals of all parties—Tory, Whig, Radical—condemned in strong terms the action of the South. . . . Not a single expression of sympathy with the South was discovered. I heard afterwards that in one monthly magazine, *Blackwood's,* there was a dissentient note, and this was considered a disgrace. . . . When twelve of England's chief newspapers, representing all parties, joined in a chorus of condemnation, when no newspaper was found which failed thus to join in reprobating the South—a conclusive proof of sympathetic feeling with the North was given. Yet in the North this conclusive proof was followed by diatribes against our assumed sympathy with the South." On the other hand, as late as March, 1863, the *Atlantic Monthly* spoke of "the sensitiveness of Northern people and statesmen to the open sympathy which the Rebellion received from the leading journals and public men of Great Britain."

Spencer's views, though far too sweeping, were supported, in April, 1863, in a reply from "the women of England" to Mrs. Stowe's charge that their sympathy was with the South. Indignantly they declared: "Wherever it has been possible to learn the feelings of the great masses, no lack of ardent feeling has ever been found in England for the Northern cause." It praised American generosity in the striking words: "We are assured that in the heart of both our nations survives unchanged that kindred regard and respect whose property it is, above other human feelings, to be indestructible. At this hour of your greatest need and direful struggle—at this hour when a pirate from our ports is ravaging your shores, as you believe (albeit erroneously) with our guilty connivance—at this very hour you have come forward with the noblest generosity, and sent us the rich vessel which has brought food to our starving people. The *Griswald* has been your answer to the *Alabama*. It is a magnanimous, a sublime one. . . . Our hearts are with you in unchanging sympathy for your holy cause, in undying abhorrence of slavery, in profound sorrow for your present afflictions, and in earnest faith in the final overthrow of the unrighteous power whose corner-stone is an injustice and a crime."

But, even yet, many English leaders and many important journals refused the crusade theory. "It is little less than a mockery," said the London *Quarterly Review*, "to ask us to believe that the Northerners are fighting solely to extinguish, and the Southerners solely to perpetuate, slavery. There is, however, a small, and we believe, diminishing, set of English men and women who are enthusiastic about Mr. Charles Sumner and Mrs. Beecher Stowe as being enlightened apostles and beneficent philanthropists. We might pause, and ask the admirers of this gifted pair in what philanthropy consists. Does it include self-denial? If so, what sacrifices has either made for the negro? How will their record read by the side of Stonewall Jackson's or Robert Lee's? The cause of the Federal Government is not a crusade," it concluded, but "the unholy dream of universal empire," revived in the West.

So far as England was concerned, financial interests would have welcomed the idea that the Southern states, which contributed to her wealth without rivalling her industries, should become the controlling power on the American continent; but the masses, whatever had been their opinion at the opening of the war, certainly did not favour that idea after Lincoln had made abolition his program, and Davis had refused to follow his example. Therefore, thenceforward, the South steadily lost its hold on England's masses; though the classes continued to express their sympathy.

In contrast with the undoubted success of the Emancipation

Proclamation in its effect upon European psychology, stood its apparent failure so far as the negro race was concerned. If Lincoln had counted upon an uprising of the negroes of the South, and a rush to arms in defence of their freedom offered by the Proclamation, he was disappointed. They showed, as a Philadelphia paper declared in surprise, "a strange aversion to freedom." "It failed to incite a servile insurrection," commented the British *Quarterly Review*, "the only way in which it could possibly produce a practical result; nor is there any reason to believe that a single negro was freed by it. . . . It retained slavery where there was power to end it, and it pretended to sweep it away where there was no power to touch it." Thurlow Weed's paper declared, "He [the slave] has not manifested that alacrity to embrace the opportunity of freedom which we had anticipated. . . . We counted upon insurrections—terrible and widespread—among the servile population, as an inevitable and almost immediate consequence of war between the Government and the secessionists. . . . But the result we anticipated has not come to pass. Slavery, so far from being an element of weakness, has been an element of strength to the rebels. The blacks have failed, except in a few cases, to embrace the opportunities of freedom. They have failed as a class to prove that they very ardently covet a change of circumstances."

Perhaps this hesitation was due to a fear that freedom must mean unequal and unprotected competition with the more advanced, more efficient white race. The able negro, Frederick Douglas, looking backward, later declared that by emancipation his undeveloped race had received "nothing but the dusty road under his feet. He was [still] . . . a slave to the rains of summer and to the frosts of winter. He was turned loose, naked, hungry, and destitute, to the open sky." And this is but a picture of what Davis had always argued against plans for a sudden emancipation before the slaves had been made fit for freedom; and Lincoln had used a similar argument.

Great as was Davis' desire for European recognition, his chief interest continued to lie in the work of the armies. In his message of January 12, 1863, already referred to, he had declared, "In Virginia, their fourth attempt at invasion . . . has met with decisive repulse. Our noble defenders, under the consummate leadership of their general [Robert E. Lee] have again at Fredericksburg inflicted on the forces under General Burnside the like disastrous overthrow as had been previously suffered by the successive invading armies commanded by Generals McDowell, McClellan, and Pope. In the West, obstinate battles have been fought with varying fortunes. . . . At Vicksburg another formidable expedition has been repulsed with considerable loss on our side and severe damage to the assailing forces. On the Atlantic coast the enemy has been unable to gain a footing beyond the protecting shelter of his fleets. . . . The anticipations with which we entered into the contest have now ripened into a conviction which is not only shared with us by the common opinion of neutral nations, but is evidently forcing itself upon our enemies themselves."

Since sending this message, he had continued to meditate upon military problems, and to plan new methods of attack and defence, and on January 29th he telegraphed to General J. C. Pemberton, at Jackson, Mississippi: "Has anything or can anything be done to obstruct the navigation from Yazoo Pass down?" a question calculated to arouse resentment in the breast of General Joseph E. Johnston, now recovered from his wounds, who had been given command of this section with headquarters at Chattanooga. In a later statement prepared for Congress, but never sent, Davis explained the situation as he saw it. Johnston, he says, had been "assigned to . . . the general supervision and control of several armies, each under an immediate commander to whom was entrusted the direct duty of organizing, disciplining, and supplying his own troops. His department included the Districts of Tennessee, Alabama, and Mississippi, with power to command in person wherever he should consider his services most needed, and to transfer troops at discretion. He thus controlled the army under General Bragg in Tennessee, those of Generals Pemberton and Gardner at Vicksburg and Port Hudson, and that of General Forney at Mobile and other points in Alabama. The new assignment was of higher grade and to a more enlarged sphere than the former—embracing within its limits my own home and those of my nearest relatives and friends. It is therefore apparent that I felt no disposition to depreciate the merits of General Johnston, or to deprive him of an opportunity of rendering such conspicuous services as would secure military fame for himself."

Johnston's orders provided that he should "repair in person to any part of said command whenever your presence might be for the time necessary or desirable," but did not specify who was to make the decision. As Commander-in-chief, Davis considered that decision his, while Johnston as the active commander felt that it belonged to him.

The question that presented itself at the moment was whether a railway should be built connecting Port Hudson, Louisiana, and Jackson, Mississippi. "The facility it would afford," wrote Davis to Hon. Edward Sparrow, of Richmond, on February 5, 1863, "for using a reserve either at Vicksburg or at Port Hudson, as the one or the other should be attacked, would be equal in value to ten thousand men. . . . If the requisite supply of iron could be immediately obtained, I should deem it proper that the work should be at once commenced and vigorously pressed to completion." The need was urgent, as Grant was massing his troops opposite Vicksburg, preparatory to another attempt to take the position upon which so much depended—the position which Admiral Farragut and General Williams had vainly assaulted the previous summer, and which, on January 11, 1863, Admiral Porter and General McClernand had partially reduced. To Davis it was "necessary and desirable" for Johnston to move rapidly to the relief of Pemberton, then commanding at Vicksburg, but, realizing Johnston's then state of mind, he proceeded cautiously.

On February 19th he sent him this message: "If circumstances permit, a visit from you might be serviceable to the defence of Vicksburg." To Johnston, a visit to Davis was never convenient, and, convinced that a President's place was in his office, not in the field, he found that circumstances did not permit.

This attitude of defiance was, at the same time, manifest in other commands as well. From Texas, on March 9th, Guy M. Bryan wrote that Sam Houston, an avowed candidate for Governor, was boldly declaring that Davis desired to be made emperor; and that offensive acts of the military "have been done by your instruments. . . . His election would be the verification of the statements of Jack Hamilton to the Lincoln Government of the existence of a strong Union sentiment in Texas, and would be regarded also as evidence of the disposition of Texas to return to the Union. At the outset of the revolution, Houston was known to be an advocate of the Lone Star in preference to the Bars and Stars; recently, he spoke in Houston, and had suspended over him the Lone Star flag only, when a flag of the Confederacy could as easily have been obtained. He fans the flame of discontent in private talks, and will be supported by all of the dissatisfied, disaffected, and disloyal."

The situation was indeed critical, and had Sam Houston known that at that moment Davis was refusing to furnish the Confederate Senate information regarding vessels of war under construction in foreign dockyards, he would doubtless have added that to his charges.

Yet this was true, and from Davis' point of view wholly justifiable. "Contracts made for the construction of vessels of war in foreign countries for the service of the Confederate States," he wrote to Senator C. C. Clay on March 10th, "can only be successfully executed by the maintenance of the utmost secrecy. . . . For these reasons, I do not think it would be consistent with the public interest or the good faith of the Government to furnish the copies you request." The Confederate Senate, therefore, remained uninformed, while Davis, Commander-in-chief of the navy as well as of the army, pressed his plans for the building of Confederate cruisers in foreign dockyards. Funds were provided by the negotiation of a £3,000,000 loan, and before the end of the month Captain Bullock, Mr. Slidell and Monsieur Arman, a member of the *Corps Legislatif* and proprietor of a large shipyard at Bordeaux—held a consultation in Paris, at which Arman renewed the assurances that such vessels of war could be constructed and sent to sea, with the consent of the government. Similar quiet ventures were and had long been in progress in England, the results of which appear in the careers of the Confederate cruisers, and the adjustment of damages in the Geneva award.

While Davis thus worked at his threefold task as head of the government, head of the army, and head of the navy, facing burdens too great for one man, rumours that the current year, 1863, would see the end of the war forced another burden upon him. The one-crop men of the South began planting cotton and tobacco on a large scale, in preparation for reopened world markets. Davis saw that, if unchecked, this movement would mean a shortage of food supplies should these rumours prove groundless, as he had to doubt they would. He therefore, after consultation with his Cabinet and his Congress, issued an address to the people of the Confederate States, urging them to continue to produce chiefly food. "We began this struggle without a single gun afloat," he said, "while the resources of our enemy enabled them to gather fleets which . . . consisted of 427 vessels, measuring 340,036 tons and carrying 3,268 guns." Despite this disparity on the sea, and a corresponding disparity on land, he wrote, the Confederacy has maintained herself and improved her relative position. "At no previous period of the war have our forces been so numerous, so well organized, and so thoroughly disciplined, armed and equipped as at present. . . . Disaster has been the result of their [the enemy's] every effort to turn or to storm Vicksburg and Port Hudson. . . . There is but one danger which the Government of your choice regards with apprehension. . . . If through a confidence in an early peace, which may prove delusive, our fields should be now devoted to the production of cotton and tobacco instead of grain and live stock . . . the consequences may prove serious, if not disastrous." He declared that at the moment the food supply was adequate, but difficult to assemble at the points of greatest need, on account of the lack of adequate transportation facilities. "Is it not a bitter and humiliating reflection," he added, "that those who remain at home, secure from hardship and protected from danger, should be in the enjoyment of abundance, and their slaves also should have a full supply of food, while their sons, brothers, husbands, and fathers are stinted?"

On April 16th Commodore Porter and General Grant succeeded in running their iron-clads and transports past the Vicksburg batteries, and Davis showed his feeling of personal responsibility for the situation by telegraphing to General Pemberton: "Have you tried the use of fire-rafts, to be set adrift from the cove, at upper batteries of Vicksburg, to float down the river when boats are attempting to pass?"

While thus seeking to direct Pemberton, Davis felt little confidence in him, or in Johnston, and longed for a second Lee; for the first Lee was doing wonderful things. On May 2nd, 3rd and 4th, he fought at Chancellorsville the most remarkable of his many battles, "more nearly a flawless battle . . . than any that was ever planned and executed by an American commander," to quote Lee's ablest biographer. With 62,500 men he forced Hooker's army, which at the beginning was two and a half times as large, to recross the Rappahannock, lacking 16,845 men. The Confederate losses were less than half that number; but they included "Stonewall" Jackson, and, as Lee lamented, "any victory would be dear at such a price."

So far, if we judge British opinion by that of *The Times*, the

English leaders remained convinced that the South would win in the end. On Saturday, May 2, 1863, in a leading article, *The Times* editor gravely advised the United States to accept the fact that the Union was divided irreparably. "We have all come to the conclusion [regarding the Revolution] that they had a right to be independent, and it was best they should be. Nor can we escape the inference that the Federals will one day come to the same conclusion with regard to the Southern states." The North "have not succeeded, simply because theirs was only the lust of empire and the rage of disappointment. They have been met by a still stronger passion—the love of independence." But it is necessary to remember that *The Times*, then as now, spoke for the political leaders and the intellectuals, rather than for the vast army of labour and proletariat. And immediate events did little to sustain the cause of independence, as *The Times* interpreted the situation, although occasional successes encouraged the South to hope for real victories. On May 4th, having received from Lee assurances that victory was his, Davis telegraphed, "Giving praise to God for the success with which He has crowned our arms."

But success in the east could not distract him from the obtrusive consciousness that Grant and Porter were slowly closing in upon Vicksburg. "To hold both Vicksburg and Port Hudson," Davis telegraphed Pemberton, on May 7th, "is necessary to our connexion with Trans-Mississippi," since, as everyone knew, they were the only fortified positions he had on the Mississippi River. On the same day, he wrote to his brother Joseph, in evident apology for Johnston's and Pemberton's slowness, "A general, in the full acceptation of the word, is a rare product, scarcely more than one can be expected in a generation, but in this mighty war . . . there is need for half a dozen."

Having vainly sought Johnston's co-operation, Davis now ventured to command it. His view was that Grant should be attacked while still in the interior, by a rapid combination of Johnston's and Pemberton's forces. Only in such a movement could he see a chance of saving Vicksburg. Therefore, on May 9th, he ordered Johnston "to repair in person to Mississippi," but, either misunderstanding the order, or allowing his resentment of Davis' assumption of military superiority to influence him, Johnston proceeded so slowly that it was May 13th before he reached Jackson. Instead of the large army which he expected, he found 5,000 panic-stricken troops, if we may trust the report of his surgeon and companion, Dr. D. W. Yandell.

Johnston immediately telegraphed to the Secretary of War: "The enemy is in force between here and Vicksburg. Communication is cut off. I am too late." He now made every effort to open communications with Pemberton in Vicksburg, urging him to "come upon the enemy's rear at once" and promising co-operation. "General Sherman, with four divisions, is between us at Clinton." Eagerly he demanded reinforcements, but it was now too late for reinforcements to be sent: and Johnston retired from Jackson as the Federal troops appeared "entering on the west." "At three o'clock the Federal flag floated from the dome of the State House," Yandell adds; and Johnston was well on his way toward Canton. "Throughout the night the twinkling stars looked down upon the merciless conflagration, kindled by the enemy."

Davis agreed that Johnston had come "too late," but was far from agreeing with Johnston's reasons for his failure. "When General Grant made his great demonstration of Vicksburg," he told Congress in a message of 1865, "General Johnston failed to perceive its significance, and did not repair to that vital point in his department until ordered from Richmond to do so. He arrived, as he reported, too late. He did not proceed to the headquarters of the forces in the field, but stopped at Jackson and undertook from there to direct the operations of the army, though, as was shown by subsequent events, he was not well informed of the situation."

Davis had intended a quick union of Johnston's and Pemberton's forces and a combined attack upon Grant. "Thus alone," he wrote a few days later, "was a complete victory expected. Now the enemy has made a junction of his forces and got to his river transportation; he has had time to entrench his position and the chances are less favourable for his overthrow."

On May 14th, the day after Johnston's tardy arrival at Jackson, Lee reached Richmond for a conference with Davis concerning military problems, East and West. He spent three days in a careful review of the situation of his own armies and of those under General Johnston, after which he announced the conviction that his own proper course was to invade Pennsylvania, with all available forces, and that Johnston's proper course was to attack Grant, promptly, with such force as he could command. He was, however, unwilling to spare any of his own men to reinforce Johnston. Threatened as he was by Hooker, who lay beyond the Potomac, with an army still twice as great as his own, and by dwindling food supplies, he believed that the only hope of the cause lay in a northward movement which would place him within reach of the rich stores of the Cumberland Valley, draw the enemy away from Richmond, his present objective, and from the Atlantic coast, where railways, indispensable to his armies, were threatened.

Thus Lee pictured the effect of what later became the Gettysburg campaign. At the end of the conference, he retired, satisfied with Davis' approval of his plan, and that of every member of the Cabinet, except Reagan. They were agreed that Johnston's demands for reinforcements must be refused, in view of the larger importance of Lee's contemplated movement. The day following Grant began closing the net which he had so patiently woven about Pemberton, and, with feverish interest, Davis sought means to aid Johnston's relieving armies without weakening those of Lee. On that day he telegraphed the former, who from Jackson had demanded cavalry reinforcements: "Have seen your dispatch of this date. The cavalry mentioned cannot reach you before weeks; others, larger and more practised cavalry, I had hoped could be drawn to you from another part of your department as suggested in telegram some time since. Several of the best infantry regiments if mounted might serve as substitute. . . . Your presence will effect much to inspire confidence and activity. The enemy will probably seek to join his fleet at Warrenton, draw the remaining forces from the camp above Young's Point and prepare for land and water attack on the defences of Vicksburg. If you could unite with Pemberton and attack the enemy in his retrograde movement toward the river, the chances would be much better."

In vain did Johnston watch for signs that Pemberton had attacked the enemy as directed. "Had he struck this blow," writes Yandell, "he would have crushed a large detachment of Grant's army and made a vast stride toward ending the campaign." Possibly. But history deals not with possibilities, but with facts, and the fact was that the "large detachment of Grant's army," instead of being crushed, tightened its hold upon the now doomed city of Vicksburg. On May 22nd, Grant attempted to finish his task, and failed, losing 2,500 men. He did not, however, relax his efforts, and on that same day Davis ventured to ask from General Bragg aid for Johnston. "The vital issue of holding the Mississippi at Vicksburg," he wrote, "is dependent on the success of General Johnston in an attack on the investing force. The intelligence from there is discouraging. Can you aid? If so, and you are without orders from General Johnston, act on your own judgment." As Johnston had expressed the opinion that no troops should be taken from Bragg, he resented this suggestion, though continuing to demand reinforcements, which Davis could not supply. On June 4th, he telegraphed: "My plan is to relieve Vicksburg. My force is far too small for the purpose. Tell me if you can increase it, and how much." To which Davis was forced to reply: "We are too far outnumbered in Virginia to spare any." But, after almost a month of what he considered Johnston's needless procrastination, he sought to bring General E. K. Smith into the picture. "I am convinced," he telegraphed Smith, on July 2, 1863, "that the safety of Vicksburg depends on your prompt and efficient co-operation. As far as practicable I desire you to move your forces to the Mississippi River and command in person operations for the relief of the besieged city." Two days after this dispatch was sent, and before General Smith could act, Pemberton surrendered Vicksburg, with its 31,600 men, 172 cannon, 60,000 muskets, and invaluable stores, thus losing a city for the Confederacy, and making a formidable Commander for the Federal armies.

After the capture of Vicksburg and Port Hudson, a detachment was sent by Grant to take Jackson, and Davis later described his success to Lee, in the words: "One army of the enemy has triumphed by attacking three of ours in detail, at Vicksburg, Port Hudson, and Jackson. General Johnston, after evacuating Jackson, retreated to the east, to the pine woods of Mississippi, and if he has any other plan than that of watching the enemy, it has not been communicated."

It is useless to speculate whether better results would have followed had Johnston accepted Davis' leadership in the Vicksburg campaign; but it is certain that they could not have been worse.

Meanwhile the rumours of pending peace had grown to the proportions of a veritable campaign for peace. On June 12, 1863, Vice-President Stephens had suggested to Davis that he be sent to Washington, to make an attempt to stop the war, upon the basis of state sovereignty. He intimated that a peace mission should not be openly attempted, only "a mission . . . on a minor point," the chief object to be, apparently, incidental. He felt that the great military ability shown by the South during the last two years had prepared the mind of the North to open to such suggestions. Davis had promptly summoned him to Richmond, and commissioned him to go to Washington, to "open the way for future negotiations that might eventually lead to an amicable adjustment," and to secure a body of correspondence which, when published, would open the eyes of the "great mass of the people in the Northern states . . . to the great danger to their own liberties." Mr. Robert Ould, Confederate agent for the exchange of prisoners, accompanied him, but before they reached Newport News, Gettysburg altered the picture, and the Washington Government announced that he would not be received, as "the customary agent and channels are adequate for all needful military communications and conference." Stephens always believed, however, that if General Meade, who led the Federal forces at Gettysburg, in succession to the removed Hooker, had been defeated, "Mr. Lincoln might have been . . . brought to entertain a proposition to treat, not only on the exchange of prisoners, but upon terms of peace, notwithstanding the fall of Vicksburg."

The story of the Gettysburg campaign, and its failure, belongs to the biographer of Lee, not Davis. As commander-in-chief, Davis had approved Lee's plans during the conference of May 14th-17th, but the venture was Lee's, and he never, by word or innuendo, sought to shift the responsibility to Davis, or any member of his Cabinet. To Davis it was only "a bold movement to attempt to transfer hostilities to the north side of the Potomac, by crossing the river and marching into Maryland and Pennsylvania": but Sir Frederick Maurice later declared that to Lee it was a grand, final stroke to end the war: and he blamed Lee for failing to make clear to his chief that this daring manœuvre was the "last throw for victory." "If he [Davis]," wrote that brilliant military critic, "had given his whole mind to strengthening Lee for that end, the campaign of Gettysburg might have had a different issue." But he places no blame upon Davis, for, as he continued, "Lee had not made him understand fully what was in his mind." It seems certain, however, that when, three days before the surrender of Vicksburg, Lee approached Gettysburg, he felt that it was the greatest, if not the last chance of the Confederate cause. He laid his plans without fear, but without over-confidence, knowing the risks and how much depended upon the results. And when on July 3rd, Pickett's survivors staggered back, and Lee knew that his first defeat had come, he accepted the full responsibility. He had planned an invasion of Pennsylvania, he had achieved a colossal defeat, and he did not close his eyes to its meaning.

Davis later thus defined Lee's objective: "The able commander who conducted the campaign in Virginia determined to meet the threatened advance on Richmond, for which the enemy had made long and costly preparations, by forcing their armies to cross the Potomac and fight in defence of their own capital and homes. Transferring the battlefield to their own soil, he succeeded in compelling their rapid retreat from Virginia, and in the hard-fought battle of Gettysburg inflicted such severity of punishment as disabled them from early renewal of the campaign as originally projected. Unfortunately, the communications on which our General relied for receiving his supplies of munitions were interrupted by extraordinary floods which so swelled the Potomac as to render impassable the fords by which his advance had been made, and he was forced to withdraw."

In his Report of July 7th Lee referred to "the unsuccessful issue of our final attack on the enemy in the rear of Gettysburg," and announced that he had withdrawn his army to the west side of the mountains, had paroled fifteen hundred of the six thousand prisoners taken, and had sent the rest to Williamsport, "where they will cross." His summary of the situation appears more intimately in a personal letter to Davis on July 8th, which seems to disprove Sir Frederick Maurice's theory that he considered Gettysburg the last throw made and lost. By that date he was certainly aware, not only that his Pennsylvania campaign had failed, but that Johnston's feeble efforts to save Vicksburg had also failed disastrously on July 4th. Yet he wrote: "I hope that Your Excellency will understand that I am not in the least discouraged, nor that my faith in the protection of an All Merciful Providence, or in the fortitude of this army is at all shaken; but though conscious that the enemy have been much shattered in the recent battle, I am aware that he can be easily reinforced, while no addition can be made to our numbers."

Impatiently he waited for the floods to subside, and allow him to cross to the Virginia shore; but the enemy did not venture to attack him again. On July 12th, he reported to Davis: "The river has now fallen to four feet, and a bridge which is now being constructed, I hope, will be passable tomorrow; should the river continue to subside our communication with the South bank will then be open. Had the late unexpected rise not occurred there would have been no cause for anxiety, as it would have been in my power to recross the Potomac on my first reaching it, without molestation."

Lee had confessed to Davis, in reporting the parole of fifteen hundred of the six thousand prisoners taken at Gettysburg, that "under the late arrangements these paroles will not be regarded." And this proved true, much to Davis' indignation. "The prisoners taken at Gettysburg," he later declared to Congress, ". . . should at once have been returned to our lines on parole, to await exchange. Instead . . . pretexts were instantly sought for holding them in permanent captivity. General orders rapidly succeeded each other from the bureaus at Washington, placing new constructions on an agreement which had given rise to no dispute while we retained the advantage of the number of prisoners."

This indignant denunciation of the Federal pretext for not carrying out the arrangement for parole of prisoners takes on a new reasonableness when we read Grant's explanation: "The prisoners in our hands," he said, "were well fed and were in better condition than when they were captured (a clear admission of Southern helplessness). Our prisoners in the South were ill fed, and would be restored too much exhausted by famine and disease to form a fair set-off against the comparatively vigorous men who would be given in exchange." In short, it was the deliberate policy of the Federal army to require their wounded and ill soldiers in captivity to continue risks as serious as, perhaps more serious than, those of their sound brethren in the line of battle. Sherman once said: "War is hell." And such a policy regarding disabled veterans goes far to justify that opinion.

The result of this policy caused the Southern prisons to be overcrowded, Davis' later explanation being that "a selfish policy which for an indefinite time would leave in captivity their countrymen . . . marked a degree of cold-blooded insensibility which we had not anticipated." The congestion, combined with the Northern policy of making medicines contraband, and the shortage of food, he says, entailed sufferings "not in our power to remove."

His desire to have them removed was indicated in the words which he addressed to the troops defending Richmond from McClellan's attack: "You are fighting for all that is dear to man, and though opposed to a foe who disregards many of the usages of civilized war, your humanity to the wounded and the prisoners is a fit and crowning glory of your valour." In commenting on these noble words, the *Richmond Examiner* declared: "The chivalry and humanity of Jefferson Davis will inevitably ruin the Confederacy."

By all considerations of humanity, and civilized warfare, a wounded or ill soldier, when captured, is in the position of one who has paid the price: and the policy expounded by General Grant explains much of the horror which history ascribes to Andersonville and which in later days was laid to the charge of Jefferson Davis.

## CHAPTER XX

# HABEAS CORPUS

IN THE early days of the Confederacy, Davis had trusted the assurances of France and England, but such difficulties had been placed in his way by the rulers of both countries that he had long since despaired of even-handed justice from either, and his experience with cruiser-building in England had led him to believe that Great Britain, "under professions of neutrality, had become subservient to the designs of the enemy." He had, accordingly, been obliged to recall the commissioners whom he had sent, thus isolating the Confederacy in what he called "the darkest hour of our political existence." Moreover, he was beset with domestic problems, growing ever graver, and was constantly under attack from "unreasonable men who think they have been neglected." He was anxious in regard to the Confederates across the Mississippi, whom the fall of Vicksburg had cut off from their Government in Richmond, and knowing that, under such conditions, his announcement of their right to secede might have dangerous consequences, set himself to prevent such secession.

Furthermore, France had entered upon her daring project, to place Maximilian upon the throne of Mexico, thus giving Napoleon that control of the destinies of an American state which the Monroe Doctrine specifically declared dangerous to America's peace and safety. Davis knew that if the attempt should succeed, the most flattering offers would be made to the people of his own Trans-Mississippi Department. While little inclined to criticize the Mexicans, should they decide to work in with Napoleon, he wished to prevent any part of the territory claimed by the Confederacy from working in with it. "Although preferring our own Government and institutions," he told Congress, ". . . we have no disposition to contest the exercise by them [the Mexicans] of the same right of self-government which we assert for ourselves. If the Mexican people prefer a monarchy to a republic, it is our plain duty cheerfully to acquiesce. . . ."

The disappointment of the Gettysburg campaign had undoubtedly told upon Davis' nerves, and even upon General Lee, who felt deeply the criticism it had brought upon his chief, as well as upon himself and who, with characteristic consideration and fairness to Davis, sought to soothe the latter's resentment of the critics who filled the press with their attacks on both. On July 31, 1863, Lee wrote: "Your note of the 27th, enclosing a slip from the Charleston *Mercury* relative to the battle of Gettysburg is received. I much regret its general censure. . . . I am particularly sorry, however, that from partial information and mere assumption of facts, injustice should be done any officer, and that occasion should be taken to asperse your conduct, who, of all others, are most free of blame. I do not fear that your position in the confidence of the people can be injured by such attacks. . . . The object of the writer and publisher is evidently to cast discredit upon the operations of the Government and those connected with it and thus gratify feelings more to be pitied than envied." And with a magnanimity that never failed, he added: "No blame can be attached to the army for its failure to accomplish what was projected by me. . . . I am alone to blame, in expecting too much of its prowess and valour. It, however, in my opinion, achieved under the guidance of the Most High a general success, though it did not win a victory. I thought at the time that the latter was practicable. I still think if all things could have worked together it would have been accomplished. . . . The unexpected state of the Potomac was our only embarrassment."

A few days later came another communication from General Lee, and one which distressed Davis more than had all the bitter letters and the widespread newspaper abuse—General Lee's resignation from command of the Army of Northern Virginia.

In this letter Lee expressed the hope that the people "may see their duty and perform it. Nothing is wanted but that their fortitude should equal their bravery, to ensure the success of our cause. We must expect reverses, even defeats. They are sent to teach us wisdom and prudence; to call forth greater energies, and to prevent our falling into greater disasters. Our people have only to be true and united, to bear manfully the misfortunes incident to war, and all will come right in the end. The general remedy for the want of success in a military commander," he added, "is his removal. . . . No matter what the ability of the officer, if he loses the confidence of his troops, disaster must sooner or later come. I have been prompted to these reflections more than once since my return from Pennsylvania to propose to Your Excellency the propriety of selecting another commander for this army. I have seen and heard of expressions of discontent in the public journals as the result of the expedition. . . . Success is so necessary to us that nothing should be risked to secure it. I therefore, in all sincerity, request Your Excellency to take measures to supply my place. I do this with the more earnestness because no one is more aware than myself of my inability for the duties of my position. . . . I hope that Your Excellency will attribute my request to the true reason, the desire to serve my country and to do all in my power to ensure the success of her righteous cause. I have no complaints to make of anyone but myself. I have received nothing but kindness from those above me, and the most considerate attention from my comrades and companions in arms. To Your Excellency, I am especially indebted for uniform kindness and consideration. You have done everything in your power to aid me in the work committed to my charge, without omitting anything to promote the general welfare. I pray that your efforts may at length be crowned with success, and that you may long live to enjoy the thanks of a grateful people. . . ."

Washington, under similar conditions, might well have written this letter, since, like Washington, Lee thought not of himself, nor of the dignity of his high command, nor of his place in history. He sought only to serve a cause which to him was above reproach, and offered himself as a sacrifice. Gallantly, but vainly, he tried to hide his distress, a distress which his ragged, barefooted, unpaid soldiers shared: and which one of them, who had read Victor Hugo, expressed with pathetic humour: "We are Lee's 'Misérables.' "

Davis' reply anticipated the verdict of history: Your achievements "will make you and your army the subject of history and the objects of the world's admiration for generations to come." "To ask me to substitute for you some one . . . more fit to command, or who would possess more the confidence of the army and of the reflecting men in the country is to demand from me an impossibility."

General Bragg, too, had suffered his full share of criticism, and when, on September 19 and 20, 1863, he scored a victory against Rosecrans, at Chickamauga—"one of the most brilliant and decisive victories of the war," as Davis called it—but allowed his opponent to retire unharassed to Chattanooga, the criticism was renewed, with increased intensity. Therefore, on October 14th, Davis took occasion to address the Army of Tennessee, which he thanked for its "glorious victory on the field of Chickamauga. When your countrymen," he said, "shall more fully learn the adverse circumstances under which you attacked the enemy—though they cannot be more thankful—they may admire more the gallantry and patriotic devotion which secured your success." "When the war shall have ended, the highest meed of praise will be due, and probably given, to him who has claimed the least for himself in proportion to the service he has rendered, and the bitterest self-reproach which may hereafter haunt the memory of any one will be to him who has allowed selfish aspiration to prevail over a desire for the public good."

With equal staunchness he stood by General Pemberton when more justifiable attacks were made upon him, and by others less conspicuously singled out for press and platform denunciations.

The October number of the *Atlantic Monthly* published an article by Charles Sumner, which shows that the centralization of power against which the states rights men had so often warned their fellow-countrymen, had already begun its work. In describing the war situation, Sumner placed the emphasis not upon the need of victory which he considered certain, but upon the question of "How to treat the rebel states," after their conquest. "Four military Governors have been already appointed [by the Executive]," he wrote, "one for Tennessee, one for South Carolina, one for North Carolina, and the other for Louisiana." "But if this can be done in four states, where is the limit? It may be done in every rebel state, and if not in every other state of the Union, it will be simply because the existence of a valid state Government excludes the exercise of this extraordinary power. But, assuming that, as our arms prevail, it will be done in every rebel state, we shall then have *eleven* military Governors, all receiving their authority from one source, ruling a population amounting to upward of nine millions. And this imperial dominion, indefinite in extent, will also be indefinite in duration. . . . And the whole region which they are called to sway will be a military empire, with all powers, executive, legislative, and even judicial, derived from one man in Washington . . . , military rule . . . in the name of a republic."

This sounded the keynote of the contest soon to come, between the executive and legislative branches of the Federal Government, as to which should rule and readjust a conquered nine millions. To the South, and especially to Davis, it must have appeared futile to debate the treatment of rebels, until it should be certain that they would not prove themselves revolutionists by achieving independence: but to one in a position to follow the division between the Washington Executive and the Federal legislature it was a timely argument.

"In undertaking to create military Governors of states," Sumner added, "we reverse the policy of the Republic, as solemnly declared by Jefferson, and subject the civil to the military authority." And he pointed to the prototype of Lincoln's state Governments, in Cromwell's plan "of parcelling the kingdom into military districts, of which there were eleven—being precisely the number which it is now proposed, under the favour of success, to establish among us." "There is no argument against that early military despotism which may not be urged against any attempt to revive it in our day." Military powers "must necessarily be subordinate to the legislative power in Congress," and "if a new Government is to be supplied, it should be supplied by Congress rather than by the President, and it should be according to the established law rather than according to the mere will of any functionary, to the end that ours may be a Government of laws and not of men."

In this article Sumner, the most learned of the Radical Republicans, threw down the gauntlet to the Executive, introducing a contest from which Lincoln never thereafter escaped, and which almost caused his successor to be removed by impeachment. Bitter as were the critics then harassing Davis, they fell short of the bitterness of those who attacked his great antagonist and ridiculed his homely costume, his simple origin, his not too refined manners. Emerson made the confidential entry in his *Journal*: "You cannot refine Mr. Lincoln, extend his horizon, or clear his judgment; he will not walk dignifiedly through the traditional part of the President of America, but will pop out his head at each railroad station and make a little speech. . . . But this we must be ready for, and let the clown appear, and hug ourselves that we are well off if we have got good nature, honest meaning, and fidelity to public interest, with bad manners."

In November, 1863, Davis sent Ambrose Dudley Mann to Rome, with a letter to Pope Pius IX, to seek to induce him to recognize the Confederacy. Mann presented the letter, and with it a manifesto which Davis had prepared. Both documents were deferential in character, for Davis' early education had given him a lasting feeling of respect for the Church of Rome. The reply was long delayed, and when it came was signed by G. Carl Antonelli and addressed, not to Mann alone, but to "Messrs. A. Dudley Mann, J. M. Mason, and John Slidell, Commissioners of the Confederate States of America." It read as follows:

"Hon. Gentlemen:

"Mr. Sutter has handed me your letter of Nov. 11, with which, in conformity to the instructions of your Government, you have sent me a copy of the Manifesto issued by the most Honourable President, in order that the attention of the Government of the Holy See, to whom, as well as to the other Governments, you have addressed yourselves, might be called to it. The sentiments expressed in the Manifesto, tending as they do to the cessation of the most bloody war, which still rages in your countries, and to the putting an end to the disasters which accompany it, by proceeding to negotiations for peace, being entirely in accordance with the disposition and character of the august head of the Catholic Church, I did not hesitate a moment in bringing it to the notice of the Holy Father. His Holiness, who has been deeply afflicted by the accounts of the frightful carnage of this obstinate struggle, has heard with satisfaction the expressions of the same sentiments. Being the Vicar on earth of that God who is the author of peace, he yearns to see these wraths appeased and peace restored. In proof of this, he wrote to the Archbishops of New York and New Orleans as far back as October 18, 1862, inviting them to exert themselves in bringing about this holy object.

"You may then, Hon. Gentlemen, feel assured that whenever a favourable occasion shall present itself, His Holiness will not fail to avail himself of it, to hasten so desirable a result, and that all nations may be united in the bonds of charity. In acquainting you with this benignant disposition of the Holy Father, I am pleased to declare myself with sentiments of the most distinguished esteem,

"Truly Your Servant,

"G. Carl Antonelli.

"Rome, December 2, 1864.
Messrs. A. Dudley Mann, J. M. Mason, and John Slidell,
(Commissioners of the Confederate States of America)—Paris."

There was little here which even Judah P. Benjamin could interpret as Papal recognition of the Confederacy, save the address to the "commissioners of the Confederate States of America." Even that, however, was a gratification to Davis, smarting under the reiterated and never-silenced charge that he was the leader of a war to perpetuate slavery. He drew greater comfort however from an earlier and more personal letter, written on December 3, 1863, to "The Illustrious and Honourable Jefferson Davis, President of the Confederate States of America," and signed by His Holiness Pope Pius IX himself. This letter was said to have been inspired by Napoleon III, and its meaning was clear to all men, especially to Abraham Lincoln. There was no "so-called" Confederacy in it; and while it only prayed for peace, and did not propose any armed action on the part of the states of the Church, the onus of responsibility for a fratricidal war was distinctly put on the North.

In the end, the Pope granted Mann a personal interview, which the latter described as "one of the most remarkable conferences that ever a foreign representative had with one of the potentates of this earth. . . . I cannot help but think how majestic was the conduct of the Government of the Pontifical States in its bearing towards me as compared with the subterfuges to which some of the European Governments had recourse in order to evade intercourse with our commissioners." The interview, however, failed to bring His Holiness to a more definite declaration in favour of the Confederacy.

On December 7, 1863, the fourth session of the Confederate Congress opened, and the President laid before it his report upon the state of the Union. He expressly informed Congress that "the partiality of Her Britannic Majesty's Government in favour of our enemies" was now being shown by the fact that "the British Government has ordered the seizure in a British port, of two vessels on suspicion that they may have been sold to this Government and may be hereafter armed and equipped in our service, while British subjects are engaged in Ireland by tens of thousands to proceed to the United States for warfare against the Confederacy, in defiance both of the law of nations and of the express terms of the British statutes, and are transported in British ships, without an effort at concealment, to the ports of the United States, there to be armed with rifles imported from Great Britain." England, once so near recognition of the Confederacy, was now, in his opinion, encouraging her subjects to lend their aid to the North.

The message showed also that, with $700,000,000 of paper money in circulation, and gold gone, the financial condition of the Confederacy was as desperate as were its military position and its chance of foreign assistance, and he urged a "restoration of the currency to such a basis as will enable the Department [of War] to purchase necessary supplies in open market." But he urged in vain. Frenzied finance was working its customary wreckage, and no word from Davis could stop or even check it. With the disappearance of gold, prices had reached the absurd heights which always follow such methods. "King Cotton," no longer king, was a prisoner on the plantations of the South where it was practically useless in the quantities existing, the blockade having checked its normal progress towards Europe. For the invading Northern armies it offered valuable plunder; but its usefulness to the South was limited.

To devise a tax system capable of raising an amount necessary to keep the $700,000,000 of paper money stable was rendered almost impossible to Davis, tied as he was to the literal construction of his Constitution. A direct tax might have helped conditions, but the Confederate Constitution, imitating the Federal Constitution, demanded that direct taxes should be apportioned among the states according to population, and taxes on land and on slaves were recognized as direct taxes. In the absence of a census, Davis saw no means of making such an apportionment, and he felt that it would be grossly unfair to impose new taxes upon other kinds of property unless these, the two chief items of wealth, could be also taxed. "A law which should exempt from the burden two-thirds of the property of the country," he said, "would be as unfair to the owners of the remaining third as it would be inadequate to meet the requirements." Thus, enmeshed in his adherence to the Constitution, he looked in vain for an adequate system of taxation which would not violate it. What the Confederacy needed was a Moses, in the shape of a second Alexander Hamilton, to lead it out of the financial wilderness in which it was wandering.

Lincoln's third annual message, delivered on December 8th, showed the happier state of the Federal Government, and was of such a character as to stir to praise even Charles Eliot Norton, who had lamented that the President had turned out to be only a cat "when one wants a Bengal tiger." Now, after reading the message, and the Proclamation transmitted with it, he wrote: "How wise and how admirably timed is his Proclamation. As a state paper its naïveté is wonderful. Lincoln will introduce a new style into state papers. . . . I conceive his character to be on the whole the great net gain from the war." Clearly Lincoln, despite the mad propaganda of enemies bent upon defeating him in the coming presidential election, was gaining the confidence of the North, while Davis, with no re-election campaign to consolidate his supporters, was rapidly losing strength. His gallant followers were affected with a sickening sense of inevitable defeat.

The last letter that we have to President Davis, in the year 1863, was from Governor Vance, of North Carolina, calling attention to a recent intimation, perhaps "meaning very little," from the Federal House of Representatives to the effect that a movement towards negotiations of peace might not be fruitless, and announcing his belief that, in view of public opinion, it was wise to keep open constantly a readiness to negotiate.

Davis, nowever, needed no such intimation. Always he had declared himself ready to negotiate for peace, but with the reservation that it must be peace between two countries, not the surrender of one to the other. In his answer to Governor Vance he wrote, on January 8, 1864:

"We have made three distinct efforts to communicate with the authorities at Washington, and have been invariably unsuccessful." The latest, the mission of Vice-President Stephens, failed before its representative "reached Fortress Monroe on his way to Washington. To attempt again . . . to send commissioners or agents, . . . is to invite insult and contumely, and to subject ourselves to indignity without the slightest chance of being listened to. . . . I cannot recall at this time one instance in which I have failed to announce that our only desire was peace." "Have we not been apprised by that despot [Lincoln] that we can only expect his gracious pardon by emancipating all our slaves, swearing allegiance and obedience to him and his proclamations, and becoming in point of fact the slaves of our own negroes? Can there be in North Carolina one citizen so fallen beneath the dignity of his ancestors as to accept, or to enter into conference on the basis of these terms? . . . I do not believe that the vilest wretch would accept such terms for himself. . . . I have seen no action of that House that does not indicate by a very decided majority the purpose of the enemy to refuse all terms to the South except absolute, unconditional subjugation or extermination. But if it were otherwise, how are we to treat with the House of Representatives? It is with Lincoln alone that we ever could confer, and his own partisans at the North avow unequivocally . . . his purpose . . . to shut out all hope that he would ever treat with us, on any terms. If we will break up our Government, dissolve the Confederacy, disband our armies, emancipate our slaves, take an oath of allegiance binding ourselves to obedience to him, and to disloyalty to our own states, he proposes to pardon us, and not to plunder us of anything more than the property already stolen from us, and such slaves as still remain. In order to render his proposals so insulting as to secure their rejection, he joins to them a promise to support with his army one-tenth of the people of any state who will attempt to set up a government over the other nine tenths."

There had been times in the past when Davis had ventured to listen to the siren voice which whispered peace by negotiation, but henceforth, his program was "peace by proven capacity to maintain independence."

Whatever may be thought of Davis' insistence that the President is the head of the army and navy, of his slavery theories, or even of his ability as an administrative officer, it is certain that he was proving himself a last-ditch leader; and under conditions of the most extreme discouragement. He still believed that the Confederacy might at last win, and a study of the leading British reviews of the period shows that he was not alone in that faith. The London *Quarterly Review*, for example, complimented the Confederacy upon its President's "rare fitness for his post," and declared "the material of the Federal armies to be infinitely less good than it was in 1862, and that is especially the case with the army under Grant." It congratulated the Confederacy upon the possession of "the only two great men (we do not even except Stonewall Jackson) whom the war has produced. . . . It is too late," it adds, ". . . to enter into a disquisition about the merits and qualities of men so well known as President Davis and General Lee. Their abilities and virtues are admitted and appreciated by all who understand what they are and what they have done."

Davis, however, knew that the tide was now running heavily

against him. On January 9, 1864, he warned General Maury, General Joseph E. Johnston, and General Polk, who were operating in the South, that "Admiral Farragut is preparing to attack Mobile, and will try to rush by the forts as was done at New Orleans." He knew that Lee was in desperate need of men and provisions which he could not send, and that the Confederacy was growing relatively weaker each month; but he accepted its weakness as a test of his strength, and hardened his heart against all thoughts of peace by concession.

By the beginning of February, 1864, both Davis and Lee appreciated Lincoln's wisdom in early ridding himself of the restrictions imposed by the writ of *habeas corpus*. Although Davis had already approved an act of the Confederate Congress which limited the embarrassments due to appeals to that ancient common-law privilege, he was conscious that it still operated to weaken conscription: and, in his message of February 3rd, urged Congress to go as far as Lincoln had gone in relieving the Administration of this embarrassment. "It has been our cherished hope," he said, ". . . that we might exhibit . . . the proud spectacle of a people . . . achieving their liberty and independence . . . without . . . sacrifice of civil to military necessity." The recent use made of appeals to the writ of *habeas corpus*, however, he explained, had greatly weakened the army, and was a serious menace to the success of the cause. "Must the independence for which we are contending . . . be put in peril for the sake of conformity to the technicalities of the law?" To this question there was but one answer, not easy for him to make, but necessary: "I therefore respectfully recommend that the privileges of the writ of *habeas corpus* be suspended." As he had been careful to recognize that suspension could only be made by Congress, his recommendation was promptly accepted, and the courts as promptly recognized the action as within the powers conferred by the Constitution upon the Congress of the Confederate States.

There were still pending, however, certain cases relating to men who had tried to escape conscription by demanding the old privilege, and Davis assured Congress that so long as the privilege is acknowledged, "every judge has the power to issue a writ. . . . And if one [judge] manifests more facility in discharging petitioners than his associates the application is made to him, however remote he may be. In one instance a general on the eve of an important movement, when every man was needed, was embarrassed by the command of a judge—more than two hundred miles distant—to bring, if in his custody, or to send if in the custody of another, . . . some deserters who had been arrested and returned to his command. In another, the commandant . . . who had a conscript in camp, was commanded to bring him before a judge more than a hundred miles distant, although there was a judge competent to hear and determine the cause resident in the place where the writ was executed. He consulted eminent counsel and was advised that, from the known opinions of the judge selected, the conscript would undoubtedly be released, and the officer was therefore advised to discharge him at once and return the facts informally; that such a return was not technically sufficient, but would be accepted as accomplishing the purpose of the writ. He acted on the advice . . . and was immediately summoned by the judge to show cause why he [the officer] should not be attached for contempt in making an insufficient return, and [he] was compelled to leave his command at a time when his services were pressingly needed by the Government and travel over a hundred miles . . . to purge himself of the technical contempt."

Thus, Davis pointed out, "if a single judge, in any state, should hold the [Conscription] Act to be unconstitutional, it is easy to foresee that that state will either furnish no soldiers from this class [conscripts], or furnish them only when too late for the pressing need of the country. [For] every application will be made to that particular judge, and he will discharge the petitioners."

The law's setting aside the privilege of the writ of *habeas corpus* had stopped this extraordinary process; but Davis now found himself embarrassed by another Constitutional provision. Clause 4 of Section 9, Article I, of the Confederate Constitution definitely forbade the passage of an *ex post facto* law. The pending cases had arisen before the writ had been suspended. How, then, should they be settled? On March 7th he announced to the Hon. Thomas Bragg of Raleigh, North Carolina, that he was willing to respect a decision of Judge Parsons, who had just released a conscript, on the ground that "the case was before him prior to the passage of the law suspending the writ," but that, while the pending case of appeal, presented before the writ had been suspended, must be decided in favour of the defendant, in all subsequent cases the writ should not serve to secure the release of the deserter. He had been compelled to this course by the knowledge that the unity and enthusiasm which had marked the early days of the war had been "impaired by the long continuance and magnitude of the struggle," and by the fact that there were now in the Confederacy men who were advocating "peace on the terms of submission and the abolition of slavery."

Although the chief argument which Davis had advanced in favour of setting aside the *habeas corpus* Act had been that it enabled men to avoid military conscription, he knew that the vast majority of the Southern men of military age were more than willing to fight, if allowed to do so in their own way. What that way was, in some cases, was brought home to him by various letters descriptive of what were dangerously like "guerilla bands." On February 15th, for example, V. Wall wrote of the plight of a number of men, some "exempt from conscription" by virtue of age or disability, and others unwilling to leave their families for the regular service. "In the regular service," he argued, "their pay would not buy bread alone for their children. Driven almost to desperation, they have formed themselves into small bands to harass and plunder the enemy. If taken, they are shot like wild beasts—in turn they seldom take prisoners. To place them in a position more safe and honourable to themselves and useful to our country is my object in writing." These bands he asked Davis to use for war purposes, in the hope "that Our Heavenly Father may make you the chief instrument in securing our independence." A few weeks later J. W. Tucker wrote of a political organization, enumerated by states and aggregating 490,000 men, "the most perfect and the most secret the world has known," which was eager to be used by the Confederacy to defend "states rights and free representative government," by means which he outlined and which had little resemblance to what is known as civilized warfare.

To Davis' "machinely crammed" military mind such suggestions were abhorrent. He would carry on the war under the rules of organized armies and had no idea of becoming the chief of disorganized land pirates.

On March 9, 1864, Lincoln had commissioned Grant Lieutenant-General. "In my first interview with Mr. Lincoln alone," wrote the latter in his *Memoirs*, "he stated to me that he never professed to be a military man, or to know how campaigns should be conducted, and never wanted to interfere in them: but that procrastination on the part of commanders, and the pressure from the people at the North and Congress, which was always with him, forced him into issuing his series of 'Military Orders'—one, two, three, etc. He did not know but they were all wrong, and did know that some of them were. All he wanted or had ever wanted was some one who would take the responsibility and act." He was content, to quote his own characteristic simile, to be a helper. "As we say out West, if a man can't skin, he must hold a leg while somebody else does."

General Halleck warned the new lieutenant-general not to let Lincoln know his plans, if they required secrecy, as "He is so kind-hearted, so averse to refusing anything asked of him, that some friend would be sure to get from him all he knew." Grant took this advice literally, and kept his plans not only from the

President, but from Halleck and the Secretary of War as well. He promptly took control of the Army of the Potomac, and thereafter was allowed to make his military decisions, unhampered by the will of his Constitutional commander-in-chief. He established headquarters at Culpepper, and began preparations for an early campaign. "My general plan," he later wrote, ". . . was to concentrate all the force possible against the Confederate armies in the field. There were but two such . . . east of the Mississippi River and facing north. The Army of Northern Virginia, General Robert E. Lee commanding, was on the south bank of the Rapidan, confronting the Army of the Potomac; the second, under General Joseph E. Johnston, was at Dalton, Georgia, opposed to Sherman, who was still at Chattanooga." Against these he directed a dogged determination which partook of genius; and Lincoln watched, with the eager hope that he would soon bring the long contest to a close by an overwhelming victory.

On April 16th Davis dispatched General Pendleton to present to General Joseph E. Johnston a detailed plan for the operations of the Army of Tennessee. After a conference, Pendleton reported: "In view of the facts exhibited and reasons urged, I did not feel justified in pertinaciously advocating the particular move into Tennessee, and could but admit that the mode of attack preferred by General Johnston might prove on the whole most effective." In this opinion, however, he soon found himself mistaken; or perhaps it would be better to say that Davis soon received news which proved its fallacy. He later complained that, despite prompt and adequate reinforcements, "Johnston made no attempt to advance. . . . The enemy commenced advancing in May and General Johnston began retreating, . . . until he was finally brought to the suburbs of Atlanta." Davis was then convinced that Johnston planned leaving Atlanta under the guard of the Georgia militia and moving his own army into the field, which "was regarded as conclusive that Atlanta was to be given up without a battle."

It has long been a matter of controversy whether Johnston was guilty of the charges against him. But no one has ever adversely criticized the manner in which Lee handled his forces, as he faced his able opponent in the last phase of the great conflict. While daily more conscious of the surpassing generalship of Lee, Grant, cautious, secretive, and supremely able, was encouraged by the now obtrusive fact that the enemy could get no more recruits, and were losing at least a regiment a day by desertions alone. "Every able-bodied man between the ages of eighteen and forty-five," as he later recorded in his *Memoirs*, "had been conscripted, while Junior Reserves had been formed out of boys from fourteen to eighteen, and Senior Reserves of men from forty-five to sixty." The South, as one critic wrote, was "robbing the cradle and the grave" to supply Lee's army.

The military situation was now so grave that a determined effort was made to induce Davis to arm the negroes, and employ them as soldiers; but he still refused to countenance such a plan. Lincoln therefore had a monopoly of this source of supply and in March, being convinced that the outcome of the war depended upon the handling of the negro problem, had sought to make it more effective by advocating the franchise for the more intelligent negroes, and for those who served in the Federal armies.

Davis, on the other hand, while fully conscious of the man power which a similar course would give to the South, still insisted that the states alone had the right to control slavery, and when his old West Point friend, the fighting bishop—General Polk—asked how he should deal with captured negro soldiers, his answer was, "If the negro soldiers are escaped slaves, they should be held safely for recovery by their owners. If otherwise, inform me." And again, on April 30th, he telegraphed Polk: "Captured slaves should be returned to their masters on proof and payment of charges. Until such time, they might be usefully employed on public works." He agreed with Ould, who had recently declared that he and his fellow-Southerners would "die in the last ditch" before giving up the right to send slaves back to slavery as property recaptured.

Immediately after this dispatch was sent, Davis returned to the White House of the Confederacy to face a domestic tragedy. His little son, Joseph, had fallen over the iron balustrade in the entrance hall, and had been dashed to death on the stones below.

On May 2nd Davis sent to Congress a brief message which contained the bitter acknowledgment that the Confederacy was isolated diplomatically, and must rely solely upon its armies, but gallantly he struggled to believe that she would yet succeed, despite the "hundred and thirty, forty, or fifty thousand coloured persons now serving . . . as soldiers, seamen, and labourers" in the Federal forces. "A naval attack on Mobile," he pointed out, "was so successfully repulsed at the outer works that the attempt was abandoned, and the nine months' seige of Charleston has been practically suspended. . . . The armies in northern Georgia and in northern Virginia still oppose with unshaken front a formidable barrier to the progress of the invader, and our generals, armies and people are animated by cheerful confidence." He expressed satisfaction that the Treasury, the second line of defence, showed a reduction of the $700,000,000 of treasury notes mentioned in his late message to about $230,000,000; and emphasized the dangers of inflation by urging Congress to forbid any increase in that volume.

On May 13th he telegraphed to Lee: "Every organized brigade in the Department of S. Carolina and Georgia has been ordered on and is supposed to have reached Petersburg. General Bragg estimates the cavalry and infantry left on the sea coast of those states as not more than a brigade of each. It may be that something more can be drawn from Florida (and possibly elsewhere) when circumstances there are more fully ascertained, and the reserves are so organized as to be available for service." And again on May 15th: "Have directed all organized infantry and cavalry to come forward from the Department of South Carolina, Georgia, and part of Florida. General Beauregard is at Drewry's Bluff. After a long conference yesterday, he agreed to bring forward Whiting from Petersburg with two brigades of infantry, two regiments of cavalry, and several batteries of light artillery, and then with the troops on the north side of the James River, in the defenses of Richmond, to attack the enemy. I hope we can cut his now extended line, and prevent him from getting back to his base, and beat him so as to prevent any further trouble from that source. If this hope be fulfilled, we can then reinforce you and enable you to close your brilliant campaign with a complete victory."

## CHAPTER XXI

# FUTILE PEACE MOVEMENTS

AS LEE'S devotion to the cause was whole-hearted, so was Davis' devotion unmarred by thought of self. He was ready, and felt that every Southern man should be ready, to make any sacrifice to help towards independence. "I ask all for the cause," he said to B. H. Hill, Senator from Georgia, "nothing, nothing for myself." It is equally true that Lincoln wanted nothing for himself, though his contemporaries seemed often ignorant of the fact and persistently represented him as an enemy to peace, since like Davis, he set his face against a peace by negotiation, knowing that the differences between the North and the South were too basic to be so solved. From time to time, however, unofficial advocates of this method to end the war endeavoured to obtain his co-operation. The most famous of such incidents occurred the following July.

Horace Greeley was at that time the leader of a group of Union men who had lost patience with Lincoln's patience. They felt that the President was neglecting what they considered the best road to speedy and honourable peace. They knew that Stephens was the leader of a Southern group which was criticizing Davis for the same fault: and the *New York Tribune*, which in those days was Horace Greeley, freely lent its columns to their criticisms. Early in the month, one of Greeley's satellites, William Cornell Jewett, who claimed close contacts with leaders both in the North and in the South, wrote to Greeley from Niagara, intimating that he was the medium of certain peace proposals from Davis' Government. He claimed that one George N. Sanders, of Kentucky, waiting at the moment on the Canadian side of the Falls, had privately assured him that "two ambassadors of Davis & Co. are now in Canada with full and complete powers for peace. . . . Mr. Sanders requests that you come immediately . . . or, if you will send the President's protection for him and two friends, they will come and meet you. He says the whole matter can be consummated by me, you, them, and President Lincoln." After a little urging from Jewett, Greeley communicated what he believed to be the facts to Lincoln, confessed doubts of the commissioner's "full powers," but urged that the suggestion be followed. He ventured to reprove Lincoln for having refused to receive Stephens' late mission of peace: and lectured him upon the widespread desire for peace which, he said, pervaded both North and South, warning him of impending insurrection at the North, and a defeat in the coming election.

Lincoln had already received many evidences of the fact that Davis' irreducible demand was independence, but Greeley's influence was great and he decided to allow the latter to discover for himself how impossible of success was negotiation under such conditions. He therefore answered: "If you can find any person, anywhere, professing to have any proposition of Jefferson Davis' in writing, for peace, embracing the restoration of the Union and the abandonment of slavery, whatever else it embraces, say to him that he may come to me with you, and that if he really brings such proposition he shall at least have safe conduct with the paper (and without publicity, if he chooses) to the point where you shall meet him. The same if there be two or more persons." Somewhat astonished at Lincoln's ready acceptance of the proposition, Greeley temporized, while he looked further into the evidence, and on July 13th wrote to Lincoln: "I now have information, on which I can rely, that two persons, duly commissioned and empowered to negotiate for peace, are at this moment not far from Niagara Falls in Canada, and desirous of conferring with yourself, or with such persons as you may appoint and empower to treat with them. Their names (given in confidence) are Hon. Clement C. Clay of Alabama, and Hon. Jacob Thompson of Mississippi."

Still doubting the authority of these men to offer, on Davis' behalf, terms short of independence, Lincoln now sent Major John Hay to Greeley's office with a letter which declared, under date July 15, 1864: "I not only intend a sincere effort for peace, but I intend that you shall be a personal witness that it is made." This letter Hay presented to Greeley on the morning of the 16th, with the announcement that the President wished Greeley to go to Niagara Falls, to prove in person his assertion, that "I now have information, on which I can rely, that two persons, duly commissioned and empowered to negotiate for peace, are at this moment not far from Niagara Falls."

Reluctantly, Greeley made the journey, carrying with him a safe conduct produced by Hay, which gave to Clement C. Clay, Jacob Thompson, James P. Holcombe, and George N. Sanders the right to come to Washington in company with Horace Greeley, exempt from annoyance of any kind. He found what Lincoln had expected him to find, that the gentlemen in question had no authority from President Davis, or from the Confederate Government. They claimed, however, that they knew the views of Davis' Government, and could easily get credentials, which facts being reported to Lincoln, he sent Hay to Niagara with the following letter to Greeley:

"Executive Mansion,
Washington, *July 18, 1864.*

"To Whom it may Concern: Any proposition which embraces the restoration of peace, the integrity of the whole Union, and the abandonment of slavery, and which comes by and with an authority that can control the armies now at war against the United States, will be received and considered by the Executive Government of the United States, and will be met by liberal terms on other substantial and collateral points, and the bearer or bearers thereof shall have safe conduct both ways.

ABRAHAM LINCOLN."

This paper Greeley and Hay delivered to Mr. Holcombe, his associates not being present, and Greeley returned to New York, to suggest that Lincoln, in some undefined way, had been responsible for the fiasco: while his co-worker, Jewett, gave to the press such items as he considered it advisable to publish.

After receiving Hay's full report, Lincoln dismissed the incident as closed: but on July 25th sent to Abram Wakeman, a Republican politician, a summary of this abortive effort at peace: "The men of the South recently (and perhaps still) at Niagara Falls tell us distinctly that they *are* in the confidential employment of the rebellion; and they tell us as distinctly that they are *not* empowered to offer terms of peace. Does any one doubt that what they *are* empowered to do is to assist in selecting and arranging a candidate and a platform for the Chicago convention?" This was an unwarranted insinuation. The President of the Confederacy was giving no attention to the selection of a Democratic opponent to President Lincoln, but the idea that the Niagara conference was part of such a plan remained in Lincoln's mind, as he awaited the verdict of the coming election, conscious of the danger that the peace party might secure McClellan's election; but resolved, in that event to co-operate with him, to the end that the Union might be saved, whatever else were lost.

Had Lincoln given full credence to the reports of two other advocates of peace by negotiation, James F. Jaquess and J. R. Gilmore, whom he had reluctantly allowed to go to Richmond, he would have been confirmed in the view that Davis would not accept any terms which he himself felt free to offer. But he would have been less confident that Davis was working to make McClellan President. The history of Jaquess' mission, as he proudly called it, and of his report, is as follows:

In May, 1863, James F. Jaquess, D.D., a Methodist minister, and colonel of the 73rd Illinois Volunteers, wrote to General James A. Garfield that the Methodist Church, South, was weary of the war and could, in his opinion, be used to bring Jefferson Davis to accept terms of peace. "God has laid the duty upon me," he explained, "of presenting these facts to the proper authorities. Therefore I will go into the Southern Confederacy and return within ninety days with terms of peace that the Government will accept." This extraordinary offer was sent on to Lincoln, with the support of Jaquess' superior commander, who felt that it might be worth consideration, and Mr. Lincoln, though having little faith in such a project, was so bombarded with letters and appeals that he at last announced that Jaquess should be allowed, without official character, to try his experiment. Jaquess then enlisted the co-operation of J. R. Gilmore, a lecturer and writer, who employed the *nom de plume* of "Edmund Kirke," and together, they started south on July 16th, the day on which Lincoln sent Greeley to Niagara.

So far the facts are beyond question, but for the rest of the story we must depend largely upon the writings of Gilmore, which have been called by some investigators, "pure fiction." The main facts of his story, however, were told so accurately that Nicolay and Hay, after comparing it with Benjamin's account, considered it "substantially correct."

"Mounted on two raw-boned relics of Sheridan's great raid," wrote Gilmore, "and armed with a letter to Jeff Davis, a white cambric handkerchief tied to a short stick, and an honest face—the last was the colonel's—we rode up to the rebel lines." The rest of the journey was made in a hack, driven by a negro, who explained that he was the only remaining one of 1,200 slaves formerly owned by his master. When asked what had become of the 1,199, he replied, "De res' all stole, massa—stole by you Yankees."

Although in their note to the Secretary of State Jaquess and

Gilmore had frankly admitted that they had no official character or authority, Benjamin arranged an interview for them in his office. On the Secretary's right, says Gilmore, "sat a spare, thin-featured man, with iron-grey hair and beard, and a clear, grey eye, full of life and vigour. He had a broad, massive forehead, and a mouth and chin denoting great energy and strength of will. His face was emaciated and much wrinkled, but his features were good, especially his eyes—though one of them bore a scar, apparently made by some sharp instrument. He wore a suit of greyish-brown, evidently of foreign manufacture, and, as he rose, I saw that he was about five feet ten inches high, with a slight stoop in the shoulders. His manners were simple, easy, and quite fascinating; and there was an indescribable charm in his voice as he extended his hand and said to us—'I am glad to see you, gentlemen. You are very welcome to Richmond.'"

Jaquess and Gilmore opened the discussion with the remark that they understood that "the dispute between your Government and ours is narrowed down to this: Union or disunion." Davis replied: "Yes, or, to put it in other words, independence or subjugation." The envoys then suggested a plebiscite upon two propositions: "Peace with disunion and Southern independence, as your proposition—and peace with Union, emancipation, no confiscation, and universal amnesty, as ours." Davis declared such a plan "altogether impracticable. If the South was only one state, it might work; but as it is, if one Southern state objected to emancipation, it would nullify the whole thing; for you are aware that the people of Virginia cannot vote slavery out of South Carolina. . . ."

The envoys then asked Davis to state how peace could be brought about. "In a very simple way," Davis replied. "Withdraw your armies from our territory and peace will come of itself. . . . You deny to us what you exact for yourselves—the right of self-government. . . . I desire peace as much as you do, I deplore bloodshed as much as you do, but I feel that not one drop of the blood shed in this war is on my hands. I can look up to my God and say this. I tried with all my power to avert this war. I saw it coming, and for twelve years I worked night and day to prevent it, but I could not. The North was mad and blind; it would not let us govern ourselves, and so the war came, and now it must go on till the last man of this generation falls in his tracks, and his children seize his musket and fight his battle, unless you acknowledge our right to self-government. We are not fighting for slavery. We are fighting for independence and that, or extermination, we will have."

Colonel Jaquess ventured to point out that "Grant has shut you up in Richmond," and that "Sherman is before Atlanta." Davis replied: "We are not exactly shut up in Richmond. If your papers tell the truth, it is your capital that is in danger, not ours. Some weeks ago Grant crossed the Rapidan to whip Lee and take Richmond. Lee drove him in the first battle, and then Grant executed what your people call a 'brilliant flank movement,' and fought Lee again. Lee drove him a second time, and then Grant made another 'flank movement'; and so they kept on—Lee whipping, and Grant flanking—until Grant got where he is now. And what is the net result? Grant has lost seventy-five or eighty thousand men—more than Lee had at the outset—and is no nearer taking Richmond than at first; and Lee, whose front has never been broken, holds him completely in check, and has men enough to spare to invade Maryland and threaten Washington."

To the argument that in the end the majority, which was with the North, must rule, Davis answered, "I am not so sure of that. Neither current events nor history shows that the majority rules or ever did rule. The contrary, I think, is true. . . . The man who should go before the Southern people . . . with any proposition which implied that the North was to have a voice in determining the domestic relations of the South could not live here a day. He would be hanged on the first tree, without judge or jury."

Here Benjamin intervened to ask whether, in offering emancipation, no confiscation, and universal amnesty, they were suggesting what Lincoln had authorized. "No, sir," the envoy replied. "Mr. Lincoln did not authorize me to offer you any terms. But I think both he and the Northern people . . . would assent to some such conditions."

At this point, Davis exlaimed: "Amnesty applies to criminals. We have committed no crime. Confiscation is of no account unless you can enforce it. And emancipation! You have already emancipated nearly two millions of our slaves; and if you will take care of them, you may emancipate the rest. I had a few when the war began. I was of some use to them; they never were of any to me. Against their will you emancipated them, and you may emancipate every negro in the Confederacy, but we will be free. We will govern ourselves. We will do it, if we have to see every Southern plantation sacked and every Southern city in flames. Say to Mr. Lincoln for me," he added, "that I shall at any time be pleased to receive proposals for peace on the basis of our independence. It will be useless to approach me with any other."

When the two Federals returned to Washington they reported that Davis was the power which held the Confederacy to its hard task of unequal warfare. "Without him the rebellion would crumble in a day; with him it may continue to be, even in disaster, a power that will tax the whole energy and resources of the Union. . . . There can be no peace so long as Mr. Davis controls the South. Ignoring slavery, he himself states the issue—the only issue with him—Union or disunion."

With this and the former abortive movements in memory, the peace party of the North continued to clamour for Lincoln's defeat, and to hail McClellan as the leader born to replace him. Davis showed an entire lack of interest in the question. He did not regard McClellan as a peace candidate in the sense in which he understood peace—that is a proper, friendly relation between independent nations. He was convinced that, whatever the outcome of the election, the only hope of Southern independence rested with its armies, and refused to devote his time to calculations of Lincoln's chances or McClellan's chances. His business was to work for military success, upon which alone he believed the issue depended.

For weeks Davis had watched General Johnston with growing concern. He knew him to be able, but felt that he showed a strange unwillingness to fight, even when numbers were approximately even. He had suggested his fears to Lee and to the members of his Cabinet, and had found that they shared them. Confirmed in his opinion, he then asked Johnston the question: "Will you surrender Atlanta without a fight?" Receiving what he considered an evasive answer, he consulted Lee upon the question of removing Johnston from command, and putting Hood in his place. Lee's reply recognized that the decision rested with the commander-in-chief: "It is a grievous thing to change the commander of an army situated as is that of the Tennessee. Still, if necessary, it ought to be done. I know nothing of the necessity. I had hoped that Johnston was strong enough to deliver battle. . . . If Johnston abandons Atlanta, I suppose he will fall back on Augusta. This loses us Mississippi and communication with Trans-Mississippi. . . . Hood is a good fighter, very industrious on the battlefield, careless off, and I have had no opportunity of judging of his action when the whole responsibility rested upon him. I have a high opinion of his gallantry, earnestness, and zeal. General Hardee has more experience in managing an army. May God give you wisdom to decide in this momentous matter."

On July 17th, having again consulted his Cabinet, all of whom were, according to Benjamin A. Hill, more anxious than was Davis himself for Johnston's removal, he made his decision, and on that day caused his adjutant to send the following dispatch:

"Richmond, Va., *July 17, 1864.*

"To General J. E. Johnston:

"Lieutenant-General J. B. Hood has been commissioned to the temporary rank of General, under the law of Congress. I am directed by the Secretary of War to inform you, that as you have failed to arrest the advance of the enemy to the vicinity of Atlanta, and *express no confidence that you can defeat or repel him*, you are hereby relieved from the command of the Army and Department of Tennessee, which you will immediately turn over to General Hood.

"S. Cooper
Adjutant and Inspector-General."

"If General Johnston had informed me that he would retreat to Atlanta," Davis wrote, a few weeks later, "he would have been sooner relieved, as it was my opinion then, as clearly as now, that Atlanta could be best defended by holding some strong positions to the north of it."

This action was deeply resented by Johnston and thence forward it became a subject of bitter controversy. Indeed, there is probably no single act of Davis' life which has been more fiercely assailed. Grant remarked to J. R. Young: "When I heard your Government had removed Johnston from command I was as happy as if I had reinforced Sherman with a large army corps. . . . Joe Johnston gave me more anxiety than any of the others. I was never half so anxious about Lee." Later, in his *Memoirs*, he gave the reason for this opinion: "Inasmuch as he had relieved Johnston and appointed Hood, . . . it is natural to suppose that Mr. Davis was disappointed with General Johnston's policy. My own judgment is that Johnston acted very wisely: he husbanded his men and saved as much of his territory as he could, without fighting decisive battles in which all might be lost. . . . Hood was unquestionably a brave, gallant soldier, and not destitute of ability, but unfortunately, his policy was to fight the enemy wherever he saw him, without thinking much of the consequences of defeat." Johnston's policy was calculated to "gain recognition in the end."

The peace party at the North lost no time in interpreting the Niagara conversations as proof that Lincoln was blocking the way to a possible peace, and Horace Greeley now requested permission to publish the documents relating to them, which request Lincoln, for sound political reasons, refused, proposing instead that the "correspondence be published, suppressing only the parts of his letters over which the red pencil is drawn in the copy which I herewith send." The deleted portions, he felt, would, if made known, add to the already alarming state of public opinion, and serve no good purpose. As Greeley indignantly declined to publish this garbled version, Lincoln assured Raymond that he thought it unwise to make an issue of the matter. "It is better for me to submit for the time to the consequences of the false position in which I consider he has placed me than to subject the country to the consequences of publishing their discouraging and injurious parts. . . ."

On August 17th Lincoln wrote to Charles G. Robinson: "If Jefferson Davis wishes for himself, or for the benefit of his friends at the North, to know what I would do if he were to offer peace and reunion, saying nothing about slavery, let him try me." But the discontented Republican leaders, led by Raymond, chairman of the National Executive Committee of the party, were not content to wait for Davis to "try" Lincoln, and proceeded to bring pressure upon Lincoln himself, to make the peace move. "Why would it not be wise," wrote Raymond, ". . . to appoint a commission . . . to make distinct proffers of peace to Davis, as head of the rebel armies, on the sole condition of acknowledging the supremacy of the Constitution—all other questions to be settled in a convention of the people of all the states?" Three days later, he and his committee went to Washington to press the question. Feeling that Davis would probably accept such a proposition, as he had been from the first the champion of the Constitution, Lincoln, supported by Seward, Stanton, and Fessenden, answered his visitors with written instructions to Raymond to go in person to Richmond and present the offer. But having thought over the consequences, Raymond became convinced that the effect of this third peace proposal would be the loss of the presidential election, and the committee withdrew their demand.

Meanwhile, the accumulation of thousands upon thousands of prisoners of war made prison conditions most distressing. In August, Colonel Chandler made a report upon Andersonville, which came into the hands of Judge Campbell, Confederate Assistant Secretary of War, who, according to the positive statement of Davis, neglected to call it to the latter's attention. "We all knew," Davis wrote later to General Chilton, "of the disease and fatality among the prisoners of Andersonville, and I remember it was attributed to the climate and corn-meal diet; and the absence of proper medicine. . . . It was under these circumstances that I sent General Lee to hold an interview with General Grant, and press on him the necessity for resuming the exchange of prisoners according to the cartel. He failed to awake any of that tender regard for the prisoners which is now [December 9, 1875] assumed for the purpose of maligning me." Having full confidence in General Winder, whom he later described as "too gallant to have oppressed anyone when at his mercy," Davis believed that the conditions were as good as Confederate resources allowed, for so he was assured by men whom he trusted, and there is nothing which gives the slightest justification for the later charges of Blaine and Garfield that he deliberately encouraged ill-treatment of Federal prisoners of war.

Moreover, Davis' position is sustained by the *New York Day Book* of January 13, 1866, which in an account of the condition of Andersonville, declared that great care had been exercised to make the prison as healthful as circumstances allowed, and that the food was "the same as that issued to the Confederate soldiers."

And the author of the *Escape of a Confederate Officer* says that he breakfasted with Lee, whose officers were eating practically the same food as that served to the prisoners at Andersonville, and that the guards had the same provisions. Such testimony is available from many sources, Northern as well as Southern. Jno. F. Frost of Maine, eleven months a prisoner of Andersonville, wrote: "Wirz was harsh and cruel to the prisoners, and deserved hanging; but I believe the Confederate authorities did as well as they could for the prisoners." And it is certain that their efforts to lessen their sufferings by exchanges were repulsed by Grant, who felt that sympathy for the captives should never be allowed to interfere with the effectiveness of war plans. Indeed, he is reported to have declared: "It is hard on our men, held in Southern prisons, not to exchange them, but it is humanity to those left in the ranks to fight our battles. Every man released on parole or otherwise becomes an active soldier against us at once, either directly or indirectly. If we commence a system of exchange which liberates all prisoners taken, we will have to fight on till the whole South is exterminated. If we hold those caught, they amount to no more than dead men. At this particular time, to release all rebel prisoners North would ensure Sherman's defeat, and would compromise our safety here."

In the absence of a proper system of exchanges, confessedly due to Grant's Spartan theories, congestion in the prisons, North and South, became steadily worse, to the undoubted regret of both Presidents; while alert propagandists sought to place the guilt upon the one side or the other, according to the affiliations of the writer. At a time when rumour was going the rounds to the effect that McClellan's election would mean a speedy peace, and Lincoln's re-election, a continuation of the horrors of war, such material as the prisons offered was skilfully used.

Davis knew that a Confederate defeat would probably cause a reaction in the North so favourable to the existing order as to ensure Lincoln's re-election. An anti-war faction was backing

McClellan, whose delegates were already preparing for the journey to Chicago, where they expected to see him chosen as the Democratic candidate who "could beat Lincoln." Eager friends deluged Davis with information about the coming contest. On August 20th S. J. Anderson wrote, with singular disregard of McClellan's right to the hereditary spelling of his name: "McLellan will be enthusiastically elected in defiance of force and fraud," and added the opinion that the misspelt candidate was ambitious "enough for Bonaparte," and would, if elected, "submit propositions to you which it would be difficult to reject." Lincoln too regarded McClellan as a peace candidate, but Davis refused to back either, believing that such a contest was of importance only to the enemy.

Such incidents were side issues for Davis, as he contemplated the wreck of hopes built upon Hood's substitution for Johnston. On July 20th-22nd, Hood had faced Sherman in the battle of Atlanta, and without doing serious damage to his opponent, had lost 8,000 men. On August 31st he abandoned the city and retired towards Newman. Sherman entered on September 2nd and began at once preparing his march to the sea. Lee, in the meantime, was urging every possible addition to the Confederate forces. On September 2nd he wrote to Davis that every man liable to military service should be at once enrolled, and that teamsters, cooks, mechanics and labourers should be employed as soldiers, their places to be supplied by negroes. "In my opinion," he added, "the necessity . . . will never be more urgent."

Though realizing the facts, as Lee presented them, Davis did not lose hope. On September 18th he wrote to H. V. Johnson: "I think it [Atlanta] can be recovered . . . if the absentees from Hood's army can be sent back, and the men of Georgia, who by operation of law are exempt from military service, will give temporary aid; that Sherman's army can be driven out of Georgia, perhaps be utterly destroyed." The extent of the exemptions is easily understood if we consider Lee's words to Bragg, written on

September 10th: "I was informed . . . that in this state alone [Georgia] there were no less than 40,000 exempts, details, and applications for detail," and added: "I recommended to the President to have an inspection made of the conscription service with a view to obtain accurate information."

Prompted by the consciousness of Lee's dire need of men, several Governors, including Brown of Georgia, now urged the President to issue a proclamation that all aliens, resident in the Confederate States, must either enlist or depart within a specified time. In reply Davis pointed to the fact that many of these aliens had been induced to come into the South "under conditions which guarantee to them immunity from the obligation of bearing arms." To him, even in his present need, that fact gave an immunity which was sacred and irrevocable, and he therefore decided instead to rally, by a personal campaign, deserters and men legally exempt, beginning in Georgia.

Governor Brown, though a bitter enemy to conscription and a violent critic of Davis, had by his suggestion in regard to aliens, given signs, Davis thought, of a readiness to co-operate with him in this hour of dire necessity. He therefore decided to make a personal visit to Georgia and an appeal for a final sacrifice in the interest of the cause and of Lee, who needed every man who could be coaxed or coerced into, or back into, his depleted ranks. He arrived at 4 A.M. on Wednesday, September 28th, at Macon. No one in the city had been informed of his intended visit; but a meeting for the relief of Atlanta refugees was scheduled for eleven that morning, and Davis decided to address it. After a conciliatory introduction, referring to the fact that his father had been a Revolutionary soldier, fighting the British as a son of Georgia, he came at once to his theme: "What though misfortune has befallen our arms from Decatur to Jonesboro, our cause is not lost. Sherman cannot keep up his long line of communication; retreat, sooner or later, he must. And when that day comes, the fate that befell the army of the French Empire in its retreat from Moscow will be re-enacted. . . ." And to bring about that day he urged that every citizen, man and woman alike, should bring pressure to induce deserters from Hood's army to return to the ranks.

A few days later, Davis addressed the legislature, and the citizens of Montgomery, "the capital in which the first notes of our existence were issued," acknowledging the recent "great disasters," in Georgia and Alabama; but pointing proudly to Virginia, where, "despite the odds . . . we have beaten Grant, and still . . . hold our lines before Richmond and Petersburg. That pure and noble patriot, the great soldier and Christian, General Lee," . . . commands "a body of men who have never known what it was to be whipped, and never stopped to cipher." In conclusion, he warned his fellow-citizens against listening to whispers of the possible victory of a candidate in the North who would bring overtures for peace. "Victory in the field," he said, "is the surest element of strength to a peace party. Let us win battles, and we shall have overtures soon enough."

Intent upon the problem of persuading stragglers and deserters to return to the ranks, Davis now became for a time a travelling propagandist. From Montgomery he proceeded to South Carolina, arriving at Columbia on October 4th. His speech here, too, was an uncompromising demand for victories, as the only road to honourable peace. Foreign intervention, once a hope, he said, "has proved an *ignis fatuus*. There is . . . but one means by which you can gain independence and an honourable peace, and that is by uniting. . . . With every Confederate victory our stocks rise in the foreign market—that touchstone of European sentiment. . . . Is this a time to ask what the *law* demands of you . . . to ask if the magistrate will take you out of the enrolling office by a writ of *habeas corpus*? Rather is it the time for every man capable of bearing arms to say: 'My country needs my services!' "

This speech was unfairly used by Vice-President Stephens, in a published letter, to give the unwarranted inference that Davis preferred Lincoln to McClellan, a letter, says Davis, "intended quite plainly to disparage me and to inspire distrust of me among the people." He bitterly resented the action, and after a hot controversy, by letter, forced Stephens to the admission that there was no just ground for the statement.

The last speech of this strenuous tour was at Augusta, Georgia, on October 5th. Employing an interruption by an Irishman who demanded three cheers for the Confederacy, Davis said, "From the accents of that voice, my friend, I see that you have come into this country from one that has lost its liberty. You may well exclaim 'three cheers for the Confederacy,' upon whose success now alone depends the existence of Constitutional liberty in the world. We are fighting for that principle; upon us depends its last hope. The Yankees, in endeavouring to coerce the states, have lost that heirloom of the Fathers, and the men of the South alone must sustain it. Ours is not a revolution . . . our struggle is for inherited rights. . . . I believe," he added, "that a just God looks upon our cause as holy, and that of the enemy as iniquitous."

When Lincoln found the argument of military necessity strong enough to overcome both his Constitutional views, and the promise of his platform, Davis had interpreted the action as dictatorship. But he now found himself toying with the same idea. He knew that Lincoln's bold declaration of freedom to the slaves in the seceded states, based upon the doctrine of military necessity, had given the North a new position in the eyes of Europe, and was inclining more and more towards Benjamin's suggestion to recapture the lost ground by taking similar action. Such a step, even at that late hour, would have a powerful effect upon foreign judgments, perhaps upon foreign action, in the direction of recognition of the South. It would also make available for military work a large number of negroes, who would doubtless join their old masters, if promised freedom as their reward. That such assistance was desperately needed was clear, from a letter which Lee wrote to Davis from Petersburg on November 2nd:

"The information contained in the notes you enclosed me, I hope is exaggerated as regards numbers. Grant will get every man he can and 150,000 men is the number generally assumed by Northern papers and reports. Unless we can obtain a reasonable approximation to his force I fear a great calamity. . . . The inequality is too great." This was the strongest intimation which Lee had yet given that, with conditions as they were, ultimate defeat was inevitable. Davis knew that Lee looked with favour upon the idea of enlisting negroes as regular troops, and of holding out the offer of freedom as an inducement to service, and he now decided that the desperate state of the Confederate army made this necessary. Accordingly, in his message of November 7th he proposed "the training of 40,000 negroes for service," and freedom for those who should fight for Confederate independence. He declared his opposition to "a general levy and arming of the slaves for the duty of soldiers," but announced that, should a general levy later appear indispensable to the winning of independence, he might alter his view. He expressed a readiness to contemplate a law "to liberate the negro on his discharge after service faithfully rendered," as preferable either to granting freedom at once or to retaining him in servitude. He was also doubtful "whether the private right of property can consistently and beneficially be continued," a startling admission for a believer in the divine origin and sanction of slavery. But he asserted again his view that the South had managed her race problem, and fulfilled her duty of Christianizing and improving the condition of her African charges better than any nation in history.

On the whole, the message is the message of a leader at bay, for only desperation could have brought him to consider training slaves for army service. It resulted in a bill embodying his slave proposition, which the Confederate Congress rejected and James Russell Lowell joyfully wrote: "The late proposal of Davis and

Lee for the arming of slaves, though they certainly did not so intend it, has removed a very serious obstacle from our path. It is true that the emancipating clause was struck out of the act as finally passed by the shadowy Congress at Richmond. But this was only for the sake of appearances. Once arm and drill the negroes, and they can never be slaves again."

What might have been the effect of so bold a handling of the slave question as Benjamin had urged, in view of the coming trial of political strength between Lincoln and McClellan, can now be but a matter of speculation. History knows only that Lincoln retained his hold upon the European mind, and kept his American political following. On November 1, 1864, C. C. Baughman wrote from the trenches at Petersburg: "I fear Lincoln has the Yankee nation so much under his power that he will force them to elect him." But Davis showed a calm indifference, refusing to admit any preference between Lincoln and McClellan; though not hesitating to show that he hated Andrew Johnson, who, as Lincoln's running-mate was soon to become President. His references to Johnson, however, were personal, rather than political.

On November 8th the newspapers announced the result: "Abraham Lincoln carries every state except Delaware, Kentucky, and New Jersey," disregarding of course the states still "out of their proper practical relation to the Union." His election ensured a continuance of the war upon the basis of his policy of complete submission as the only condition of peace—a situation which the London *Times* interpreted as the end of the Republic. "The case of the Democratic minority is soon stated," it declared on November 24, 1864. "They were denied the franchise the Constitution gave them by the Generals of the President. What fate have they to expect now the election is decided? What right will be held sacred, when the right of election is set at naught? Henceforth, we may consider the Democratic party as expelled from the arena of politics, and destined to submission, or to suffer all the miseries that tyranny can inflict. We can regard the appointment of Mr. Lincoln as little less than an abdication by the American people of the right of self-government; as an avowed step towards the foundation of military despotism; towards the subversion of popular government, which may still exist in form, but which in substance is gone. . . . Future historians will probably date the second presidency of Mr. Lincoln as the period when the American Constitution was thoroughly abrogated, and had entered on the way by which Republics pass from Democracy to tyranny."

Those who had hoped for peace by negotiation in the event of McClellan's election soon found that Lincoln interpreted his victory as a mandate from the people to trust nothing to negotiation, but to press for complete victory. "It seems to me," he said to Congress, in his message of December 6, 1864, "that no attempt at negotiation with the insurgent leader could result in any good. He would accept nothing short of severance of the Union, precisely what we will not and cannot give. His declarations to this effect are explicit and oft-repeated. He does not attempt to deceive us. He affords us no excuse to deceive ourselves. He cannot voluntarily re-accept the Union; we cannot voluntarily yield it. Between him and us the issue is distinct, simple, inflexible. It is an issue which can only be tried by war, and decided by victory. If we yield, we are beaten; if the Southern people fail him, he is beaten. Either way, it would be the victory and defeat following war.

"What is true, however, of him who heads the insurgent cause, is not necessarily true of those who follow. Although he cannot re-accept the Union, they can. Some of them, we know, already desire peace and reunion. The number of such may increase. They can, at any moment, have peace simply by laying down their arms, and submitting to the national authority under the Constitution. After so much, the government could not, if it would, maintain war against them. The loyal people would not sustain or allow it."

After referring to his earlier offer of "general pardon and amnesty . . . to all except certain designated classes," who though thus excepted were "still within contemplation of special clemency," he added, significantly, "I retract nothing heretofore said as to slavery. I repeat the declaration made a year ago, that 'while I remain in my present position I shall not attempt to retract or modify the Emancipation Proclamation, nor shall I return to slavery any person who is free by the terms of that proclamation, or by any of the acts of Congress.'"

## CHAPTER XXII

# HAMPTON ROADS CONFERENCE

AT THIS juncture, Francis P. Blair, Sr., who had helped Andrew Jackson to defeat South Carolina's plan of nullification, urged Lincoln to allow him to go to Jefferson Davis and seek a peaceful settlement. "Come to me after Savannah falls," was the reply. When therefore Sherman entered Savannah, on December 22, 1864, Blair renewed his request, and, six days later, obtained from Lincoln a card with the words:

"Allow the bearer, F. P. Blair, Sr., to pass our lines, go south, and return.

"A. Lincoln."

It is difficult to determine, after so many years, how much Blair knew of the group in the South, headed by Vice-President Stephens, whom Lincoln's message had described as those who "already desire peace and re-union," but he was convinced that he had a plan which would cause Davis himself to desire both.

From Lincoln's papers it is clear that Blair's visit was entirely an affair of his own planning. "When he applied for a passport to go to Richmond, with certain ideas which he wished to make known to me," Lincoln wrote, "I told him flatly that I did not want to hear them. If he desired to go to Richmond of his own accord, I would give him a passport; but he had no authority to speak for me in any way whatsoever." "Nor was I," he later assured Congress, "informed of anything he would say or do, on his own account or otherwise." Blair's pass, therefore, is no indication that Lincoln agreed with his views, or indeed that he had troubled to inquire into them. He was probably following the policy which had sent Greeley to Niagara and Jaquess to Richmond; namely to let the advocates of negotiation find out for themselves what he himself already knew, that Davis would consider nothing less than independence.

Tom Paine, at the opening of the American Revolution, urged direct action, in the words, "The time for debate is over," but Davis knew better. The time for debate is never over since it always offers greater possibilities of a just settlement than can ever be obtained by the breaking of heads. He therefore consented to receive Blair and hear his proposition. Blair opened the conversation with the frank declaration of his lack of authority to speak for Lincoln, but gave Davis the impression that Lincoln understood his plans and would act in accordance with them. With that understanding, according to Stephens, Davis heard his suggestions, which had been reduced to writing and which Blair read aloud. They proposed that having obtained the benefit of enlarged amnesty, Davis should transfer a portion of the Confederate armies to Texas, and thence to Mexico where Juarez could be induced to rally the liberals to join him in expelling Maximilian. Juarez, explained Blair, "is intimate with my son, Montgomery, who is persuaded that he could induce him to devolve all the power he can on President Davis—a dictatorship, if necessary—to restore the rights of Mexico and her people." If more force should be required, "multitudes of the army of the North, officers and men," could be found ready to embark in an enterprise vital "to the interests of our whole Republic." "He who expels the Bonaparte-Hapsburg dynasty from our southern flank . . . will ally his name with those of Washington and Jackson as a defender of the liberty of the country." He held up before the astonished eyes of Davis, a vision of completing the work of Jefferson, by "rounding off our possession on the continent at the Isthmus, and opening the way to blending the waters of the Atlantic and

Pacific, thus embracing our Republic in the arms of the ocean," and "restoring the equipoise between the Northern and Southern states—if indeed such sectional distinctions could be recognized, after the peculiar institution which created them had ceased to exist," since as the memorandum had stated, "slavery no longer remains an insurmountable obstruction to pacification."

When he had read his proposal to the end, Blair said: "There is my problem, Mr. Davis. Do you think it possible to be solved?" And Davis answered, "I think so."

The remainder of the conversation, as reported by Blair, leaves the impression that Davis was prepared to venture, if the matter were conducted through Lincoln, and not Seward. "As to Mr. Seward," Blair later explained, Davis "had no confidence in him . . . and . . . did not know any man or party in the South that had." Davis stated that he did not know Lincoln, but was inclined to accept Blair's assurance that he could be trusted "to maintain his word inviolate," and that he cared not for the glory held out to him, nor what his name might be in history. If he could restore the prosperity and happiness of his country that was the end and aim of his being.

As a result of the conference, Blair returned to Washington, armed with the following letter:

"Richmond, Va., *January 12, 1865.*

"F. P. Blair, Esq.

"Sir: I have deemed it proper, . . . to give you in this form, the substance of the remarks made by me, to be repeated by you to President Lincoln, etc. I have no disposition to find obstacles in forms, and am willing now, as heretofore, to enter into negotiations for the restoration of peace; and am ready to send a commission whenever I have reason to suppose it will be received, or to receive a commission, if the United States government shall choose to send one. Notwithstanding the rejection of our former offers, I would, if you could promise that a commission, minister, or other agent would be received, appoint one immediately, and renew the effort to enter into a conference with a view to secure *peace to the two Countries*. Yours, etc.

"JEFFERSON DAVIS."

Having placed this message in Lincoln's hands, Blair received, for immediate transportation to Davis, the following:

"Washington, *January 18, 1865*.

"F. P. BLAIR, ESQ.

"Sir: You having shown me Mr. Davis' letter to you of the 12th inst., you may say to him that I have constantly been, am now, and shall continue ready to receive any agent whom he, or any other influential person now resisting the national authority, may informally send me, with a view of securing peace to the people of our common country.

"Yours, etc.,

"A. LINCOLN."

The same day Blair wrote to Greeley: "My faith is strong that we shall have a happy deliverance, and that soon. There is good will for it on both sides." He was convinced that in view of an offer of compensation for the slaves, Davis would not deny the statement that "slavery no longer remains an insurmountable obstruction," though less confident in regard to Davis' phrase, "peace to the two Countries," since Lincoln had countered with the words, "peace to the people of our common country." Still buoyant despite a difference which would have discouraged most men, Blair returned to Richmond. Though conscious that Lincoln would not countenance the plan for a joint invasion of Mexico, he hoped that a conference at least could be agreed upon and that out of it might come terms of peace. "The simple truth is," says the Nicolay and Hay biography of Lincoln, ". . . Mr. Blair was, as best he might, covering his retreat from an abortive intrigue."

After reading Lincoln's reply twice over, in Blair's presence, Davis raised a question about the meaning of the words, "our common country," and received the reply that it related to the part of Mr. Davis' letter about "the two countries." Knowing that he himself would never return the Confederate States to the Union, even could he do so, and confident that Lincoln would never recognize them as independent, he however decided to give Vice-President Stephens, and those who with him so ardently clamoured for negotiations, an opportunity to try out their program. He therefore sent R. M. T. Hunter, now President *pro tempore* of the Confederate Senate, to invite Stephens to express his views upon the subject of accepting Lincoln's offer to "receive any agent whom he . . . may informally send me." "I called at the hour," writes Stephens, "and found Mr. Davis alone. . . . The substance of what he then stated was, that Mr. Blair . . . had suggested to him a course by which a suspension of hostilities might be effected. This was to be done by a *secret military convention* between the belligerents, embracing another object, which was the maintenance of the Monroe Doctrine, in the prevention of the establishment of the then projected empire in Mexico by France.

"I told him that I thought the program suggested by Mr. Blair should be acceded to, at least so far as to obtain, if possible, a conference upon the subject."

Stephens declared that in his opinion, President Davis should himself conduct the negotiations, face to face with President Lincoln, but Davis had no mind to undertake such a mission. Stephens then suggested a commission of three, Judge Campbell, Assistant-Secretary of War; General Henry L. Benning, ex-Justice of the Supreme Court of Georgia, now commanding a Confederate brigade; and Thomas S. Flournoy, a prominent Virginian, well known to President Lincoln. Davis, however, was determined, as Lincoln had been in the case of Greeley, that the leader of the party urging negotiation should himself head the commission, and Stephens' many objections were overruled. Finding escape impossible, he at last consented to serve with R. M. T. Hunter and Judge Campbell, and, on January 29, 1865, they started for Petersburg, with the following instructions, more specific than Benjamin thought advisable, as he feared the issue clearly raised by the final words:

"Richmond, *January 28, 1865.*

"In conformity with the letter of Mr. Lincoln, . . . you are to proceed to Washington City for an informal conference . . . upon the issues involved in the existing war, and for the purpose of securing *peace to the two Countries.*

"With great respect, your obedient servant,

"JEFFERSON DAVIS."

Although the greatest secrecy had been observed throughout this preliminary correspondence, rumours of a coming peace had begun to be heard as soon as Lincoln had consented to receive a commission: and with them the fear that Mr. Davis was contemplating submission. On January 19th, C. C. Baughman wrote, from Camp Walker, that the rumours of peace were considered anything but pleasant. "We have no idea," he declared stoutly, "of submitting after having endured all these hardships." And five days later, "If we are true to ourselves, we will gain our independence despite present gloomy prospects."

Had the writer of this letter known how gloomy the prospects were, he would have been less optimistic. Davis' inability, due to states sovereignty, to adopt a comprehensive abolition program to match that of Lincoln, had destroyed the last vestige of hope of British intervention. Charles Francis Adams reported to Lincoln a few days later, that the election had put an end to the chief reliance of the Confederacy. "Foreign assistance is less likely than ever. Cotton has ceased even to pretend to sovereign power. . . . The object of the struggle had in fact been to withdraw slavery from the dangers apprehended, by the political revolution of 1860, and to fence it round with a new barrier . . . formed of the material interests of the Old and the New World, and sustained by physical force. As an incident to this result, political independence was regarded as indispensable. The failure in gaining the hoped-for sympathy from abroad has arisen from that very cause. . . . Sensible too late of the commission of this fatal mistake, the last and most desperate cast of the die has been resorted to, a reversal of the order has been proposed. Slavery is offered as a sacrifice, provided some advantage may be gained by it to independence. But even then it is too late to expect foreign nations to hazard anything simply for the recognition of an abstract principle by a distant community. Something more must be offered. It is nothing less than a petition for a protectorate. Away then goes the other object of the struggle, independence. And thus is once more verified the moral of the fable of the dog who, clutching at the shadow in the water, lost the bone which had been safe in his mouth."

President Davis and his hard pressed followers would have scorned the idea that political independence had ever been regarded by them as "an incident" compared with the protection of slave property. He was ready to yield to the pressure for negotiation, but only with the reservation that independence, not slavery, would be the ultimate basis of agreement.

The original plan had been that the Confederate commissioners should go, via Grant's headquarters, to Washington, to confer with Lincoln in person, and the change which landed them at Hampton Roads is thus explained by Grant: "On the last of January, 1865, peace commissioners from the so-called Confederate States presented themselves on our lines around Petersburg, and were immediately conducted to my headquarters at City Point. They proved to be Alexander H. Stephens, Vice-President of the Confederacy, Judge Campbell, Assistant-Secretary of War, and R. M. T. Hunter, formerly United States Senator and then a member of the Confederate Senate. . . . I at once communicated by telegraph with Washington and informed the Secretary of War and the President of the arrival of these commissioners and that their object was to negotiate terms of peace. . . . I was instructed to retain them at City Point until the President, or some one whom he would designate, should come to meet them." They were accordingly kept for several days as guests, but Grant adds, "I never admitted . . . that they were the representatives of a government, though every courtesy was shown them."

Informal discussions with his guests convinced Grant that their intentions were good and that they sincerely desired to restore peace and union; which opinion he reported to Stanton. "I have not felt myself at liberty," he added, "to express . . . views of my own, or to account for my reticence. This has placed me in an awkward position, which I could have avoided by not seeing them in the first instance. I fear now their going back without any expression from any one in authority will have a bad influence. At the same time I recognize the difficulties in the way of receiving these informal Commissioners at this time, and I do not know what to recommend. I am sorry, however, that Mr. Lincoln cannot have an interview with the two named in this dispatch [Stephens and Hunter], if not all three now within our lines. Their letter to me was all that the President's instructions contemplated to secure their safe conduct, if they had used the same language to Major Eckert.

"U. S. Grant, Lieut.-General."

Grant's desire for peace was not due to any doubt of the strength of his position or of his power to compel peace, which latter Lee himself had practically admitted in a letter to Davis, on January 29th, which stated that Grant's forces are now "so superior to ours that if he is reinforced to any extent I do not see how . . . he can be prevented from enveloping Richmond." He had added the opinion that reinforcing Sherman would be "almost as bad in consequences as reinforcing Grant."

Major Eckert, whom Lincoln had sent to City Point, found the commissioners willing to confer at Fortress Monroe, and Lincoln, upon the receipt of Grant's letter, sent the following dispatch:

"War Department. Washington.
*February 2, 1865*

"To Lieut.-General Grant, City Point, Va.,

"Say to the gentlemen that I will meet them personally at Fortress Monroe as soon as I can get there.

"A. Lincoln."

He also telegraphed Seward: "Induced by a dispatch from General Grant, I join you at Fortress Monroe as soon as I can come." Grant too reported that the Confederate commissioners were willing to confer at Fortress Monroe or Hampton Roads, and were starting at 9.30 A.M. on February 2nd.

This unexpected delay which kept the Confederate commissioners in Grant's camp for two days, seemed to Davis adequately explained by Lincoln's change of plans, despite the fact that Lee had offered a different interpretation in a confidential dispatch on January 30th: "Probably the delay in receiving Messrs. Stephens, Hunter, and Campbell is occasioned by the arrival of some . . . troops in James River which they do not wish to disclose."

When Lincoln reached Hampton Roads, on the night of February 2nd, he found Seward and Eckert awaiting him in one steamer, and the commissioners in another. Seward reported that he had had no communication with the latter, and showed Lincoln a letter which they had sent to Eckert that day, announcing their readiness to negotiate upon terms "not inconsistent with the essential principles of self-government and popular rights, upon which our institutions are founded."

Lincoln could have seen in these words little to give value to Grant's view, that Stephens and Hunter were eager "to restore peace and union," for he knew that the power back of them was Jefferson Davis, whose view of self-government and popular rights was not peace and union, but peace and Southern independence. Nevertheless, being at the scene of the conference, he decided to hear the proposals of the commissioners.

Many accounts have been written of the Hampton Roads conference, most of them built upon speculation or tradition. The actual witnesses, so far as the South was concerned were only Stephens, Campbell, and Hunter; and Lincoln adds that he and Seward were the only Federals present. From the reports of these five men, therefore, the story must be constructed. Stephens' *War Between the States* gives the fullest and most interesting picture of the Conference, which, though complicated in origin, proved a singularly straightforward discussion of pending issues.

The three Confederate commissioners were conducted to the saloon of Lincoln's vessel, the *River Queen*, and were there joined by Lincoln and Seward. Stephens opened the conversation with a reference to experiences which he and Lincoln had had in common when working for Taylor's election in 1848. Lincoln responded cordially. Stephens then asked: "Is there no way of putting an end to the present trouble, and bringing about a restoration of the general good feeling and harmony then existing between the different states? . . ."

Lincoln answered that "there was but one way . . . for those who were resisting the laws of the Union to cease that resistance."

"Is there no continental question . . . which might . . . temporarily engage their attention? We have been induced to believe that there is," said Stephens.

Lincoln replied: "I suppose you refer to something that Mr. Blair has said. . . . Whatever he said was of his own accord and without the least authority from me. . . . The restoration of the Union is a *sine qua non* with me."

With these words the great issue was disposed of; the issue which had been defined by Davis' "peace to the two countries" and Lincoln's "peace to the people of our common country." For four hours longer the conference continued, touching upon many vital matters, but the hope of peace had been destroyed. Lincoln discussed the slavery issue frankly, but as a subordinate question, a position to which Davis had always relegated it. He declared that his Emancipation Proclamation was "a war measure, and would have effect only from its being an exercise of the war power." As soon as the war should cease, "it would be inoperative for the future. It would be held to apply only to such slaves as had come under its operation while it was in active exercise." This, he declared, was his individual opinion, "but the Courts might decide the other way, and hold that it effectually emancipated all the slaves in the states to which it applied at the time."

Seward pointed out that the Constitutional amendment (later the thirteenth) which Congress had recently proposed, and which provided for the immediate abolition of slavery throughout the United States, was also a war measure. "If the war were then to cease," he suggested, pertinently, "it would probably not be adopted by a number of states sufficient to make it a part of the Constitution." Stephens says that Seward left on the minds of the commissioners the impression that, "if the Confederate States would abandon the war, they could themselves defeat this amendment. . . . The whole number of states . . . being thirty-six, any ten of them could defeat it."

Lincoln's opinion was that it was not wise for the South to attempt thus to defeat the amendment. "Stephens," he said, using the same intimate address as in the old days, ". . . if I resided in Georgia, with my present sentiments, I'll tell you what I would do. . . . I would go home and get the governor of the state to call the legislature together . . . and ratify this amendment *prospectively*, so as to take effect—say in five years. Such a ratification would be valid in my opinion. . . . Whatever may have been the views of your people before the war, they must be convinced now that slavery is doomed." He assured the commissioners, that as President he would use the utmost liberality in dealing with the South, if it would return to the Union, and declared, adds Stephens, that he would himself "be willing to be taxed to remunerate the Southern people for their slaves. He believed the people of the North were as responsible for slavery as the people of the South, and if war should then cease, with the voluntary abolition of slavery by the states, he would be in favour, individually, of the Government's paying a fair indemnity for the loss to the owners. He believed this feeling had an extensive existence at the North. He knew some who were in favour of an appropriation as high as four hundred millions of dollars for this purpose." Seward added that he believed the people of the North "would be willing to pay as an indemnity for the slaves what would be required to continue the war"—an astonishing statement, from the heads of a nation now so near to final victory, especially from men regarded by the South as leaders of a fanatical abolitionist group, bent upon robbing the South of liberty, and of property guaranteed to them in the Constitution.

The commissioners knew, however, that the price demanded was submission and the utter abandonment of the dream of final independence; and this price they were neither willing nor authorized to promise. They therefore declared, through Stephens, that they must regard the conference as a failure, and retired, to prepare their report to President Davis.

Campbell, in his *Recollections*, says that the "chagrin" of the commissioners was great; and Nicolay and Hay add that Davis' "chagrin was as great as theirs." But in this they were clearly mistaken. Neither Davis nor Lincoln had expected from the negotiation any outcome save to still the insistent demand for negotiation from the peace parties, both North and South. Davis feared, however, that by having agreed that the conference should be confidential, the Confederate commissioners had made it possible for Seward, whom he regarded as wholly unscrupulous, to convince France that the Confederacy was using the Mexican situation to check friendliness between the Federal Government and France; and to the end of his life cherished the belief that Seward had actually so employed it. Only a few years before his death, he expressed the opinion that the dispatches between Seward and Dayton, following the Hampton Roads conference, had served to induce the subsequent unfriendly attitude of Louis Napoleon towards the Confederacy.

On February 6, 1865, Davis wrote to Senator Hill, "The commissioners have returned. They met Lincoln and Seward at Fortress Monroe, were informed that neither the Confederate States nor the individual states could be recognized as having power to enter into any agreement prescribing the conditions of peace. Nothing less would be accepted than unconditional submission." On the same day, he sent to Congress his interpretation of the conference, in which he said, "the enemy refused to enter into negotiations with the Confederate States, or with any of them separately, or to give to our people any other terms or guarantees than those which the conqueror may grant, or to permit us to have peace on any other basis than our unconditional submission to their rule, coupled with the acceptance of their recent legislation on the subject of the relations between the white and black populations of each state. . . ."

The failure of the conference he proposed to make the theme of an address at the African Church, in Richmond, a favourite place for public meetings; and he invited Stephens to join him in urging the people to a resistance which might yet mean victory and independence. "I declined," says Stephens, "because I could not undertake to impress upon the minds of the people the idea that they could do what I believed to be impossible." Undaunted by this refusal, or by the fact that opposition to his leadership was increasing rapidly, Davis, however, appeared at the meeting, determined to recover lost ground and to prove that though peace by negotiation was impossible, there was still hope of victory and independence. Stephens mingled with the crowd, eager to hear, though unwilling to speak. Reviewing Davis' speech in the light of retrospect, he wrote: "It was not only bold, undaunted, and confident in its tone, but had that loftiness of sentiment and rare form of expression, as well as magnetic influence in its delivery, by which the passions of the masses . . . are moved to their profoundest depths." It "caused the minds of not a few to revert to like appeals by Rienzi and Demosthenes." And he added the striking, but now hackneyed comment: "It is brilliant; it is grand; but it is not war!"

Shortly after this meeting, Stephens, hopeless of the future, retired to "Liberty Hall," his country home, where he remained, in seclusion, until arrested on the 11th of May. His departure was a relief to Davis, who, conscious of the existence of a Congressional cabal to remove him and make Stephens President, had remarked to James Lyons that he was ready to resign if Stephens would, but that he would never yield the Executive office to a man who would immediately surrender to the enemy.

Although knowing also that another cabal was working to make Lee Dictator, a plan which included his own elimination, Davis knew that the most important service which he could render to the Confederacy was that of persuading Lee again to accept the post of commander-in-chief of all its armies. This position Davis had once already assigned to him and had only relieved him of it at Lee's own request, as the latter argued that he could not give his best services when holding at the same time the active command of the Army of Northern Virginia. On January 18th, in his reply to a demand from the Virginia Assembly, that he should again give Lee supreme command, Davis had explained that situation: "The opinion expressed by the General Assembly in regard to General R. E. Lee has my full concurrence. Virginia cannot have a higher regard for him, or greater confidence in his character and ability, than is entertained by me. When General Lee took command of the Army of Northern

Virginia, he was in command of all the armies of the Confederate States by my order of assignment. He continued in this general command, as well as in the immediate command of the Army of Northern Virginia as long as I could resist his opinion that it was necessary for him to be relieved from one of these two duties. . . . He left it for me to choose between his withdrawal from the command of the army in the field, and relieving him of the general command of all the armies of the Confederate States. It was only when satisfied of this necessity that I came to the conclusion to relieve him from the general command. . . . He has always expressed his inability to assume command of other armies than those now confided to him, unless relieved of the immediate command in the field that now opposes General Grant."

In view of the military situation, Lee's direct command was evidently the only safeguard for Richmond, and Davis continued to hold the opinion that under no consideration should he be allowed to relinquish it. In the end, Lee yielded to Davis' urging and consented to hold both positions. Accordingly, on February 6th Davis again appointed him commander-in-chief and upon receiving Lee's definite acceptance, wrote:

"Richmond, *February 10, 1865.*

"Sir:

"Yours of yesterday received. I have not failed to appreciate the burden already imposed on you as too heavy to enable an ordinary man to bear an additional weight. Your patriotic devotion I knew would prompt you to attempt anything which was possible, if it promised to be beneficial to the country.

"The honour designed to be bestowed has been so fully won, that the fact of conferring it can add nothing to your fame. . . .

"Jefferson Davis."

There is no evidence here or elsewhere to justify the view, which some writers have advanced, that Lee's restoration to supreme command was delayed because President Davis "was still thinking of himself as another Washington," nor is there any foundation for the belief that Davis was jealous of Lee. On the contrary, there was, to the very end of the Confederacy, now close at hand, and to the end of Lee's life, warm friendship and absolute confidence between them.

CHAPTER XXIII

# THE FALL OF RICHMOND

THE conversations of the Hampton Roads conference, just reviewed, again make it clear that neither Lincoln nor Seward regarded abolition as the dominant question at issue between the North and the South. Both had shown a readiness to see even the pending Thirteenth Amendment defeated, if by its defeat the South could be restored to its proper, practical relation to the Union; and the developments of the weeks immediately following the return of the Confederate commissioners also proved, beyond doubt, that Davis and his fellow-Confederates were as ready to give up slavery to secure independence, as Lincoln and Seward were to tolerate it if thereby they could secure re-union. Indeed, Benjamin had sent Duncan F. Kenner, of Louisiana, to Paris and London, to discover whether such a policy would be likely to induce France and England to help the Confederacy, and had authorized him to co-operate with Slidell and Mason, or, if necessary, to supersede them, and to declare that his powers emanated from President Davis himself. These powers reached to a promise that the Confederacy would abolish slavery, if that should be found to be an obstacle to recognition.

The notorious Vallandingham, "ablest member of the Democratic party at the North after the death of Douglas," as Alexander H. Stephens calls him, had apparently heard of this plan when, on January 23, 1865, he wrote to Greeley, "Depend upon it . . . just as soon as it becomes absolutely necessary, and perhaps before, it may be this year, she [the South] will agree with England and France for recognition and material aid, upon the condition of remote or even contingent emancipation—sufficient to satisfy appearances. . . . The South will even, if necessary, abolish slavery absolutely. Then she will have gained the greatest moral victory for ages and exhibited the sublimest spectacle in history." Vallandingham doubtless knew that the sentiment in France encouraged the hope that such a concession on the part of the South might be sufficient to turn the tide in favour of the Confederate cause; and if Davis had any doubts upon the question they were soon relieved; for, on February 25th, George M. Henry reported from Europe, that "the Emperor Napoleon's movement in reference to Mexico was very unpopular in Paris until the French arms achieved success. His people have now become impatient at the delay on the part of the United States in the recognition of the new empire. May he not then desire to join forces with the South? A pro-slavery man himself, the 'peculiar institution' of these states has not stood in the way of his acknowledging their independence; but, there is no denying, that among many of the masses in France there is a strong abolition feeling. A further question then arises: may he not be induced to humour that feeling by insisting upon emancipation as the price of recognition, now that some of the journals of the Confederacy, unwisely in my belief, have intimated that such a bargain could be made? We have," he added, "a good friend in Austria in consequence of the opposition of the Southern members of the Federal Congress to the recognition of the independence of Hungary, so strongly urged by the Senators and Representatives from the Northern states. Austria, then, being interested in the Mexican question, the Emperor Maximilian being Austrian, has no doubt pressed France, as much as she could, to act on behalf of this Confederacy.

"England will probably look on for a while longer. She owes France a grudge for the position that Power took last year in reference to the Danish question. But she may eventually be drawn into the conflict. A very erroneous notion prevails in the public mind here in regard to the course of England towards this Confederacy. The slavery question has not for one moment or in any degree retarded her recognition of the independence of these states. Abolitionism in England is as dead as Unionism in the South."

The recent instructions given to Kenner show that this had not been the opinion of Davis and Benjamin when they were drawn, but reports of Kenner's experiences gave confirmation to Henry's opinion. In company with Mason, Kenner had discussed the situation with Lord Palmerston, had read to him the closing paragraph of his instructions which declared the Confederacy's willingness to abolish slavery if slavery was an obstacle to recognition, and had received Palmerston's assurance that England's refusal to recognize the Confederacy was due to no obstacles which had not already been pointed out. Little therefore was to be hoped for now by offering abolition in return for recognition; for France had made clear to Kenner that the Emperor would not take any step except in concert with England.

Pending these developments, and before he was certain that Kenner's mission had failed, Davis had consulted Lee upon the pressing question of how to increase the man-power of the Confederacy. Lee's opinion had been given: the time had come to enlist the slaves as soldiers, coupling with the call a definite promise of freedom to those who should join in the fight for self-government. Davis agreed with this view, knowing that the conscription system, so helpful in earlier and more hopeful days, had broken down. He was painfully conscious of the fact that his Government was now not able to supply recruits sufficient to counterbalance desertions, which had become alarmingly numerous. "Enrolling officers," complained the *Examiner*, "are always pouring our fighting material into a tub of the Danaides, pierced with an hundred auger-holes." Davis, however, was far more conscious than Lee that such a policy depended upon public opinion;

and, much as he desired the added power which the enlistment of negroes would give, he doubted whether the "sovereign states" were ready to support it. On February 21st, he wrote to John Forsyth, who had written to urge it: "It is now becoming daily more evident . . . that we are reduced to choosing whether the negroes shall fight for us or against us, and that arguments as to the positive advantages or disadvantages of employing them are beside the question. . . . I can see no discordance in the views you express and what wise policy would dictate. . . . The influence of your journal in the line which you propose to take would be of valuable assistance."

These, and many similar letters, show that Davis was ready, if public opinion could be properly prepared, to announce a policy of emancipation for such negroes as should enlist in the army. Without the support of public opinion, he knew that such an announcement would only increase prevailing discontent. He was fighting for state sovereignty, and could not without abandoning that cause emancipated slaves held within sovereign states, unless public opinion in those states could be brought to his assistance. He therefore had little hope of being able to bring about even "contingent emancipation sufficient to satisfy appearances," while the possibility of "absolute" emancipation which Vallandingham had predicted was quite out of the question. "It was," he later explained, "out of the power of the Confederate Government to act on the subject of the domestic institutions of the several states, each having jurisdiction on that point."

It is difficult, if not impossible, to make a union of complete individualists, and the theory that the states were free to determine their own domestic institutions later embarrassed Lincoln, as it was now embarrassing Davis. When the law requiring reconstructed states to prohibit slavery was presented for his approval, Lincoln declared that he could not sign it. Chandler warned him that "if it is vetoed, it will damage us fearfully. The important point is that one prohibiting slavery in the reconstructed states."

"That," answered Lincoln, "is the point on which I doubt the authority of Congress to act." To the argument of his opponents that he had already so acted by issuing his Emancipation Proclamation, he replied: "I conceive that I may, in an emergency, do things on military grounds which cannot be done constitutionally by Congress," though later he added: "I do not see how any of us now can deny and contradict what we have always said, that Congress has no Constitutional power over slavery in the states." By his doctrine of military necessity, he had overcome the limitations of his Constitutional theory, thereby greatly increasing his fighting force; but he had also created a problem for his successor, who found over 85,000 negroes still in the army in October, 1865, after vigorous efforts had been made to reduce the forces.

Toward the middle of March, 1865, the Confederate Congress, in response to the suggestions which Davis and Lee had made, passed a law providing for the enlistment of slaves as soldiers, but without the promise of freedom which they had recommended. It was a weak bill, little calculated to be received as an answer to the charge that the South was fighting to preserve slavery, and not, in Davis' opinion, likely to add much strength to the army, but it was a step in the right direction, and he decided to approve it. He reported his decision to Lee, as follows:

"Richmond, *March 13, 1865.*

"GENERAL:

"I am in receipt of your favour in regard to the bill for putting negroes in the army.

"The bill was received from Congress today and immediately signed.

"I shall be pleased to receive such suggestions from you, as will aid me in carrying out the law, and I trust you will endeavour in every available mode to give promptitude to the requisite action.

"Very respectfully and truly yours,

"JEFFN. DAVIS."

To some of his friends it was a disappointment that, in signing the bill he had not stated, for the benefit of European opinion, that emancipation would soon follow. In answer to this criticism, he wrote, on March 22nd, to J. D. Shaw: "Your proposition in regard to negotiating with European powers respecting the slavery question has been attentively considered. There would be difficulty, however, in carrying it into effect. In the first place, the Confederate Government can make no agreement nor arrangement with any nation which would interfere with state institutions, and if foreign governments would consent to interpose in our behalf upon the conditions stated, it would be necessary to submit the terms to the different states of the Confederacy for their separate action.

"It cannot be doubted that the obstacle to the recognition of the Confederacy has been an unwillingness to be embroiled in a quarrel with the United States. If slavery or any other cause had been the impediment, our advances to European governments would have led to the disclosure of their reasons for not acknowledging our independence. As soon as these governments are willing to negotiate with us upon terms to which we can honourably accede, the declaration of their conditions will probably be made known to our commissioners, so that the terms proposed may be submitted to the people, states and Government of the Confederacy."

Thus only a couple of weeks before the final collapse of his fighting-machine, Davis felt compelled to respect the sovereignty of the states which made abolition by the Confederate Government impossible. And even in carrying into effect the law just signed, enlisting negroes, he waited on the states. "My idea has been," he wrote to Governor Smith of Virginia, on March 25th, "that we should endeavour to draw into our military service that portion of the negroes which would be most apt to run away and join the army of the enemy, and this would be best effected by seeking for volunteers. If this plan should fail to obtain the requisite number, there will still remain the process of compulsory enlistment." On March 30th, he wrote again to Governor Smith: "I am happy to receive your assurance of success, as well as your promise to seek legislation to secure unmistakably freedom to the slave who will enter the army, with a right to return to his old home when he shall have been honourably discharged."

Meanwhile Davis, having persuaded Lee to accept the responsibility of commander-in-chief of all the armies of the Confederacy, without relinquishing the immediate command of the Army of Northern Virginia, had consented, at Lee's request, to make Johnston commander of the Army of Tennessee, and to give him charge of a district which included also South Carolina, Georgia, and Florida. The appointment had been followed by orders from Lee directing Johnston to concentrate all his available forces against Sherman, and, if possible, to prevent him from reinforcing Grant near Petersburg. For some weeks Johnston had prepared to face Sherman and at last on March 19 and 20, 1865, he had engaged him at Bentonville, capturing four pieces of artillery and nine hundred prisoners. It was hardly a victory, as Johnston retreated before Sherman to Raleigh and then moved over to the neighbourhood of Greensboro. Davis, however, received the news with great satisfaction, as a harbinger of greater achievements by the man who had so often disappointed him. "I have been much gratified by the success of General Johnston at Bentonville," he commented, "and hope that is only the first of the good tidings we may receive from that quarter. It is a plain case for the application of the maxim with regard to the employment of a small army against a large one. Sherman's forces, worn by long marches, and necessarily comparatively ignorant of the country in which he is operating, must offer opportunities for surprises and attacks in detail. . . . I hope General Johnston will find the opportunity to destroy at least to a great extent Sherman's army before it makes a junction with the other."

This, however, did not prove to be the case. Johnston and Lee were being slowly enmeshed in Grant's web, from which escape was impossible, and on March 23rd, Lee sent Davis a report from Johnston to the effect that, "Sherman's course cannot be hindered by the small force I have. I can do no more than annoy him." Three days later Lee reported a disappointing engagement near Petersburg. "I fear . . . it will be impossible to prevent a junction between Grant and Sherman, nor do I deem it prudent that this army should maintain its position until the latter shall approach too near." Estimating Sherman's forces at some 60,000, and Grant's at more than 100,000, he concluded that, if the junction should be effected, there would be scant hope indeed of preventing an overwhelming catastrophe for the Confederates.

Despite such vast disparity in numbers, however, Lee maintained his position, while prudently working out plans for evacuating the Richmond line and establishing a new base at some suitable point farther south. He later told Gordon of a conversation which he had had with Davis over the question of an early evacuation of Richmond. "Of Davis," says Gordon, "he spoke in terms of strong eulogy; of the strength of his convictions, of his devotion, of his remarkable faith in the possibility of still winning our independence, and of his unconquerable will power."

Knowing from Lee's confidential dispatches that this move would have to be made whenever Sherman should join Grant, and that then Richmond would be captured, Davis had sent his family south. "Mr. Davis came to me," says his wife's *Memoir*, "and gently but decidedly announced the necessity of our departure. He said that for the future his headquarters must be in the field, and that our presence would only embarrass and grieve, instead of comforting him. . . . I argued the question with him and pleaded to be permitted to remain, until he said, 'I have confidence in your capacity to take care of our babies, and understand your desire to assist and comfort me, but you can do this in but one way, and that is by going yourself and taking our children to a place of safety.' He was very much affected and said, 'If I live, you can come to me when the struggle is ended, but I do not expect to survive the destruction of Constitutional liberty.' " Mrs. Davis then yielded, and later wrote, "Mr. Davis gave me a pistol and showed me how to load, aim, and fire it. He was very apprehensive of our falling into the hands of the disorganized bands of troops roving about the country, and said, 'You can at least, if reduced to the last extremity, force your assailants to kill you, but I charge you solemnly to leave when you hear the enemy approaching; and if you cannot remain undisturbed in our country, make for the Florida coast and take a ship there for a foreign country.' "

In preparation for Mrs. Davis' departure, the more valuable articles of furniture were disposed of through a dealer, and Major Echols was dispatched to secure a house at Charlotte, North Carolina, suitable for her reception. When these preparations had been completed, Burton Harrison, the President's secretary, was directed to conduct her to Charlotte, and at the station, just before the train started, Davis confided the most recent information from Lee: "Sheridan has been ordered to move with his cavalry to our right flank, and to tear up the railroad; he is to remain there . . . until driven off by Hampton, or by lack of supplies; he is then to rejoin Grant in front of Petersburg, if possible; otherwise, to go to Sherman in North Carolina."

After watching the train disappear, Davis distributed among the hospitals the scanty stores remaining in the White House of the Confederacy, but though forced to accept the prospect of a speedy departure from Richmond, he cherished the hope that he might rejoin his family and eventually bring them back to the restored capital. The plan for voluntary, negro enlistment had proved a failure; yet his courage never failed. The shadow of Appomattox was over him; but he staunchly continued to hope for the "miracle of recruiting" which Lee had indicated as the only remaining hope. That miracle did not come to pass. The dead still came in faster than the living could be induced to go out.

The fatal disaster of Five Forks which gave Grant control of the direct line of retreat to Danville left open to Lee only the line of retreat upon the northern side of the Appomattox, which was longer. Thus Grant had the advantage of operating upon an interior line. As a result, on April 1st, Lee reported that he was preparing "for the necessity of evacuating our position on the James River," a clear indication that Richmond must soon be abandoned.

Although Davis carefully guarded this warning, the evil news could not be kept secret, and, as it mysteriously circulated, becoming ever more alarming with each repetition, he decided to address the citizens of Richmond and attempt to quiet their fears. He therefore let it be known that he would appear at a certain hour on the steps of the African Church to speak to such of his fellow-citizens as cared to come. To the throng which gathered he addressed himself in terms of courage and hope. Alexander H. Stephens again joined the crowd to hear what was to be heard. "I pushed myself through the crowd," he says, "and got so near to him that I heard every word he said. . . . Mr. Davis calmly and earnestly said, and the expression of his face carried conviction of his sincerity: 'That the disasters of today are temporary. They will be reversed. We will soon come back to establish the capital in this city. The ultimate success of the Southern Confederacy cannot be questioned, but we must have courage and fidelity to meet the situation.' There was no word, look, or tone to indicate fear or misgiving. His faith was sublime."

With this certainty of the speedy fall of Richmond in mind, Davis appeared at St. Paul's, the next morning, to join in the celebration of the Holy Communion. According to Mallory, his face was closely scrutinized as he entered and quietly sought his pew; but its expression varied not from that cold, stern sadness which four years of harassing mental labour had stamped upon it; and as he raised his head after a brief interval from its devotional position, and turned toward Dr. Minnegerode, the calm eyes, the sunken cheek, the compressed lip were all as impenetrable as an iron mask. Not a devotee in all that congregation seemed more gravely attentive than he to the morning service or responded to its exhortations more fervently; and yet his heart was agonized, and his brain sorely perplexed by Lee's dispatches of the early hours of the day, telling of Grant's overwhelming charge through his centre, of heavy losses, of his inability to re-establish his lines, and suggesting the abandonment of Richmond. The dull, booming sound of distant guns was mingled with the impressive words of the service, forming strange and startling responses to its invocations for peace on earth and good will to men.

After the procession had entered and the choir had taken their accustomed places, Dr. Minnegerode, the rector, began the service, Davis devoutly following. As he knelt, with bowed head, writes Mrs. Gorgas, wife of the famous soldier-engineer, who sat near him, "a messenger came into the church and walked quickly to the President's pew. He said something in great excitement. Mr. Davis' face grew pale, but in a moment he controlled his emotion, arose, and with his usual dignity of bearing, walked out of the church."

Davis' own simple account was given in a letter to his wife three days later: "On last Sunday, I was called out of church to receive a telegram announcing that General Lee could not hold his position longer than till night, and warning me that we must leave Richmond, as the army would commence retreating that evening."

Upon leaving the church, Davis walked to his office, "assembled the heads of departments and bureaus, so far as they could be found, on a day when all the offices were closed, and gave the needful instruction for our removal that night, simultaneously with General Lee's from Petersburg. . . . This occupied myself and staff until late in the afternoon. By this time the report that

Richmond was to be evacuated had spread through the town, and many who saw me walking toward my residence left their houses to inquire whether the report was true. Upon my admission of the painful fact, qualified, however, by the expression of my hope that we should under better auspices again return, they all, the ladies especially, with generous sympathy and patriotic impulse responded, 'If the success of the cause requires you to give up Richmond, we are content.' "

Upon his arrival at the White House, Davis calmly completed preparations for its abandonment. "Nothing," he later reported to Mrs. Davis, "had been done after you left and but little could be done in the few hours which remained before the train was to leave.

"I packed the bust and gave it to John Davis, who offered to take it and put it where it should never be found by a Yankee. I also gave him charge of the painting of the heroes of the valley. Both were removed after dark. The furniture of the house was left, and very little of the things I directed to be put up, bedding and groceries, were saved. . . .

"The auctioneer returned account of sales $28,400. Could not dispose of the carriages. Mr. Grant was afraid to take the carriage to his house &c &c. I sent it to the depot to be put on a flat. At the moment of starting it was said they could not take it in that train, but would bring it on the next train. It has not been heard from since. . . . I had short notice, was interrupted so often and so little aided that the results are very unsatisfactory."

The special train which had been arranged for him and the other Government officials was ready at eight o'clock that evening: and for three hours crowds surged round it, hoping to be taken on board. With the exception of many terrified women, however, only those "indispensable to the operations of the Government" could be allowed to enter. At eleven o'clock Davis appeared, accompanied by the Secretary of War and other prominent members of his Government. At once the signal was sounded and the train moved out of Richmond towards Danville, which had been selected as the temporary capital. "No man who saw Mr. Davis on that trying occasion," said Reagan, "but was impressed with his calm and manly dignity, his devotion to the public interest, and his courage."

Courage too was required of those left behind: for the departure of the Government had left the city at the mercy of Grant's advancing armies. Mrs. Fontaine, writing to a friend, with the picture fresh in her memory, tells what she saw on that night: "We returned to our rooms to prepare those who were to leave. . . . All through that long, long night we worked and wept and bade farewells, never thinking of sleep. In the distance we heard the shouts of the soldiers and mobs as they ransacked stores; the rumbling of wagons, and beating of drums, all mixed in a confused medley. Just before dawn explosions of gunboats and magazines shook the city, and glass was shattered, and new houses crumbled beneath the shocks. Involuntarily, I closed the shutters, and then everything became still as death, while immense fires stretched their arms on high all round me. I shuddered at the dreadful silence. Richmond was burning, and no alarm. . . . I cannot describe my feelings as I stood at a window overlooking the city, in that dim dawn. I watched those silent, awful fires; I felt that there was no effort to stop them, but all like myself were watching them, paralysed and breathless. After a while the sun rose . . . a great, red ball, veiled in a mist. . . . The streets were alive with hurrying men and women, and the cry of the 'Yankees.' . . . I did not move, I could not, but watched the blue horseman ride to the City Hall, enter, with his sword knocking the ground at every step, throw the great doors open, and take possession of our beautiful city; watched two blue figures on the Capitol, white men . . . unfurl a tiny flag, and then I sank on my knees, and the bitter, bitter tears came in a torrent."

In this letter we have a composite photograph of every Confederate woman left in Richmond. To them the marching soldiers, the crackling flames, and the destructive explosions were but parts of one stupendous plot to efface the capital of the Confederate States. But calmer judgment has long ago absolved Grant's armies of the charge of aiming deliberately to destroy the city. His own later account is probably much nearer the truth. He says in his *Memoirs* that he "found the city on fire in two places. . . . Up to the very hour of the evacuation the people had been led to believe that Lee had gained an important victory somewhere round Petersburg. . . . Our troops were directed to extinguish the flames, which they finally succeeded in doing." His opinion that "the fire had been started by some one connected with the retreating army" is, however, probably a mistake. Mr. Douglas Freeman, a very careful authority, declares that "the destruction of tobacco (a policy which Lee had advocated on January 28, 1865) probably led to the memorable fire that laid in ashes the business section of the city."

There was a tradition, which has been perpetuated by Thomas Dixon's "Victim," that when Davis "crossed the Savannah River . . . he dropped the Seal of the Confederate Government in the depths of its still, beautiful waters"; an appealing story, reminiscent of the day when King James II, fleeing from his capital, threw the Great Seal of England into the Thames. We now know, however, that in the case of the Confederacy the story is fiction. James Jones, Davis' trusted mulatto servant, with an inordinate thirst for notoriety, gave to the press a carefully elaborated narrative which declared that President Davis had entrusted the Great Seal to his care, and that he had sunk it in the James River near Richmond. He claimed that he had been entrusted also with a treasure amounting to $13,000,000, which he had hauled round on a freight-car "from one point to another in the South until Captain Parker . . . relieved me of it at a point near Washington, Georgia." Both statements were entirely false; but the story appealed to the public love of adventure, and for many years it continued to be repeated as history. As late as June 4, 1907, the New York Daily *Tribune* printed three columns of Jones' "Memories," which had still lost nothing of their popular appeal. Unfortunately for his memory, however, the facts about the Great Seal have since been made known.

At the evacuation of Richmond, it was carried away by Mrs. Bromwell, wife of a clerk in the State Department. For a time it was hidden in a barn near Richmond, and later in Washington. In 1872, John J. Pickett acting for Bromwell sold to the United States Government for $75,000 a mass of Confederate archives which he had taken from Richmond. The sale was promoted by Lieutenant Thomas O. Selfrage, and in recognition of his help, Pickett gave him the Great Seal of the Confederacy. Years later, Congress acquired also the papers of Pickett himself; and in preparing these for deposit in the manuscript department of the Library of Congress, Galliard Hunt came across a reference to the Seal. A careful search was instituted, and resulted in its discovery. The news was sent to Mr. Eppa Hunton, Jr., of Richmond, who, with William H. White and Thomas P. Brown, made up a purse of $3,000 for its purchase, subject to positive identification. It was sent to England, in charge of M. J. St. George Bryan, where J. S. Wyon, successor to the firm which had made it, examined it carefully and declared it to be "the Great Seal of the Confederacy, which was engraved in silver by my uncle, Mr. J. S. Wyon, in the year 1864." It was then deposited in the museum of the White House of the Confederacy, where it is cherished among the most valued relics of the Lost Cause.

## CHAPTER XXIV

# COLLAPSE OF THE CONFEDERACY

AS DAVIS' train approached Danville, he knew that he was an object of great interest to the hovering myrmidons of Sherman and Grant, who were eager to capture him. His chief anxiety, however, was for his family, who were less protected than he. His wife's first letter, however, greatly reassured him. Writing on April 3rd from "20 miles south of Washington," she reported that she was making good progress and was "well-provided in every respect, but of course proceeding cautiously. I have," she added, "2,500, some things to sell, and have heart, and a hopeful one, but above all, my precious only love, a heart full of prayer. May God keep you and have his sword and buckler over you. Do not try to make a stand this side [of the Mississippi]. . . . Leave your escort and take another road often. There are only enough men to point attention. Let them follow you. . . . Alabama is full of cavalry, fresh and earnest in pursuit. May God keep you. . . ."

That same day Davis entered Danville without unpleasant incident. He established offices at the residence of Colonel Southerlin, and set himself to the difficult task of composing a proclamation which should hearten the people for renewed and persistent resistance. Uneasy lest his work be interfered with by wandering bands of Federal troopers, but reassured by promises of a proper guard, he wrote to General Beauregard, on April 4th: "The cavalry you ordered here [to Danville] will be of special value at this time, and with the infantry en route will probably serve the immediate necessity. Have sent courier to General Lee, from whom I have no communication."

The next day he issued his "Proclamation to the People of the Confederate States of America," one of the strangest of his papers. Himself a fugitive, his capital in the hands of the enemy, his greatest generals meshed in Grant's net, he yet spoke of the evacuation of Richmond as a bit of military strategy: "The General-in-chief of our Army has found it necessary to make such movements of the troops as to uncover the capital, and thus involve the withdrawal of the Government from the City of Richmond. . . . The loss which we have suffered is not without compensation. For many months the largest and finest army of the Confederacy, under the command of a leader whose presence inspires equal confidence in the troops and the people, has been greatly trammelled by the necessity of keeping constant watch over the approaches to the capital, and thus has been forced to forego more than one opportunity for promising enterprises. . . . Relieved from the necessity of guarding cities and particular points, important but not vital to our defence, with our army free to move from point to point and strike in detail the detachments and garrisons of the enemy, operating in the interior of our own country, where supplies are more accessible . . . nothing is now needed to render our triumph certain, but the exhibition of our own unconquerable resolve. Let us but will it, and we are free. . . ."

"If you would know why Rome was great," says a student of her history, "consider that Roman soldier whose armed skeleton was found in a recess near the gate at Pompeii. When burst that sulphurous storm the undaunted hero dropped the visor of his helmet and stood there to die." Davis too was beaten, but not conquered.

In the meantime, and within a few hours of Davis' departure, Lincoln entered Richmond from a Federal gunboat. He walked from the docks to the White House of the Confederacy, and swung his long legs from the chair in which Davis had so lately sat. After conversing with General Weitzel, upon the strange fortunes of men and the grim conflict which had seated him in Davis' chair, he wandered through the house, now Federal property. Later, standing in Capitol Square, he studied the equestrian statue of Washington, with right hand raised and eyes fixed upon every beholder, and remarked: "Washington is looking at me, and pointing to Jeff Davis."

After completing his inspection of the city, Lincoln paid a visit to Grant's headquarters to discuss the conditions of surrender which should be offered to Lee when the now inevitable end should come. The terms that he directed were generous terms, conceived with the intent to make peace palatable. He intimated also a desire that Davis should be induced to leave the country, and suggested that a Federal boat should be placed at his disposal upon which he should be allowed to carry away such of his private possessions as he wished, hoping, according to Sherman, that Davis might escape "unbeknownst to me."

Meanwhile the object of this strategy, as wise as it was generous, was preparing not for flight, but for further struggle, although his circumstances were indeed desperate. Three days earlier, the Treasurer of South Carolina had returned to Davis his cheque for $28,244, drawn on the Bank of Virginia, with the explanation that he was "not authorized to pay cheques." But though troubled by this, and desperately anxious in regard to the condition of his family, gone he knew not whither, and with funds which must be growing scanty, he was still intent upon his purpose, to reorganize resistance to the armies of the United States.

It would have confirmed Davis in his belief that success was still possible could he have read an entry, made in his private files on January 12, 1865, by John Bigelow, American minister to France, which declared that Napoleon III, disregarding the third article of his Declaration of Neutrality, had encouraged the building of Confederate war vessels in France, but had never been quite willing to allow them to be delivered to a Government as hard pressed as the Confederacy had been. At this last moment, however, one had escaped to Copenhagen, under the name *Stoerkodder*. There she had assumed two aliases, the *Olinde*, and the *Stonewall*, and had prepared for her deadly work against American commerce. "Had the war continued but a month longer," commented Bigelow at a later date, "the *Stonewall* would have had possession of Port Royal, and if two months longer, the City of New York would probably have lain at her mercy. One more defeat, or one less victory of the Union arms, would certainly have given the Confederates one, and probably four vessels, each more formidable than anything which floated the Union Jack. The French Government intended these vessels should in some way be placed at the disposal of the Confederate Government. They only waited for it to show strength enough, or the Union weakness enough, to establish a reasonable presumption that these vessels could decide the contest."

Mrs. Davis had now reached Charlotte, and wrote that she was "very well off and very kindly treated"; and a few days later Burton Harrison returned, reported that his charges had been safely lodged in a rented house, and praised the delicacy and hospitality of their landlord, Mr. Wielie. He later recorded that at Danville he "found several Bureaus of the War Department, with other departments of the Confederate Government organized for work in regular quarters in the town, and a separate and commodious house occupied by the President and his staff. The chief secretary, M. H. Clark, had started the work of organizing the Executive Offices: and the President was planning military activities with apparent calm and confidence."

News of the evacuation of Richmond, and of its occupation by Grant's army, now caused Mrs. Davis to make a sudden change in her plans, a change which caused her to lose touch with her husband. Anxious for the safety of the Confederate treasure carried by her escort, she decided to leave Charlotte, but before making her preparations, dispatched a messenger to Davis, with a letter declaring that "the news from Richmond came upon me like the 'abomination of desolation,' the loss of Selma like the 'blackness thereof.' Trans-Mississippi seems our ultimate destination." Before selecting her own immediate destination and planning her retreat, she received news of Lee's surrender of April 9th, which caused her to fear for the treasure train. In an article, later contributed to *Spare Moments*, she graphically sketches the details of the journey which followed: "At Charlotte . . . I heard . . . of the surrender of Lee and the rumour that the President and the Cabinet were coming to Charlotte to meet General Johnston. He [the President] had charged me solemnly to take the utmost care of our children and I felt that I must obey him and remove myself still farther from the immediate zone of danger. The night we heard of Lee's disaster it was decided to move the treasure train of the Confederacy and the Richmond banks, which was escorted by the midshipmen under Captain Parker. Among the escort I had two relatives, one being my own brother, Jefferson, and the other a grand-nephew of Mr. Davis. I . . . placed my family and servants in an extra train that had been supplied, which was to travel as far as Chester, the railroad beyond that point being impassable. There I managed to secure an ambulance . . . and after spending the day in preparation, we started on in the wake of the wagon train for Abbeville. Of the rigours of that trip it is hard to speak. The roads were so deeply covered with soft sticky mud that we were for the most part compelled to walk, until my nurse, who had charge of the youngest child, refused to farther continue in the mire. I think I walked about five miles that night in the darkness, with the mud over my shoe tops and my baby in my arms.

"Imagine that passage through the night, with alarms at every turn in the road; for the Yankee pickets and scouts were everywhere, and it was not known definitely in what direction they were reconnoitring. These alarms happily turned out to be groundless, and about one o'clock we managed to reach a little church that . . . had been pre-empted by the men of the treasure train, as it furnished something tangible in the way of defence were we to be attacked. To say the small structure was crowded would be to express its condition but faintly. It was literally packed and none of us obtained much rest that night. Early in the morning we moved on again, and after a journey that even now has not lost its terrors, and from which time has not taken the sting, we moved into Abbeville and were warmly welcomed. . . . We remained for a time at Abbeville, and the treasure train moved on immediately to Washington [Georgia]." Here, where she was hospitably entertained by Mr. Armistead Burt, Mrs. Davis received more detailed news of Lee's surrender, rumours that Johnston was preparing to surrender, and the comforting assurance that her husband had reached Charlotte in safety.

Before abandoning his new capital at Danville, Davis had written to Lee, warning him of a rumour that Sherman planned to concentrate his forces there. "We have here," he added, "about 3,000 infantry and artillery, are constructing defences and should have an experienced engineer, the ground being unfavourable.

"I had hoped to have seen you at an earlier period, and trust soon to meet you. The Secretary of War, Quartermaster-General, Commissary-General and Chief Engineer have not arrived. Their absence is embarrassing. We have here provisions and clothing for your army and they are held for its use. You will realize the reluctance I feel to leave the soil of Virginia, and appreciate my anxiety to win success north of the Roanoke. The few stragglers who come from your army are stopped here and at Staunton bridge. They are generally, however, without arms." There followed a brief description of recent dispositions of commands for the defence of Georgia and Alabama, and the letter closed with the words: "May God preserve, sustain, and guide you."

At the very hour in which this letter was written General Lee was preparing for the last scene of his brilliant military career, the surrender of Appomattox. Davis did not know that on April

7th Grant had asked Lee to aid him in stopping "any further effusion of blood," by surrendering "that portion of the Confederate States' army known as the Army of Northern Virginia." When asked his terms, Grant replied: "There is but one condition, . . . that the men and officers surrendered shall be disqualified for taking up arms again against the Government of the United States until properly exchanged."

It is not possible to discover how far this generous condition was the result of Lincoln's presence in Grant's camp: but it breathes his spirit. A conversation is recorded during which some one expressed to Lincoln the hope that, whatever else should result from Lee's coming surrender, Jefferson Davis would reach the gallows. Lincoln's rebuke followed, in the quiet words: "Let us judge not, that we be not judged."

Lee's reply to Grant's request had been, "I do not think the emergency has arisen . . . for surrender. But, as the restoration of peace should be the sole object of all, I desire to know whether your proposals would tend to that end. I cannot . . . meet you with a view to surrender the Army of Northern Virginia, but, so far as your proposition may affect . . . the restoration of peace, I should be pleased to meet you at 10 A.M., tomorrow, on the old stage-road to Richmond, between the picket lines of the two armies."

Grant answered that he had no authority to treat on the subject of peace, and felt that a meeting upon the basis which Lee had suggested would "lead to no good. I am," he added, "equally anxious for peace with himself; and the whole North entertains the same feeling. The terms upon which peace can be had are well understood. By . . . laying down their arms," the South "will hasten that most desirable event, save thousands of human lives, and hundreds of millions of property." Upon this basis, Lee consented to the meeting which resulted in the famous surrender of April 9, 1865, at Appomattox Court House, and before

Davis' letter of April 9th reached him the famous surrender had become history.

Lee's decision to discuss surrender was born not of despair, but of human sympathy; for he was confident of his ability to defy Federal authority indefinitely, should he adopt the methods of guerilla warfare. He had recently said to Davis, "With my army in the mountains of Virginia I could carry on this war for twenty years longer." And Davis later approvingly explained, "when he found the line which obstructed his retreat could not be broken, he said there was nothing to do but surrender." He knew that independence, the cause for which he had fought, was lost, and refused to sacrifice his men upon the altar of pride disguised as patriotism.

It was long before Davis knew the details of that memorable Palm Sunday: but they are now a part of American history. Until the agreement for the meeting at Appomattox was reached, Grant had enjoyed the advantage of Lincoln's presence in his camp: but at this point, the latter, feeling that the next day's meeting would mark the end of effective resistance by the South, returned to his waiting vessel and started back to Washington. "His only preoccupation," according to the later testimony of one of his companions, "was the necessity of wiping out the consequences of the war," but he had no intention of countenancing a treaty of peace. To him, as at the commencement of the contest, the seceded states had conducted a domestic insurrection, "too powerful to be suppressed by the ordinary course of judicial proceedings, or by the powers vested in the marshals by law"; it was this interpretation which had caused Grant to say: "I have no authority to treat on the subject of peace."

On the boat Lincoln devoted himself to the entertainment of his guest, the Marquis of Chambrun, who was returning with him to Washington. He was, apparently, in high, even boisterous spirits. After directing the military band to play the "Marseillaise," he asked if the Marquis had ever heard "Dixie." When a negative answer was given, Lincoln said: "That tune is now Federal property. It belongs to us"; and added that he would have it played for the Marquis, to prove that "with us they will be free to hear it again."

The next morning, the day of the surrender, while Grant and Lee were preparing for the auspicious meeting, and Davis was writing his dispatch to Lee, just quoted, Lincoln conversed quietly with the Marquis and Senator Sumner, choosing literature rather than war as his topic. Producing a well-thumbed quarto volume of Shakespeare, he read aloud a number of his favourite passages from Macbeth. One passage he read twice:

> Duncan is in his grave;
> After life's fitful fever he sleeps well.
> Treason has done his worst; nor steel, nor poison,
> Malice domestic, foreign levy, nothing,
> Can touch him further.

Meanwhile Lee, immaculately clad and imperturbable, met the leader who had conquered at last. Tradition has shown him handing his sword to Grant under an apple tree at Appomattox; but, as Grant wrote later, "war produces many stories of fiction, some of which are told until they are believed to be true . . . and the story of the apple tree is one of those fictions based on a slight foundation of fact. . . . There was an apple tree, hard on the side of the hill occupied by the Confederate forces." But Lee's surrender did not take place there. The scene was enacted within the four walls of a house. "When I went into the house," the *Memoirs* continue, "I found General Lee. We greeted each other, and after shaking hands took our seats." Grant was dressed in a soldier's blouse, with only "shoulder straps of my rank to indicate to the army who I was." General Lee, with characteristic regard for the dignity of the occasion, "was dressed in a full uniform which was entirely new, and wearing a sword of considerable value." Grant carried no sword. "The much-talked-of surrender of Lee's sword and my handing it back . . . is the purest romance. The sword . . . was not mentioned by either of us, nor is it mentioned in the terms of surrender."

Grant suggested that, as the most influential general in the South, Lee should advise the surrender of all the armies remaining in the field, and thus save fruitless and unnecessary loss of life. Lee answered that he could not do this without first consulting President Davis. He, too, understood, that the settlements of peace belonged to the Executive.

Thus, the problems of peace being confessedly outside their provinces, Grant and Lee finished the terms of surrender, and signed them. The original text of Lee's General Order No. 9, announcing the news to his army, and preserved in the Confederate Museum at Richmond, declares: "by the terms of the agreement, officers and men can return to their homes and remain until exchanged." The hero of the Confederacy and his heroic followers of the Army of Northern Virginia were now prisoners on parole. And when, some months later, President Johnson and Secretary Stanton proposed to arrest all Confederate officers of the rank of colonel or higher, Grant boldly resisted, declaring, according to Bingham: "You will have to whip me and my army before one hair of one head of the men whom we captured, and to whom I promised protection, shall perish."

Those who had seen Lee at Seven Pines, on June 1, 1862, riding beside the President of the then hopeful Confederacy, had admired the general; but as yet they did not know the reserves of patience, power, imagination, and daring which ripened him into a figure which the world will not forget; and as he rode away from Appomattox, a paroled prisoner of war, he was a man even more worthy of admiration than he had been at the beginning, or at the zenith of his great career. In Douglas Freeman's fine sentence, Appomattox had shown that great as Lee had proved himself, as a soldier, "Lee the man and the Christian was greater by far." In such fashion did the South's great leader, the idol of all hearts, become a prisoner of war, as he gave his parole to the North's great leader, who then, as thereafter, was surprisingly considerate of both Lee and Davis. Had the rest of the North been as generous, and as just, America would have been spared the horrors of Reconstruction which needlessly perpetuated sectional hostility and created what has since been called "the Solid South." General French correctly described the facts upon which a wise statesman, such as Lincoln, might easily have built at once a reunited nation, when he wrote: "The soldiers on either side understood each other. . . . They had traded tobacco for coffee too often on the picket line not to fraternize, and they were imbued with the common feeling of humanity. . . . And numbers of the highest officers on either side had been school companions and devoted friends. . . . But there was a large class of people in the North who knew us only by report . . . and they urged relentless war." Even Emerson wrote in his *Journal* on news from Appomattox: " 'Tis far best that the rebels have been pounded instead of negotiated into a peace. . . . General Grant's terms certainly look a little too easy." As for the politicians of the North, they deliberately played politics, using "God's image in ebony" as helpless pawns in their fight for power. Sumner spoke the motives which many obeyed when he declared, while urging the enfranchisement of all freedmen, "We need the votes of all, and cannot afford to wait," and Gerrit Smith demanded that for a dozen years "the rebel masses shall not . . . be allowed access to the ballot-box or be eligible to office."

Colonel Robert Bingham declared later that the sympathy of Grant's men for their fallen antagonists was very apparent, as the latter stacked their arms for the last time. "I saw tears of sympathy and pity streaming from the eyes of the Federal soldiers who stood in line on each side of us. They had pursued us and overwhelmed us, but they were touched with the feeling of our infirmity, and the victorious Americans mingled their tears with the tears of the vanquished Americans."

The news of Lee's surrender brought to the majority of Southern hearts a grief quite disconnected from personal interest or slave property. "There were those in the South," wrote Basil L. Gildersleeve, in later years, recalling the fight in which he had stood among the defeated, "who, when they saw the issue of the war, gave up their faith in God, but not their faith in the cause." And, looking backward, after over seventy years, we see that the same staunch faith in the cause that was, remained with many Englishmen who had steadfastly refused to believe that the South fought to perpetuate slavery. "I broke my heart over the surrender of Lee, the greatest General the world has ever seen, with the possible exception of Napoleon," wrote Lord Acton, historian, scholar, and friend of Gladstone. And later, in acknowledging the receipt of Miss Emily V. Mason's *Life of Lee*, he said: "Your book on your hero, and mine, was valuable to me as about the only Englishman left who is true to the Lost Cause, and can never turn to its records, even now, without emotion." The two English scholars, George Long and Philip Stanhope Worseley, had been also staunch supporters of the South; and the former, writing in his last year of life, said: "It is strange how fresh the Southern States are in my memory. I shall die thinking of them." And in his *Thoughts on Marcus Aurelius* he turned aside to eulogize General Lee. Worseley dedicated to Lee his translation of the Iliad, in verses of great charm and pathos, and described him as "the most stainless of living commanders and, except in fortune, the greatest." And there were many others, equally eminent, who manifested an abiding faith in the principle for which Lee and his armies had contended, insisting to the end of their lives that it was not slavery, but the inalienable right to self-government.

The public mind, accustomed to peace treaties for the settlement of war questions, has grown to regard the surrender of Appomattox almost as an agreement which put an end to the war: but such was not the case. To Davis it was a terrible disaster, but by no means the end of the struggle for independence.

On the afternoon of April 9th while Lee busied himself with preparations for dispersing his paroled army, a son of General Wise, who had refused to be paroled, started for Danville, where he gave to Davis the first news of Lee's surrender. Mallory, in his *Last Days of the Confederate Government*, writes: "It fell upon the ears of all like a fire-bell in the night. . . . They carefully scanned the message as it passed from hand to hand, looked at each other gravely and mutely, and for some moments a silence more eloquent of great disaster than words could have been, prevailed. The importance of prompt action, however, was evident, and in a short time preparations for moving south, before the enemy's cavalry could intervene and prevent escape, were in rapid progress. The hour of departure for Greensboro, North Carolina, was fixed for eight o'clock that evening [April 9th], but, as usual, there was delay. Nothing seemed to be ready or in order, and the train, with the President, did not leave until nearly eleven o'clock. Much rain had fallen, and the depot could be reached only through mud knee deep. With the utter darkness, the crowding quartermasters' wagons, the yells of their contending drivers, the curses, loud and deep, of soldiers, organized and disorganized, determined to get upon the train in defiance of the guard, the mutual shouts of inquiry and response as to missing individuals or luggage, the want of baggage arrangements, and the insufficient and dangerous provision made for getting horses into their cars, the crushing of the crowd, and the determination to get transportation at any hazard, together with the absence of any recognized authority, all seasoned by *sub rosa* rumours that the enemy had already cut the Greensboro road, created a confusion such as it was never before the fortune of old Danville to witness.

"At ten o'clock, Cabinet Officers and other chiefs of the Government, each seated upon or jealously guarding his baggage, formed near the cars a little silent group by themselves in the darkness, lighted only by Mr. Benjamin's inextinguishable cigar.

It was nearly eleven o'clock when the President took his seat and the train moved off."

The strategic change of base had become in fact a flight. But Davis, unlike the men whom Basil Gildersleeve described, had lost faith neither in God nor in the cause. Lee, his great reliance, might be a prisoner on parole; but there were yet Confederate armies and leaders unsurrendered, and he determined to rally them beyond the Mississippi and continue the fight for terms compatible with the dignity of his nation. Mrs. Davis, he decided, was right, when she said: "Trans-Mississippi seems our ultimate destination." His letters, even now, showed no signs of panic, or belief that the end had come. Before leaving Danville, he wrote to L. E. Harvie, concerning the defences in process of construction: "You will perceive that to leave the defences incomplete may shorten the time with which your rolling stock must be removed." He then arranged to have General Walker take the forces on hand to Greensboro, North Carolina, and telegraphed General Johnston that they were to join his army there. He took time to send to the Mayor of Danville a courteous note of thanks "for your kindness . . . under that pressure of adversity which is more apt to cause the loss of friends than to be the occasion of forming new ones. May God bless and preserve you," he added, "and grant to our country independence." His views then were those which he later expressed in the words: "Force may prevail over right, but cannot destroy truth. The exercise of a power to coerce a state cannot give to that act Constitutional authority, but it has been so acquiesced in, that the remedy of secession by an oppressed minority must be considered impracticable. The South never asked more than a fair construction of the Constitution as interpreted by the men who made it. . . . We cannot surrender a right even while admitting our inability to maintain it."

Meanwhile, as Lincoln's little boat passed the historic mansion of Washington at Mount Vernon, the Marquis de Chambrun remarked: "Mount Vernon and Springfield, the memories of Washington and your own, those of the Revolutionary and Civil Wars; those are the spots and names America shall one day equally honour." To which Lincoln responded, wearily: "Springfield! How happy, four years hence, will I be to return there in peace and tranquillity."

A little later the steamer brought them in sight of Washington, and Mrs. Lincoln exclaimed, petulantly, "Hateful city; it is full of our enemies!" Lincoln replied: "That is not so—now. We must never think of that." Had he known that in Washington was Wilkes Booth, who, burning with indignation over his belief that Lincoln had promised to save Captain John Beall of the Confederate army from a spy's death, had, after the execution, sworn that "no such traitor to his word should longer rule the nation," he might have shared Mrs. Lincoln's anxiety.

Upon landing, Lincoln, noticing with surprise the wild excitement and joy which filled the Capital city, inquired the reason. The answer came exultantly, "Lee has surrendered."

The next day, April 10th, Lincoln was interrupted by crowds in the street, accompanied by a band, demanding a speech. Too discreet to make an impromptu address at such a time, he repeated the witticism of the previous day: "You have a band with you. There is one piece of music I have always liked. Heretofore it has not seemed the proper thing to use it in the North, but now, by virtue of my prerogative as President and Commander-in-chief of the army and navy, I declare it contraband of war and our lawful prize. I ask the band to play 'Dixie.' If you will come to the White House tomorrow evening, I will have something to say," he added.

When, on April 11th, the crowd assembled, Lincoln appeared at the window and read from manuscript the speech he had prepared. In its spirit, kindness, and breadth of vision, it is a model. The question whether the so called seceded states "are out of their proper practical relation with the Union," he declared a matter of common agreement. Whether they "are in the Union or out of it," he characterized as a question "bad as the basis of a controversy, and good for nothing at all—a mere pernicious abstraction. . . . Finding themselves safely at home, it would be utterly immaterial whether they had ever been abroad."

He wisely advocated not the wholesale enfranchisement of the freedmen, but the conferring of the suffrage "on the very intelligent, and on those who serve our cause as soldiers," and a sympathetic attitude towards those persons who were seeking to bring states back into proper practical relations with the Union. "Concede," he said, with characteristic levity, "that the new Government of Louisiana is only to what it should be as the egg is to the fowl, we shall sooner have the fowl by hatching the egg than by smashing it."

Standing in the crowd of listeners outside, John Wilkes Booth remarked to Lewis Payne as they turned away, "That is the last speech he will ever make."

There is a quaint and characteristic story concerning Lincoln and the Cabinet meeting which he held on April 14th, shortly before starting to Ford's Theatre, where he was to attend a performance of "Our American Cousin," and to meet his death. After listening to various views, he had remarked in his inimitable manner, "I am a good deal like the Irishman who had joined a temperance society, but thought he might take a drink now and then, if he drank unbeknownst to himself. A good many people think that the big Confederates ought to be arrested and tried as traitors. Perhaps they ought to be; but I should be right glad if they should get out of the country, 'unbeknownst to me.'" Gideon Wells later reported an additional kindly remark, "We must extinguish our resentments if we expect harmony and union."

On the same day, Assistant-Secretary of War, Charles A. Dana, called to consult Lincoln about the advisability of arresting Jacob Thompson, a former Secretary of the Interior and later chief

Confederate agent in Canada. Lincoln listened, and remarked: "No, I rather think not. When you've got an elephant by the hind leg, and he's trying to run away, it's best to let him run." And to another visitor he declared: "No one need expect me to take any part in hanging or killing these men, even the worst of them. Frighten them out of the country, open the gates, let down the bars, scare them off. Enough lives have been sacrificed." But, if we may trust a story quite consistent with his mystical temperament, he had in mind, as he started to the theatre, the thought that at least one more life must be sacrificed. "Do you know, Crook," he said to a guard who attended him, "I believe there are men who want to take my life. And I have no doubt they will do it. . . . It is impossible to prevent it."

Within three hours the shot was fired by Booth: and the world will never forget the result. He was carried by loving hands to a little house near the theatre, where he died the next morning, (Good Friday) April 15, 1865.

That day, Edward Everett Hale wrote from Boston in the first gloom of the great calamity, "To think that it is in the same world, and in the same week of our victory and gratulation. It is a picture on the largest human scale, of the eternal and divine contrast between the triumph of Palm Sunday—and the wretchedness and glory of the Crucifixion."

## CHAPTER XXV

# JOHNSTON'S SURRENDER

SO PASSED the pacific hero of America's civil war: the man who had planned "the generous policy which would have restored the state and made a new Union possible," to quote the opinion of the still unreconstructed Basil Gildersleeve. And at once Davis' bitter, personal enemy, Vice-President Andrew Johnson, took the oath that made him President. Upon receiving the news of his accession to power, the British *Quarterly Review* introduced him to its readers in the words: "An ardent defender of slavery, a slaveholder himself to the extent of his means; a believer in 'manifest destiny.' . . . We have sought in vain for one noble sentiment, for one generous emotion. . . . [His] cry is vengeance, confiscation, blood."

The official announcement of Lincoln's death, as received by the American minister in London from Secretary Stanton, indicated the man marked for Johnson's vindictiveness. The deed, it said, resulted from a "conspiracy deliberately planned and set on foot by rebels under the pretence of avenging the South and aiding the rebel cause." From such a statement, in an official paper, to the charge that Davis had procured Lincoln's assassination was an easy step, and Johnson quickly took it. Within three weeks he issued a proclamation offering a reward of $100,000 for the capture of Jefferson Davis, and declaring that the War Department had proofs sufficient to place upon him the guilt of Lincoln's assassination.

In strange contrast with this fantastic accusation, however, he at once adopted Lincoln's views upon Reconstruction, declaring,

"The true theory is that all pretended acts of secession were from the beginning null and void. The states cannot commit treason nor screen individual citizens who may have committed treason any more than they can make valid treaties or engage in lawful commerce with any foreign power. The states attempting to secede placed themselves in a condition where their vitality was impaired, but not destroyed." And as soon as Congress assembled, he reported that all the seceded states, save Texas, were ready for readmission to their proper places in the Union, under the ten per cent plan which Lincoln had devised.

Lincoln had, however, announced in his last public speech, that he claimed no "right to say when or whether members should be admitted to seats in Congress from such states." The crisis which had forced him to assume powers, practically dictatorial in character, being now over, he had frankly acknowledged that, by the Constitution, the legislative branch of the government possessed delegated powers which the Executive must respect. Had Johnson been wise enough to adopt this view also, his career as President would have been less strife-producing.

Upon reaching Greensboro on April 11th, Davis had learned that a body of Federal cavalry had cut the railway tracks at a point which his train had passed only a few minutes before. Upon which he remarked, "a miss is as good as a mile." Although Greensboro was, or had been, a flourishing town, and contained many commodious houses, it seemed at first that no door would be opened to the chief of the Confederacy and the members of his staff and Government. The fear of Federal vengeance had apparently dried up the springs of its traditional hospitality. Davis was frail in body and exhausted by excitement, disappointment, and anxiety for the cause and for his family, again lost. Trenholm was seriously ill. After some delay, however, Colonel Wood, a member of his staff, came to the rescue and provided Davis with a bed in a little house which he had rented for his family. Quarters were found for Trenholm in the mansion of Governor Morehead, and the staff and Cabinet contented themselves as best they could, with the meagre comfort afforded by the leaky railway coaches in which they had arrived, and with such food as could be prepared in the open air by a negro boy. Here they received and entertained such visitors as cared to come, "with a cheerfulness and good humour seasoned by a flow of good spirits which threw a charm round their wretched shelter," to quote Mallory's *Last Days of the Confederate Government.*

In this atmosphere of courage, Davis spent most of his waking hours, and from here transacted the business still falling to him. But the days of the Confederacy were numbered. Sherman was slowly surrounding Johnston, with the cavalry leaders, Sheridan and Stoneman, closing the gaps, and despite the fact that he himself commanded scarcely less than 45,000 men, Johnston knew that the end was approaching.

Sherman, terrible in war, now confident of success, was planning for the wise use of victory. His aim was peace, and for its speedy establishment he made his plans, commanding that "The inhabitants be dealt with kindly, looking to an early reconciliation."

In Sherman's army, and throughout the nation, wild rumours were now current, concerning Davis, who was supposed to be seeking safety by attempting to escape from the country. Nothing was farther from his thoughts, however. Wholly uninformed of the course of events since his departure from Richmond, he was intent upon rallying the remaining Confederate forces beyond the Mississippi, and before his first day at Greensboro was over had written to Johnston, now falling back before Sherman, "As your situation may render best, I will go to your headquarters immediately after the arrival of the Secretary of War, or you can come here; in the former case our conference [would have to] be without the presence of General Beauregard. I have no official report from General Lee; the Secretary of War may be able to add information heretofore communicated. The important question first to be solved is at what point shall concentration be made?"

Meanwhile, rumours of a raid on Charlotte had caused Mrs. Davis to retire to Chester, but here too there seemed no safety, and on the day of her arrival she wrote: "A threatened raid here induces me to leave . . . without making an hour's stay. . . . I go with the special train because they have a strong guard and are attended by two responsible men. I am going somewhere, perhaps to Washington, Ga., perhaps only to Abbeville, I don't know; just as the children seem to bear the journey, will I decide. . . . Would to God I could know the truth of the horrible rumours I hear of you. One is that you have started for General Lee, but have not been heard of."

To this Davis replied on the day of Lincoln's assassination, of which he had not heard, "I will come to you if I can. Everything is dark. You should prepare for the worst by dividing your baggage so as to move in wagons. If you can go to Abbeville it seems best, as I am now advised. . . . God bless, guide, and preserve you."

The next day, April 15th, Davis prepared for the conference with Johnston, who had elected to come to Greensboro as he too wished Beauregard to be present. Conscious of the presence of the Federal cavalry who had cut the railway line, his plans included preparations for moving southward as soon as the conference should be ended, and arrangements had also to be made for the safety of the scanty contents of the Confederate Treasury now presided over by Hendren. He therefore ordered the latter to report to General Beauregard with the treasure "that he may give to it due protection as a military chest to be moved with his army train." He was, as was his custom, clearing the decks for action, realizing that he must for the moment accept the unwelcome rôle of a fugitive. His intended destination was Texas, and when General Preston Johnston objected that it would be difficult for him to cross Mississippi without being recognized, he replied, "It is true—every negro in Mississippi knows me."

Had Davis known that at seven o'clock that morning Lincoln had died of an assassin's bullet, and that Secretary Stanton and President Johnson were laying the atrocious crime at his door, he would have understood the danger of delaying flight even for so important a conference. Being, however, completely ignorant of these facts, he awaited the arrival of General Johnston and the formation of plans for a new campaign. Nor did he know that Johnston had requested Sherman to grant a temporary suspension of active operations, until after the conference, and that Sherman had willingly consented. He knew, however, that his hostess, Mrs. John Taylor Wood, was alarmed lest Stoneman's cavalry should discover his presence in her home and descend upon it, and his sensitive nature shrank from the rôle of unwelcome guest. It was, however, for the cause, and so he waited until General Johnston appeared, and the conference assembled. Nor was the alarm of his hosts allayed when they saw General Johnston, General Beauregard, John C. Breckinridge, Benjamin, Mallory, and Reagan, added to their risks, as each entered the house and disappeared into Davis' bed-sitting room. They were entertaining the entire executive department of the Confederate States, except Trenholm, who was too ill to attend.

After a few words of greeting, Davis turned to General Johnston and said, in his usual quiet manner, "I have requested you and General Beauregard . . . to join us this evening, that we might have the benefit of your views upon the situation of the country. Of course we all feel the magnitude of the moment. Our last disasters are terrible; but I do not think we should regard them as fatal. I think we can whip the enemy yet, if our people will turn out. . . ."

Johnston at once replied: "My views are, sir, that our people are tired of the war, feel themselves whipped, and will not fight. Our country is overrun, its military resources greatly diminished, while the enemy's military power and resources were never greater and may be increased to any extent desired. We cannot place another large army in the field, and, cut off as we are from foreign intercourse, I do not see how we could maintain it in fighting condition if we had it. My men are daily deserting in large numbers, and stealing my artillery teams to aid their escape to their homes. Since Lee's surrender, they regard the war as at an end. . . ." Johnston's tone and manner were bitter, "almost spiteful," according to Mallory's account.

Davis listened quietly, but his hands were nervously folding and unfolding a scrap of paper which he held and when Johnston ceased speaking, he turned to Beauregard and said, in low, even tones: "What do you say, General Beauregard?" "I concur in all General Johnston has said," was the reply.

Davis then asked Johnston, "What do you propose? You know, of course, that the enemy refuses to treat with us. How do you propose to obtain terms?" Johnston explained that, in his opinion, Sherman would consent to treat with him. "Well, sir," said Davis, with evident reluctance, "you can adopt this course, though I confess I am not sanguine as to the ultimate results."

In the end, Davis dictated a letter, which was taken down by a Cabinet member, and signed by Johnston, who hastened back to his headquarters, to open negotiations with Sherman.

According to "The Case of Jefferson Davis," in *Chase's Decisions,* Davis' act represented not conviction, but submission to the wishes of his advisers. He knew Lincoln's views too well to suppose that Sherman would be allowed to do more than accept Johnston's army upon terms quite unconnected with peace agreements. But had he known that Andrew Johnson was now President he would have expected even less from negotiations with Sherman.

The chief reason for his delay being removed, Davis was now free to search for his wife and family before starting upon his long ride to Texas, and without waiting to learn the outcome of

Johnston's plans, which he believed doomed to ignominious failure, he left Greensboro, attended by a cavalry escort composed of detachments from Ferguson's and Dibbrell's brigades of Wheeler's Division. His immediate objective was Charlotte, North Carolina, distant some ninety miles, where he hoped to overtake Mrs. Davis. The conditions of travel were difficult. The roads were seas of mud: and twenty miles represented a hard day's march. Davis and his immediate staff were on horseback. The rest of the party, including Benjamin, used ambulances, army wagons, and such other vehicles as could be secured. "During the march," says Burton Harrison, "Mr. Davis was singularly equable and cheerful; he seemed to have had a great load taken from his mind. . . . He talked of men and of books . . . of horses, dogs, and sports; of the woods and the fields. . . . His extraordinary memory made him a charming companion."

When they reached the neighbourhood of Lexington, North Carolina, according to Reagan, "Mr. Davis received a dispatch from General Johnston, requesting him to send him assistance in his negotiations with General Sherman. General Breckinridge and myself were then sent back by him to join General Johnston . . . near Hillsboro." Burton Harrison adds that Davis gave them "large discretion as to what should be agreed to." His aim was peace, and negotiations for peace were in accordance with his theory of how the war should be ended; but he still believed that only another Hampton Roads disappointment awaited them.

His first information concerning the negotiations was the following letter:

"Greensboro *9.30 A.M.*
*April 17, 1865.*

"President Davis:

"I have arrived. General Johnston returned last night to Hillsboro. He received an answer from Sherman, the exact character of which I can't ascertain: but Gen. Beauregard says its tone was conciliatory. I have telegraphed General Johnston to know if he desires me to go on and will dispatch you when I receive his answer.

"J. C. BRECKENRIDGE,
"Sect'y of War."

[Endorsed: April 17, 1865.
Breckinridge to Davis]

A second dispatch from Breckinridge followed almost immediately:

"Greensboro
*11 A.M. April 17, 1865.*

"PRESIDENT DAVIS:

"General Johnston has just dispatched me from Hillsboro that he is about to confer with General Sherman and he will know in two or three hours whether I will be required there.

"JNO. C. BRECKENRIDGE,
"Sect'y of War."

The next day, April 18th, came the astonishing news that Johnston and Sherman had signed an agreement, and Davis telegraphed in reply to Breckinridge: "Yours received. Join me at Charlotte." General Johnston had been right when he declared that Sherman would treat with him. For the latter had agreed to a general pacification, and the document announced "the war is to cease." It, however, contained the additional clause: "Not being fully empowered by our respective principles to fulfil these terms, we individually and officially pledge ourselves to promptly obtain necessary authority and to carry out the above program."

To Davis the news seemed incredible; but, according to Stephen's statement, presented after careful study, Sherman had but carried into effect instructions which Lincoln had himself given him before returning to Washington to his death, and which Andrew Johnson had approved in a joint resolution, agreed to by every Senator, and by every Congressman save two. Sherman later declared that Lincoln had also given him the hint that Davis should be allowed to escape; and Reagan adds that Sherman had intimated during the conference that, according to Lincoln's suggestion, Davis would be given free passage on a Federal vessel, with whatever he might care to take of his private possessions.

But circumstances alter cases, and the circumstances of April 18th were startlingly different from those under which these generous instructions had been given. Lincoln was now dead, and his successor, Andrew Johnson, believed, or professed to believe, that Davis had been an instigator of the plot of which Lincoln's assassination was but a part. Under these conditions, there was small chance that the Federal Government would approve the document which Sherman and Johnston had signed.

Meanwhile Mr. Davis was eagerly seeking news of his wife. "When within some miles of Charlotte," writes Burton Harrison, "I sent forward a courier with a letter to Major Echols, the Quartermaster of that post. My letter asked him to notify Mrs. Davis of our approach and to provide quarters for as many of us as possible. The Major rode out to the outskirts of the town . . . with the information that Mrs. Davis and her family had hastily proceeded towards South Carolina, several days before. . . . She had fled when the railway south of Greensboro had been cut by the enemy's cavalry." The Major also confided to Harrison that, while the members of the President's party could be housed in comfort at Charlotte, "he had as yet been able to find only one person willing to receive the President," because of rumours that Stoneman's cavalry had threatened to burn any house which should dare to shelter him.

The one willing host was a certain Mr. Bates, "a man said to be of Northern birth, a bachelor of convivial habits, and the local agent of the Southern Express Company," and although it was considered "not at all the place for the President to be," there seemed no alternative and he was conducted to the Bates house, in the main street of the town.

Bates, expecting the arrival of his distinguished guest by train, had gone to the station to meet him, and the house was closed when Mr. Davis' party arrived. Major Echols therefore went to the back door, and came through to open the front one. While the party waited, as William Johnston, a business man of Charlotte, later reminded Mr. Davis, "a large concourse, principally citizens, had assembled in front of the house, and loudly greeted and called for you. Your address was calm and brief. As you concluded, standing on the second step to the door, Major John Courtney . . . then telegraph agent here, handed you a dispatch from General Breckinridge. . . . You read it in perfect silence."

"Greensboro.

*April 19, 1865.*

"His Excellency President Davis:

"President Lincoln was assassinated in the theatre in Washington on the night of the 11th inst.

"Seward's house was entered on the same night and he was repeatedly stabbed and is probably mortally wounded.

"Jno. C. Breckenridge."

After reading the telegram, Davis passed it to William Johnston, with the remark, "Here is a very extraordinary communication." The words being heard by those in the front of the crowd, the cry passed through the assemblage, "Read it, read it!" "Thereupon," says Johnston, in a later letter to Davis, "I read it aloud. . . . My voice could not reach the limit of spectators—all did not hear it. One or two cheers were uttered on the street, but I do not think their authors had heard or knew the substance of the dispatch. Your presence had excited a lively interest in the town, and I think the cheers were intended as complimentary to you. The effect of the dispatch on those in hearing was silence and wonder, as Humboldt describes the first effects of an earthquake on men and animals.

"In the meantime the graceless scamp, Bates of Massachusetts, appeared, opened the door behind us, and you walked in, without making a remark about the contents of the dispatch which he did not hear read. . . ."

Davis then handed the telegram to Burton Harrison, and said: "I am sorry. We have lost our noblest and best friend in the court of the enemy." According to Mallory, a few minutes later he added: "I certainly have no special regard for Mr. Lincoln, but there are a great many men of whose end I would much rather hear than his. I fear it will be disastrous to our people, and I regret it deeply." A. K. McClure, in *Our Presidents and How We Make Them*, records that Davis, ten years later, said to him: "Next to the destruction of the Confederacy, the death of Abraham Lincoln was the darkest day the South has ever known." Had he known the story of Lincoln's last days, his regrets would have been even greater, for they left no doubt of the latter's determination to befriend the conquered South. Davis knew, however, Lincoln's great kindness of soul, and to him the news of his death was "the last crowning calamity of a despairing and defeated though righteous cause."

The new President, Andrew Johnson, Davis knew also. He had debated with him too often in the United States Senate to be ignorant of his qualities. He knew that Johnson had not forgotten the debate of January 25, 1859, for example, when Davis had banteringly accused him of Presidential ambitions. Johnson, flushed and resentful, had intimated that "minds as nicely balanced and as well trained" as that of Davis might also have ambitions. "I assure the Senator," he had said, rather heavily, that "I am willing to widen the field so that . . . he may have a chance." "I have disclaimed in your favour already," Davis had replied. A little more play of wits, stiletto against broad-ax, and

Johnson had lost his temper and exclaimed: "I prefer to discharge my duty faithfully as an honest representative of the states or the people. Occupying that position . . . when contrasted with being President of the United States, I say damn the Presidency; it is not worthy of the aspirations of a man who believes in doing good. . . . The Presidency! I would rather be an honest man, an honest representative, than be President of the United States forty times. . . . The idea of President-making ought to be scouted out of the halls of Congress."

Davis later confirmed the story that Colonel Alston of Morgan's staff had written to him offering to assassinate Lincoln. In answer, Davis sent the letter to the Confederate War Office, with an order that Alston be arrested and court-martialled. With such sentiments and such memories flooding his mind, the last thought likely to come to him was that he might be suspected of complicity in the plot which had made Johnson President. But war psychology is quick at inference, and many men with little or no knowledge of the particulars of the crime were already raising the cry that it was but another instance of Southern barbarism, another reason why Jeff. Davis should be captured and hanged.

Edward Everett Hale declared, when the news of the end of the Confederacy reached him: "This has not been a work against slavery, but against barbarism: it was civilization against barbarism. It has been impossible to make your English friends understand this." And blandly assuming, without a thread of evidence, that the South had procured Lincoln's assassination, he added: "This is a very patent illustration of it before man and God."

Before further news reached Davis, General Basil Duke appeared, leading 600 bare-backed cavalrymen, the remnant of Morgan's raiders. As they passed Bates' house, they halted and demanded a speech. Davis came out, praised the gallantry of the Confederate cavalrymen, expressed his determination to remain with the last band which upheld the Confederacy, and retired.

"I distinctly heard every word," writes Harrison, and "he said nothing" about Lincoln. But the report was spread abroad that he had declared, 'If it was to be done, it is well it was done quickly,' and Bates was later induced to testify to that effect before a military tribunal."

A subsequent dispatch from General Joseph E. Johnston corrected the date of the assassination which Breckinridge's telegram had given as April 11th, but added other errors. The following account of its arrival is given by a Northern officer: "I was sent from our camp at Lincolnton to Charlotte, N. C., under a flag of truce. . . . I was conducted to General Echols' headquarters, in a large upper room, evidently a schoolroom. . . . Glancing round, I saw about sixteen or eighteen gentlemen, all with one or two exceptions, in military uniform. . . . The cold stare of a glass eye caught my attention, and the features were somewhat familiar. 'Ah! Jeff Davis, and you here, pressed to the wall,' was my first thought. But I saw a much pleasanter-faced man than our Northern papers had pictured him. A dispatch was handed to General Echols, who read and re-read it, with an anxious, earnest look upon his face. Half rising, he passed the paper to Mr. Davis, who read it slowly, and, handing it back, remarked, 'Well, we have lost a generous enemy.'" General Echols was asked, a little later, by Colonel Cal Morgan, brother of General John Morgan, whether he might show the dispatch to Lieutenant Thompson. Consent was given and Thompson read:

" 'Greensboro, N. C., April ——

" 'Lincoln was assassinated the night of the $14^{th}$ in Ford's Theatre. Seward was assassinated about the same time in his own house. Grant has marched his army back to Washington to declare himself military dictator.

" 'J. E. JOHNSTON.'

"I cannot recall the exact date of the dispatch," Thompson

continues. "But it necessarily travelled slowly, as we had cut all the telegraph wires, burned bridges, torn up railroads and impeded travel all we could."

Thompson further says that Davis soon left the room, and that he said to General Echols: " 'I see you have President Davis with you, General.' " Looking around the room, the General said, 'No. Mr. Davis is not here.' 'But,' I said, 'he was here a minute ago.' . . . 'Mr. Thompson,' said the General, 'I am surprised at your asking such questions while here under a flag of truce.' But in the end, he said, smiling, 'Yes, President Davis is with us.' "

Davis' undaunted idea that victory was still a possibility was now strengthened by the receipt of a letter from Wade Hampton, dated Hillsboro, April 19, 1865, declaring: "The military situation is very gloomy, I admit, but it is by no means desperate, and endurance and determination will produce a change. . . . There are now not less than 40 to 50 thousand men in arms on this side of the Mississippi. On the other, there are as many more. Now the question presents itself, shall we disband these men at once, or shall we endeavour to concentrate them? If we disband we give up at once and for ever all hope of foreign intervention. Europe will say, and say justly, 'Why should we interfere if you choose to re-enter the Union?' But if we keep any organization, however small, in the field, we give Europe the opportunity of aiding us." He painted a dark and prophetic picture of the fate of the South should she allow herself to be reannexed to the Union. "We shall live," he said, "under a base and vulgar tyranny. No sacrifice would be too great to escape this train of horrors, and I think it far better for us to fight to the extreme limit of our country, rather than to reconstruct the Union upon any terms."

Hampton's idea was to change infantry into cavalry, cross into Texas and thence send cavalry forces into "the country of the enemy and they will soon show that we are not conquered. If I had 20,000 mounted men here, I could force Sherman to retreat in twenty days. Give me a good force of cavalry and I will take them safely across the Mississippi, and if you desire to go in that direction it will give me great pleasure to escort you. My own mind is made up. . . . I shall fight as long as my Government remains in existence; when that ceases to live I shall seek some other country, for I shall never take the 'oath of allegiance.'" His closing words must have cheered the heart of Jefferson Davis, discouraged as it was, but not despairing: "I can bring to your support many strong arms and brave hearts, men who will fight to Texas and will seek refuge in Mexico, rather than in the Union."

Three days later Hampton wrote a similar letter from Greensboro, adding the interesting suggestion that Texas be induced to "seek the protection of Maximilian," France's puppet Emperor of Mexico. That same day Davis telegraphed Hampton: ". . . Wish to see you as soon as convenient. Will then confer."

There is no record of the conference, but there can be no doubt that Hampton's suggestions had reached Davis by April 23, 1865, for on that day the latter wrote to Mrs. Davis from Charlotte: "Governor Vance and General Hampton propose to meet me here, and General Johnston sent me a request to remain at some point where he could communicate with me. Under these circumstances I have asked Mr. Harrison to go in search of you. . . . Your brother William telegraphed . . . that you were at Abbeville." He confessed that Lee's surrender had "destroyed the hopes I entertained when we parted. Had that army held together, I am now confident we could have successfully executed the plan which I sketched to you and would have been today on the high road to independence."

That this task, not yet relinquished, had been made far more difficult, he did not attempt to conceal: "The loss of arms has been so great, that, should the spirit of the people rise to the occasion, it would not at this time be possible adequately to supply them with the weapons of war." But he left no doubt concerning his intention to fight on, despite all losses and discouragements, although his letter indicated a hope that the Federal Government might confirm the Johnston-Sherman agreement. "The terms," he added, "are secret, and may be rejected by the Yankee Government. To us they are hard enough, though freed from wanton humiliation, and expressly recognizing the state Governments, and the rights of person and property as secured by the Constitution of the United States. General Breckinridge was a party to the last consultation and to the agreement. Judge Reagan went with him and approved the agreement, though not present at the conference. Each member of the Cabinet is to give his opinion in writing today, first, upon the acceptance of the terms, second, upon the mode of proceeding if accepted. The issue is one which it is very painful for me to meet. On the one hand is the long night of oppression which will follow the return of our people to the 'Union'; on the other, the suffering of the women and children, and carnage among the few brave patriots who still oppose the invader. . . . I have prayed to our Heavenly Father to give me wisdom and fortitude equal to the demands of the position in which Providence has placed me. . . . I can measure my ability to make any further sacrifice required, and am assured there is but one to which I am not equal. My wife and children—how are they to be saved from degradation or want is now my care.

"During the suspension of hostilities you may have the best opportunity to go to Mississippi, and either to sail from Mobile for a foreign port or to cross the river and proceed to Texas, as the one or the other may be more practicable. . . . For myself, it may be that a devoted band of cavalry will cling to me and that I can force my way across the Mississippi, and if nothing can be done there which it will be proper to do, then I can go to Mexico, and have the world from which to choose a location."

It seems likely that rumours of President Johnson's accusation had reached Charlotte, for, as Davis and Burton Harrison came out of the little church on Sunday morning, Davis said, "I think the preacher directed his remarks at me; and he really seems to fancy I had something to do with the assassination." Had he had access to the mind of the North at that moment, his belief would have been changed to certainty, for the charge which Stanton had made on April 15th was now freely made by many, if less eminent persons, including the President himself.

Benjamin's memorandum, of April 22, 1865, concerning the Johnston-Sherman agreement, was long and carefully reasoned, and declared that the terms offered by Sherman were "the best and most favourable that we could hope to obtain by a continuance of the struggle." He defined it as "an agreement that if the Confederate States will cease to wage war for the purpose of establishing a separate Government, the United States will receive the several states back into the Union with their state governments unimpaired, with all their Constitutional rights recognized, with protection for the persons and property of the people and with a general amnesty." He further declared that while, as President, Davis was "powerless to act in making peace on any other basis than that of independence," he could, as commander-in-chief "ratify the military convention . . . and execute its provisions. He can end hostilities." Under the Confederate Constitution, "the states alone can act in dissolving the Confederacy and returning to the Union." He warned Davis that the army which Johnston commanded had dwindled from 70,000 to 20,000, and added: "We could not at the present moment gather together an army of 30,000 men, by a concentration of all our forces east of the Mississippi River. . . . We have lost possession in Virginia and North Carolina of our chief resources for the supply of powder and lead. We can obtain no aid from the Trans-Mississippi Department, from which we are cut off by the fleets of gunboats that patrol the river. We have not a supply of arms sufficient for putting into the field even 10,000 additional men, if the men themselves were forthcoming."

Benjamin's advice went so far as the suggestion: "The President should by proclamation inform the states and the people of the Confederacy of the facts above recited; should ratify the convention so far as he has authority to act as commander-in-chief, and . . . should declare his inability with the means remaining at his disposal to defend the Confederacy or maintain its independence, and should resign."

Shortly after submitting this memorandum, Benjamin took his own counsel, by resigning his post in the Cabinet. He then presented himself, disguised as a Frenchman, "having" no English; and taking leave of the President and his fellow-Cabinet officers, started for the coast, where a boat carried him to England and a new career—a career still remembered as one of the most brilliant and successful ever won by an alien at the English bar.

Before Benjamin's departure, Davis had in his hands the memorandum of the Attorney-General, George Davis, dated Charlotte, N. C., April 22, 1865, which declared: "Taken as a whole, the convention amounts to this: that the Confederacy shall re-enter the old Union upon the same footing on which they stood before seceding from it." He estimated that "the Army of Tennessee contains now about 13,000 effective men . . . and is daily melting away by desertion. It is confronted by one of the best armies of the United States, 50,000 strong. Manifestly, it cannot fight; and if it retreats, the chances are . . . that, like the Army of Northern Virginia, it will dissolve, and the remnant be forced to capitulate. . . . It cannot be recruited. Volunteering is long since at an end, and conscription has exhausted all its force. . . . Observation has satisfied me that the states of Virginia and North Carolina are finally lost to our cause." It was his opinion that both these states would "make terms for themselves" if the convention were rejected. "This melancholy array of facts," he continued, "leaves open but one conclusion . . . that the convention ought to be ratified." And he re-echoed Benjamin's opinion that the time had arrived for President Davis to resign his office. "Issue your Proclamation," he urged, "plainly setting forth the circumstances which have induced you to assent to the terms proposed, disbanding the armies of the Confederacy, resigning your office as Chief Magistrate, and recommending to the people of the states that they assemble in convention, and carry into effect the terms agreed on."

Reagan, the Postmaster-General, who had been with Breckinridge and Johnston when the convention with Sherman was negotiated, though not when it was actually signed, also sent his advice on April 22nd. It re-echoed Johnston's opinion that "the enemy's forces, now in the field, exceed ours . . . probably ten to one." Selma, Montgomery, Columbus, and Macon, he sadly reminded the President, are gone, "with their magazines, workshops, and stores. . . . Probably all of the states will make separate terms with the enemy," if this settlement is allowed to fail. He further pointed out that "the agreement contains no direct reference to the question of slavery—requires no concession from us in regard to it, and leaves it subject to the Constitution and laws of the United States and of the several states, just as it was before the war." His advice also was, prompt acceptance. "If the terms . . . should be rejected [by the Federal Government]," he added, "or so modified as to refuse a recognition of the right of local self-government, and our political rights . . . or as to refuse amnesty for past participation in this war, then it will be our duty to continue the struggle."

Memoranda from the other members of the Cabinet came within a few hours. Breckinridge, Secretary of War, wrote, on April 23, 1865: "Our ports are closed, and the sources of foreign supply lost to us. The enemy occupy all, or the greater part of Missouri, Kentucky, Tennessee, Virginia, and North Carolina, and move almost at will through the other states, to the east of the Mississippi. . . . I do not think it would be possible to assemble, equip and maintain an army of 30,000 men at any point east of the Mississippi River." He also advised Davis to "return to the states and the people the trust which you are no longer able to defend."

Mallory, Secretary of the Navy, expressed the conviction that "nine-tenths of the people of every state of the Confederacy" would advise accepting the terms, if able to express themselves. "They are weary of war and desire peace. . . . I do not believe that by any possibility we could organize, arm, and equip . . . 15,000 men within the next sixty days; and I am convinced that both General Beauregard and General Johnston are utterly hopeless of continuing the contest. . . . The loss of Selma and Columbus, where much valuable machinery for the construction of ordnance and ordnance stores was collected, must materially circumscribe our ability in this respect. Our currency is nearly worthless. . . . The arms of the United States have rendered the great object of our struggle hopeless; have conquered a reconstruction of the Union. . . . The propositions signed by the opposing generals are more favourable . . . than could justly have been anticipated. . . . I advise their acceptance."

One cannot read these memoranda of Davis' Constitutional advisers without the feeling that it would have been madness for him to refuse such terms, under such conditions. And that was the conclusion which he himself now reached; reluctantly but definitely. As soon as the last memorandum had been read, therefore, he sent to General Johnston the following communication, dated, Charlotte, North Carolina, April 24, 1865: "The Secretary of War has delivered to me the copy you handed him of the basis of an agreement between yourself and General Sherman. Your action is approved. You will so inform General Sherman; and if like authority be given by the Government of the United States to complete the arrangement, you will proceed on the basis adopted."

General Lee once declared that "True patriotism sometimes requires a man to act exactly contrary, at one period, to that which he does at another, and the motive which impels him, the desire to do right, is precisely the same." Pitt said that no man can serve Great Britain in high office, without sacrificing the "minor virtues," among which he considered consistency. In accepting the terms of the Sherman-Johnston agreement, Davis had followed both precepts; and now awaited the decision of President Andrew Johnson, whose fame had suddenly become so great that the Press was proclaiming him the most popular man in America—so great that Senator Doolittle of Wisconsin declared: "the sceptre of power passed from a hand of flesh to a hand of iron."

Johnson, studying the agreement that had given him his brief glimpse of popularity, remarked that it was more like a treaty of peace than a memorandum of the surrender of a rebel army. Lincoln had often refused to allow generals in the field to negotiate upon subjects political rather than merely military; and Johnson adopted the same point of view, and rejected the agreement.

At once the fickle public accused General Sherman, its author, of the most sinister motives in granting it; and Secretary Stanton issued a bulletin to the Press which declared that Sherman's action had probably opened the way for "Jefferson Davis to escape to Mexico or Europe, with his plunder, which is reported very large." The radical press of the North bristled with denunciations of Sherman, the Judas who had been bribed by Jeff Davis' gold. According to other excited critics, he was ambitious to become Dictator. General Halleck went so far as to order that no commands from Sherman should be obeyed, and that Federal armies should push forward as rapidly as possible; which extraordinary command Secretary of War Stanton published in a bulletin.

In order to save Sherman, however, and to stay the tide of denunciation to which his fellow-Unionists were subjecting him, Grant now ordered him to accept Johnston's surrender upon the terms granted to Lee. As all acts of war on the part of Johnston's troops had ceased from the date of the rejected agreement, and his army had melted perceptibly, the desertions being estimated at 8000, a renewal of warfare, on the part of the Confederates, was impossible. Johnston therefore agreed to reopen negotiations upon the terms suggested, and the result was a surrender acceptable to President Johnson.

According to the Psalmist, God makes the wrath of man to praise Him: but He did not select this instance of man's wrath for that purpose. Its immediate effect was to make more difficult the task, inherited by President Johnson from President Lincoln, of receiving into the Union the states already reconstructed according to Lincoln's ten per cent plan. Gone in a moment was all hope that the latter's generous spirit would still direct the affairs of the nation. He had loved justice. His successor was bent upon vengeance.

## CHAPTER XXVI

# "SARTOR RESARTUS": THE ARREST AND THE CLOTHES

DAVIS had by now grown very anxious in regard to his wife and children and started in pursuit of them. As it was his intention to join the forces west of the Mississippi as soon as he had assured himself of their safety, his personal staff, with the few available troops, including two detachments of cavalry, and all his Cabinet, save Benjamin, who had started for England, and Trenholm, too ill to travel, moved with him. The news of Johnston's final surrender still caused him burning indignation. Lee's surrender, upon similar terms, he had accepted as necessary. Johnston's first agreement with Sherman he had accepted in deference to the opinions of his Cabinet and because he realized that they were generous and as favourable as he was likely to receive. But in the Sherman-Johnston agreement of April 26, 1865, he saw neither necessity nor generosity. "His [Johnston's] line of retreat, as chosen by himself . . . ," he later explained, "was open and supplies were placed upon it at various points. He had a large force of which over 36,000 were paroled. At Greensboro, North Carolina, we had other forces in the field, and we were certainly in a position to make continued resistance. This was all the more important as such a course would have been of service in securing better terms in bringing the war to an end." Johnston's unauthorized action had now rendered this impossible, but it had not caused Davis to abandon hope. He was still determined to continue resistance, but must make certain of Mrs. Davis' safety before moving west. This was made easier by the arrival of a letter from Mrs. Davis, written at Abbeville on April 28th, and stating her plans:

"My own dear old husband:

"Your very sweet letter reached me safely by Mr. Harrison, and was a great relief. I leave here in the morning at 6 o'clock for the wagon train going to Georgia. Washington will be the first point I shall 'unload' at—from there we shall probably go on to Atlanta or thereabouts, and wait a little until we hear something of you. Let me now beseech you not to calculate upon seeing me unless I happen to cross your shortest path towards your bourne, be that what it may. It is surely [as he had said] not the fate to which you invited me in brighter days, but you must remember that you did not invite me to a great Hero's home, but to that of a plain farmer. I have shared all your triumphs, been the *only* beneficiary of them. Now I am but claiming the privilege for the first time of being all to you, now these pleasures have passed for me.

"My plans are these, subject to your approval: I think I shall be able to procure funds enough to enable me to put the two eldest to school. I shall go to Florida, if possible, and from thence go over to Bermuda or Nassau, from thence to England, unless a good school offers elsewhere, and put them to the best school I can find, and then with the two youngest join you in Texas—and that is the prospect which bears me up, to be once more with you—once more to suffer with you if need be. . . . God loves those who obey him, and I know there is a future for you." Overcome by bitterness caused by anxiety, she added: "These people are a craven set; they cannot bear the tug of war," a statement as unjust as was ever made concerning the gallant Southland which had borne the tug of war for four long years, with an heroic courage that astonished the world.

"Be careful how you go to Augusta," continued the letter. "I get rumours that Brown is going to seize all Government property, and the people are averse—and mean to resist with pistols. They are a set of wretches together, and I wish you were safe out of their land. God bless you, keep you. I have wrestled with God for you. I believe he will restore us to happiness.

"Devotedly—

"YOUR WIFE."

The day after this letter was sent, Mrs. Davis started for Washington, Georgia, "whence," Harrison reported, "we shall go towards Atlanta, there to halt until we see or hear from you. This movement was determined by your telegrams and by the belief that you would move westward along a line running north of this place." On the road a smallpox scare caused Mrs. Davis to inspect her party. She found that all had been vaccinated except the Davis' baby daughter, and there being no doctor at hand, they halted at a farmhouse and had the planter vaccinate her, taking "a fresh scab from the arm of a little negro called up for the purpose."

At Washington they stopped for two nights while Harrison procured additional wagons, and before another start Captain Moody and Major Victor Maurin joined the party, already consisting of Mrs. Davis, Miss Howell, four children, three mounted Kentuckians, Lieutenant Hatheway, Mr. Monroe, and Mr. Messick. On May 2nd, Harrison wrote to some one whose name does not appear:

"Washington, Ga.

*"May 2, 1865, 10:15* A.M.

"My dear Sir:

"We had intended to move this morning and had prepared our wagons and ambulances, which are now standing ready to start. We have excellent drivers, teams, and conveyances . . . and are prepared for a long and continuous march. . . . Our route was changed by the tidings of General Johnston's surrender of the department east of the Chattahoochee; Wilson was ordered by Sherman to execute the terms of the capitulation 'at Macon and in western Georgia.' Gilmore was ordered to take charge in the 'Department of the South,' which seems to include this place and Abbeville—Wilson has a mobilized cavalry column which could readily blockade the roads thro' western Georgia—and thus make the route thro' Atlanta dangerous. . . . The safest route seems to lie between Macon and Augusta running through Sandersville and thence south and southwest into Central Florida whence we can strike for the coast."

Harrison further informed his anonymous correspondent that news had come that forage had been sent by the quartermaster to Starkville for "the President's cavalry escort, which was to halt there last night. We have thence supposed that the President is in Abbeville today and that this town (Washington) may be on his line of march. If so he will probably be here tomorrow. . . . Mrs. Davis is very anxious to see him if she can do so without embarrassing his movements. . . . She is willing to start without seeing him, however, if necessary."

Owing to sudden alarms, Mrs. Davis finally decided not to wait for her husband, but sent a letter to Abbeville, by special messenger, asking his plans. It opened with a characteristic reference to Johnston's capitulation: "I cannot refrain from expressing my intense grief at the treacherous surrender of this Department. May God grant you a safe conduct out of this maze of enemies. I believe you are safer without the cavalry than with it, and I so dread their stealing a march and surprising you. I left Abbeville against my convictions but agreeable to Mr. Burt's and Mr. Harrison's opinions. Now the danger of being caught here by the enemy and of being deprived of our transportation if we stay, is hurrying me out of Washington. I shall wait here this evening until I hear from the courier we have sent to Abbeville." In a hasty note, undated, but evidently written very shortly afterward, however, she added: "We thought we had better move for fear our transportation would be stolen. . . . We will make a march tomorrow of 25 miles to pass beyond the point of positive danger. . . . Do not try to meet me. I dread the Yankees' getting news of you so much. You are the country's only hope, and the very best intentioned do not calculate upon a stand this side of the river. Why not cut loose from your escort? Go swiftly and alone with the exception of two or three—Oh! may God in his goodness keep you safe, my own."

Fearful that an attempt would be made to capture his wife, non-combatant though her party was, Davis hurried on towards Washington, hoping that he might arrive before her departure. Just before he crossed the Savannah river a company of Confederate troops, commanded by Walter Acker, on picket duty, presented arms, "the last organized body of Confederate troops that ever had the honour of presenting arms to you," wrote its captain in later years. He entered Washington on May 2nd only to find Mrs. Davis gone. While preparing to follow her he wrote to a friend, "I expected to cut my way through to a place of safety with the two detachments of cavalry along with me, but they have become so much demoralized . . . that I can no longer rely on them in case we should encounter the enemy. I have therefore determined to disband them and try to make my escape, as a small body of men can elude the vigilance of the enemy easier than a larger number. They will make every effort in their power to capture me, and it behooves us to face these dangers as men. We will go to Mississippi, and there rely on Forrest, if he is in a state of organization, and it is to be hoped that he is; if not, we will cross the Mississippi River and join Kirby Smith, where we can carry on the war for ever. Meet me south of the Chattahoochee, as this Department has been surrendered without my knowledge or consent."

After leaving Washington, Davis' diminished party stopped at a farmhouse to purchase fresh eggs, and Mr. Davis was recognized. "Mrs. Davis passed here this morning," remarked the farmer, "and there are a number of fugitive Confederate soldiers through this portion of the state who have been heard to boast that they mean to rob her. . . . I fear there is going to be trouble." This news greatly excited Davis, who was already overstrained and ill, and he insisted upon hastening forward, without a stop until one o'clock in the morning. At times he was waylaid by women who had lost sons, brothers, or husbands, and who pressed forward, weeping, to greet him. Upon Colonel Johnston's remarking that it must be gratifying to find that he still had the confidence of such people, he replied, with tears in his eyes, "It is that which makes me most miserable of all."

As they approached Abbeville, Georgia, his alarm caused him to send forward a swift rider warning Mrs. Davis to leave at once, and assuring her that he was close behind and would reach Abbeville on May 3rd. She at once obeyed, moving toward Pensacola, where she hoped to secure a boat.

At Abbeville, according to Burton Harrison, Davis found the papers and records of the President's office, which had been sent forward just before the fall of Richmond. "They were culled over by Colonel Johnston, Colonel Wood, and (perhaps) Colonel Lubbock, of the President's staff; many papers were there destroyed; the others were put, some into a bag and left at Abbeville with the ladies (the Monroes) of the family of Col. Leovey, of New Orleans, temporarily residing at Abbeville, and some into my trunk which the party carried on to Washington, in Georgia, and there left in charge of a friend of mine, who sent it to me in New York nearly two years later. The papers left at Abbeville were taken by Mrs. Leovey and the Misses Monroe (her sisters) to New Orleans, with great difficulty and most devoted interest and care. In the spring of 1866, I went to New Orleans, ascertained that the papers were at Col. Leovey's summer house at Pass Christian, and there recovered them, taking them aboard a steamboat under the nose of an officer of the United States army who stood at the gangplank to keep the rebels in subjection. . . . The very interesting and valuable papers of the State Department at Richmond were sold to the Government of the United States, early in the seventies, by one, Bromwell, who had been a clerk of that Department, the transaction being in the name of Colonel Pickett; those archives had never been farther south than N. C.—I think had never left Virginia."

All arrangements having been completed for his contemplated movement to the west, Davis now dissolved his Cabinet, after directing the Secretary of War to pay the soldiers with the money that remained. He declared that he required only a small band of volunteers to accompany him in his long journey which even he could now consider nothing less than flight, deeply as he had hitherto resented the term. However, he assured General Duke that he would listen to no suggestion of leaving the country nor to any proposition aiming only at his own safety. "Of all present," said Duke, in a later interview, "Mr. Davis alone urged, and seemed to think a longer resistance practicable. Everyone else expressed the opinion that such a course was futile."

Many officers and soldiers volunteered to accompany him, but he selected only ten; and these, with his confidential clerk, M. H. Clark, his aides, Colonel William Preston Johnston, Colonel John Taylor Wood, and Colonel John Lubbock of Texas, and his one remaining Cabinet officer, Reagan, turned southward with him. Reagan tried to persuade him to create the impression that he was still with his party, while he should escape to Florida and take a boat for Brownsville, to join them beyond the Mississippi. "I was influenced to make this suggestion," says Reagan, "because we thought him so exhausted and enfeebled that we did not think he could make the trip by land." He refused, however, "on the ground that he would not abandon Confederate soil."

As news of disaster after disaster arrived, Davis retained not only his courage, but his calm and his cheerful exterior. Clark declared: "I saw an organized government disintegrate and fall to pieces little by little, until there was only left a single member of the Cabinet, his private secretary, a few members of his staff, a few guides and servants, to represent what had been a powerful government. . . . Under these unfortunate circumstances, his great resources of mind and heart shone out most brilliantly. He was calm, self-poised; giving way to no petulance of temper at discomfort; advising, consoling, laying aside all thought of self; planning and doing what was best . . . for our unhappy and despairing people, and uttering words of consolation and wise advice to every family where he entered as guest." One story of many which survive illustrates both his generosity and his financial condition after his guarded treasury had been disbursed. He stopped at a little cabin on the roadside and asked a woman who stood in the doorway for a drink of water. She turned to comply with his request, and while he drank, a baby barely able to walk crawled down the steps towards him. The mother smiled. "Is this not President Davis?" she asked. "It is, madam," he answered. She pointed proudly to the child. "He's named for you." The President drew a gold coin from his pocket and handed it to the mother: "Please keep it for my little namesake and tell him when he is old enough to know." As he rode away with Reagan, he added, "The last coin I had on earth, Reagan. I wouldn't have had that but for the fact I'd never seen one like it and kept it for luck."

His luck had left him before this generous impulse took his lucky coin, but he added, cheerfully, "My home is a wreck, Benjamin's and Breckinridge's are in Federal hands, Mallory's residence at Pensacola has been burned by the enemy, your home in Texas has been wrecked." He paused and drew from his pocket-book a few Confederate bills: "That is my estate at the present moment."

So far Davis had been spared the greatest shock of all; for he still did not know that, on May 2nd, President Johnson had issued the following proclamation:

"Whereas, it appears from evidence in the Bureau of Military Justice, that the atrocious murder of the late President, Abraham Lincoln, and the attempted assassination of the Honourable William H. Seward, Secretary of State, were incited, concerted, and procured by and between Jefferson Davis, late of Richmond, Virginia, and Jacob Thompson, Clement C. Clay, Beverly Tucker, George N. Sanders, W. C. Cleary, and other rebels and traitors against the Government of the United States, harboured in Canada:

"Now, therefore, to the end that justice may be done, I, Andrew Johnson, President of the United States, do offer and promise for the arrest of said persons, or either of them, within the limits of the United States, so that they can be brought to trial, the following rewards: one hundred thousand dollars for the arrest of Jefferson Davis; twenty-five thousand dollars for the arrest of Jacob Thompson, late of Mississippi; twenty-five thousand dollars for the arrest of George N. Sanders; twenty-five thousand dollars for the arrest of Beverly Tucker; and ten thousand dollars for the arrest of William C. Cleary, late clerk of Clement C. Clay. The Provost-Marshal General of the United States is directed to cause a description of said persons, with notice of the above rewards, to be published."

The hasty nature of this Proclamation is attested by the fact that the list of rewards did not include Clay, who had been mentioned in the first paragraph.

Mr. Justice Chase's opinion on the case of Jefferson Davis, as given on page 5, of Johnson's *Reports*, declares that it was clearly "the intention of the Government of the United States at that time to try him before a military commission on the charge of having procured the assassination of Mr. Lincoln." And the famous jurist added the opinion: "According to the philosophy of government, all punishments are inflicted by the Executive. The Judicial investigates, ascertains the guilt or innocence, and advises the Executive of the fact. The latter then discharges the accused from bonds or inflicts punishment as the case may require. Strictly speaking, the judicial power, as a branch of the Government, has no office in any criminal proceeding except to advise as to the law, and to inform the Executive concerning facts not previously known." President Johnson, at this stage of the case, was ready to accept the powers thus defined and to punish the man who, as he believed, despite Davis' denial and apology, had once scorned and ridiculed him as a mere tailor.

The proclamation placed the pursuit of Davis upon a new basis. It was now a hunt for a supposed assassin, branded as such by the voice of the Chief Executive, and carrying on his head a fortune which any man might win. According to Johnson's *Decisions of Chief Justice Chase*, it was generally supposed that Davis had escaped from the country, and the proclamation was telegraphed wherever wires would carry it. Moreover, that he might be recognized as a criminal in any land which he might reach, his photograph was sent to every general police headquarters in Europe. Furthermore, the rumour that he carried with him vast treasure was given the colour of fact in the following handbill, issued by General J. H. Wilson:

"$100,000 Reward in Gold.

"Headquarters Cav. Corps, Military Division, Mississippi.

"Macon, Ga., *May 6, 1865.*

"One hundred thousand dollars Reward in Gold, will be paid to any person or persons who will apprehend and deliver Jefferson Davis to any of the military authorities of the United States.

"Several millions of specie reported to be with him will become the property of the captors.

"J. H. Wilson."

It is idle to speculate whether, had these facts been known to him, Davis would have deferred, as he did, his projected flight in order to seek his wife in that vast region. That he did so is clear proof, however, that he was not suffering from extreme caution. So far as he knew, he was only the leader of an almost overwhelmed nation, seeking to carry out to the uttermost the responsibilities of his office. He therefore turned south, instead of west, following the vague intimations which had been conveyed to him of Mrs. Davis' plans. Burton Harrison thus describes his arrival at her camp:

"About the middle of the night, I, with two teamsters, constituted a picket. . . . We heard the soft tread of horses . . . approaching over the light sandy soil of the road. The teamsters . . . ran off to arouse the camp, having no doubt that the attack was about to begin. I placed myself in the road, to detain the enemy as long as possible and, when the advancing horsemen came near enough to hear me, called 'halt.' They drew rein instantly. I demanded, 'Who comes there?' The foremost of the horsemen replied, 'Friends,' in a voice I was astonished to recognize as that of the President, not suspecting he was anywhere near us. . . . He had happened to join us . . . only because Colonel Johnston had heard . . . that an attempt was to be made to capture" a party in the neighbourhood, which Davis had feared might be that of Mrs. Davis.

Davis spent that night with his wife's party, rode with them the following day, and camped with them the following night. After breakfast he bade them good-bye and led his own little party forward. "My purpose," he wrote upon Harrison's proof of *The Capture of Jefferson Davis*, which the latter had sent to him for correction, ". . . was to cross the Chattahoochee below the point at which the enemy had garrisons, and [as] Taylor and Forrest were still maintaining themselves in the field, to join them and await reinforcements, or otherwise to cross the Mississippi immediately."

Mrs. Davis, under Harrison's guidance, continued her journey to the south, fearful of attack, yet valiant in flight. Through mud, forest and heavy storms they pressed forward, Mrs. Davis wondering, no doubt, how Davis was faring on his hazardous journey. As they neared the Ocmulgee River, in southern Georgia, Davis' party, which had become lost in the fog, unexpectedly rejoined them. "He continued with us until about 5 o'clock," says Burton Harrison, when it was decided to camp for the night. "Immediately after crossing the little creek just north of Irwinsville, . . . " camp was made. As there were now fully fifty miles between them and Hawkinsville, where the pursuing Federal cavalry were supposed to be, it seemed safe for Mr. Davis to take a good night's rest. But Harrison, Wood, and Thornburn, who had a boat at the Indian River in Florida, ordered thither in the hope that Davis might consent to use it, united in urging him to move forward at least ten miles farther as soon as the much-needed evening meal was over. Reluctantly he agreed, and Harrison wearily sought his bed on the ground without waiting for food. After he was gone, Davis decided that it was unnecessary to ride that night, and made his plans for an early start next morning. "He seemed entirely unable," Harrison later wrote, "to apprehend the danger of capture."

In view of Davis' ignorance of the circumstances, however, this carelessness is not astonishing. He believed that he was still only the leader of a nation at war, deserting sections held by the enemy, and seeking to reach other sections still under arms; and lay quietly down to sleep in a district in which the people had been fully informed that, on May 8th, Brevet Major-General Wilson had transmitted to General Upton the details of President Johnson's proclamation, and that Captain F. W. Scott, acting adjutant-general, had issued, by command of General Minty, the following order to Lieutenant-Colonel Howland, who commanded a brigade of Federal troopers: "You will have every port and ferry on the Ocmulgee and Altamaha rivers . . . well guarded, and make every effort to capture or kill Jefferson Davis, the rebel ex-President, who is supposed to be endeavouring to cross. . . ."

Although ignorant of these facts, Davis had, however, been

warned by Colonel Johnston that marauders were about and likely to attack the camp that night. "As they would probably be, for the most part, ex-Confederate soldiers," Davis later explained, "I thought they would so far respect me as not to rob the encampment of my family. In any event, or whoever they might be, it was my duty to wait the issue. . . . I lay down in my wife's tent, with all my clothes on, to wait for the arrival of the marauders; but, being weary, fell into a deep sleep, from which I was aroused by my coachman, James Jones, telling me that there was firing over the creek."

The firing, as Davis later learned, was caused by the fact that two bodies of his pursuers had met in the dark, the one Colonel Pritchard's Fourth Michigan Cavalry, and the other Colonel Harnden's First Wisconsin Cavalry. Confident that they were close upon the heels of the fugitive, each had mistaken the other for the enemy, a mistake which cost two lives. Discovering their error, they concerted plans for closing in upon Davis' camp, now known to be very near.

Mr. Chief Justice Taft once declared that his legal practice had convinced him that the most unreliable testimony is that of the "eye-witness": and the testimony which has survived concerning Mr. Davis' capture goes far towards establishing the truth of that statement. Andrew Bee, a Norwegian tanner, enlisted in Colonel Pritchard's Fourth Michigan Cavalry, tells this story:

"We started south and on the evening of the 9th came up with the Ninth [apparently meaning the First] Wisconsin, Col. Harnden commanding. The officers held a consultation and, finding they were on the same mission, concluded to each take a number of picket men and proceed by different routes . . . Col. Harnden took 44 men from the First Wisconsin, and then we rode off some odder ways. . . . It was about 1 o'clock in the morning that we came in sight of their tents. . . . Col. Pritchard gave orders to surround the camp and not to disturb the sleepers." Bee adds that he watched until about daylight when Davis raised the tent flap and came out. "I knew him from his pictures. He had on a military suit, cavalry boots and all, and a grey flannel blouse. As he stepped out he was pulling on an ulster without sleeves. Mrs. Davis followed him and threw his travelling shawl over his shoulders. You know all men who went about a good deal used to have them. . . . So that's all there is to that story. He started towards his horse when I lifted my carbine and pointed it at him, saying out loud: 'Sheff. Davis, you stay dare.' . . . Anybody who think Sheff. Davis a coward to run away mit woman's clothes should have seen him then. He turned right square around and came towards me fast. He had no show, and he knew I would shoot if he try to get away on his own horse, so he come up to me. He say afterwards he been going to knock me off my horse and get my carbine. There'd been a fine fight pretty quick, but his wife got between us and say, 'For God's sake don't shoot! He won't try to get away.' . . . Sheff he laughed kind of bitter, and walked back to the tent mit his arm round his wife. He stood by the fire, head down, thinking. Pretty soon Mrs. Davis gave him a tin bucket to get some water and he started off, but I covered him and again I say, 'Sheff. Davis, you stay dare,' and I walk up to der tent. Then he put his hand on his sword and got mad. 'Haven't you any better manners, you —— Yankee, than to come into a lady's bedroom?' That made me feel pretty bad, because I got some pretty good manners. . . . He shust stayed there quiet until Col. Pritchard came up and took him prisoner."

The higher critic will not fail to mark the discrepancy in style in this quaint narrative, and to question its authenticity upon that ground. But, though manifestly built, at points, upon knowledge not possessed by Bee at the time, it has been substantiated in large part. Clark Seely, of the First Wisconsin Cavalry, later assured the *National Tribune* that "no one soldier captured Jeff. Davis. . . . One soldier . . . halted Jeff . . . and turned him back to his tent, but . . . did not know who he was until Colonels Harnden and Pritchard rode back to the camp after the firing ceased; and then one of them asked him if he was Jeff Davis. He answered, 'I am President Davis.'" Colonel Johnston adds this detail: Pritchard "came up and addressed Davis in insolent language, something like this, 'Well, old Jeff, we have got you at last.' Mr. Davis replied, 'The worst of all is that I should be captured by a band of thieves and scoundrels . . .' I somewhat regretted that Mr. Davis had lost his temper, but he was in a very excited state of mind."

We have also, in certain notes on Burton Harrison's *Capture of Jefferson Davis*, Davis' own account of his actions, from the moment when he was roused by his coachman. "The idea with which I had fallen asleep was still in my mind when, stepping . . . out of the tent, I saw the troopers deploying from the road down which they came, and immediately turned back to inform my wife that these were not the expected marauders, but were cavalry, having recognized them as such by the manner of their deployings. . . . My wife urged me to leave immediately, the way being still open to the eastward. My horse (left saddled the night before) and arms, however, were near to the road down which the assailants came, so that I must go on foot. As I started, the foreman of the deploying troopers advanced towards me and ordered me to halt, at the same time aiming his carbine at me and ordering me to surrender, to which I replied with angry defiance." "My wife," declares one of Davis' notes on Burton Harrison's account, ". . . rushed after me and threw her arms round my neck. Whether it would have been possible for me to escape the trooper's fire and get his horse by a very sudden movement, it was quite certain that the instant's delay, with the hurrying approach of the other troopers, rendered the case hopeless; I therefore walked back with my wife to her tent, and passed on, without entering it, to the fire in the rear of it, where I sat down, as the morning was chilly."

These notes show that Harrison's account was revised by Davis, and, in view of their relationship, it is probable that Mrs. Davis helped with the revision. Harrison may therefore be trusted when he says, naturally excepting Davis' own knowledge of what occurred: "I have not found there was any one except Mrs. Davis, the single trooper at her tent, and myself, who saw all that occurred and heard all that was said at the time. Any one else who gives an account of it has to rely upon hearsay or upon his own imagination."

In an article contributed to "Belford's Magazine," Davis later wrote that his wife urged him to start to the woods as if going for water. "After some hesitation, I consented, and a servant-woman started with me, carrying a bucket, as if going to the spring for water. One of the surrounding troopers ordered me to halt, and demanded my surrender. I advanced towards the trooper, throwing off a shawl which my wife had put over my shoulders. The trooper aimed his carbine, when my wife, who witnessed the act, rushed forward and threw her arms round me, thus delaying my intention, which was, if the trooper missed his aim, to try to unhorse him and escape with his horse."

This testimony lends a semblance of accuracy to Bee's account, and Jones, too, the negro servant who had warned Davis, later gave an interview, sworn to on July 8, 1907, before a notary public, in which, whether from memory or from information gathered later, he confirmed the main points of both Bee's and Davis' narratives.

Colonel Pritchard's official report, dated May 11, 1865, was specific as to details of the capture, but said nothing concerning Davis' clothes, a topic soon to be eagerly discussed throughout the world; and on May 12th, when Brevet Major-General Wilson telegraphed his first report from Macon, he also failed to mention them:

"I have the honour to report that at daylight of the 10th instant, Col. Pritchard Cmdg. 4th Michigan Cavalry captured Jeff. Davis & family, with Reagan, postmaster-general, Col. Harrison, private secretary, Col. Johnson A. D. C., Col. Morris, Col. Lubbock, Lieut. Hatheway, and others. Col. Pritchard surprised their camp at Irwinsville in Irwin County, Georgia, seventy-five miles southeast of this place. The prisoners will be here tomorrow night and will be forwarded under strong guard without delay. I will send further particulars at once."

At this point imagination, that great confuser of history, proceeded to furnish the public with a myriad of interesting details. On May 13th, General Wilson sent a dispatch to Stanton, based upon hearsay: "The captors report that he [Davis] hastily put on one of Mrs. Davis' dresses and started for the woods": and General Halleck, commanding the Department of the James River, suggested to the Secretary of War, "If Jefferson Davis was captured in his wife's clothes, I respectfully suggest that he be sent north in the same habiliments." On May 14th, Wilson reported, again from hearsay: "The device adopted by Davis was even more ignoble than I reported at first." And as he did not specify "the device" it was promptly supplied by the press. The *New York Herald* printed in large headlines:

"Davis disguises himself in his wife's clothing, and, like his accomplice, Booth, takes to the woods. He shows fight and flourishes a dagger in the style of the assassin of the President. He fails to imitate Booth and die in the last ditch. His ignominious surrender."

Another enterprising reporter, learning that hoopskirts had been found in the tent which Davis and his wife had occupied, gleefully announced that Davis was wearing them when taken, and his enemies found the story too good to be untrue. Upon the not unusual war maxim, "What are facts among enemies?" the tale, with a hundred variations, was broadcast to an eager world. The press of many lands employed cartoonists to depict the exiled "rebel" as his enemies wished to see him, skirted and bonneted, intent upon escape at any cost. The Northern press of America, not satisfied with mere newspaper space, printed cartoons upon large sheets and dispatched them to the four winds. One of especial merit presents Davis half over a fence, with his hoopskirts caught on the post, exposing a wilderness of bare wires, and beneath a pair of military breeches, finished off with shining army boots, tipped with gleaming spurs; while the stiff figure of Mrs. Davis standing by uttered the words: "Don't irritate the 'President'—He might hurt somebody!"

The story of the hoop skirts was skilfully capitalized by P. T. Barnum, the famous showman, who delighted his circus-minded audiences, says Mallory, by "a graphic life-size representation of Mr. Davis, thus habited, resisting arrest by Federal soldiers. Many thousands of children, whose wondering eyes beheld it, will grow to maturity and pass into the grave, retaining the ideas thus created as the truth of history."

Defenders appeared, however, even among those who had shared the glory of capturing Davis. Captain James H. Parker, who contested with Bee the honour of being the first to recognize him, flatly denied the story in a statement to the *Argus*, of Portland, Maine: "I am no admirer of Jefferson Davis. I am a Yankee, full of Yankee prejudices, but think it wicked to lie about him.

"I was in the party that captured Jefferson Davis and saw the whole transaction from its beginning. I now say, and hope that you will publish it, that Jefferson Davis did not have on, at the time he was taken, any garments such as are worn by women. He did have over his shoulders a water-proof article of clothing something like a 'Haverlock.' It was not in the least concealed. He wore a hat and did not carry a pail of water on his head, nor kettle in any way.

"His wife did not tell any person that her husband might hurt somebody if he got exasperated. She behaved like a lady, and he as a gentleman, though manifestly he was chagrined at being taken into custody. I know what I am writing about. I saw Jefferson Davis many times while he was staying in Portland several years ago, and I think I was the first one to recognize him at the time of his arrest.

"I defy any person to find a single officer or soldier who was present at the capture of Jefferson Davis, who will say upon honour that he was disguised in woman's clothes. I favour trying him for his crimes, and, if he is found guilty, punish him. But I would not lie about him when the truth will certainly make it bad enough."

Stanton, however, "rolled the statement under his tongue as a sweet morsel," as Captain Parker expressed it, and on May 23rd, ordered that Pritchard be sent to bring to Washington "the woman's dress in which Jefferson Davis was captured." Pritchard's account of his mission follows: "On the afternoon of May 23, 1865, I received orders from the War Department, through General Miles, directing me to procure the disguise worn by Davis at the time of his capture and proceed to Washington and report to the Secretary of War. Accordingly I went to the steamer, *Clyde,* and received from Mrs. Davis a lady's water-proof cloak, . . . which Mrs. Davis said was worn by Davis . . . at the time of his capture, and which was identified by the men who saw it on him at the time. On the morning following, the balance of the disguise was procured, which consisted of a shawl, which was identified and admitted to be the one by Mrs. Davis. These articles I brought to Washington and turned over to the Secretary of War, and this closes my account of the capture and custody, up to the time of his being turned over to the United States authorities, of the great conspirator and traitor, Jefferson Davis." During President Taft's administration, his Secretary, F. W. Carpenter, discovered in the War Department, a box marked "Shawl, waterproof and spurs worn by Jeff. Davis on the day of his capture, May 10, 1865." The label was signed Edwin M. Stanton. A smaller seal bore the lines, "Deliver only to order of Secretary of War, or General E. D. Townsend. A.A. Gen. E.D.S."

These facts complete the evidence, substantiating Davis' own story of the costume in which he was captured, as given in his *Rise and Fall of the Confederate Government:*

"As it was quite dark, I picked up what was supposed to be my 'raglan,' a water-proof, light overcoat, without sleeves; it was subsequently found to be my wife's, so very much like my own as to be mistaken for it; as I started, my wife thoughtfully threw over my head and shoulders a shawl." On August 14, 1879, Davis enclosed in a letter to Governor Stone of Mississippi a photograph of himself, "taken in the identical clothes worn when I was captured. Every article I then had on appears in the portraiture, except a pair of large spurs, which were stolen from me after my capture. I had a water-proof 'raglan' and a shawl about my head when I left the tent, but on being hailed by a cavalryman, who rode a considerable distance before his comrades, I dropped both the 'raglan' and the shawl while advancing on my challenger, and thus appeared before my captors in the exact costume reproduced in the portrait."

To a collection of Davis cartoons in the Boston Public Library is attached a picture of the suit in which he was captured. It was sent in protest by Miss Harrison, keeper of the Confederate Museum in Richmond, where the suit itself is preserved, and shows a coat cut in the style prevalent in the sixties, and made of grey cloth. The trousers are of the same material and bag perceptibly at the knees. The suit bears unmistakable evidence of long service. The preservation and display of this picture is an eloquent witness that the Library authorities have no desire to offend the susceptibility of the South, or to do injustice to the leader of the Lost Cause.

As soon as the fantastic tales of Davis' capture began to circulate in the South, he had reason to pray, "Lord, deliver us from our friends." Stung by the attack upon their leader, they rushed to his rescue with accounts of other heroes who had sought to escape arrest by adopting female disguise, or others equally humiliating: Charles the Second at Woodstock; the Young Pretender after leaving Flora McDonald. Convincingly they argued that King Alfred had sought safety for his royal person by adopting the clothes of a cowherd, and that the Lion-hearted Richard had donned pilgrim's attire in the hope of eluding pursuit. Even Lincoln was introduced as a proper precedent entering his capital disguised with "Scotch cap and cloak."

"Behold, how great a matter, a little fire kindleth." For the rest of his life Davis resented the thought that friend or enemy could believe him guilty of seeking safety by a method so "unbecoming a soldier and a gentleman." Probably no single incident of his career caused him such poignant anguish.

Another of General Wilson's strange imaginings, or cullings from the imaginings of others, was the story of a wild, and certainly never-conceived plan of Davis' to join the *Shenandoah*: "In order to secure the escape of himself and principal officers," it ran, "Davis had many weeks before Lee's catastrophe made the most careful and exacting preparations for his escape, discussing the matter fully with his Cabinet in profound secrecy, and deciding that . . . the *Shenandoah* should be ordered to cruise off the coast of Florida to take the fugitives on board. These orders were sent to the rebel cruiser many days before Lee's lines were broken."

The Honourable George Davis, once attorney-general in Davis' Cabinet, thus pilloried the story: "The *Shenandoah* was then, and long had been, on the broad bosom of the Pacific Ocean, hunted on all sides by Federal cruisers, and without a single friendly port in which to drop her anchor. Were these orders sent round the Horn, or overland from Texas? . . . The narrative deals in pure fiction, too absurd for the wildest credulity. No such orders were issued. There were no discussions in the Cabinet, no 'careful and exacting preparations for escape,' and no preparations of any kind until the fall of Petersburg rendered them necessary; and then the anxiety was for the preservation of the Government, and not for the safety of its individual members. . . . As to Mr. Davis, it was well known in Richmond that his unnecessary and reckless exposure of himself was the cause of frequent and earnest remonstrances."

In view of the absurd accusation, however, the later career of the *Shenandoah* seems a fitting ending to the actual war. With Johnston's surrender, as we now know, the war was over. The battle flags of Union and Confederacy alike became relics, centres of memories, sweet or bitter. But the *Shenandoah*, Commander, J. I. Waddell, still held her adventurous course, too far from the lines of news to know the situation. On May 10, 1865, the day of Davis' capture, Lining's *Journal* showed Lat. (D. R.) 40-17 N. Long. 150-23 E., with heavy winds recorded. On June 22, 1865, the Journal recorded: "Sight and capture the ships *William Thompson* and *Euphrates*. . . . Heard through papers which were on board a batch of bad news, which if it proves true will be terrible. First that Charleston was captured. This, I was expecting, as I did not think we could hold it against Sherman's army. Next that Richmond and Petersburg were taken. I was looking for their evacuation, so it did not surprise me much. But when I heard that General Lee had surrendered with the whole of the Army of Northern Virginia, I was knocked flat aback—can I believe it? And after the official letters which are published as being written by Grant and Lee, can I help believing it? It is either true or the Yankees are again publishing official lies. God grant that it may not be true!" Acting upon hope rather than probability, the *Shenandoah* continued her course, and the *Journal* that night recorded: "Sight six ships—capture of bark *Milo*—the *Sophia Thornton* takes to the ice—but returns—capture the *Jireh Swift*—burn her at once—the *Milo* bonded for $48,000 to carry the prisoners ashore." Thus from day to day the *Journal* records war captures on the high seas when war was no more.

On August 2nd, appeared this entry: "Lat. 16-20-10 N. Long. 121-11-16 W. This is doomed to be one of the blackest of all the black days of my life, for from today I must look forward to begin life over again, starting where I cannot tell, how I cannot say—but I have learned for a certainty that I have no country." The crushing truth had been conveyed to Commander Waddell by an English bark which he had boarded "thirteen days out from San Francisco," that "the Southern Confederacy was a thing of the past, all her armies having surrendered, Mr. Davis and Mr. Stephens prisoners, which was also the case with most of the prominent men. I now see no reason to doubt it and it remains for us to see what we ought to do. It is the opinion of the majority of the officers that we ought to take her to Australia, turn her over to the Government, and we ourselves leave for England." Waddell himself at last came round to this opinion and the ship's course was changed for Sydney "much to the delight of everybody—or nearly everybody, for some still think we ought to go to England with her. Thus ends our dream! But I am too sad to think of it."

Waddell, however, changed his mind; and the next day headed the *Shenandoah* for England, declaring that it "would be foolish to land the crew penniless in Australia." Next day he informed the crew that "the South had been conquered; they were in a position such as no ship had ever occupied; their cruise would go down to history; he would run into the first English port," the decision which the crew had itself urged in a petition.

On November 6th, the *Shenandoah* anchored off Liverpool, and two days later Lining closed his *Journal* with the exultant entry: "We were the last thing that flew the Confederate flag and that is something to be proud of."

Still ignorant of the fact that he was regarded as one of Lincoln's assassins, Davis with his fellow-prisoners started, under guard, towards Macon, he and his family in an ambulance, and his friends riding their own horses. On the second or third day they passed a cavalry camp, and as Davis came abreast of it, its band struck up "Yankee Doodle." "It was at that camp," says Harrison, "that we first heard of the proclamation offering a reward of $100,000 for the capture of Mr. Davis, upon the charge invented by Stanton and Holt, of participation in the plot to murder Mr. Lincoln." Colonel Pritchard had himself just received it, and considerately handed a printed copy of the proclamation to Mr. Davis, "who read it with a composure unruffled by any feeling other than scorn."

When the party arrived at General Wilson's headquarters, Davis was asked whether he preferred to call on the General or to receive him in his own apartments, and, having chosen the former alternative, was conducted into Wilson's presence. Here he was again shown a copy of the President's proclamation and scornfully commented, "There is one man at least who knows the charge to be false," and when Wilson asked who that was, Davis answered, "The man who signed the proclamation, for he well knew that I greatly preferred Lincoln to himself."

There were, however, other men high in the public service who shared President Johnson's and Secretary Seward's view of Davis' complicity in the murder. Charles Sumner, for example, wrote to a friend in England, at about this time: "You enjoy the overthrow of belligerent slavery. In assassinating our good President it acted naturally, logically and consistently, and yet there are foreigners who are astonished that Jefferson Davis can be thought guilty of such an atrocity."

The idea that there was anything ignominious about Mr. Davis' surrender has been long since dissipated. But it is not strange that the generation which had been shocked by the assassination of a President, the first of a now long series, should have yielded to hysteria when the man whom war propaganda had painted as the chief assassin was in their hands. It was inevitable that for a period, Davis should be looked upon as a fiend incarnate, and blamed for every catastrophe, including the crimes of starving helpless Federal prisoners at Andersonville and assassinating President Lincoln. War psychology always produces such results, as no one who has lived through the period of the World War will be disposed to deny.

General Joseph Wheeler, the dashing cavalry leader, captured a little later than Davis, in describing his experiences as a prisoner, says that at Augusta he was placed on a tug, where he found himself as fellow-prisoner "with a most distinguished company; for there were on board Jefferson Davis and his family; . . . Alexander H. Stephens; C. C. Clay . . . and Mrs. Clay; . . . Colonel Lubbock, of Texas; Colonel Burton Harrison; . . . Postmaster-General Reagan; and Colonel William Preston Johnston, . . . aide to President Davis. . . . We soon started down the river, and upon reaching Savannah were transferred to a large river steamboat, which conveyed us to Hilton Head. . . . We were guarded on the steamboat by men of Colonel Pritchard's force, who . . . were in high spirits over the knowledge that the reward of one hundred thousand dollars for the President's capture would be theirs, as indeed it was, after some trouble in the division."

As the voyage continued, and the precautions of the guard became more lax, General Wheeler conceived a bold plan for releasing his fellow-prisoners and himself. "There were ten of us, able-bodied men," he later wrote, "and with . . . guns in our hands we should soon [have] been masters of the situation." He therefore suggested that they seize the arms of the guards, carelessly stacked on deck when they went to meals, and make themselves masters of the situation. It would be easy, he argued, to get ashore before help could arrive. The objection was raised that Mr. Davis would not countenance such a revolt, and while Wheeler went below to consult Davis, and be confronted with the expected refusal, "our opportunity passed."

Thus, without exciting incident, the prisoners arrived at Hilton Head, where they were transferred to the *Clyde*, which conducted them to Fortress Monroe, the gunboat, *Tuscarora,* attending. Many felt, with Stephens, the fear that Davis was being conveyed to his execution; but "President Davis himself," according to General Wheeler, ". . . showed not the slighted trepidation, but reviewed the situation as calmly as if he had no personal interest in it. He discussed the war, its men and its incidents, in the same dispassionate way that a traveller might speak of scenes and incidents in some foreign land. He was affable and dignified as usual, and if he felt any fear, he certainly showed none. Nor would his fine sense of honour and propriety allow him to take advantage of another plan that we made for his escape."

And so, refusing all suggestions of escape, did this august prisoner of war (for the world today does not deny him that title) approach his prison days, destined to last, without the benefits of *habeas corpus*, without trial, without being confronted by witnesses, either for defence or prosecution, for two years, less six days.

CHAPTER XXVII

# THE SCAPEGOAT

IN OLD TESTAMENT days it was customary for the Priest at the Altar to lay his hands upon the body of a he-goat, and then send him into the wilderness bearing the sins of the people. As Davis approached Virginia, on his way to prison, he bore upon his shoulders the major part of the "sin" of secession. Others the radical leaders of the North might consent to pardon but not him whom unfair propaganda had made the chief instigator of the war, now at an end.

On May 19th the *Clyde* docked at Old Point Comfort, where the captives were divided, as Stephens and Reagan were to be sent to Fort Warren; Wheeler and his staff, with W. P. Johnston and Lubbock, to Fort Delaware; Harrison to Washington, and Davis and Clay to the grim recesses of Fortress Monroe. The anxiety of the Federal authorities concerning Davis' security, is shown by the fact that General Grant telegraphed Halleck that Brevet Major-General Miles was to be sent to Old Point Comfort, "the object being to put an officer at Fort Monroe who will by no possibility permit the escape of the prisoners to be confined there." The order was at once sent to General Meade, Army of the Potomac, and three days later, Miles entered upon his duties, conscious that the safety of Jefferson Davis was to be the chief of them.

On May 22nd, the *Clyde* landed her cargo of captives, and at 2 P.M. Charles A. Dana, Assistant Secretary of War and Stanton's confidential witness, who had been sent to report on the landing, telegraphed his chief that the "two prisoners [Clement C. Clay and Jefferson Davis] have just been placed in their respective casemates." He further reported that "Davis bore himself with a haughty attitude. His face was somewhat flushed, but his features were composed and his step firm," as he descended the gangplank, his right arm firmly held by General Miles, resplendent in his handsome uniform. "In Clay's manner there was less impression of bravado and dramatic determination." Dana further assured his chief that the prisoners were now perfectly safe. "The arrangements for the security of the prisoners seem to me as complete as could be desired. Each one occupies the inner room of a casemate. The window is heavily barred. A sentry stands within before each of the doors leading to the outer room. These *doors are to be grated but are now secured by bars* fastened on the outside. . . . Two other sentries stand outside these doors. An officer is constantly . . . in the outer room, whose duty is to see his prisoners every fifteen minutes. The outer door of all is locked on the outside, and the key is kept exclusively by the general officer of the guard. Two sentries are also stationed without that door. A strong line of sentries cuts off all access to the vicinity of the casemates. Another line is stationed on the top of the parapet overhead, and a third line is posted across the moats on the counter-scarfs opposite the places of confinement. The casemates on each side and between those occupied by the prisoners are used as guard-rooms, and soldiers are always there. A lamp is kept burning in each of the rooms."

That Davis' conduct was less bravado than resignation to the will of Heaven is shown in a letter from Reagan to the Reverend J. W. Jones: "It was a very sad leave-taking. Mr. Davis requested me to read the 16th Psalm. He said it gave him consolation to read it." And Reagan adds: "I loved him as I never loved any other man."

The *New York Herald* of May 23rd described the incarceration from its own point of view: "At about three o'clock yesterday afternoon, 'all that is mortal' of Jeff'n Davis, late so called 'President of the alleged Confederate States,' was duly, but quietly and effectively, committed to that living tomb prepared within the impregnable walls of Fortress Monroe. The 22nd day of May, 1865, may be said to be the day, when all the earthly aspirations of Jeff'n Davis ceased. . . . No more will Jeff'n Davis be known among the masses of men. . . . His life has been a cheat. His last free act was an effort to unsex himself and deceive the world. He keeps the character, we may say, in death, and is buried alive."

The same paper reported later: "Davis can never escape. He is not allowed to speak to any one. He is literally in a living tomb. Over all the state prisoners, the same guard, numbering 70 officers and men, is now kept on watch. It may, in fact, be said, that neither the great Napoleon at Elba or St. Helena, the lesser Napoleon at the Fortress of Ham, nor any other state prisoner of the centuries, was subjected to greater surveillance than that to which Jeff'n Davis is subjected here. The great Corsican escaped from Elba, Napoleon the lesser escaped from Ham, but no such hope for Davis. He can never escape."

Not content with these arrangements for securing men whose paroled word would have sufficed—the inner casemate, the barred window and doors, the line of sentries, outside and in, the well-nigh four score officers and men on guard and the ever-burning lamp—Dana telegraphed, on the day that Davis was brought to the fortress: "Brevet Major-General Miles is hereby authorized and directed to place manacles and fetters upon the hands and feet of Jefferson Davis and Clement C. Clay whenever he may think it advisable in order to render their imprisonment more secure. By order of the Secretary of War." The next morning Miles sent an order for irons, and that evening in the hundredfold guarded chamber in Fortress Monroe, a dramatic, humiliating and totally unnecessary scene took place.

In the Confederate Museum at Richmond can be seen a letter from the man who shackled Jefferson Davis:

"Roanoke, S. D., July 4.—My Dear Son: There has been much said and written about Jefferson Davis in relation to putting fetters on him at Fortress Monroe, Virginia. Some statements are in great part true and others are false, and some say he never was shackled.

"On the morning of May 23, 1865, I was detailed as officer of the day, and after guard mount I reported to General Nelson A. Miles for special orders in regard to the three state prisoners —Jefferson Davis, C. C. Clay, and John Mitchel—who were confined in separate gunrooms or casemates, the embrasures of which were closed with heavy iron bars looking out on the moat or ditch, which is about sixty feet wide. The first room, or casemate, had but one door and two large windows facing the inside of the court. The gunroom had two doors leading in from the casemate; these were closed by heavy iron grating doors and locked with padlocks, and at each door, in the gunroom with the prisoner, were two sentinels with loaded muskets, and in the casemate were two more sentinels and officers of the guard, all of whom were under lock and key, the officer of the day having charge of the keys. The guard was relieved every two hours, and that could only be done in the presence of the officer of the day. The windows of the casemate were also grated with iron bars. The prisoners occupied every other gunroom and the guards not on duty the intervening ones.

"There was a special guard mounted of eighty men for these three prisoners and the commandant of the fort could not give any orders of any kind to that special guard; in fact, he could not come within the lines. There were four sentinels on the parapet overhead, four on the glacis beyond the ditch, and six in the fort in front of the casemates. The above statement is just as I found things the day that Davis was shackled.

"I reported to General Miles as the new officer of the day. The general said he had special orders for me as to Jeff Davis. Having heard it rumoured that morning that Davis was to be put in irons, I said to the general, 'I think I can guess what it is, General.' 'Well, what is it, Captain?' 'To put irons on Davis.' He said, 'That is it.' I said, 'When do you wish it done?' He said, 'The irons are not ready.' Then I said, 'Had we not better put them on towards evening?' He said, 'Yes,' and I could send my orderly to the blacksmith's and have him meet me at that time with the leg irons, and at the same time he—General Miles—showed me part of a letter he had from Secretary Stanton, in which he said that if he thought the safety of Davis required it he could put irons on Davis, or words to that effect. The matter was left optional with General Miles as to whether Davis should be put in irons or not.

"Just before the sundown relief I sent my orderly out for the blacksmith to meet me with the leg irons at the casemate. Soon after I went down I found the smith and his helper there. I then unlocked the door and told the guard to let them pass, that is, smith and helper.

"As I entered the gunroom Davis was sitting on the end of his cot, or hospital bed, reading his Episcopal Prayer Book, and as he looked up I said, 'Mr. Davis, I have an unpleasant duty to execute.' At the same moment, seeing the blacksmith with the irons, he said, 'You do not intend to put fetters on me?' I said, 'Those are my orders.' He said, 'Those are orders for a slave, and no man with a soul in him would obey such orders.' I then said, 'Those are my orders.' Mr. Davis said, 'I shall never submit to such an indignity.' He then asked if General Miles had given that order. My answer was in the affirmative. He said he would like to see General Miles. I replied the general had just left the fort. Davis then asked that the execution of the order be postponed, and I should telegraph to the President in his name. I said, 'Mr. Davis, you are an old soldier and know what the orders are; it is needless to say that an officer is bound to execute an order given him.' Davis said it was obvious that there could be no necessity for such an order to make his imprisonment secure. I said, 'My duty is to execute this order and it is folly for you to resist.' Davis' answer was that he was a soldier and knew how to die, and, pointing to a sentinel, said, 'Let your men shoot me at once.'

"A few moments after he placed his foot on a stool and his quiet manner led me to think he would not resist. I then said, 'Smith, do your work.' As the blacksmith stooped to place the clasp of the shackle round his ankle Davis struck him a violent blow that threw him on the floor. He recovered and at once made for Davis with his vise and hammer and would have struck him if I had not caught his arm as he was in the act of striking. A moment after that I saw Davis and one of the sentinels struggling, both having hold of the musket, Davis just below the shank of the bayonet. The next instant the sentinel had wrenched the musket from Mr. Davis' hands. I then ordered the soldier to his post and reprimanded him for leaving. I now saw there would be trouble, so I ordered the officer of the guard to go out and get four of the best men of the guard, with outside arms, and have them report to me at once. A few minutes after four stalwart soldiers made their appearance. I said, 'Men, I wish you to take Mr. Davis, with as little force as possible, and place him on that cot and hold him there till the smith is through with his work.'

"As the men advanced Davis struck the first or foremost man, but all four instantly closed on him and shoved him on the cot. Davis showed unnatural strength; it was all the four men could do to hold him while the blacksmith riveted the clasp round his ankle, his helper holding a sledge hammer. The other clasp was locked on with a brass lock, the same as in use on freight-cars. I ordered the men to their quarters, and they passed out. Davis lay perfectly motionless. Just as I was going out Davis raised from his cot and threw his feet to the floor, and with the clanging of the chains he gave way. I will say here that it was anything but a pleasant sight to see a man like Jefferson Davis shedding tears, but not one word had he to say.

"Two hours after I called to relieve the guard and found Davis lying on his cot. I said, 'Mr. Davis, you can't rest well that way; if you will give me your word of honour that you will give no more trouble in this matter I will unlock the shackles so you can take off your clothing.' 'Captain, I assure you there will be no more trouble. I was very much exasperated at the time; never expected to be subjected to such an indignity.' I then unlocked the shackle, he taking off his clothing and locking it again himself.

"JEROME TITLOW,

"Late Captain Third Pennsylvania Regiment Artillery."

The following letter was written by the blacksmith who forged the fetters and put them on:

"Granville Centre

"Bradford Co. Pa.

*"Nov. 1, 1911.*

"MR. ST GEORGE T. C. BRNYAN

"Dear Sur

"in reply to your letter, I forged the irons and put them on Mr Davis I reveted them on his angles not on boot. Yes he ressested: we laied him on cot while puting them on he saied he would as soon be shot he only had them on 2 weakes A man naim John Redm tuck them off As I was A way that day the order came from Washington to put them on Dr. Craven from New Jersey saiad the ingerd his halth and truy him the wear [they were] taken off and then he was mooved from casmat to Carroll hall Gen Miles has the Shackles

"I was post Blacksmith from April 61 to March 66 when I

came hear whear I have Lived and Worked at my trad ever Sence I am 71 years old

"yours truly

"H C ARNOLD"

The next day, May 24th, General Miles wrote to Dana:

"Yesterday I directed that irons be put on Davis' ankles, which he violently resisted, but became more quiet afterward. His hands are unencumbered. Both he and Clay are well." [He showed his lack of sensitiveness by adding] "The females were sent to Savannah today.

"NELSON A. MILES

"Brevet Major-General of Volunteers

"Commanding.

"To C. A. DANA

"Assistant Secretary of War."

Dr. John J. Craven, who, as surgeon of the Fort, saw Davis that day for the first time, reported less favourably concerning his health. "He presented a very miserable and affecting aspect. . . . Stretched upon his pallet, and very much emaciated, Mr. Davis appeared a mere fascine of raw and tremulous nerves —his eyes restless and fevered, his head continually shifting from side to side for a cool spot on the pillow, and his case clearly one in which intense cerebral excitement was the first thing needing attention."

Having intervened in behalf of his patient, Dr. Craven secured permission to return at evening and brought with him a package of tobacco. When Mr. Davis had lighted his pipe, the only article, save the clothes he wore, which he had been able to bring from the *Clyde*, he remarked: "This is a noble medicine." And, after speaking of the inconveniences caused by the presence of two sentries within his chamber, he added that "with this"—touching his pipe—he "hoped to become tranquil."

Tranquillity under the circumstances would have been even more difficult had he known what he later learned, and reported to an old West Point friend, that, "the staff officers, sent on the ship where my wife and children were detained after I was incarcerated . . . plundered her trunks, carrying off many articles of value, and among other things a hoopskirt which the knaves were said subsequently to have sold as the one worn by me. . . ."

The Confederate Records quote Stanton as having ordered "the women and children, constituting the families of Davis and Clay, and other females in the company, to such places in the South where we have transports going." Mrs. Davis' destination proved to be Savannah, and upon being landed, she read in the *Republican* the grim details of the shackling of her husband, with thoughts, as she later said to Dr. Craven, that stopped her "heart's vibrations." She was later allowed to see a letter which he had written to her in one of his blackest hours, and which shows a spirit little akin to that of a murderer, too dangerous to be left unshackled: "Every day, twice or oftener, I repeat the prayer of St. Chrysostom, 'Tarry there the Lord's leisure; be strong and He will comfort thy heart.' "

For five days Davis endured his chains, obedient to force; while the press was flooded with details of the shackling, and with censure of the Government which had ordered so needless an insult to the ex-President of the Confederacy, and to the people of the South. On the sixth day Stanton, moved by the widespread protest, sent the following dispatch to General Miles:

"War Department,
"Washington, D. C.
*"May 28, 1865.*

"MAJOR GENERAL MILES, Commanding etc.
"Fort Monroe:

"Please report whether irons have or have not been placed on

Jefferson Davis. If they have been, when was it done, and for what reason, and remove them.

"EDWIN M. STANTON,
"Secretary of War."

Miles' reply was as follows:

"FORT MONROE, VA., *May 28, 1865*—2.30 P.M.—Hon. Edwin M. Stanton, Secretary of War: I have the honour to state, in reply to your dispatch, that when Jeff'n Davis was first confined in the casemate, the inner doors were light wooden ones without locks. I directed anklets to be put upon his ankles, which would not interfere with his walking, but prevent his running should he endeavour to escape. In the meantime I have changed the wooden doors for grated ones with locks and the anklets have been removed. [The dispatch does not say whether before or after Stanton's order.] Every care is taken to avoid any pretence for complaint as well as to prevent the possibility of his escape. I remain, with the highest respect, your obedient servant,

"N. A. MILES, Brigadier General."

A feeble effort was made in the administration press to convince the public that the "temporary" shackling of Davis had been made necessary by the work of removing the "wooden door," now preserved in the Confederate Museum at Richmond, but it made little impression on a public who had read the details of the extraordinary care with which he was guarded, day and night. They knew that his safekeeping had not required the humiliation under which he had suffered, a humiliation felt by every Confederate heart, and which increased the already bitter sectional hatred.

The [London] *Times*, meanwhile, though absurdly crediting Davis with a desire to make himself king, urged clemency. "The inhabitants of these islands," it said, "have little reason to sympathize with Jefferson Davis. He has been one of the most inveterate calumniators of this country; his policy has been to stir up the feelings of every class of his countrymen against us. For the person who could speculate on the miseries he would bring upon us, as his means of success, we have little respect, and if we plead for his life, it is not from any respect for his motives or sympathy with his character. It is purely in the cause of the American Union that we urge . . . the impolicy of shedding the blood of a man whom a little success would have transformed from a traitor into a monarch. The stake has been played fairly, it has been lost entirely, and the victor should be content with success."

Whether or not this article came to Stanton's attention, the outspoken opinion of the English press did, and he brought it to the notice of J. C. Hamilton, who replied on May 29th, warning Stanton to beware of British intrigues, which might endanger him and other Federal officials: "May not a probable theory of the murder [of Lincoln] and attempted assassination [of his advisers] be this? The *Times* published some weeks since an article showing the confidence of the South in S——n's politics? [obviously General Sherman is meant.] . . . A friend who has returned from Savannah informs me that S——n habitually rejected the advances of the blacks who complained of his non-encouragement of them. . . . The paper you showed me is a paraphrase with addenda of his conversation with Johnson. The letter stating his expectation [that] the Government would *not outlive* the Rebellion has meaning. Keep these in view, and let us proceed. The condition of the South was desperate. Mr. Lincoln, though kind, was true to the country. His Cabinet were committed. The Vice-President's vigour of character and intellect they were aware of. General Grant would prove a rampart insuperable. What could be done? Through Sherman a light opened and at the last gasp of their [the South's] political life what else presented if not a probable, at least a possible, relief, to their discomforted fortunes? That Sherman knew what was to follow, it would be highly criminal to suppose. But the solution of what did follow, and of the motive for the whole scope of life-destruction may be read thus: 'We (the South) will put out of the way the P——t —— the V. Pt —— the Secretary of War —— of State —— and General Grant.' The door of access will be before Sherman. . . . Sherman can clutch the key, as the deliverer of the nation. This policy will save our wreck. The expectation of Sherman that the Government would not survive the Rebellion would be fulfilled, the prophet would become the destiny! The change in the villainous plan must have had a motive. At first Mr. Lincoln was to be kidnapped to extort terms—but why not pursue it? Why proceed to assassination? The assassins . . . were mere hirelings. . . .

"This is a painful picture, but when we are dealing with the life or death of nations we must penetrate deep into all the wickedest recesses of policy. The whole is a shrouded scene.

"Are there not some conclusions to be drawn from this theory? Is it probable, if Davis and others are not executed, that the lives before in jeopardy will be permitted to exist? General Grant told me, you thought there was some danger; —— that he *did not*. If there is a scintilla of doubt as to the safety of you all or of any one of you, has the Government a right to question with its safety?"

Absurd as was this letter in its insinuations against both General Sherman and the South, it was calculated to make Stanton still less sympathetic in his treatment of his prisoner; and there followed a period of the kind of confinement which has driven many a prisoner mad. Davis' room was kept lighted, day and night, and two soldiers stood guard, with orders to inspect his person every fifteen minutes. Davis protested to Dr. Craven: "The consciousness that the Omniscient Eye rests upon us in every situation is the most consoling and beautiful belief of religion, but to have a human eye riveted on you in every moment of waking or sleeping, sitting, walking, or lying down, is a refinement of torture on anything the Comanches or Spanish Inquisition ever dreamed. . . . The lamp burning in my room all night, shooting its rays . . . into my throbbing eyeballs, one of them already sightless from neuralgia, is torture of most intense agony."

Dr. Craven complained to the authorities that the treatment was endangering Davis' life, whereupon General Miles removed Craven and substituted Dr. George Cooper, who soon expressed the same fear. Yet Davis endured, supported, as he himself declared, "by the conscious rectitude of my course, and humbly acknowledging my many sins against God, and confidently looking to His righteous judgment for vindication in the matter whereof I am accused by man. . . ."

At first opinion in the North had seemed to approve, even to demand, harsh treatment of Davis, but it was not long before his sufferings began to rouse sympathy, and Northern champions appeared for him. On May 29th Thurlow Weed protested: "The world is now with us. But this wholly unnecessary severity with a state prisoner will lose us a great advantage. If a mistake has been made I am sure it must have been without authority, and I pray that you will immediately correct it."

The obvious method of making the correction was, of course, trial of the prisoner, and about the beginning of June the rumour was spread abroad that Davis was to be removed to Washington for that purpose; whereupon certain leading citizens of New York urged George Shea to volunteer for the defence. Too cautious to venture upon such a course without careful investigation, Shea set to work to find and interpret the facts and the law, and being soon convinced that Davis could no more be convicted either on the charge of treason or of complicity in Lincoln's assassination, than on that of cruelty to prisoners, was ready to do what he could to procure a speedy trial, or release.

Meanwhile, Daniel Lord and other eminent New York lawyers, who, though entertaining strong opinions against the right and act of secession, were indignant at the law's delays, united in a similar request to Charles O'Conor, the premier of the American bar. O'Conor had also convinced himself, by a preliminary study, and, on June 2nd, dispatched the following letter:

"Hon. Jefferson Davis:

"Dear Sir:

"Gentlemen who have no personal acquaintance with yourself, and who never had any connexion by birth, residence, or otherwise with any of the Southern states, have requested me to volunteer as counsel for the defence in case you should be arraigned upon an indictment which has been announced in the newspapers. No less in conformity with my own sense of propriety than in compliance with their wishes I beg leave to tender my services accordingly. I will be happy to attend at any time and place that you may indicate in order to confer with yourself and others in relation to the defence. The Department of War having given its assent to the transmission of this open letter, through the proper military authorities, I infer that if my professional aid be accepted you will have full permission to confer with me in writing and orally at personal interviews, as you may judge to be necessary or desirable. I am, dear sir, yours respectfully,

"Ch. O'Conor."

This letter, after due inspection, was delivered to Davis, but its contents, reported by the censor, so disturbed General Miles that he wrote to his superior officer, on June 6th:

"General Townsend:

"General: Shall I furnish Jefferson Davis writing material to answer Mr. O'Conor's letter received this A.M.?"

Permission having been given, Davis dispatched the following reply:

"FORTRESS MONROE, VA.,
*7 June, 1865*

"CHARLES O'CONOR, ESQ.
"NEW YORK CITY.
"My dear Sir:

"Yours of the 2d inst. was laid before me yesterday, and today permission has been granted to me to make a specific reply to your offer. Formally, then, I accept your tender of services as my counsel, and offer my grateful acknowledgment of your kindness. Please oblige me still further by giving my thanks to those generous men who, though personally unacquainted with me, and wholly unconnected with the Southern states, nevertheless have had their regard for law and their love of justice quickened into action by a knowledge of my present condition.

"After my capture as a prisoner of war the proclamation publicly accusing me and offering a reward for my arrest reached the section where I then was; since my arrival here all knowledge of passing events has been so rigorously excluded, that I am quite ignorant as to any proceedings instituted against me, as well as the character of the evidence on which they could have been founded; and consequently cannot judge what kind of testimony will be required for my vindication.

"Though reluctant to tax you with the labour of coming here, I must, for the considerations indicated, request you to obtain the requisite authority to visit me for the purpose of a full conference.

"Again tendering to you my sincere thanks, I am, very respectfully and truly yours,

"JEFFERSON DAVIS."

Despite the harmless character of this reply it was held for several days by the censor and then returned to Davis' cell for revision. Davis complied with the demand and re-wrote the letter, but it was never sent to Mr. O'Conor. On June 15th the latter complained to Secretary Stanton that ten days had passed without reply, and requested for himself and his associate, Edwin A. van Sickle, Esq., permission "to have a personal interview with the accused." The interview was refused on the ground that Davis was "not in civil custody."

The State of Mississippi now offered O'Conor a fee of $20,000 in compensation for his proffered services; but O'Conor's intention was to serve his country, by furthering prompt justice, and he would accept no financial compensation.

Soon other able lawyers volunteered to join Shea and O'Conor in their effort to bring about a speedy trial. Charles H. Fowler offered his services on June 22nd; and on June 30th Davis replied: "Before the receipt of yours, a similar offer had been made by Mr. O'Conor of New York and replied to, accepting his services." Knowing this, Fowler had already written to O'Conor, who had answered: "Mr. Davis' letter to me in reply to my tender of services was returned to him as an improper communication. Permission to visit him and confer upon his case orally has been for the present denied by both the Attorney-General and the Secretary of War . . . doubtless we will find occasion to make your services available."

These complications illustrate how difficult a matter it was to give Jefferson Davis the fair and speedy trial to which, upon every ground, he was legally entitled, and Chase's *Decisions* clearly formulate other complications: "According to the philosophy of Government, all punishments are inflicted by the Executive. The Judiciary investigates, ascertains guilt or innocence, and advises the Executive of the fact. The latter then discharges the accused from bonds and inflicts punishment as the case may require. Strictly speaking, the judicial power, as a branch of the Government, has no office in any criminal proceeding except to advise as to the law, and to inform the Executive concerning facts not previously known. . . . Concerning acts which have reached such a measure of notoriety that they cannot lawfully be gainsaid, judicial investigation or trial is impossible."

In the case of Mr. Davis, every material fact was of a public nature, and therefore common knowledge. That he had been chief of the hostile belligerents being universally known and admitted, to seek to prove it in a court of law was obviously an absurdity. To these complications was added the fact that the Legislative, namely the radical Republican majority of Congress, and President Andrew Johnson, were in deadly conflict over the question of which had the right to reconstruct the South; and that Chief Justice Chase was determined that Davis should not be tried for treason is clear from the following extracts from Johnson's *Reports* of his decisions:

"If you bring these leaders to trial, it will condemn the North, for by the Constitution secession is not rebellion."

"Trials for treason in the civil courts are not remedies adapted to the close of a great civil war. Honour forbids a resort to them after combatants in open war have recognized each other as soldiers and gentlemen engaged in legitimate conflict. . . . It would be shockingly indecorous for the ultimate victor in such a conflict to send his vanquished opponent before the civil magistrate to be tried as if he were a mere thief or rioter."

At this point certain ingenious minds suggested a solution: Let Mr. Davis ask for a pardon, President Johnson grant it, and all complications would be solved. "I was solicited," Davis later wrote to Mr. James Lyons of New Orleans, "to add my name to those of many esteemed gentlemen who had signed a petition for my pardon, and an assurance was given that on my doing so the President would order my liberation. Confident of the justice of our cause and the rectitude of my own conduct, I declined to sign the petition." He shared the opinion which Gerrit Smith had recently proclaimed at Cooper Institute: "To be pardoned for a great crime, as, for instance treason or piracy, is the next thing to being punished for it. . . . For one, I am not willing to have it go over the earth, and down to posterity, that millions of my countrymen were pardoned traitors."

In the meantime, the War Department had been advised that Davis' servant, James Jones, had gone to Raleigh to secure two bags of money said to have been concealed near where Mr. Davis was captured; and intent upon securing the evidence which Johnson's proclamation had declared to be already in its possession, had sent Captain Bryant, assistant provost marshal of Florida, to arrest Jones and endeavour to find "the wagon and baggage" abandoned near Gainesville. The result of this search had been reported to the Secretary of War on June 17, 1865, by General Vogdes, who said that he had recently captured a portion of the private baggage of Mr. Davis, near Gainesville, Florida, and furnished a list of the articles which it contained, chiefly "letters from members of his family, and confidential letters from members of his staff and political associates." Vogdes had expressed the opinion that "the most important papers are the original replies of the several members of the rebel Cabinet to the question of Mr. Davis as to acceptance of the terms of the armistice [Sherman and Johnston] 17th and 18th of April, 1865."

This was a disappointing report for those eager to find evidence to discredit Mr. Davis. The baggage, however, was sent and eagerly examined for incriminating clues: but such failed to appear. The absence of evidence, however, did not prevent eminent Northern politicians and hostile Northern papers from confidently prejudging the case. Speaker Colfax declared: "If there is justice left in this country we will see him hanging between heaven and earth as not fit for either." It was not many years, however, before Colfax's connexion with frauds and official plunder disqualified him as a censor of morals. The *Philadelphia Press*, on July 7th, presented again the picture of Davis as the power back of Lincoln's assassination. "Had there been no

Jefferson Davis, there had been no Booth, and while we thirst for no man's blood, justice demands that, when the underlings of the Great Criminal are ignominiously executed [Herold, Payne, Atzerodt, and Mrs. Surratt had been that day put to death on decision of a military commission], he should not be exempted from the fate he accepted for himself, even as he forced it upon them."

President Johnson, acutely conscious that the evidence of treason was unconvincing, and unwilling to yield to the demand for trial which Davis' counsel urged, now asked Chief Justice Chase's views as to the advisability of allowing the case to come to trial. Chase's opinion was as disconcerting as that of O'Conor himself. "Lincoln," he said, "wanted Jefferson Davis to escape, and he was right. His capture was a mistake; his trial will be a greater one. We cannot convict him of treason. Secession is settled. Let it stay settled." For such a trial, bristling with such problems, the Chief Justice was no more anxious than the President. Committed as he himself was to the doctrine of states rights, he saw the case as the British *Quarterly Review* saw it, when it declared: "If this trial is to be conducted calmly, as an affair of state, the difficult task must be encountered by disproving the right of a sovereign state to withdraw from its Union with others; does any counsel dare use the argument?"

Although Davis had refused to ask for pardon, his counsel wished to discover whether the President would consent to settle the matter by discharging him on bail or parole. A letter containing this suggestion was accordingly dispatched to Johnson, who referred it to his attorney-general. No definite reply was made; but O'Conor received an intimation that such a method would have a better chance of success if leading Unionists should offer to sign Davis' bond. The hint was not lost upon O'Conor and Shea whose minds now naturally turned to the idea of asking Horace Greeley to perform this service.

At this point Mrs. Davis might well have complicated the

situation, as she wrote to Greeley, bitterly denouncing both the treatment to which her husband was subjected, and the attitude of the Press. Greeley, however, read the letter sympathetically, but thought it best to show it to Shea, who had undertaken the case partly at Greeley's solicitation, and on July 3rd, Shea wrote to Mrs. Davis that he had been assured by Secretary Stanton that "there was no truth in the newspaper stories" about Davis' cruel treatment.

The harsh treatment continued, however, and even Davis' counsel were still refused the privilege of visiting him. To O'Conor's protest the attorney-general, James Speed, answered: "The Government cannot consent to allow any one to visit" him, but added that his counsel would be allowed conference with him as soon as he should be handed over to civil custody. Perfectly innocent and normal requests were still coldly disregarded, even that of his rector.

Meanwhile, Mrs. Davis used every art of her capable brain to win sympathy for the prisoner at Fortress Monroe. On July 14th she wrote to Shea from Savannah: "Ever since Mr. Davis' incarceration, I have been detained here. I was brought here against my will, have never been here before, and knew no friend to whom I could turn. Left with no other support than the small sum which the cupidity of the enemy, our captors, had failed to ferret out and steal—I have been forced to spend as much in one month as I could have lived upon in a cheap place for a year, or until Mr. Davis' case should be decided. Denied the comfort of telling him how his baby prisoners are or of sending one word of love to him. When his life was apparently hanging upon a thread, the Government had not the humanity to send me notice of it, but every agony of his was published accompanied with jeers of the valiant editors, and hawked about the streets in extras. I applied three days ago to go to Augusta to see my family, leaving all my children in Savannah, but was refused permission, because a prisoner within the limits of Savannah. Yet the Government does not pay my expenses. I am accused of no wrong, yet I am confined here without redress, as I was conveyed here guarded by men armed with Spencer rifles, and bayonets, and up to the hour of leaving Fortress Monroe, they guarded my door. . . . Is it sought to prevent me from communicating with the outer world lest the plea for justice may not be overpowered by the cry of 'crucify him.' For our downtrodden people I crave the 'amnesty' whatever that may be; it is Protean and I cannot define it, unless it is their Adamic legacy confirmed to them by President Johnson—permission to breathe God's air, and gain their bread by the sweat of their brows. But for me, and for mine, we crave no amnesty. We have been robbed of everything except our memories—God has kept them green. . . . There is no bond uniting us to the Northerners. A great gulf of blood rolls between and my spirit shrinks appalled from attempting to cross it. I am strong to suffer, but quite unable to offer friendship, or receive amnesty at the hands of the Federal 'many-headed monster thing' which has usurped the place of our grand old compact. If we get justice, I desire no favours. Mr. Johnson may pardon us like the Revd. Mr. Chadband, whether we wish it or not, but he will never be asked."

This letter showed also how fully Mrs. Davis had entered into her husband's Constitutional theory for it cleverly characterized his "offence" as "an inexpedient assertion of an undeniable right," and declared Davis to have been "falsely accused of every baseness and inhumanity which could disgrace mankind, without a shadow of proof," an assertion which in time was fully admitted. With the definiteness which characterizes strong characters she pinned the responsibility upon one individual, and he, the President of the United States, "by accident dressed in a little brief authority." Scornfully she flayed also the Chief Justice of the United States, who, according to Colonel Pritchard's report, had answered the question, "what will be done with Mr. Davis?" by the words, "I do not know, it remains to be seen what the feelings of the people will indicate"—words little consonant with the idea of justice. "They are mousing among the achives," Mrs. Davis continued, bitterly, ". . . for something upon which to support accusations. . . . And combining business with pleasure, *Quid nuncs* are polluting with their unhallowed gaze the precious records of my few happy hours, and turning an honest penny by selling garbled extracts from my husband's letters, and mine, to those papers whose readers, needing a gentle excitement, are willing to pay for 'readable matter.'"

Thus bitterly did Mrs. Davis demand a justice which never came, and unburdened her heart, in confidence, to the champion who had undertaken the heavy task of securing justice for the leader of the Lost Cause, now the "scapegoat" of a subverted nation. "I am unhinged by sorrow," she continued, "and forget you have not lived in an invaded country and that . . . your ire has not been lighted at the funeral pyre of friends and homes lost for ever." And desiring to show her appreciation of the disinterested service of O'Conor and Shea, and other Northern friends who were seeking justice for her husband, she continued,

> "The poor make no new friends,
> But Oh! they love the better, far,
> The few the Father sends."

For some time Mrs. Davis had been seeking permission to go North, and as this was steadily refused, she had quietly planned to get her children out of the country. On July 24th she sought the assistance of a friend, the widow of President Tyler, in the following letter:

"Savannah, Ga.,
*July 24th, 1865.*

"Mrs. Tyler,

"My dear Friend,

"My Mother will hand you this letter or send it to you. She goes on to New York for the purpose of taking my poor little children to school in Canada, as I am a prisoner in Georgia until Mr. Stanton sees fit for me to go out of the country. I have thought it better to send them out from under Yankee influences. . . . As we are very poor, economy is a great item in our calculations, so I must beg of you to get them a cheap and quiet place if you can by your superior knowledge of the New York locality. They do not know any one and are quite unused to a large city. Will you take the trouble to be their cicerone?

"In what a maze of horrors have we been groping for these two months. As for me, I sometimes wonder if God does not mean to wake me from a terrific dream of desolation and penury, to a beatified conviction of freedom achieved, and government established on the best, and surest foundation—I cannot trust myself to speak of my husband. I feel so sure you sympathize with me that I can say to you that the light is gone from my house & the strength with it. . . ."

By the beginning of August Mrs. Davis had won the coveted privilege of going North, and on August 3rd, Shea wrote: "Welcome to New York—while here are your husband's chief political enemies, you will find your chief personal friends. . . . Whatever may be the future [we] will do our best." Greeley, he said, had bidden him say that "he had just received assurances that all was right at last at Washington, and that he felt very comfortable as to the result." "He is a good and firm friend of those who need a friend, and unswerving in the day of defeat and danger." The next day Shea received from Mrs. Clay a letter enthusiastically re-echoing his own opinion: "Blessings on Greeley, for his efforts for justice and peace." It is "so strange that only 'an hour ago' he was regarded as the most implacable foe and fanatic."

Slowly, the pleas of able lawyers, and other men of eminence and political influence in the North were having their effect upon the popular mind also, perhaps even upon the official mind; and the failure to find evidence which a jury would accept as a demonstration of treason, gave pause even to those who could not be moved by appeals to reason and justice. Time was required for war hysteria and war blood lust to abate; but there were signs that they were abating. Even James Russell Lowell, bitter though he still was against "Davis and his fellow-conspirators," argued that "the South has received a lesson of suffering which satisfies all the legitimate ends of punishment."

This changing temper was reflected in practical manner, by the relaxing of the rigour of Mr. Davis' confinement, and visitors were at times allowed him. General Gordon, one of the first who saw him after the rules of his confinement were relaxed, was greatly impressed by the interview. Years later, in a speech at Montgomery, Alabama, he declared that he had seen Davis "on the battlefield of the first Manassas, the Constitutional commander-in-chief of a victorious army," and "in Fortress Monroe, the vicarious sufferer for this vanquished people. . . . To my mind," he added, "great and grand as he was in the hour of his most splendid triumph, he was greater and grander still in the hour of his deepest humiliation."

As the months passed, the weakness of the case against Davis became so apparent that President Johnson began to realize the wisdom of Lincoln's desire that Davis might escape. Every method had been, and was still being, employed to discover evidence sufficient to enable the Government safely to try its prisoner. Even the private letters of his counsel were not safe in the United States post office, and on August 16th, O'Conor wrote to James M. Mason: "Without any previous experience of the sort, I have met with much delay and some loss of letters entrusted to the mails since my announcement as one of the counsel of Mr. Davis. I have therefore become very cautious in my correspondence not only as to the mode of transmission, but as to the matter communicated. Letters should be sent under cover to some inconspicuous person with instructions to make delivery to myself in person. . . . The Chief Executive is often *sick*, his advisers do not all concur in opinion nor are their objects alike. Consequently, the future action of the Government with respect to the state prisoners can only be conjectured." "No trial for treason or any like offence will be had in the civil courts. Notwithstanding the Surratt murder and its flagitious concomitants, the managers at Washington are not agreed as to the safety of employing military commissions to colour a like outrage upon any eminent person. Neither treason nor any ordinary belligerent act can be tortured into a military offence and hence arises a doubt as to the most expedient course."

Nevertheless, as a good attorney, and a sworn servant of even-handed justice, O'Conor employed every available method of securing evidence, and Shea travelled widely in search of documents, which were studied for light upon the main issues.

On August 22nd, the latter wrote from Saratoga to Greeley: "I received from Mr. O'Connor and want you to read a letter which in the fulness of time ought to be published. It is an exculpation of Davis from any participation by act or word in the abuse of our prisoners, and a most interesting and valuable historical testimony coming from the highest and best informed source. I am glad to possess this, as it relieves Davis' case from that odious feature. And I notice with pleasure that the charges and specifications preferred against Wirz (printed in this morning's *Tribune*) do not state the name of Davis among the persons with whom Wirz is therein said to have confided."

Nine days later, he wrote to Mrs. Davis: "Whenever a trial upon indictment is announced fair weather has set in. A civil trial, even before Chase, is most fervently hoped for." He expressed confidence that there would be none before a military tribunal, as the "government has unequivocally declared this. . . . Before a civil tribunal, we are safe in our defence."

That a speedy trial was unlikely, however, appears from the statement of Chase, which Aiken reported to Shea on September 10th, that "he had no knowledge of any arrangements for the trial of Mr. Davis, and that he had no expectation of presiding at such a trial at Norfolk, as the newspapers have represented. He intimated that he could not preside in any of the seceding states until there had been some legislation in relation to them by Congress," and said to Mr. Sutton, official reporter of the Senate, "if you wait for that purpose [reporting Davis' trial] until I try the case, you will wait a long time." He added, however, that he would not absent himself from the bench of the Supreme Court, which was to assemble in December, which fact was reported to Shea as an indication "that there might not be any trial," of Jefferson Davis. Perhaps as a warning to Davis' counsel, Aiken added: "The Wirz trial is getting . . . more interesting, from the fact that . . . they are now implicating 'bigger fish.'"

Meanwhile, Davis had sent his wife this comforting message: "I am now permitted to write to you under two conditions, viz., that I confine myself to family matters, and that my letter shall be examined by the United States Attorney-General before it is sent to you. . . . Confidence in the shield of innocence sustains me still. . . . You can rely on my fortitude. God has given me much of resignation to His blessed will. . . . It has been reported in the newspapers that you had applied for permission to visit me in my confinement; if you had been allowed to do so, the visit would have caused you disappointment at the time, and bitter memories afterward. You would not have been allowed to hold private conversation with me. Remember how good the Lord has always been to me, how often He has wonderfully preserved me, and put your trust in Him."

On September 26th, he wrote: "It is true that my strength has greatly failed, and loss of sleep has created a morbid excitability, but an unseen hand has sustained me, and a peace the world could not give and has not been able to destroy will, I trust, uphold me to meet with resignation whatever may befall me.

"If one is to answer for all, upon him it most naturally and properly falls. If I alone could bear all the sufferings of the country, and relieve it from further calamity, I trust our Heavenly

Father would give me strength to be a willing sacrifice; and if, in a lower degree, some of those who call me (I being then absent) to perform their behests, shall throw on me the whole responsibility, let us rejoice at least in their escape, excepting for them a returning sense of justice when the stumbling-blocks of fear and selfishness shall have been removed from their paths. . . . The great mass . . . would bury the inevitable past with the sorrow which is unmingled with shame. . . ."

To a friend he wrote: "I care nothing for my own sufferings, but I do care for the way my people were made to suffer," and to Mrs. Davis again, on October 2nd, that he still had "no communication with the outer world except with you, and in that restricted by the judgment of the Commanding Officer. . . . My daily walk continues, the hour dependent upon General Miles' engagements, as I only go out when he can be present. . . . I am not allowed to keep stationery. When it is specially granted, it has to be accounted for, the whole being returned, written or blank."

From Mill View, on October 10th, Mrs. Davis begged Dr. Craven to "prevail upon the authorities to let him sleep without a light. He is too feeble to escape and could not bear a light in his room when in strong health." But Dr. Craven was already doing what he could to improve Mr. Davis' surroundings, and the next day, before her letter was received, Mr. Davis wrote: "On the second of this month I was removed to a room on the second floor of a house built for officers' quarters. The dry air, good water, and a fire when requisite have already improved my physical condition. . . . I am deeply indebted to my attending physician, who has been to me much more than that term usually conveys. In all my times of trouble, new evidences have been given me of God's merciful love. . . . I have lately read the *Suffering Saviour*, by the Rev. Dr. Krumacher, and was deeply impressed with the dignity, the sublime patience of the model of Christianity. . . . Misfortune should not depress us, as it is only crime which can degrade. . . . Our injuries cease to be grievous in proportion as Christian charity enables us to forgive those who trespass against us, and to pray for our enemies."

Evidences of a new sentiment on the part of his captors now became frequent. Davis was allowed to send an "unrestricted letter" to his wife, and to receive visits from her and from sympathetic friends. The madness which had turned an honest gentleman into the murderer of a President had passed, even for Andrew Johnson. This easier accessibility had its disadvantages, however; for the merely curious were eager to see "the traitor." One instance is recorded of the visit of two rough characters who rang the bell at Davis' quarters and said to his faithful negro manservant who answered: "We want to see 'Jeff.' Davis." "I am sorry," was the courteous reproof, "the President is not receiving."

O'Conor and Shea now were encouraging Mrs. Davis to hope that their constant demands for a speedy trial would soon bear fruit. "I think," Shea wrote, on October 20th, that "the Government will enter civil prosecution, from which Mr. Davis need fear nothing." From such a trial, however, President Johnson had much to fear. Having rashly declared his administration in possession of facts which would convict Davis of complicity in the murder of President Lincoln, he was painfully conscious of the fact that he had no evidence and that his charge would be absurd if dragged into the light of open court. Furthermore, his bitter quarrel with the leaders of his own party rendered such an outcome dangerous to himself.

As Davis was now allowed to see the papers, he was able to form some idea of the rising tide of anger in the relationship between the radical Republican leaders and President Johnson; and the news drew from him many expressions of contempt. On December 7th he wrote to Mrs. Davis: "I see that the North as represented in Congress stands quite united to keep the South out of the legislative halls of the Union, and the South, wistfully looking at the closed entrance, stands outside, and then she is told she has all the time been inside." He feared what O'Conor feared when he wrote: "There is but one ground on which a doubt of . . . early trial would be warranted. A game of cross-purposes in Congress between the President's own proper party and the extreme radicals might arise, and might lead to delays, and an ultimate abandonment of the prosecution. Strange as it may seem, the persons most likely to urge the prosecution are of that faction in the Republican party which is likely to be the Republican wing of Mr. Johnson's legion."

This made Johnson's position difficult. He could neither rebuff his new half-attached Republican allies, who only desired him to produce the evidence which he had claimed to have, nor could he produce it. Davis had all along been conscious of this fact, and thus described his view of the situation: "A fair inquiry will show how 'false witnesses have risen against me and laid to my charge things that I knew not of.' . . . Sometimes I feel that there is a real compliment in the trust displayed by some of my slanderers, to whom it must occur that with a single breath I could topple over their miserable fabric. There is an unseen hand which upholds me."

The situation was without precedent: a man branded by the Chief Executive as the murderer of a President, eagerly seeking a trial; and his accuser delaying trial upon the most flimsy pretexts. On December 26th, O'Conor wrote to Mason: "Everything which, in ordinary cases, could be treated as a sign of coming events would indicate that a trial will be had ere long; yet so little confidence seems due in this matter to signs and indications of any sort that I can scarcely form a conjecture on the subject. About ten days ago Mr. Stanton himself assured a friend of Mr. Mallory's that that gentleman would be tried for treason in a civil court 'within thirty days.' . . . It is a suggestive fact that after murdering poor Wirz by military commission, they should first try their newly-to-be-constituted courts upon a subordinate officer before venturing to strike at 'the head of the rebellion.' It indicates the character of the men who conduct the assassination bureau at Washington."

But though growing sceptical as regarded a trial, O'Conor, Shea, and Horace Greeley pressed forward their preparation for Davis' defence. They were satisfied that there was no evidence which would convince a jury that he was in any way connected with the assassination of Lincoln, but wished to know more about his connexion with the ill-treatment of Federal prisoners. This they felt could be gathered from the Confederate records, now in Canada; and accordingly Shea was chosen to go as searcher, and sent back the following account of his trip:

"I went to Canada the first week in January, 1866, taking Boston on my route, there to consult with Governor Andrew and others. While at Montreal, General John C. Breckinridge came from Toronto, at my request, for the purpose of giving me information. There I had placed in my possession the official archives of the Government of the Confederate States, which I read and considered, especially all those messages, and other acts of the Executive with the Senate in its executive sessions, concerning the care and exchange of prisoners. I found that the supposed inhuman and unwarlike treatment of their own captured soldiers by agents of our Government [the Federal government] was a most prominent and frequent topic. That these reports, current then, perhaps even to this hour, in the South, were substantially incorrect is little to the practical purpose. From these documents, not made to meet the public eye, but used in secret session . . . it was manifest that the people of the South believed these reports to be trustworthy, and they individually, and through their representatives at Richmond, pressed upon Mr. Davis, as the Executive and as the commander-in-chief of the army and navy, instant recourse to active measures of retaliation, to the end that the supposed cruelties might be stayed. . . . It was equally and decisively manifest, by the same sources of information, that Mr. Davis steadily and unflinchingly set himself in opposition to the indulgence of such demands, and declined to resort to any measures of violent retaliation. It impaired his influence and brought much censure upon him from many in the South, who sincerely believed the reports."

Having thus got the facts, Shea reported to O'Conor: "The business upon which I am here is already satisfactory in results—have much to say—had better deliver it in person."

The day after this report was written, James Speed, Johnson's attorney-general, and Stanton, the Secretary of War, filed a report suggesting that Davis should be tried for treason, and that "the proper place for such a trial was in the state of Virginia." "That state," they pointed out, "is within the judicial circuit assigned to the Chief Justice of the Supreme Court, who has held no court there since the apprehension of Davis, and who declines for an indefinite period to hold any court there." When Johnson mentioned this suggestion to the Chief Justice, Chase declared again that he would hold no court in Virginia so long as the judicial proceedings there were subject to military control.

Before Shea returned from Canada, to report in person upon the details of his study of the Confederate records, Johnson and Stanton had prepared a reply to a repeated demand of the United States Senate for information concerning Davis' case. It was dated, January 7, 1866, signed by Stanton, and declared that Mr. Davis had not been arraigned, "but has been indicated for the crime of high treason by the grand jury of the District of Columbia, which indictment is now pending in the Supreme Court of said District." Stanton also declared that the President was of the opinion, given by his legal advisers, that "the proper place for such a trial was in the state of Virginia." Such a reply was little calculated to satisfy a Senate disposed to criticize Johnson quite as much as Davis; but for the time being it held its peace.

Shea's report, on the other hand, was definite enough to silence all doubts in the minds of Greeley, Wilson, and others who had sent him in search of evidence that Mr. Davis, despite great pressure from friends, had steadfastly refused to countenance harsh treatment of Northern prisoners, in return for what they erroneously believed had been malicious cruelty towards Southern prisoners. "The result," Shea later wrote, "was [that] these gentlemen, and those others in sympathy with them, changed their former suspicion to a favourable opinion and a friendly disposition," and with characteristic energy, increased the pressure for a speedy civil trial of Mr. Davis. The *Tribune* demanded it editorially, but on January 16, 1866, Senator Howard of Michigan offered a joint resolution recommending that Davis and Clement C. Clay be tried before a military tribunal or court martial.

"Treason," declares the Federal Constitution, "shall consist only in levying war against the United States or in adhering to their enemies." "The latter word," reasoned the judicial mind, "means the public enemy, and such enemy himself cannot be the traitor. The characters are incompatible. This is a thoroughly established construction; and, consequently, in order to charge the Southern Confederates with treason under the municipal law it would have been necessary to establish that they were not public enemies in the judicial sense of that phrase, and also that they had levied war against the United States. Neither fact could have been truly asserted. Levying war means setting it on foot. Waging war is a different thing. It is only in the original conspiracy and in adapting its means to the purposes of active resistance that war can be *levied*. The offence of treason by levying war, as defined in the Constitution, stops there. Subsequent acts may, indeed, sometimes serve to show that this offence has been committed, but those subsequent acts cannot have that effect if in themselves they amount to waging a formal regular war by a public enemy, and are accepted as such by the government." So far as the Civil War was concerned, it was, therefore, as Chase's *Decisions* expressed it, "a clearly defined and officially acknowledged public territorial war."

Such theories, and they were in every legal mind at that time, led many leading lawyers of the North, and even many officials of the Federal Government, to the conviction that no properly constituted court of justice would convict Jefferson Davis of treason, and, moreover, that a conviction under the circumstances would be highly discreditable to the nation. To convict him of treason would have been tantamount to convicting the people of eleven states—an imperial area. "We have neither moral nor legal right to put on trial, under the Constitution, those whom we have recognized as belligerents, and under the protection of the law of war," commented Gerrit Smith. And he added: "The South, in her vast uprising, reached the dignity and rights of a party to a civil war." Even James G. Blaine, in the midst of his fierce denunciation of Davis, of later date, conceded that it would have been without reason to indict him for things done in common with the people of his whole section.

Clearly, an attempt to convict Davis of treason before a civil tribunal presided over by Chief Justice Chase was the council of despair, a fact which Senator Howard of Michigan may have been seeking to avoid when he offered his joint resolution recommending that Davis and Clay be tried before a military tribunal, or court martial. It is not unreasonable to believe, however, that this move was aimed at Johnson rather than at Davis.

Meanwhile, Davis endured the endless, dreary monotony of prison life. On the night of January 13, 1866, as he sat by the fire lost in thought he "had a startling optical illusion," as he later told his wife. ". . . I saw little Pollie walk across the floor and kneel down between me and the fire in the attitude of prayer. I moved from consequent excitement, and the sweet vision melted away. . . . I am hungry for the children's little faces, and have habitually to resist the power of tender feelings which may not be gratified . . . to look only to those hopes of which man cannot deprive me."

On February 12th, O'Conor declared to Shea that he regarded the Government as "remediless in the premises, unless it dares to slay without form or ceremony." And this remark is fairly illustrative of the bitter, contemptuous tone that was creeping into the confidential correspondence between Davis' counsel. "Our sincere thanks are due to the enemy," wrote O'Conor on February 14th. "By and by, we may think it prudent to have them presented. A leather-medal is the form usually suggested in vulgar speech as suitable for such cases; but a hempen collar might be at once more decorous and more appropriate."

It is not clear to whom this bitter witticism was meant to refer, but there were many in Congress, especially among the radical Republicans, who felt that it was not a bad diagnosis of President Johnson's plight as his fight with his party developed.

Davis' distress and confinement were now telling heavily upon him. "I am in the condition to give the highest value to quiet," he wrote to Mrs. Davis, on March 22nd, "it being the thing never allowed to me by day or night. . . . I strive to possess my soul in patience and by every means attainable to preserve my health against undermining circumstances. The officers of the guard treat me with all the consideration compatible with their position." Dr. Cooper grew more and more anxious, and in May, notified Mrs. Davis, that despite his best efforts her husband was steadily failing. "The only thing left," he added, "is to give him mental and bodily rest, and exercise at will. This can be [obtained] only by having the parole of the fort, with permission to remain with his family . . . He will then probably recuperate."

These better conditions however were alarmingly denied, and the search for evidence continued. On April 10, 1866, Boutwell of Massachusetts had introduced in the Senate a resolution instructing the Judiciary Committee of the House to ascertain the facts regarding the wild charges which had been made by irresponsible rumour about the ex-Confederate President, and a committee set itself the task of collecting and sifting the evidence. This committee secured from the war department such material as it had on file, and set Lieber to the task of sifting it, and reporting how far it seemed likely that a verdict of guilty could be made against Davis in connexion with the murder of Lincoln. Lieber examined "some 270,000 letters," and declared that "Davis will not be found guilty, and we shall stand there completely beaten."

Meanwhile, preparations for presenting the case of Davis and Lee before a grand jury in Virginia, had gone forward, and in the *Decisions* of Chief Justice Chase, appears the following startling account of the proceedings: "He [President Johnson] and Mr. King expressed the desire, and believed it to be the duty of the court, to present to the grand jury the views of the Supreme Court of the United States, as expressed by Mr. Justice Greer, that the late Civil War was a rebellion, and that those who had been engaged in it were . . . guilty of treason, and that the more prominent and guilty leaders ought to be indicted, for their conduct, resulting, as they thought, and culminating in the assassination of Mr. Lincoln.

"Although Judge Underwood had previously taken the position that the great conflict had outgrown the character of a rebellion, and had assumed the dimensions of a civil war, and that sound policy and humanity demanded that the technical treason of its beginning should be ignored . . . he consented to charge the jury as they advised.

"After this interview he proceeded to Norfolk, opened the court there, and did charge the jury in the precise language suggested by the President and Mr. King. . . . Upon this, the grand jury, on May 8, 1866, found an indictment against Mr. Davis and others for treason. . . ."

The original intention of the Washington Government had been to proceed against both Lee and Davis, on this charge, and the process had started early. "Soon after the close of the war," says Davis, "a grand jury found bills of indictment against General Lee and myself. General Grant, with manly integrity and soldierly pride, insisted that he had accepted the parole of General

Lee, and could not consent to his arrest and trial in violation of the pledge on which the parole was given. The United States suspended the prosecution of Lee." The chief concern was now a new indictment against Davis, and a jury was soon sworn in and charges presented. The indictment found by the grand jury, composed of whites and blacks, waking and sleeping, declared that Jefferson Davis, "not having the fear of God before his eyes, nor weighing the duty of his . . . allegiance but . . . moved and seduced by the instigation of the devil," had committed certain specified overt acts of treason.

## CHAPTER XXVIII

# SECOND YEAR OF PRISON LIFE

THE indictment found against Davis, by the Circuit Court at Norfolk, on May 8, 1866, one year after his incarceration in Fortress Monroe, offered the opportunity for which his counsel had waited, and on May 14th Shea started to Washington with a letter of introduction to Secretary Seward, from Truman Smith, judge of the Slave-trade Court in New York, which urged that Davis' counsel be given "the ordinary privilege of counsel," and allowed access to the prisoner at Fortress Monroe. His mission was successful, and a few days later, he reported to Mrs. Davis that he and O'Conor would "in a few days go together to Fortress Monroe to confer with Davis. . . . We are assured at least one month's previous notice of trial." No trial followed, however, as, to quote Chief Justice Chase, the indictment had been "lost from the records of the court," and although another indictment had been found in the District of Columbia, no process had been issued on it.

At about the same time Thaddeus Stevens told Shea that the chief of the military bureau had shown him the evidence upon which the Administration was relying for connecting Davis and Clay with the assassination of Lincoln. Having read it, Stevens declared the evidence insufficient, the guilt incredible. "I am not likely ever to forget," he wrote, in later years, "the manner in which Mr. Stevens then said to me: 'Those men are no friends of mine. They are public enemies; and I would treat the South as a conquered country and settle it politically upon the policy best suited for ourselves. But I know these men, sir. They are gentlemen and incapable of being assassins.' " And with spectacular suddenness Stevens volunteered his services as counsel for Davis.

Burton Harrison, in a letter to his mother, dated June 13, 1866, thus commented on the news:

"Thaddeus Stevens recently sent an offer to become one of Mr. Davis' counsel, if it were agreeable to us to have him serve, though the wily old rascal has a purpose of his own to accomplish. His doctrine is that there is no treason in the war after it had once been set on foot, that the opposing enemies represented independent belligerent governments, and that the Southern communities are now not states . . . but merely conquered territories which may be disposed of as he and the radical party in the North see fit. In order to get that doctrine established, he wants Mr. Davis tried for treason and acquitted; then he thinks his nice little political schemes will come along as a natural consequence."

Whatever the reason, or reasons (for historic events usually result from many causes), for Stevens' offer, the Federal Government had long since lost its desire to try Jefferson Davis upon the charge so confidently made in the President's proclamation. If there were evidence, as that proclamation declared, "that the atrocious murder of the late President," had been "incited, concerted, and procured by Jefferson Davis," it strangely failed to appear, or to hearten the Administration for the trial, as Johnson's *Decisions* point out, adding that the charge itself had been "crushed out under the common, general, and uncontroverted belief in its utter falsity, absurdity, and groundlessness." The charge, however, was never withdrawn, although it was never seriously revived.

Emboldened by her husband's suffering, Mrs. Davis, now determined to go to the President himself and demand more humane treatment for him, and after some failures, managed to gain a promise of audience. "My object," she writes, "was to obtain from him permission to take the lamp out of Mr. Davis' room, and other little ameliorations of his sufferings. . . . I asked by a respectful note an audience from the President. He sent me a verbal message of discourteous character. . . . Mr. Reverdy Johnson, Mr. Voorhies, and Mr. Saulsbury, always quick to espouse the cause of the helpless, went to him and remonstrated rather sharply. Under this pressure he appointed an hour to see me. General Grant also set an hour for an audience, but the President was so late in giving audience after my card was sent up that General Grant, after waiting an hour, courteously left his aide-de-camp to explain that he had an engagement he must keep, but would be glad if he could serve me in any way, and Mr. Davis never forgot the courtesy, nor did I."

Finally Mrs. Davis was invited into Johnson's office and stood face to face with him, "My first and last experience as a suppliant. . . . The President was civil, even friendly, and said, 'We must wait; our hope is to mollify the public towards him.' " This evasion from the man who had connected the name of her husband with the crime of assassination apparently caused the question of removing the lamp from Mr. Davis' prison to pass from her memory, now occupied with more bitter memories. "I told him that the public would not have required to be mollified but for his proclamation that Mr. Davis was accessory to assassination, and added, 'I am sure that, whatever others believed, *you* did not credit it.' He said he did not, but was in the hands of wildly excited people, and must take such measures as would show that he was willing to sift the facts. I then responded that there was never the least intercourse between Mr. Davis and Booth . . . and remarked that, 'if Booth had left a card for Mr. Davis, as he did for you, Mr. President, before the assassination, I fear my husband's life would have paid the forfeit'; to which the President bowed assent, and after a moment of silence remarked, now this was all over, and time was the only element lacking to Mr. Davis' release. I remarked that, having made a proclamation predicated upon the perjury of base men suborned for that purpose, I thought he owed Mr. Davis a retraction as public as his mistake. To my astonishment, he said that he was labouring under the enmity of many in both Houses of Congress, and if they could find anything upon which to hinge an impeachment they would degrade him; and with apparent feeling he reiterated, 'I would if I could, but I cannot.'" At this moment Thaddeus Stevens appeared, "a lop-sided man who stood on one leg by preference," and he "threatened the President in such a manner as would have been thought inadmissible to one of the servants." When the intruder was gone, the President remarked, "I am glad you saw a little of the difficulty under which I labour. Trust me, everything I can do will be done to help Mr. Davis. Has he thought of asking pardon?" "No, and I suppose you did not expect it," replied Mrs. Davis, frankly.

Probably no incident in this strange interview so much astonished Mrs. Davis as Johnson's suggestion that her husband should ask pardon for having been leader of a cause which had been and ever remained in his mind, both right and noble. "It was a new phase of humanity to me," she concludes. "I felt sorry for a man whose code of morals I could not understand."

On June 13th, Burton Harrison wrote to his mother: "President Johnson himself told Mrs. Davis, in the conversation he had with her, three weeks ago, that he never had believed that Mr. Davis had anything to do with, or knew anything about, this hideous murder, that he had been compelled by Stanton and Holt to issue that proclamation."

Meanwhile, on May 20th, Dr. Cooper's official reports of Davis' failing health got into the Press, and indignant letters appeared from all sides. So bitter were the attacks upon the "cruelty of Mr. Davis' jailors," that six days later General Miles undertook to defend his actions as mere obedience to orders. But the grim Secretary of War did not relent. To Dr. Minnegerode, who sought an interview to ask more freedom of movement for Davis on account of his ill-health, Stanton replied: "It makes no difference what the state of Jeff Davis' health is. His trial will soon come on, no doubt. Time enough till that settles it."

But still no trial came to "settle it," and the weary months passed, with bitterness towards President Johnson increasing. In the Senate, Sumner likened Johnson to Davis, declaring to his fellow-Senators: "You have already conquered the chief of the Rebellion. I doubt not you will conquer his successor also."

On June 5, 1866, the Court in Richmond opened, with James T. Brady, William B. Reed, James Lyons, and Robert Ould, as counsel for Mr. Davis; and, after the formal preliminaries, Reed addressed to the Court, Mr. Justice Underwood presiding, a demand to know: "What is to be done with this indictment? . . . We came here prepared instantly to try that case, and we shall ask for no delay at Your Honour's hands further than is necessary to bring the prisoner to face the court." He declared that nothing was desired on the prisoner's behalf save "a speedy trial on any charge that may be brought against Mr. Davis, here or in any other civil tribunal in the land. We may be now here representing, may it please the Court, a dying man. For thirteen months he has been in prison. The Constitution of the United States guarantees to him not only an impartial trial . . . but a speedy trial."

To this bold demand for a trial of strength, the assistant United States district attorney, Major Hennessey, replied that, in the absence of the district attorney, Mr. Chandler, the question could not be answered at once. He promised, however, to answer the following morning, whether his chief should arrive in the meantime or not. Judge Underwood asked Mr. Davis' counsel whether they were satisfied to wait: and, an affirmative answer being received, adjourned the court. The next day, Mr. Chandler being still absent, his assistant, Hennessey, declared that he believed the indictment would be tried, but not at once, for various reasons, the first being that the prisoner "never has been in the custody of this court, but is held by the United States Government, as a state prisoner . . . under the order of the President, signed by the Secretary of War. The second reason for delay, he declared to be the "pressing engagements" of the attorney-general. And the third "the delicate state of health" of Mr. Davis, which would make it "nothing less than cruel" to expose him to a protracted trial. He assured Mr. Davis' counsel that, "the hour Mr. Davis comes into the custody of this court, they shall have full and prompt notice when it is intended to try him"; not a very great concession in view of the historic rights of counsel.

James T. Brady, of Davis' counsel, protested that if the court would only serve the indictment, and carry out the further requirements of law, Mr. Davis' would soon come under the jurisdiction of the court. He insisted that Mr. Davis wished to claim the benefits of no technicalities, but only to have "an immediate trial. . . . Although it may be very hot in Richmond," he added, "it is infinitely worse where he is." Judge Underwood announced that, "the Chief Justice, who is expected to preside at the trial, has named the first Tuesday in October as the time that will be convenient for him. . . . Under all circumstances the court is disposed to grant the motion of the said district attorney, and I think I may say to the counsel that Mr. Davis will in all probability at that time be brought before the court, unless his case shall in the meantime be disposed of by the Government, which is altogether possible. It is within the power of the President of the United States to do what he pleases in these matters." He added: "I am happy to know that the wife of the prisoner is permitted to be with him, and that his friends are permitted to see him."

Mr. Davis' friends also were not disposed to accept Mr. Hennesey's view as to the comforts of a summer in the dungeon of Fortress Monroe; and on June 7th, O'Conor, and Ex-Governor Pratt of Maryland, accompanied by the Hon. James Speed, Attorney-General of the United States, waited upon Chief Justice Chase, to learn whether he would entertain an application for the release of Mr. Davis, on bail. Chase answered specifically that "whenever it should become apparent, either by the proclamation of the President or by the legislation of Congress, or by clear evidence from other sources, that martial law was abrogated and the writ of *habeas corpus* fully restored in Virginia, he would unite with the district judge in holding the courts in that district." While admitting that subordinate courts might properly function, in Virginia, under existing conditions, "the highest judicial authority of the nation could not properly join in holding the Circuit Court under such circumstances." Chase added that "application to discharge Mr. Davis on bail might very properly be addressed," to the district judge. For himself, he felt bound to "decline to entertain the application to admit Mr. Davis to bail." He also declared the opinion that an application for a writ of *habeas corpus* was an indispensable preliminary proceeding. He, however, apparently suggested, as the attorney-general had already done, that, even under existing conditions, Davis' release might be secured by getting Horace Greeley to sign his bail bond.

An article published in the *Telegraph and Messenger* during Mr. Greeley's presidential campaign of 1872 indicates how this hint was followed up: "Mrs. Davis went to New York to consult Charles O'Conor . . . as to the best manner of effecting Mr. Davis' release from prison. Mr. O'Conor told her that in his opinion there was but one way . . . to get the representative man of the Republican party to sign his bond. Mrs. Davis inquired who that man was. Mr. O'Conor replied that it was Horace Greeley. . . . She went to his office, sent in her card, and was invited into his private office. She said to him: 'Mr. Greeley, my husband is confined in a casemate at Fortress Monroe. He has been there for many long, weary months. He is a feeble old man, and he is gradually sinking under his rigorous imprisonment. He will die if he remains there much longer. I came here to consult Mr. O'Conor as to the means of getting him released. He has told me that there is but one way . . . and that is to get the representative man of the Republican party to sign his bond, and says that you are that man. He advised me to apply to you. He says that you have a kind heart and that you will do it if you believe it to be right. . . . Mr. Greeley may I hope that you will favourably consider my application?'

"Mr. Greeley arose, extended his hand to Mrs. Davis, and said: 'Madame, you may, for I will sign his bond.' Mr. Greeley was then a prominent candidate before the legislature for the United States Senate. Some of his friends heard that he had agreed to sign Mr. Davis' bond, and went to him to protest against it. They told him that they had made a count, and that he would be elected by six majority, but if he signed this bond it would defeat him. He replied, 'I know it will.' They told him that . . . this bond . . . would lose [the *Tribune*] thousands of subscribers. He replied, 'I know it.' They said: 'Mr. Greeley, you have written a history of the war; one volume you have out, and have sold large numbers of it. Your second volume is nearly out and you have large orders for that. If you sign this bond, these orders will be countermanded and you will lose a large amount of money.' He replied, 'Gentlemen, I know it, but it is right and I'll do it. . . .' "

Greeley now prepared and delivered to Mr. Davis' counsel the following document, to be used when needed: "I authorize George Shea to appear in behalf of me and in my name to enter into a recognizance in such sum as he may think proper for the due personal appearance of Jefferson Davis in any court of the United States at any term during the present year, 1866, to answer to anything which may be alleged against him by the United States."

This action of Greeley's is declared by Oberholtzer to have been "a mixture of charitableness of heart and the showman's instinct, part pity and part Dutch courage." This, however, is hardly fair to Greeley, whose action was a recognition of the fact, boldly proclaimed by Gerrit Smith less than a month later, that it was "neither legal nor moral right to try the rebels for treason."

At the time Mr. Davis had known nothing of his wife's efforts with Mr. Greeley. "If she had written to me of the effort she was making," he later explained, ". . . her letter would undoubtedly have been suppressed, as was my grateful letter to Mr. O'Conor acknowledging his voluntary offer to act as my counsel. . . . Mr. Greeley was moved solely by his sense of justice. . . . His claim to consideration, therefore, rests upon his self-sacrificing devotion to justice and the laws and the Constitution of the United States. . . . Judge Shea . . . who . . . twice visited President Johnson, can tell how his selfish fears caused him to insist on having the name of Mr. Greeley on the bond, and how Mr. Greeley, when informed that his name was a prerequisite to permitting the writ to be issued . . . agreed, despite the prospect of pecuniary loss. . . ."

Armed with Mr. Greeley's authorization, Davis' counsel filed on June 11th, with Judge Underwood, at Alexandria, Virginia, an application for bail; but the petition was denied, on the ground that Davis was "a military prisoner." "He is not, and never has been, in the custody of the marshal for the district of Virginia," he added, "and he is not, therefore, within the power of the court. While this condition remains, no proposition for bail can be properly entertained." In view of these facts, it is strange to read in Johnson's *Decisions of Chief Justice Chase*, the statement: "Why bail was not accepted in June, 1866, or earlier . . . is not known. . . . In 1866 Mr. Davis was ready to give bail in one million dollars, or more, if required. . . ."

The next day, June 12th, Congress drastically put an end to Chase's excuse when, on motion of Mr. Boutwell, of Massachusetts, by a vote of 105 to 19, it resolved "that . . . Davis should be held in custody as a prisoner and subject to trial according to the laws of the land." It also resolved: "That there is no defect or insufficiency in the present state of the law to prevent or interfere with the trial of Jefferson Davis for the crime of treason, or any other crime for which there may be probable ground for arraigning him before the tribunals of the country," and that it was the duty of the Executive to push the accusation made in the President's proclamation of May 2, 1865, regarding Davis' complicity in the assassination of Lincoln, that he "may be put upon trial and properly punished if guilty, or relieved from the charges if found to be innocent." As Congress had just re-examined the witnesses whose affidavits had been taken by the judge-advocate general to prove that interviews had taken place between Surratt, Davis, and Benjamin, and had heard them "retract entirely the statements which they had made," it is evident that their aim, like that of Thaddeus Stevens, when volunteering for Davis' defence, was not service to Davis but disservice to the detested President Johnson.

Thereafter, by rapid stages, the rigours of Davis' confinement were further relaxed. A bridge was constructed to connect Carroll Hall with the top of the ramparts so that Davis could go directly thither from his quarters on the second floor. His wife, her sister, Miss Howell, and his daughter "Winnie" were allowed to live with him: and their friends were freely admitted.

During that same June, 1866, Greeley suddenly appeared in Washington, and later paid a visit to Judge Underwood at Richmond; but no details of his actions are preserved. It is safe to conjecture, however, that he was pressing the cause to which he was now ardently committed, the speedy trial of Jefferson Davis, as shortly after his return to New York, he wrote a leader for the *Tribune*, asking: "How and when did Davis become a prisoner of war? He was not arrested as a public enemy, but as a felon, officially charged, in the face of the civilized world, with the foulest, most execrable guilt—that of having suborned assassins to murder President Lincoln—a crime the basest and most cowardly known to mankind. It was for this that $100,000 was offered and paid for his arrest; and the proclamation of Andrew Johnson and William H. Seward offering this reward says his complicity with Wilkes Booth & Co. is established 'by evidence now in the

Bureau of Military Justice.' So there was no need of time to hunt it up.

"It has been asserted that Davis is responsible for the death by exposure and famine of our captured soldiers; and his official position gives plausibility to the charge. Yet while Henry Wirz—a miserable wretch—a mere tool of tools—was long ago arraigned, tried, convicted, sentenced, and hanged for this crime—no charge has been officially preferred against Davis. So we presume none is to be."

On July 19th, Mrs. Davis made a second impassioned plea to President Johnson for mercy until justice could be given; and followed it by an attempt to persuade Reverdy Johnson to plead with him for Davis' release on bail. "He is so patient, so uncomplaining—so entirely quiescent in this death in life," she wrote. "It breaks my heart. Could the President be induced to parole him until his trial? If not, will you follow up my letter to him with entreaties that Mr. Davis may be given *entire* parole of the fort to which he may be removed, and that he be removed immediately to some of the forts in New York Harbour where he can see his counsel? . . . When I look at the husband of my youth, now beautiful by such holy resignation, slowly dying . . . I feel it is a bitter cup, and doubt if my Father wills that we should drink it. I would not trouble the President, . . . but I feel assured that a month's, perhaps less, delay will be fatal."

This pathetic and powerful appeal was in its turn refused, but it is only fair to remember that Johnson was convinced from confidential reports of competent medical men that Mrs. Davis' fears for her husband's life, natural though they were, were exaggerated. Soon after the appeal was refused, he again inquired about Davis' condition, and on August 14th, Doctors C. H. Crane, Assistant Surgeon-General, U. S. A., and J. Simpson, Brevet Colonel and Surgeon, U. S. A., reported to Major-General Barnes, Surgeon-General of the United States Army, that they had inspected Fortress Monroe and found it excellently maintained. "We visited Prisoner Davis and met him returning from a walk at the casemate now occupied by Mrs. Davis. . . . His health has improved in every respect during the last few weeks." Davis told them that the improvement was due to the arrival of his wife, who saw that he got proper food.

Davis had, however, undoubtedly suffered greatly in health, and on August 16th, Shea started for New England, armed with a document which he had drafted at Greeley's suggestion, urging Davis' release upon the ground of his physical condition. His mission was to have the document signed by as many leading Abolitionists as possible. O'Conor urged him to use as much speed as was consistent with "securing strength among the opponents of the President and his Democratic supporters. The moment it is ready," he added, "let it go by some sure hand who will himself deliver it to the President."

After a week's work, and "success not equal to what had been hoped," Shea returned to New York, disappointed but not disheartened; as he had read in the morning papers Johnson's Proclamation of Peace, which he considered to have removed Chase's reason for not presiding at a trial of Davis in the Virginia courts. He found O'Conor not inclined to urge a writ of *habeas corpus* upon Chase, but determined that the petition should be sent to Johnson, even "if it has only one name on it." Shea therefore continued his search for signatures, and on August 24th, Gerrit Smith, who had acted with the American Colonization Society, contributed large sums to the Kansas Emigrant Aid Society, given pecuniary aid to John Brown, and could therefore not be suspected of pro-Southern sympathies, wrote to President Johnson: "I have this day subscribed a memorial to yourself in behalf of Jefferson Davis. I have done so with great satisfaction, for I deem his very long confinement in prison without trial a very deep injustice to the South, a very deep injustice to himself, and a no less deep dishonour to the Government and the country. I trust that Mr. Davis may either have a speedy trial or be admitted to bail. There are many men who have no sympathy with his political views, and who opposed slavery as strenuously as he upheld it, that would eagerly become his bail. I am one of them."

One week later, Davis' keeper, Miles, was mustered out of the volunteer service and returned to the regular army with the rank of colonel. This, too, was regarded as a victory for Davis, as Miles had expressed the hope that he might remain in charge of the prisoner until the latter's removal from Fortress Monroe. To the end, Miles had made his custodianship as drastic as possible, even standing in the anteroom while Dr. Minnigerode administered the Holy Sacrament to his prisoner.

One of the first acts of Davis' new custodian, Brigadier-General Henry S. Burton, was to give him the "parole of the fort by day." But even that privilege failed to bring the return of strength which the doctor and Mrs. Davis had hoped for. On September 2nd, Mrs. Davis wrote to Horace Greeley: "For thirteen months I have prayed, and tried to cheerfully grope through the mist to find the end, and now it seems no nearer. I see my husband patiently, uncomplainingly, fading away, and cannot help him. Those who represent him as being well . . . stay a few moments, and are deceived by his spirited self-controlled bearing. A slight illness would kill him." And, in ignorance of the fact that Greeley had himself launched Shea's memorial to the President, she added: "Will you not procure signatures enough to that paper which Mr. Shea has to arrest Mr. Johnson's attention?"

By September 12th, Davis' friends were convinced that Mrs. Davis was right with regard to his physical condition. On that day Howell Cobb wrote to Major-General Daniel Sickles a strong plea for Davis' release and reinstatement in full citizenship. "Consider the situation of the dying man," he said, "whose only fault that is greater than his associates' is the prominence he was summoned to occupy." On September 26th, O'Conor suggested that Shea go to Washington, see "Chase, Underwood, Ashton, and the Attorney-General, or some of them [and] find out the actual condition of things." Here Shea learned that Underwood, Chase, and other eminent legal lights were convinced of "a conspiracy to murder Underwood," and that therefore Underwood would not go to Richmond, nor was his court likely to be held within the near future. He learned also that Johnson would make no movement for trial, and still based his refusal upon the claim that such trial was the affair of the Judicial Department of the Government.

When this news reached Mrs. Davis she wrote to Greeley: "The information . . . of Mr. Johnson's decision with regard to my husband's case fills me with anxiety. It seems to promise so long a postponement of his trial as to extend the time of his durance to more than two years. Can you do nothing to help? . . . Does not this reference of the case to the Judiciary place it within your power to assist us? . . . I am satisfied this impending postponement will destroy him. . . . Will you not, my dear sir, do all in your power to secure his early release? . . . I have been now fifteen months separated from my children, all babies in years, and must continue to be so as long as their father languishes here, as his claims are first upon me."

But even Greeley's influence was not sufficient to bring the Administration to the point of allowing the case to go to trial. "There seemed some influence—some 'power behind the throne' —that kept its eye upon Mr. Davis and vetoed all attempts in his favour," to quote again Johnson's edition of Chase's *Decisions*. Whose eye this was must remain, apparently, a mystery, but the President received the blame, and fully conscious of the fact, he at last asked his Attorney-General, Henry Stanbery "what further steps, if any, should be taken by the Executive with a view to a speedy, public, and impartial trial of the accused, according to the Constitution and laws of the United States?" Stanbery at once inquired of the United States district attorney for Virginia (L. H. Chandler) "why no demand has been made upon the military authorities for the surrender of Jefferson Davis, in order that he might be tried upon the indictment found against him in the

United States Circuit Court at the term held at Norfolk in May last." Chandler replied: "I have never had any doubt but that he would be delivered to the United States marshal of the district whenever he should have demanded him on a capias or other civil process." The reasons why such demand had not been made, he said, were two: "Safe keeping" and "personal comfort and health." Therefore Stanbery, on October 12th, informed the President that, "there is nothing in the present condition of Virginia to prevent the full exercise of the jurisdiction of the civil courts," and that the regular term of the Circuit Court was to be "holden on the fourth Monday of November, and if there had been no further legislation by Congress, no doubt could exist as to the competency of the Chief Justice and the district judge of that court to try Mr. Davis." He also made the following definite suggestion: "That to avoid any misunderstanding on the subject, an order be issued to the commandant of Fortress Monroe to surrender the prisoner to civil custody, whenever demanded by the United States marshal, upon process from the Federal court."

Before President Johnson had decided upon his attitude towards this recommendation, Governor Humphreys, of Mississippi, in accordance with a resolution passed by the legislature of that state, sent to Washington a commission of two, Colonel Giles M. Hillyer and Robert Lowry, to seek to persuade the President to release Mr. Davis from prison. In announcing their appointment, Governor Humphreys wrote, "We do not ask for an unconditional pardon, nor that the pending prosecutions shall be dismissed. We do not seek to screen him from trial. . . ." All the commissioners were instructed to ask was "to admit him to bail, or enlarge him on parole."

Upon their arrival, the commissioners found the President quite ready to hear, but unwilling to act. "You are not unmindful," Lowry argued, ". . . that we regard Mr. Davis as the embodiment of the Southern people, and that he is suffering for us all. . . . We can only look to you for that relief to which we know

Mr. Davis entitled. . . ." When the President still insisted that he could not act, they pointed out that under a statute passed in 1862, he had power to act; and ventured to suggest: "within ten days after Congress meets this law will be repealed, and you will be powerless." Still Johnson refused to act. "Then I said," reports Lowry, ". . . 'why not advise the authorities to at least grant him bail, and not let him die by inches? The bail would be promptly given if it did not exceed in amount the value of all the property in the Southern States.' " Still Johnson was obdurate, and the utmost that they could secure was a promise to see them later.

When, after ten days, they were again summoned into Johnson's presence, "He was alone," says Robert Lowry, "and as the door closed he arose from his chair and approached us, seemingly excited, and gesticulating with both arms, and said, 'Don't you see, don't you see, don't you see, gentlemen, that I can't do anything in the matter of Mr. Davis?'

"I replied, 'No, Mr. President . . . I can't see it, but I can see, with a plain statute authorizing it, that you could pardon President Davis, who is made to suffer for us all, and who is no more culpable than the humblest of his many thousand followers.' This ended our last interview with President Johnson."

When Mr. Lowry reported this conversation to Mr. Davis, in his prison, the latter remarked: "I shall not be surprised if President Johnson is tried for treason before I am." Davis knew of the mad rage with which the radical Republicans, bent on power, were pursuing the President, who had dared to thwart them. He knew of the wild words which Johnson had used in his "swing round the circle," and of the efforts, now in progress to prove that Johnson himself had been a partner with Booth in the plot to assassinate his predecessor in office. He was also conscious of the fact, which Johnson refused to concede, that the recent elections had been a real defeat, a popular repudiation of Johnson's leadership; and felt confident that impeachment proceedings were close at hand.

On November 9, 1866, the *Tribune* printed another leader: "Eighteen months have nearly elapsed since Jefferson Davis was made a state prisoner. He has been publicly charged, by the President of the United States, with conspiring to assassinate President Lincoln. . . . He has also been popularly, if not officially, accused of complicity in the virtual murder of Union Soldiers while prisoners of war. . . . A great Government may deal sternly with offenders, but not meanly; it cannot afford to seem unwilling to repair an obvious wrong."

The next day General R. Taylor reported to Mrs. Davis: "I saw Mr. Johnson last night for three hours, and had a full conversation with him about Mr. Davis and our unhappy people. Mr. Davis will be paroled to appear whenever the Government is ready to try him and a general amnesty will be announced. Of course this is *for you and Mr. Davis alone*. I presume it will occur within a fortnight. . . . I take it Mr. Davis will go abroad, at least for the present, and I think wisely."

Buoyed by this hope, Mrs. Davis waited expectantly for eleven days for signs of the relief which General Taylor promised. Then she again appealed to Greeley: "Allow me to thank you for the article in the *Tribune*. . . . Everything seems to fall pointless which is essayed in Mr. Davis' behalf. The last nineteen months that I have been part of the time a prisoner in Georgia, and part of the time a voluntary exile from my poor little children, has quite unhinged me, and I feel unable to bear further torture. Can you not, will you not, get such pressing recommendations for my husband's release as will move Mr. Johnson? . . . To sentence a man to a year's close, and nearly thirteen months solitary, confinement, groaning at the same time under the affluence of observation which is not sympathy, would be a dreadful punishment if proven guilty, but to be chained, starved, kept awake systematically, almost blinded by light and tortured by the ingenuity of a cruel and irresponsible jailor . . . before one has been tried, is cruel indeed. . . ."

But still the mysterious "power behind the throne" blocked the way to a trial. On November 22nd, Giles M. Hillyer wrote to Reed: "Mr. Johnson is very ready with language but very slow in action. . . . Mr. J. wants to do right, but is not bold enough."

There was, however, no lack of boldness on the part of his subordinates, who were eager beyond righteousness to find some evidence upon which they might convict Davis. Ever since November 10, 1865, when Wirz, an officer who had served at Andersonville prison, had been executed after a trial before a military commission, tales regarding the circumstances of the trial had constantly reached Davis, who never wavered in his view that the evidence had been deliberately fabricated. "Arrested while under the protection of a parole," he wrote, in later years, "tried in time of peace by a military commission of officers, in a service to which he did not belong, denied the favourable testimony of those who came, and subpoenas for other witnesses of like character—without these ordinary means, granted to the accused in all civilized countries, he died a martyr to conscientious adherence to truth."

On January 9, 1867, R. B. Winder, recently released from prison, reported to Mrs. Davis: "The door of the room which I occupied while in confinement at the Old Capitol Prison, Washington, D. C., was immediately opposite Capt. Wirz's door, both of which were occasionally open. About two days before Capt. Wirz's execution I saw three or four men pass into his room, and upon their coming out, Capt. Wirz told me that they had given him assurances that his life would be spared and his liberty given to him if he could give any testimony that would reflect upon Mr. Davis, or implicate him, directly or indirectly, with the condition and treatment, of prisoners of war, *as charged* by the United States authorities,—that he indignantly spurned these propositions and assured them that, never having been acquainted with Mr. Davis, either officially, personally, or socially, it was utterly impossible that he should know anything against him, and that the offer of his life, dear as the boon might be, could not purchase him to treason and treachery to the South and his friends. I do not know the names of the party making these propositions to Captain Wirz but . . . I am quite sure that Father Boyle, of Washington City, who was Capt. Wirz's priest, must know all these facts." In later years Father Boyle sent Davis a letter in which he said: "I attended the Major [Wirz] to the scaffold, and he died . . . praying for his enemies. I know that he was indeed innocent of all the cruel charges on which his life was sworn away."

Mrs. Davis reported Winder's story, so eloquent of the fate which seemed pending for her husband, to Mr. Davis' counsel: and, early in January, 1867, Shea sent the following letter to Chief Justice Chase:

"If convenient to the Chief Justice, will he please state a time and place where he will see Mr. George Shea during this day? He wishes to make application for a writ of *habeas corpus* to have Jefferson Davis before the Court at Richmond on the 6th inst. Or, if it be agreeable to the Chief Justice, Mr. Shea will leave the petition so that the application can be considered and passed upon now."

The Chief Justice agreed to the interview, during which he declared that the application would have to be made to Judge Underwood, the district judge in whose district the court was to be held, beginning on May 1, 1867. The application was made accordingly, and the day after the court assembled at Richmond, O'Conor wrote to Shea: "It would be well to give immediate attention to procuring the attendance of loyal anti-slavery recognizers for Mr. D. at the return day. Unless Underwood kick, the deed will be done. And there is not a great deal of time to see Mr. Greeley and to communicate in some way with Mr. Smith. We may want some of that influence to induce assent on the part of Judge U.

"Of course you know I will make proper arrangements to pay travelling expenses. It might be well to consider whether the gentlemen would prefer a trip by land or a voyage by sea. At all events let the matter receive prompt and full attention."

At the appointed hour, Davis' petition, "that a writ of *habeas corpus* may issue from this honourable court to be directed to Brigadier-General Henry S. Burton" was presented "by George Shea, his attorney in fact." Judge Underwood at once agreed to the writ, reading as follows:

"The President of the United States to Brigadier-General Henry S. Burton, and to any person or persons having the custody of Jefferson Davis, greeting:

"We command that you have the body of Jefferson Davis, by you imprisoned and detained, as it is said, together with the cause of such imprisonment and detention, by whatsoever name the said Jefferson Davis may be called, or charged, before our Circuit Court of the United States for the district of Virginia, at the next term thereof at Richmond, in said district, on the second Monday in May, 1867, at the opening of the court on that day, and so do and receive what shall then and there be considered concerning the said Jefferson Davis.

"Witness, Salmon P. Chase, our chief justice of the Supreme Court of the United States, this first day of May, 1867.

"W. H. Barry,
"Clerk of the Circuit Court of the
United States, district of Virginia."

On Saturday, May 4, 1867, the *Evening Bulletin* announced the decision, in a singularly hostile article which declared: "If the writ granted by Judge Underwood is recognized and obeyed by General Burton, Jeff. Davis will vacate his lodgings by the sea and take up his quarters in the Richmond jail. . . . The removal of the arch-traitor . . . will not add particularly to his personal comfort, unless the prisons of Richmond have been greatly improved since they were used to torture and starve Union prisoners. The fact that Judge Underwood has granted the writ of *habeas corpus* indicates nothing of his future course in the case. It is not likely that he is prepared to take the responsibility of trying Davis. . . . It is suggested that Judge Underwood's course will have the effect of removing Davis out of the President's control and placing him at the disposal of the court; but it is not easy to set bounds to Mr. Johnson's interference in behalf of criminals, whether convicted or not. The President's extraordinary partiality for forgers and counterfeiters extends itself to rebels and traitors, and there is no reason to doubt that he will gladly set Davis at liberty, whenever he believes he can do [so] without compromising his own political aspirations."

This strange announcement of a purely legal decision caused Davis' counsel, Wm. B. Reed, always suspicious of Underwood, and his colleagues, to suspect some sinister move, and to take every possible precaution against it. On May 5th, he wrote to Burton N. Harrison: "Mr. O'Conor says he wishes you to go in advance to Norfolk and Fortress Monroe and have the H. C. writ properly attested. . . . It seems to me that this matter of Mr. Davis' removal to Richmond requires very delicate handling. I have always an eye . . . to the dignity of his position."

How impressive that dignity was appears in a narrative, preserved by chance, of a visit made to Mr. Davis' prison quarters by Miss Day, sister of one of his guards, Captain Selden Allen Day: "I was speechless with amazement, as I gazed at the thin, strong features framed with grey locks, one eye faded a little more than the other, but both lightened with a smile that was almost angelic! And the most arresting of all was a quality in his voice that seemed to go directly to one's heart. Back in Ohio, we had been singing with great enthusiasm, 'Hang Jeff. Davis on a sour-apple tree.' I had expected to see Mr. Davis a most unlovable creature, almost with hoofs and horns, so strong had been the feeling against him in the Middle West, and more especially as my three brothers had been fighting in opposition to him throughout the entire war. . . . I understood why the doctor of the post, who attended Mr. Davis when he was first imprisoned, had lost his position on account of friendship and deep interest in his patient, and why another physician who succeeded him very soon developed the same friendly feeling towards the prisoner."

The order from the President was issued, in the following form:

"War Department
"Washington, D. C., *May 8, 1867.*

"Brevet Brigadier-General H. S. Burton, United States Army, Commanding Officer at Fortress Monroe:

"The President of the United States directs that you surrender Jefferson Davis, now held confined under military authority at Fortress Monroe, to the United States marshal or his deputies, upon any process which may issue from any Federal Court in the State of Virginia. You will report the action taken by you on this order, and forward a copy of the process served upon you to this office.

"By order of the President: E. D. TOWNSEND,
"Assistant Adjutant-General."

For some days before this writ was served upon Brigadier-General Burton, a missionary, Paul Bagley, had been urging Davis to ask for pardon, intimating that President Johnson had all but promised a pardon should one be requested; but Davis continued to insist that what he demanded was not a pardon, but a trial.

On May 10, Robert Lowry wrote to Burton Harrison, suggesting that Mr. Davis' friends had ample funds for the defence in bank at Jackson, Mississippi, but that in the not unlikely contingency of the removal of the friendly Governor, and the appointment of "a new incumbent" the money might be unsafe. He advised, therefore, that "at least $10,000 should be sent" to New York, where it would be "out of the reach of our enemies,"—a statement which shows, with painful clearness, the political conditions in the South under Reconstruction machinery. On that same day

General Burton prepared for the journey to Richmond, to present in court "the body" of Jefferson Davis, on May 13th.

Shea continued to work on his task of assembling "loyal anti-slavery recognizers," to the very last moment. On May 12th, Gerrit Smith telegraphed from New York: "Too late to get proxy to you—will be in Richmond Tuesday—I sign bond." Greeley too decided to come to Richmond and sign the bond in person. Commodore Vanderbilt, who had recently received the thanks of Congress for his superb work for the Government during the war, was unable to come in person, but empowered his son-in-law, Horace F. Clark, and his friend, Augustus Schell, to sign for him. By May 13th, the defence was ready for the hearing, but the work for "anti-slavery recognitions" still went on, for Shea and O'Conor were determined that no possible source of influence should be unassembled. The friendly Press, led by the *Tribune*, did its best to keep up public interest in the coming trial, and their success was such that James Russell Lowell complained that it "occupies for the moment more of the public mind and thought than the question of Reconstruction."

Upon his arrival at Richmond, conducted by General Burton, and accompanied by Mrs. Davis, Dr. Craven, and Burton Harrison, Davis was assigned, at the Spottswood Hotel, the very rooms which he had occupied six years before as President of what he fondly believed to be a new sovereign nation. His return as prisoner was marked by eager throngs, gathered to cheer him; for Virginia had not deserted their defeated and captive leader. Less than a year before, Goddard had assured the readers of the London *Daily Post* that "since his fall not a line has been written in the whole South in his favour. . . . Not a lamentation for his fall has arisen from any quarter, and not a single petition for his pardon has come to the President, except from Unionists. Could anything be more conclusive of the disfavour in which he is held by his former 'subjects' "—a statement as false and partisan as could well have been made, if the intent had been to deceive.

Promptly at 11 A.M., May 13, 1867, O'Conor and Shea, with

their able associates, William B. Reed, of Philadelphia, John Randolph Tucker, Robert Ould, and James Lyons, entered the court and took their places before the bench. Facing them was an equally distinguished array of talent, present on behalf of the Government, and headed by Mr. Evarts, Attorney-General of the United States. When these were seated, the doors were thrown open and an eager crowd rushed in, filling every inch of available space. Next the striking figure of Horace Greeley appeared and was seated, amid a buzz of whispers.

Judge Underwood then entered, and the proclamation was made, after which there were a few moments of tense excitement as the court waited for the appearance of the prisoner. So great had been the crowd in front of the Spottswood Hotel, that Davis had been taken out by a rear entrance, placed in a carriage which waited in the court, and guarded by a company of United States infantry, had been driven by a circuitous route to the Custom House. Upon arrival, he was taken into a conference room, by a private entrance, and thence came into court, attended by General Burton, Dr. Cooper, and Mr. Burton Harrison. The crowd stirred with excitement as the General conducted his prisoner to a comfortable chair, where he waited, feeble but calm, bowing to many friendly faces in the audience, and shaking hands with such friends as happened to be within reach.

Judge Underwood formally opened court with the words: "The Court is honoured on this occasion by the presence of so many of the nation's noblest and bravest defenders that the usual morning routine will be omitted." General Burton advanced, and announced:

"I now here produce before the . . . Circuit Court of the United States . . . the body of Jefferson Davis, at the time of the service of the writ held by me in imprisonment at Fortress Monroe. . . ."

Judge Underwood declared the prisoner "under the protection of American Republican law," and in proper custody of the marshal.

O'Conor now rose:

"We are advised that there is an indictment against the prisoner in this district, and that Your Honour will take such course as may be proper in the case."

Judge Underwood replied: ". . . The marshal will now serve on the prisoner the writ of indictment now in this court," whereupon a deputy marshal advanced and handed a paper to Mr. Davis, who arose and gave it to his chief counsel, Mr. O'Conor. O'Conor acknowledged the receipt of the indictment, and declared, "We hope the Court will now order such proper course as justice may require."

Turning toward Mr. Evarts, Underwood then said: "The Court would be pleased to hear from the representatives of the Government."

There followed a tense moment as the great attorney rose to his feet, but it was only a moment, for he declared at once: "It is not its intention to prosecute the trial of the prisoner at the present term of the Court."

O'Conor next gave a brief account of Davis' imprisonment, and the indictments which had been brought against him, and declared:

"Jefferson Davis is now here, under your exclusive direction, and I ask that he have the liberty of free locomotion until you are prepared to try him."

The district attorney, Mr. Chandler, raised the question of bail, suggesting that the Government was prepared to have the amount set at $100,000. O'Conor replied: "There are ten gentlemen willing to go surety ten thousand dollars each."

The matter having been thus adjusted, Judge Underwood announced: "The gentlemen proposing to offer themselves will please come forward." As their names were called, beginning with Horace Greeley, the sureties advanced to the clerk's desk, and signed the following bond:

# The Bail Bond of Mr. Jefferson Davis,

## LATE PRESIDENT OF THE CONFEDERATE STATES,

## WITH ALL THE ORIGINAL SIGNATURES THERETO.

At a stated term of the Circuit Court
of the United States for the District of Virginia
held at Richmond on the First Monday of May
One thousand Eight hundred and Sixty seven

Be it remembered that on this Thirteenth (13th) day of May in the year of our Lord one thousand eight hundred and sixty seven before the Honorable the Circuit Court of the United States for the District of Virginia at the Court House in Richmond in the said District came Jefferson Davis and acknowledged himself to owe to the United States of America the sum of One Hundred Thousand dollars lawful money of the said United States and Gerrit Smith, Horace Greely, Cornelius Vanderbilt, Augustus Schell, Horace F. Clark, A. Welch, David K. Jackman, William H. Macfarland, R. B. Haxall, Isaac Davenport Jr, Abraham Warwick, Gustavus A. Myers, William W. Crump, James Lyons, John A. Meredith, William H. Lyons, John Minor Botts, James Thomas Jr, Thomas R. Price, William Allen, Benjamin Wood, Thomas W. Doswell, each of whom acknowledged himself to owe to the United States of America the sum of Five thousand dollars of like lawful money. The said several sums to be made to the use of the said United States, of the goods, chattels, lands and tenements of the said parties respectively. The condition of this recognizance is such that if the said Jefferson Davis shall in his proper person well and truly appear at the Circuit Court of the United States for the District of Virginia to be held at Richmond in the said District on the fourth Monday of November next at the opening of the Court on that day and then and there appear from day to day and stand to abide and perform whatsoever shall be then and there ordered or adjudged in respect to him by the said Court and not depart from the said Court without the leave of the said Court in that behalf first had and obtained then the said recognizance to become void, otherwise to remain in full force.

Taken and acknowledged this 13th day of May
AD 1867 in open Court, before me
W. H. Barry, clerk.

Jefferson Davis.

W. H. Barry clerk

Gerrit Smith
Horace Greely
Cornelius Vanderbilt by Schell
Augustus Schell
Horace F. Clark per A. S.
A. Welch
David K. Jackman
Wm. H. Macfarland
R. B. Haxall
Isaac Davenport Jr
Abraham Warwick
Gustavus A. Myers

attest W. H. Barry
attest W. H. Barry
Geo. Rhea

W. H. Crump Jr
James Lyons
John A. Meredith
Wm. H. Lyons
Jno. M. Botts
Thomas W. Doswell
James his x mark Thomas Jr.
Thomas his x mark R. Price
William Allen
Benjamin Wood

In the Clerk's office of the Circuit Court
of the United States for the District of
Virginia. Richmond November the 8th in
the year of our Lord 1867

The above is a true and correct copy of the original recognizance
of Jefferson Davis, now remaining on file in this office, with
a fac simile of the signatures thereto.

Teste
Wm. H. Barry
clerk.

It was a strange list of bondsmen for a man who had, for four long years led the Confederate Government against the nation which they all loved; so strange that Mr. Davis later felt it only fair to write, in his autobiography: "Entirely as a matter of justice and legal right, not from motives of personal regard, Mr. Greeley, Mr. Gerrit Smith, and other eminent Northern citizens, went on my bond." And almost at the end of his life he assured George L. Ford that he had never had even "a speaking acquaintance" with Greeley.

When the last name had been signed, the Court announced: "The marshal will discharge the prisoner," and Mr. Davis found himself a free man, with crowds madly cheering, both inside and outside the courtroom.

He left the court, attended by Mr. O'Conor and Mr. Ould. His guard of infantry had vanished before he emerged from the door but the crowd was still in Bank Square; and it greeted him with the "rebel yell" which had been first heard at Manassas.

The streets through which the carriage passed were crowded, and the "rebel yell" re-echoed again and again from every side. Then, as the carriage approached its destination, a voice resounded, "Hats off, Virginians," and Davis entered the refuge of his hotel in a deep silence. He would have been more iron than human had not tears dimmed his eyes.

Arrived at his hotel, he found Mrs. Davis waiting with Dr. Minnegerode, and turning to the latter, Mr. Davis said: "You have been with me in my sufferings, and comforted and strengthened me with your prayers. Is it not right that we now once more should kneel down together and return thanks? . . ." Mrs. Davis led the way into the adjoining room, and there in deeply-felt prayer and thanksgiving, closed the story of Jefferson Davis' prison life.

---

In every instance of public excitement, there is what Theodore Roosevelt characteristically called "a lunatic fringe," which distorting motives, sees danger where no danger exists, and the signers of Davis' bond were denounced by such short-sighted patriots. Upon his return to New York, Greeley received from John Jay, president of the Union League Club, a copy of the following letter, signed by thirty-four members:

"JOHN JAY, ESQ.
"Pres$^{t}$. Union League Club.
"Sir:

"We have the honour to request that you call a special meeting of this club at an early day for the purpose of taking into consideration the conduct of Horace Greeley, a member of the club, who has become a bondsman of Jefferson Davis, late chief officer of the Rebel Government."

Greeley's reply might well be bracketed with Catherine of Russia's answer to George III's request to furnish troops to subdue the rebellious American Colonies, and which His Majesty filed away at Windsor Castle, labelled "not genteel." Greeley wrote: "I do not recognize you as capable of judging or even fully appreciating me. . . . You evidently regard me as a weak sentimentalist, misled by maudlin philosophy. I arraign you as narrow-minded blockheads, who would like to be useful to a great cause, but don't know how."

Gerrit Smith's comment took the form of a pamphlet entitled, "The Bailing of Jefferson Davis," in which he declared that if the Federal Government had "carried on the war under the Constitution, she would have had the right to hold the South guilty of treason. But . . . as she elected to carry it on under the law of war—under international instead of municipal law—she lost this right." He further declared that in accepting the surrender of the Southern armies, the Northern Government practically agreed "that we should treat each other not as traitors under constitutional law, but as belligerents under the law of war. The Supreme

Court of the United States unanimously held that this was the bargain. Alas, the ineffable meanness, the revolting infamy, of our breaking this bargain, now, when we have it in our power to break it! The shame of defeat is as nothing compared with the shame of abusing the power of success. . . . I have ever held that a sufficient reason why we should not punish the conquered South is that the North was quite as responsible as the South for the chief cause of the war. The North did quite as much as the South to uphold slavery; and let me add that she did it more wickedly because more calculatingly. Slavery was an evil inheritance of the South, but the wicked choice, the adopted policy, of the North. The unfortunate South felt that she must take slavery for better or for worse, for gain or for loss. But the mercenary North coolly reckoned the political, commercial, and ecclesiastical profits of slavery, and held to it."

"War is hell"; but at times, in the present state of the world, "the price of peace is war." But peace never requires, nor is it ever promoted, by carrying on the spirit of bitterness after the decision has been reached by force. In the case of the American Civil War, the spirit which Greeley, Gerrit Smith, and their courageous associates dared to display, in a reasoned patriotism, did not overcome the spirit of continuing hatred: and the result was Reconstruction, which remained warlike, hell-like, until the act of President Hayes, in 1877, restored "normalcy," and gave the South back to her people.

For Davis, alone of all the South, that period was one of vindictive, personal persecution, which he bore, as he had borne his long imprisonment, irritably at times, but always with a continuing faith in God, and in the justice of the cause which he had served. DeLeon spoke truly when he wrote, in later years, "History shows no man who has faced such fierce and sweeping blasts of indictment, calumny and malice, and so long stood erect."

## CHAPTER XXIX

# WHY DAVIS WAS NEVER TRIED

THE great incidents of history are never susceptible of simple explanations. Adequate explanations are always complex. The crossing of the Rubicon, the "shot heard round the world," the murder of an Austrian archduke, are but catchwords which explain nothing.

And when one seeks to understand why the leader of the greatest civil war in history up to that date, a man declared by presidential proclamation to have conspired to assassinate the President of the opposing Government, a man indicted as the leader of a treasonable conspiracy to destroy the American Union, was never put on trial, simple explanations are equally inadequate. Back of that simple fact there lies, and must lie, a very complex explanation.

The release of Mr. Davis on bail by a civil court was a clear indication that both President Johnson, and the Federal Judiciary held that peace now prevailed in what had been the rebellious Confederate States, and that again law reigned supreme over mere military power. But "Congress held that the status of war still existed, and by a series of legislative acts assumed command of the army, and through it exercised military law over all those states and people," to quote the words of Johnson's *Decisions of Chief Justice Chase*. The generals whom Congress placed in control of those states "were the Executive, the Legislative, and the Judicial Departments of the government concentrated into one hand, under what is known historically as the Reconstruction measures of Congress."

This condition was resented alike by the Executive and the Judiciary, and Chief Justice Chase remained firm in his determination not to sit as judge in a region "in which a soldier was the ultimate arbiter, and a bayonet the sole symbol of law."

As the released prisoner studied the condition of the country, he saw many things which seemed to mark the fulfilment of the prophetic fears with which he had regarded Lincoln's election. Then he had believed that the aim of the Republicans was domination; now their actions left no possible doubt that they were dominant. On November 9, 1860, Horace Greeley had written: "We hope never to live in a Republic whereof one section is penned to the residue by bayonets." Davis, unacquitted but now free to walk in wonder and horror in a republic actually exhibiting that condition, began to understand why he had not been tried, and to fear that he would never be. But it was a satisfaction to him to read the opinion of the Press, expressed with singular unanimity, that his release had done more to restore normal conditions of peace and Reconstruction than all the armies that infested the South, and all the Federal statutes of Reconstruction. His release had also won high praise in Europe for the "humane" President, though Davis' friends felt that Johnson's refusal to try him upon the charge of assassination was not human but inhuman.

With the burden of this charge and that of treason still heavy upon him, Davis went to Canada, to see his children, though knowing that any day might bring a messenger to claim him for the court and renewed proceedings. There he found himself inundated with letters of congratulation, and messages of affection, such as had become conspicuously lacking during the last days of the Confederacy. These letters were supremely welcome. He had long accepted the fact that, as the leader of the Lost Cause, he had been singled out for blame, while the chief praise and adulation had followed General Lee. His own deep affection for that Southern hero, whose admirers swarmed also in the North and in every civilized land, had robbed that fact of bitterness. But each new letter of affection, as it came to him, in exile, an accused criminal under bond, caused new joy.

J. M. Mason, on May 14, 1867, wrote fervently of the satisfaction with which he had read the news of his release, under "circumstances in which I confidently rely that you will not again be molested."

The same day, ex-President Franklin Pierce wrote to Mrs. Davis:

"Concord, N. H., *May 14, 1867.*

"My dear Mrs. Davis:

"I reached home last evening and found the telegraphic announcement that the Govt. declined to proceed with the trial of Genl. Davis and that he has been released upon bail. I do not know whether this will reach you at Richmond, but send it at a venture, to the care of Governor Wise, who will know how to change the direction, if you have left. I infer from a remark of General D. that you may all, in the first instance, proceed to Canada to see your boys. I would not influence your husband with regard to his movements, but I am strongly impressed with the conviction that his state of health, if no other consideration, should settle the question of his remaining at the North during the summer months now near at hand. My cottage at Little Boon's Head will be ready to receive all your family by the middle of August. The latter part of that month and the whole of September is usually delightful there. The place will be as quiet as could be desired—and I need not express how much pleasure I should find in trying to make every thing agreeable to you. Pray write and let me know how I shall direct letters to you and what I may expect. I think, upon reflection, that this note had better be directed to the care of Judge Lyon, as Gov. Wise may be absent on professional engagements.

"The package of books will be committed to the express tomorrow.

"Always and truly yours,

"FRANKLIN PIERCE.

"MRS. DAVIS
"Richmond, Va.

"P. S.—One of the photographs of dear Mrs. Pierce was taken during the last year of her life, when she was very feeble. Shall send them with the books."

A letter from Reagan, on May 21st, declared: "The feeling of relief and joy, on account of your release, is universal and strong here [in Texas]; and all feel that both justice and good policy required that this feeling should have been allowed to be perfect by your unconditional release . . . It will no doubt be a great consolation to you to know that the great mass of our people regarded you as suffering in your own person for and on account of them. . . . No patriot, or statesman, or soldier, enjoying the highest honours of success and good fortune, was ever honoured by stronger sympathy and more earnest affection from the people he represented or served than you have received from our people during your period of misfortunes. . . ."

But the letter which doubtless gave him most satisfaction was the following:

"Lexington, Va., *1 June, 1867.*

"My dear Mr. Davis:

"You can conceive better than I can express the misery which your friends have suffered from your long imprisonment and the other afflictions incident thereto. To none has this been more painful than to me, and the impossibility of affording relief has added to my distress. Your release has lifted a load from my heart which I have not words to tell, and my daily prayer to the great Ruler of the World is that He may shield you from all future harm, guard you from all evil, and give you that peace which the world cannot take away.

"That the rest of your days may be triumphantly happy is the sincere and earnest wish of your most obt. faithful friend and servt.

"R. E. Lee.

"Honble. Jefferson Davis."

Canada was well stocked with Southern refugees, who deluged him with invitations for visits, for dinners, and for fishing expeditions into the glorious virgin wilderness. These he accepted whenever he found it possible, and did his best to enjoy the sunshine of "God's out-of-doors." After his visit to Mason, that fellow-exile wrote: "I hope you had a safe and pleasant run down the lake. . . . How unfortunate that you left us so soon. Had you remained till now, you would better have understood the early summer climate of Western Canada—the thermometer at 11 A.M. today, stood . . . at 81°. Then again I brought with me from Toronto a supply of fishing-tackle, and yesterday and today, in an hour or two, caught herrings enough to supply my table for a week—Ah! what you have lost by the perverse habit of having your own way—I hope however that indulging the like inclination, you will soon come back with Mrs. Davis and your family, to remain for the summer. . . ."

Mr. Davis' thoughts, however, were occupied with more serious matters than fish and sunshine. "Deprived of the means for the support of my family," he wrote from Montreal on June 12th, to C. J. McRea, "I have had it in contemplation to form a business connexion at Liverpool by which subsistence might be earned. Here there is nothing for me to do, and until the pending prosecution of me is settled, it would be impossible for me to engage in any pursuit in our own country. . . . The spirit of vengeful persecution seems unmitigated in regard to myself, in which, however, I seem to be an exception, and this for the reason that persistent falsehood has made a widespread impression that I was accessory to the assassination of Mr. Lincoln and that cruelty was practised on prisoners at the South by officers acting under my orders. The higher officers of the United States Government, if they ever believed either, have certainly long since known both to be false, but have not the fairness to make the avowal and withdraw the infamous accusation." He wrote also that he could not afford to go to Europe with the prospect of being soon recalled to answer his accusers before the court, and was, like other Southern leaders, "waiting like Micawber" for something to turn up.

As Mr. Davis watched, from the distance, the process of Reconstruction, he lamented its obvious unwisdom. "The consolation which I derived from the intense malignity shown to me by the enemy," he wrote to General Chilton, from Montreal, on July 20, 1867, "was in the hope that their hate would, by concentration on me, be the means of relieving my countrymen. That hope has been disappointed, and the worst fears which I entertained as the consequence of a surrender of the armies without terms . . . have been fully realized. Each concession has been but the means of securing further progress in the destruction of the South. My trust in earthly powers is lost, but my sorrow is not without hope, for God is just and omnipotent. His ways are inscrutable, and history is full of examples of the greatest good being conferred upon a people by events which seemed to be unmitigated evil. Nations are not immortal, and their wickedness will surely be punished in this world." Good he believed equally destined to the reward of justice, and declared his fellow-Confederates "the best people who have ever had a place in history."

"The minds of men," he wrote to his brother, two days later, "seem to have been unsettled as to equity, but I have hoped there would still be a public sense against those who attempt to enforce contracts made under one state of circumstances, after they all had changed, so as to make private citizens bear the burden of public calamities. I will leave in a few hours to visit a copper mine in which I have been offered an interest, and hope to be able to make something out of it; of course not much, as I have no capital to put in; but in mining I think there is profitable employment to be found, and if free from the trammels of the courts of Richmond, I believe I could make more than a livelihood in that way."

On August 29th, Paul Bagley, the missionary who had long taken an active interest in Mr. Davis' case, sent a protest to President Johnson declaring: "You are aware that more than two years ago, upon the evidence of witnesses who have since sworn that they were false, a proclamation was issued by the President offering a hundred thousand dollars for the arrest of Jefferson Davis, that he was two years in prison, and some time in chains, that he has never been indicted or tried upon that charge, and that he is now only released on bail to answer at court in November next.

"You are aware of the efforts of myself and others to induce Jefferson Davis to apply for pardon. Permit me to say, sir, as a result of our labours, that it appears to be impossible in the nature of the case that Jefferson Davis should apply for pardon so long as that proclamation stands out against him, without admitting that to be true which those who made it have sworn to be false." In view of these facts, he urged the President to "enter a *nolle prosequi*" in the case of Mr. Davis.

Two days later Bagley reported to Mr. Davis that the President's reply to his letter had been the question, "How would a proclamation of amnesty do?" The same day, Bagley wrote again to Johnson: "In the name of God, the President is this day entreated to *withdraw that* proclamation. . . . Then your prisoner would stand on equal ground with others who rebelled and like them could apply for pardon."

To that point, however, Johnson could neither be led nor driven. The proclamation remained, and Davis, as steadfastly refused to apply for pardon. What he desired was trial and vindication and his devoted counsel steadily worked to that end. On October 18th, Shea wrote to Gerrit Smith, from New York: "We are just informed, and officially, that Mr. Davis will have to appear in Richmond on November 25th; and that the trial will commence on that day. Of course the accused and his counsel are ready. . . . It is clear to me that a great public benefit can even at this late date be elicited from the trial itself of Mr. Davis; and in this view of the case I wish to solicit your patriotic services. Their effective performance may need your personal attendance in Baltimore, for a day or so, and not later than next week. It will not do to commit it to letter-writing. The object is important and its success would be a great triumph for you personally, and a great benefaction to the nation. . . . I am sure the object is one that you will promptly and, indeed, enthusiastically, undertake. Our friend H.[orace] G.[reeley] fully approves of the idea."

Gerrit Smith answered, on October 21st: "I am pained to learn . . . that Mr. Davis is really to be put upon trial. I feared, from what the newspapers were saying, that it would be so, and yet I continued to hope that this great wrong would not be done him; that our nation would be saved from the dishonour of charging treason in the case of a civil war; and saved from setting, in this respect, an example for the despots to plead and profit by."

Davis, meanwhile, finding the autumnal cold of Canada too severe, had gone to Havana, but, soon weary of its monotony, sailed for New Orleans, where a hearty welcome waited him. Thence he proceeded to "Brierfield," the desolation which had been his home. His distressing visit was cut short by a summons to Richmond to face trial, and he responded gladly. Scarcely was he settled, however, when he received a letter from Mason, containing the unwelcome statement: "I see that the letter writer from Washington to the New York *Herald* . . . announces it as 'definitely settled' that the trial . . . will be postponed until May, for reason, that the chief justice can then certainly be present— that the postponement was asked by the counsel for the Government and acceded to by yours. . . ."

This evidence proved near-truth. When the date set for the court, November 25th, arrived, Shea had authorizations from Greeley, Augustus Schell, Gerrit Smith, Benjamin Wood, H. F. Clark, and Cornelius Vanderbilt, to renew the bond formerly given; and the demand for a trial was presented to Judge Underwood; but the Government declared itself not yet ready, and the case was postponed to the succeeding March. Before adjournment, Judge Underwood stated that "he believed it to be due to the defendant that two judges should preside at the trial, as in that case the defendant would have the advantage of an appeal to the higher court, in case of a disagreement between the judges upon any important question."

Left thus still uncertain of the exact date on which his presence might be demanded, and painfully conscious of the lack of means for properly supporting his family during the months of waiting, Davis returned to the neighbourhood of "Brierfield," only to discover that suspicion still dogged his footsteps. "It is alleged," he wrote to Colonel George H. Young, from Vicksburg, on February 25, 1868, "that the people have conferred with me as to armed resistance; the falsehood will be met at every corner. I start this evening for Richmond, but it is probable the trial will be again postponed. Having robbed me of everything I had, my enemies do not now allow me the poor privilege of going to work."

At Richmond Davis found his fear of further postponement realized. Evarts and Dana, leading counsel for the Government, had no wish to try so dangerous a case in the midst of the more dangerous contest between President Johnson and the radical Republicans. On January 25th Dana had written to Evarts that Johnson's administration would "gain very little by a verdict, and will be disgraced by a failure." Evarts had agreed that it might be well to prepare a letter to the attorney-general, suggesting a way out, but felt it wise to reserve it for a time, in view of the imminence of a move to impeach President Johnson. Before the date set for Davis' trial, this imminence had merged into reality, and Johnson the hunter had become the hunted; for on February 25th the House of Representatives voted to impeach the President. Evarts was now removed from the position of counsel for Davis' prosecution to that of counsel for Andrew Johnson's defence. The situation was as strange as that of earlier days when Aaron Burr, under charge of treason, presided in the Senate over the trial of Mr. Justice Chase, then being impeached.

Under such conditions it was doubtless a great comfort to the Government's counsel to be able to plead, when Davis' case was called, that the old indictment against him was defective, and that a new one must be substituted. This was found, on March 26, 1868, and it charged him with many acts of treason, among which was "conspiracy with Robert E. Lee, J. P. Benjamin, John C. Breckinridge, William Mahone, H. A. Wise, John Letcher, William Smith, Jubal A. Early, James Longstreet, William H. Payne, D. H. Hill, A. P. Hill, G. T. Beauregard, W. H. C. Whiting, Ed. Sparrow, Samuel Cooper, Joseph E. Johnston, J. B. Gordon, C. F. Jackson, F. O. Moore, and with other persons whose names are to the grand jury unknown, to the number of one hundred thousand, to levy war against the said United States. . . ." This indictment was "found on the testimony of Robert E. Lee, Lexington, Rockbridge County, Va., and seven others whose names appear at its end.

"It was expected," wrote Davis, at a later date, "that Lee would seek safety by transferring to me any responsibility which was his own; the expectation belonged to a lower standard of honesty and chivalry than that by which General Lee was governed. To the inquiries whether he was not acting under my instructions, enumerating several of his movements and battles, he answered that he had always consulted me when it was practicable to do so, and that we had always finally reached the same conclusion on any question we discussed; that his actions had therefore been in conformity to his judgment and he could not say that he would have acted differently if there had been no conference with me, and must, therefore, himself bear the responsibility attaching to his acts. . . . A less able man might have availed of the opportunity to avoid danger by transferring the responsibility to one on whom it would certainly gladly be placed. He met me immediately after leaving the jury-room, and reported what had occurred there. . . ." The evident purpose of the procedure "was to offer Lee a chance to escape by transferring to me the responsibility for overt acts. Not only to repel the suggestion, but unequivocally to avow his individual responsibility, with all that, under existing circumstances, was implied in this, was the highest reach of moral courage and gentlemanly pride."

In another article on the same subject Davis writes: "He [Lee] said he had endeavoured to present the matter as distinctly as he could, and looked up to see what effect he was producing upon the grand jury. Immediately before him sat a big black negro, whose head had fallen back on the rail of the bench he sat on; his mouth was wide open and he was fast asleep. General Lee pleasantly added that if he had had any vanity as an orator, it would have received a rude shock."

Lincoln's original contention, that the war was a "domestic insurrection," was of course sustained by the indictment, as otherwise there could have been no reason for charging Davis with treason; and an order was then entered continuing Davis' recognizance "until Saturday, the second day of May next."

But when that day arrived, it was evident that the counsel for the accused was still far more eager for trial than was the Government, and it was agreed that Davis should "be tried at a special session . . . to be held in June, 1868." On May 28th, the date was again changed by the following announcement:

"Circuit Court of the United States
for the District of Virgina.
"The United States
against
Jefferson Davis.

"This case will not be called for trial on the third day of June next, but counsel will then appear on behalf of the United States, and also on behalf of the defendant, and an order will then be entered by consent . . . giving the defendant time to appear until such day in the month of October next as may be agreeable to the court.

"New York, May 28, 1868.

"Wm. M. Evarts,
"of Counsel for the United States.
"Ch. O'Conor,
"of Counsel for defendant."

---

This gave Mr. Davis assurance that from May 28, 1868, to October, 1868, he was free to travel as far as business interests might require, without fear of a sudden call to court, on pain of the forfeiture of his bail. He therefore rejoined his family in Canada, where he was deluged with letters of indignant comment, and often bitter invective against a Government which would neither try nor acquit. On June 13th J. M. Mason wrote: "Knowing that you were summoned to Richmond for the 3rd of this month, and inferring from your last letter that you were obliged to go, I had supposed you in Virginia, until I saw in the Richmond *Enquirer* the résumé of proceedings in court there, of which I enclose the slip, as it may not have met your eye. . . . What a miserable set of poltroons and cowards they are, and without one instinct that marks the gentleman. They dare not bring you to trial, and convening before the mob, dare not release you."

This latter reflection was manifestly unfair, as the only "mob" near the court had been composed of Virginians and had had certainly no disposition to prevent Mr. Davis' release. The truth was that the court was acting under very complex and difficult conditions, and the Chief Justice, whom Mason had correctly described, in a letter of April 22, 1868, as "undoubtedly an able lawyer and responsible for the character and reputation of the Department," was trying to find a way out, while preserving both the dignity of his Department and justice which he honestly desired to follow. Indeed, the very document which Mason had enclosed to Davis explained that the postponement had been granted by the Chief Justice and accepted by Mr. Davis' counsel in view of the fact that "the wife of the district attorney was in a dying condition, and the case could not go on without him," and because "the accused was in Canada, or somewhere else." Under these conditions, the Chief Justice had announced, "the court has ordered a continuance . . . until the next November term of the court, unless . . . reason for applying for trial at an adjourned term is given."

And so with the fair prospect of several free months before him, Davis resolved to try his luck in England, and, on July 6, 1868, sent the following letter:

"Lennoxville, C. E. *July 6, 1868.*

"Hon. Howell Cobb:

"My dear Sir:

"The proceedings against me having left a longer interval in which to cast about for some employment . . . I have decided to go to Liverpool to see what may be done in establishing a commission house, especially for cotton and tobacco. An Englishman of very high character and social position who has been extensively engaged in the India trade as a commission merchant, has proposed to me a partnership under the belief that I could obtain assurance of shipments of the staple of our own country. With such assurance I would be willing to attempt a new pursuit, confident that if the business was strictly that of commissions, my friends would incur no risk, and I might hope for an increasing income. I write to you to inquire what may be expected in regard to shipments by your friends and neighbours.

"I expect to leave here on or before the $20^{th}$ inst. and to take passage the $25^{th}$ from Quebec. . . ."

Mrs. Davis, who, owing to the fact that her husband had fallen and broken two ribs, acted as his amanuensis, annexed the following postscript: ". . . I trust that at last we see our way clear . . . to be raised above the wretched sense of idle dependence which has so galled us. . . . I beg that you will write us plainly what has been your success in trying to get promises of cotton. I am sorry to say that Mr. Davis' health has not improved; he looks wretchedly, and I think much of his indisposition is induced by his despair of getting some employment which will enable him to educate our children. There are many things in our visit to the South which convince me that for a year or more, until at least civil law prevails, Mr. Davis could not quietly remain there. If it should please God that we should ever meet I will tell you. . . ."

Upon landing in England, Davis received an invitation from A. J. Beresford Hope, member for Cambridge University and son-in-law of the Marquis of Salisbury, asking him to bring his family for a visit. "Your very kind letter of the $6^{th}$ inst.," he answered from Liverpool, "has added to the happiness given by the welcome of others on my arrival in England. The desire to see and be personally known to yourself and Lady Mildred has been long cherished, and I regret that for the present my movements are so contingent that it is not possible for me to answer your kind invitation by naming the day when you may expect me. . . ." Pleasant as was this personal recognition, he did not dare turn aside from the pressing problem of securing business recognition, a difficult thing for a man under indictment for treason and still bearing the stigma of President Johnson's proclamation connecting him with Lincoln's assassination. In Mrs. Davis' mind there were other reasons too. She knew that upon such a visit the signs of their poverty must be apparent, and shrank from the thought of allowing even friendly foreigners to see it. To Mrs. Cobb she wrote a little later: "We are too poor to travel. . . . It costs so much to dress decently that I have decided not to try, and I never accept any invitations. . . . I feel hourly the necessity of pinching at every turn."

Meanwhile in America, more and more men of influence, North as well as South, were coming to the conclusion that Mr. Davis could never be convicted of treason, while the President's advisers, conscious of the trend, were considering how best to convince him that a trial should not be ventured. "It only requires one dissentient juror to defeat the Government and give Jefferson Davis and his favourers a triumph," argued Evarts in a carefully planned letter to Johnson; and he strongly advised that no trial should be allowed. After reading the advice, Johnson inscribed upon it the words, "This opinion must be filed with care. A. J." Obviously, the arguments advanced fitted well with those which had long been in his own mind regarding Jefferson Davis.

"While these various proceedings were being had," comments the *Decisions of Chief Justice Chase*, "the Congress of the United States had amended the Constitution of the United States by forcing the late Confederate States to accept certain amendments proposed by it, refusing to allow them any rights under the laws until they had so agreed to the propositions submitted to them. In this way Congress secured the vote of states sufficient to accept Constitutional amendments, and thus actually changed the organic law for states which had always adhered to the Union and which protested against the change, by the votes of states held under martial law and which were made at the point of the bayonet to repeat the words required of them. Thus the lately loyal states made the Constitution for the states always loyal." "Among these amendments," significantly remarks the reporter of the Chief Justice's views, "was the one imposing perpetual disfranchisement for aiding in rebellion, after having held certain offices."

Many strange things have since been done in the name of the Fourteenth Amendment, here referred to; but the use made of it to secure the quashing of the inconvenient indictment against Davis is among the strangest. Soon after its passage Chief Justice Chase suggested to Shea and O'Conor that it might be interpreted as repealing the statute upon which that indictment was based. This hint was not lost upon Davis' keen-witted counsel, who saw that it offered a chance to secure the quashing of Davis' indictment. Therefore, on November 30, 1868, Robert Ould, acting for that counsel, filed in open court his own affidavit that on December 8, 1845, Mr. Davis had "taken the oath as a member of Congress," and moved for a rule on the Attorney-General of the United States to show "why the indictment should not be quashed." Mr. Dana, speaking for the Attorney-General, protested that this was to him an entirely new suggestion, but the motion to quash the indictment was sustained, and on Thursday, the third day of December, 1868, the Circuit Court for the Virginia District, sitting at Richmond, proceeded to try it, with Chief Justice Chase sitting with Justice Underwood, in conformity with the latter's earlier suggestion that two judges should preside, as in that case the defendant would have the advantage of appeal to the higher court, in the event of disagreement.

Judge Underwood was so detested among Mr. Davis' counsel that O'Conor ignored his very existence, and addressed himself exclusively to the Chief Justice, who himself at times seemed to have forgotten the presence of his colleague.

The Chief Justice suggested that, as the Supreme Court would meet soon, it was highly desirable that the arguments in the Davis case be strictly confined to the exact issue involved, namely the plea for and against quashing the indictment. He therefore directed Mr. Davis' counsel to prepare at once an exact statement of their contention, and after the brief recess granted for the purpose, Mr. O'Conor presented the following:

"Circuit Court of the United States for the Distirct of Virginia.
"The United States *vs.* Jefferson Davis.

"The indictments in these cases were framed on the alleged fact that the defendant had engaged in the insurrection and rebellion against the United States, known to the Court and to the several departments of the Government as having existed at the several times mentioned in the said indictment in the State of Virginia and elsewhere, and thereby given aid and comfort to the enemies of the United States engaged in said insurrection and rebellion.

"And the defendant alleges that prior to such insurrection and rebellion, and in the year 1845 he, the said defendant, was a member of the Congress of the United States, and as such member took, in said year, an oath to support the Constitution of the United States in the usual manner, and as required by law in such cases.

"And the defendant alleges, in bar of any proceedings upon said indictments, or either of them, the penalties and disabilities denounced against and inflicted on him for his said alleged offence by the third section of the fourteenth article of the Constitution of the United States, forming an amendment to such Constitution.

"And he insists that any judicial proceeding to inflict any other or further pain, penalty, or punishment upon him for such alleged offence is not admissible by the Constitution and laws of the United States.

"Wherefore he, the said defendant, moves the Court now here

to quash and set aside the said indictments, or to dismiss the same and the prosecution thereon, or to render such other relief in that nature as the aforesaid facts and circumstances shall require, and as may seem proper.

"Charles O'Conor
William B. Reed
Robert Ould
James Lyons."

The District-Attorney, Mr. Beach, then submitted a reply for the Government, agreeing "that the Court may assume as facts" that Jefferson Davis "previous to the alleged commission of the offences set forth in the indictment, did take an oath . . . to support the Constitution of the United States."

Both papers were then filed, and Judge Ould was called upon to open the case for the quashing of the indictment. In a speech of great clearness, he argued that the third section of the Fourteenth Amendment "affords the only rule of punishment in the case of Mr. Davis, who is at this moment suffering under that penalty." "True," he said, "there is no distinct provision in the Constitution that no man shall be punished twice for the same offence; but there is a principle in the Anglo-Saxon heart, and acknowledged everywhere, which forbids such a monstrous thing. It is not less than a Constitutional provision. However slight the punishment may be, when a man receives that he goes free. Jefferson Davis has been punished, and is now undergoing punishment. The law under which he is punished, and is now undergoing punishment, is its own interpreter, and executor, and the district-attorney has nothing to do with it. The punishment . . . is now being inflicted by the voice of the American people, who have tried him and pronounced the sentence that he shall be disqualified for holding any office, state or federal. . . . It was the design of the lawmakers to make disqualification for office the only punishment for engaging in the late rebellion." This astonishing position was nothing less than the claim that the third section of the Fourteenth Amendment had repealed the act under which indictments had been found against Jefferson Davis. If it could be shown that that act had been repealed, there could, of course, be no prosecution under that act. His only punishment must be disqualification for office.

Mr. Dana at once declared on behalf of the counsel for the United States, that "the motion had been on a point unexpected to them, and probably to the court," and asked time to study it and to consult authorities, as "this was an entirely new proposition in law, for which there is no precedent." A recess was granted; but, before adjournment, Chief Justice Chase "thought proper to say that the court had not been surprised, as intimated by Mr. Dana, at the ground taken by the defendant. The course of the argument was anticipated, and it was expected that the point to be urged was the common principle of constructive repeal." From this it was evident that at least one of the two judges presiding was inclined, at this point in the debate, to accept the argument as conclusive. Quite naturally so, for he had himself suggested it.

After the brief recess, Mr. Beach opened for the Government, and Mr. Wells and Mr. Dana followed on the same side, the latter declaring that "probably nothing would more surprise the people of the United States than to learn that, by adopting Amendment Fourteen, they had repealed all the penalties against treason, insurrection, or rebellion. The construction contended for by the defendant," he said, would "relieve persons holding high office . . . from the penalties of death or imprisonment, and leave those penalties in full force against all persons engaged in a rebellion who did not . . . hold public office. It is in the highest degree improbable that the people have established a discrimination so unjust and absurd. . . ."

O'Conor, in closing for the defendant, indulged in a species of rhetoric surprising in view of the character of the case and the unemotional character of the judges. He eloquently depicted the horrors of the penalty which the Fourteenth Amendment had already inflicted upon the accused. "Most other penal inflictions," he said, "touch only the person; this wounds the mind. It condemns the proud-spirited leader of his countrymen in peace and war henceforth to walk his native soil in a rank far below the humblest of his former servants—a moral leper stigmatized in Constitutional law as unworthy of any trust, however trifling. In case of a foreign invasion, he is indeed allowed to bare his bosom on the field of his country's defence, but this must be done, if at all, in the ranks as a private. . . . He may not be able to serve in the ranks, for physical strength is not always an accomplishment of intellectual excellence. In such a case, the glorious privilege of contending for his country and surrendering life, if needful, in her behalf, is virtually denied him." The rush of eloquence had apparently caused O'Conor to overlook the fact that the subject of this pathetic appeal, Jefferson Davis, was not in a mood to grieve overmuch at having been deprived of the right to die for the nation that had overwhelmed him.

O'Conor also argued that the Sixth Amendment to the Constitution had been a deliberate attempt to render for ever impossible such punishments for rebellions as Sir Michael Foster's Treatise on Crown Law described as having been visited upon the Scots for supporting the Stuarts: and he declared that it also covered the case of the Southern rebels. "The Sixth Amendment was framed expressly to prevent this precise mischief . . . and the third section of the Fourteenth Amendment was framed in the same spirit." He therefore asked that a decision be given declaring the indictments against Jefferson Davis invalidated by the very words of the Constitution. "Such," he declared, "was, undoubtedly, the intent of its framers; and if so expounded by the courts its operation will be as benign as its conception was just, wise, and politic."

It is doubtless true that a clear decision upon the line urged by

O'Conor and his colleagues, and suggested by Chief Justice Chase himself, would have gone far towards healing the breach which four years of civil war had made. Unfortunately, there was no such decision. On December 5th Chase announced that the court had failed to agree upon the motion "to quash the indictments against Mr. Jefferson Davis." At the request of Mr. Davis' counsel, that fact was formally certified to the Supreme Court of the United States, the Chief Justice having instructed the reporter to record him as having been of the opinion, on disagreement, that the indictment should be quashed, and barred from all future proceedings by the effect of the Fourteenth Amendment. Among the records of that court it was thereafter allowed to remain undisturbed. So ended the case against Jefferson Davis. "No further proceedings," says Johnson's *Reports of the Decisions of Chief Justice Chase*, "were held in the cause."

On December 25, 1868, President Johnson terminated all prosecutions by a proclamation of amnesty "which included Davis." Later, Carl Schurz claimed for the victorious nation high praise for this action. "There is not," he said, "a single example of such magnanimity in the history of the world, and it may be truly said that in acting as it did, this Republic was a century ahead of its time."

One other item is needed in the story. "I was invited to meet Justice Chase and the United States district attorney, Beach, at dinner at Mr. Lyons'," writes John Wilcox Brown. ". . . I went there in company with Mr. Macfarland and noted that we were starting a good deal in advance of the hour named. On arrival I found that there was a consultation to be held between the various men who had Mr. Davis' case in charge. They soon began the discussion, and I learned that the subject before them was whether or not they should accept a proposition made by the Government to have a *nolle prosequi* entered on the next day. There could be no doubt on this point, and the papers were even then being prepared. The men were all of the opinion that there should be no hesitation on their part in assenting. I felt, of course, that the responsibility was entirely on them, but I could not help holding another view, convinced also as I was that Mr. Davis would agree with me. I did not consider that he was any more guilty of treason than I was, and that a trial should be insisted on, which could properly only result in a complete vindication of our cause, and of the action of the many thousands who had fought and of many thousands who had died for what they felt to be the right."

But the agreement was reached, and the next day, February 15, 1869, the district attorney, by leave of the court, formally announced that he would not prosecute further on behalf of the United States. The case was then marked "dismissed," and the bondsmen declared for ever released.

One cannot read the reports of this interesting case without the conviction that, despite all their protestations of indignation that the Government refused to try Davis, his counsel in the end were eager to secure his release without trial, but it is even more certain that John Wilcox Brown had been right in the opinion that Mr. Davis would have preferred a fair and full trial of his case, which he believed then, and for ever after, would have resulted in his complete exoneration from the charges which had been made against him.

From a letter, written by O'Conor after the case had been disposed of without trial, we learn what he would have argued, had the case been tried. "With so admirably prepared and so overwhelmingly conclusive a brief [as Rawle's *View of the Constitution*]," he said, "my task would have been easy indeed." And another of Mr. Davis' counsel, Wm. B. Reed, remarked: "If the case had come to trial, the defence would have offered in evidence the textbook on Constitutional Law [Rawle's *View of the Constitution*] from which Davis had been instructed at West Point by the authority of the United States Government, and in which the right of secession is maintained as one of the Constitutional rights of a state." Had this plea been made, there is little doubt that it would have been refuted by Government's counsel, for records, even then available to them, make it clear that Davis was not instructed from Rawle's *View of the Constitution* at West Point.

What they had actually been content to argue was this: "Admitting everything you say in the indictment is true, no offence under the law has been committed."

It is safe to say that erudition did what it could to find a basis for convicting Davis of treason. But, when erudition had done its work, there was not found in the provisions of the Constitution, or the statute law, or the precedents established by the Supreme Court, one sentence which could be tortured into a warrant of law for sustaining the charge.

## CHAPTER XXX

# HOPE DEFERRED

As Davis' presence in court had not been required during the final proceedings just described, he had remained abroad, vainly searching for a business opening, but finding none. Always impatient under criticism, he found the English part of his trip very trying. The Press had come, almost universally, to favour the victorious North, and he was often irritated by what he considered unfair statements from travellers returning from America. Especially was he incensed by the appearance of a book written, after a hasty visit to America, by F. Barham Zincke, Vicar of Wherstead and Chaplain in Ordinary to the Queen. This book severely reprimanded Mississippi for its act of repudiation, which had injured not a few Englishmen, and it also revived the long disproved accusation that Mr. Davis had been a repudiation leader. After reading it, Davis prepared a letter to the editor of the *Standard*, in which he argued again the injustice of such a charge, and proved again that he had been in no way responsible for or connected with the incident. He also sought to defend his state by explaining the conditions of the various issues and minimizing the repudiation feature. "More than eighteen years since," he wrote, "I published a defence of Mississippi against the accusation that she had repudiated a debt due by the state. I then showed that no action had been taken by the state to discredit any claim made against her, except that for the Union Bank bonds . . . and that in that case the only question . . . was whether those particular bonds . . . could constitute a valid obligation. . . ." The letter was a detailed discussion of a subject in which the average Englishman had no interest whatever; while the few who had lost in the Union Bank bonds repudiation were in no mood to read a debate upon why they had lost. It proved, however, that two years of prison life had not broken Davis' spirit. He was as ready to take up arms against all comers, in defence of Mississippi, as he had been when, resigning his seat in the Senate, he had set himself to the task of organizing her armies. Before sending the letter, however, he submitted it to Benjamin for criticism, and the latter's advice shows the wisdom, and insight into British character, which had helped him to rise to eminence at the English bar.

Benjamin urged Davis not to publish the letter, giving reasons "derived chiefly from an experience of three years spent in that close observation of men and things in England which has been indispensable to one who is driven to seek a livelihood in a new land. . . . I feel convinced that any statement from you in relation to the Mississippi debt would involve consequences deplorable to your repose and tranquil existence in this country. I have had a dozen arguments and discussions on that subject in England. People will not listen to reason on the subject. They cannot understand our Constitutional theories. Parliament is *omnipotent*, and they have but one answer, 'If our Parliament passes a law to issue bonds, and the bonds are issued, no one is bound to inquire further. If the Chancellor of the Exchequer signs a bond, no man is bound to inquire into his authority. The Mississippi bonds were signed and sealed in the name of the state. Foreigners had a right to consider the faith of the state as pledged, and if the legislature or the Governor or Secretary of State did wrong, the people of the state ought to have made them responsible, and not to have punished innocent third holders of the bonds.' " Davis wisely accepted the advice, but his resentment against his critics remained.

It is impossible to trace in detail the course of Davis' experiences in Europe. His later articles, and other writings, show, however, that in England he made many interesting acquaintances, and a few friends. In France, also, he was shown marked courtesy. It has even been claimed by some of his American admirers that Napoleon III offered to receive him at Court, and that Davis commented, that he wanted "no interview with the man who had played us false," a story certainly in character, if not convincingly established. He spent the last days of his voluntary exile in London, where, shortly before starting back to America, he received a letter from A. Dudley Mann, now in Paris, with the important suggestion: "that you will, at your earliest convenience, prepare your *book*. This is a requisition which the world of enlightened mankind makes upon you."

Much as this suggestion appealed to Davis, his circumstances did not encourage the hope of the leisure needed for such a task. He was returning to his native land, a man without a country. The stern enactments of the Fourteenth Amendment had robbed him of the normal rights of a citizen. His search for business connexions abroad had proved fruitless, and his funds were alarmingly low. He knew that there were many among his former followers who would gladly contribute to his need: indeed, just before sailing he received a letter from R. W. Graham, containing an account of "an attempt . . . making in Bourbon county, Kentucky, to raise a fund for the purchase of a home" for him in his native state. But he knew also that his pride would not allow him to accept such a gift. Even under these conditions, however, one thought brought him comfort: he had done his duty as he had understood it, and found within himself no shadow of repentance.

As it chanced, while he was in midocean, homeward bound, General Robert E. Lee, now president of Washington College, later to become Washington and Lee University, was writing a letter to R. S. McCulloch which showed that Lee too was in the same unrepentant state. "Every brave people who considered their rights attacked and their Constitutional liberties invaded," it ran, "would have done as we did. Our conduct was not caused by any insurrectionary spirit, nor can it be termed rebellion; for our construction of the Constitution under which we lived and acted was the same from its adoption, and for eighty years we had been taught and educated by the founders of the Republic, and their written declarations, which controlled our consciences and actions. The epithets that have been heaped upon us of 'rebels' and 'traitors' have no just meaning, nor are they believed in by those who understand the subject, even at the North. . . ."

Like the Saladin of history, or perhaps of fiction, Lee had proved himself capable of unsheathing his sword without anger, and he was now showing that he could sheath it without bitterness. On March 22, 1869, he wrote: "I was not in favour of secession and was opposed to war. . . . I was for the Constitution and the Union established by our fathers. No one now is more in favour of that Union and that Constitution, and as far as I know it was that for which the South has all along contended, and if restored, as I trust they will be, I am sure there will be no truer supporters of that Union and that Constitution than the Southern people." In referring to certain heirlooms of Washington belonging to his mother, which had been taken from her home and which the Federal Government had expressly forbidden to be returned to her, he continued: "They were valuable to her as belonging to her great-grandmother. . . . But as the country desires them, she must give them up. I hope their presence at the capital will keep in remembrance of all Americans, the principles and virtues of Washington." Even the mad course, called Reconstruction, which rejected governments built upon the consent of the white men of the South, and substituted a ruthless military system based in part upon a nominal negro consent, failed to tempt him to bitterness. "His St. Helena, at Lexington," justly comments Douglas Freeman, "was more glorious than his Austerlitz at Chancellorsville."

One can picture a Washington or a Lincoln bearing the sorrows of defeat as Lee bore them, but not Jefferson Davis. It would, however, be unjust to assume that he did not strive to attain Lee's spirit and there is abundant evidence to show how faithful was his striving. There is in the Department of Archives and History of Mississippi a small, worn copy of Thomas à Kempis' *Imitation of Christ*, the gift of Miss Lovell of Natchez. It is inscribed: "This copy . . . was presented to me by Mr. Jefferson Davis in July, 1879, at my own home in Beauvoir, Mississippi, he bringing the book to me. Mr. Davis told me that he had used this book constantly during his imprisonment at Fortress Monroe, also in Canada." It is marked throughout, at paragraphs which had served best the spiritual needs of the lonely prisoner. One underlined might have been written especially for him: "It is good for us to have sometimes troubles and adversities, for they make a man enter into himself, that he may know that he is in a state of banishment and may not place his hope in anything of the world. It is good that we suffer contradictions, and that men have an evil or imperfect opinion of us, even when we do and intend well. These things are often helps to humility, and defend us from vainglory. We better turn to God, our inward witness, when outwardly we are despised of men. . . . Therefore should a man establish himself in such a manner in God as to have no need of seeking many comforts." Another: "All is not lost when anything falls out otherwise than thou wouldst have it. Thou must not judge according to thy present feeling, nor give thyself up in such manner to any trouble from whencesoever it comes, nor take it so, as if all hope were gone of being delivered out of it."

An even more striking marked passage runs: "I offer up also to thee my prayers, and this sacrifice of propitiation" (Mr. Davis marked out the words "and this sacrifice of propitiation") "for them in particular, who have in anything wronged me, grieved me, or abused me, or have done me any damage or displeasure." One cannot study this little book, the spiritual comforter of many generations, without a new sense of the nobility of spirit of Mr. Davis, despite his many faults, and his self-deceptions regarding the righteousness of slavery.

Neither Davis nor Lee ever regained his lost citizenship: but both honestly sought to persuade the South to accept defeat, and to devote itself to the task of making the new type of Union, a Union based upon demonstrated power of coercion, as great as the old Union of voluntary confederation had been. With Davis, however, the controversial was ever uppermost. While the North early believed that Lee had fulfilled to the letter the promise given at Appomattox, to "devote his whole effort to pacifying the country, and bringing the people back to the Union," it has never been willing to concede as much to Davis. Yet there is abundant evidence that, with due allowance for differences of temperament, Davis strove as earnestly for the upbuilding of a new Union as did Lee. On the other hand, there is no evidence for Carl Schurz's statement that Davis, "used his influence, not as General Lee did in his frank and generous way, to encourage among his friends a loyal acceptance of the order of these things, and a patriotic devotion to the restored public, but rather to foment in a more or less concealed way, a sullen animosity against the Union. He stimulated the brooding over the past disappointments rather than a cheerful contemplation of new opportunities. He presented the sorry spectacle of a soured man who wished everyone else to be soured too."

As Davis landed in America after his fruitless journey, he must have recalled that on March 30th of the previous year, the trustees of Randolph-Macon College had offered to make him president, and that his answer had been, "I am a prisoner of state, released on bail. I feel that I cannot risk the fortunes of any institution by becoming connected with it until the odium cast upon me has been removed. . . . If I were free, I would cheerfully consider your proposition." The temptation to accept the offer had been great, as his excellent training and studious habits made it highly attractive to him, and had he accepted, as Lee, not having Davis' reason to refuse, had accepted a similar offer, he would have been returning to a useful, congenial work, and a safe and certain future.

On January 7, 1870, he declined another educational post of distinction, as it came after he had at last found a position, though of different character. "I am grateful to you and the others you mention in connexion with the 'University,'" he wrote to General Gorgas on that day. "The necessity for an income was such as to require [me] to consider the question of salary as the important feature in any proposition which was made to me. This company [The Carolina Life Insurance Company] was the first to invite me to join it and offered the largest compensation for my services. The first proposition was that I should establish a branch office at Baltimore, but when I came here this was changed into an offer of the presidency of the company, and done in such a mode that I accepted it."

Meanwhile the problem of finding time to write the book which Mann had suggested was still in the background of Davis' mind, but the exactions of a new business claimed most of his time. He had soon formed plans for establishing branches in Alabama, Georgia, and Virginia, and with such confidence in the future that he expected to be able to bring his family home from England before the arrival of another summer.

Davis' friends, however, felt that his position was not proportionate to his ability, and from one of them, Mann, still in Paris, he received a letter expressing this feeling and suggesting a course of conduct which he seemed to consider worthier. "I had fondly indulged in the hope of a different pursuit for you . . ." he wrote. "I wished to see you so situated that you would benefit mankind by your rare wisdom and your general knowledge. Strange, strange indeed, are the ways of earth when such a Light as yours is concealed under a Bushel.

"My thoughts still linger . . . round the homes of the faithful sons and daughters of the South. Often in the stillness of the night, in my little chamber do I fancy that I can behold, in the not far distant future, a high destiny for their native land: when the states over which you presided will again be states . . . examples for the emulation of those of the North. . . ."

The method which Mann suggested to bring about this result, was "for all true patriots to commence, . . . to wean themselves from Federal attractions and to resist Federal temptations—to consider Federal office as disreputable and the Federal capital as the abode of murderers and robbers. . . . As the Federal Government . . . forced black political equality upon the South, the South in return should force black political and social equality upon the administrators of the Federal Government. Let negroes be sent, exclusively by her to both branches of Congress and enjoy every Federal office within her limits. Let the white citizens, thereof, solemnly resolve . . . to view every Federal place of trust or profit as too much dishonoured for their acceptance. Let not a solitary state position be conferred upon a negro. In a word, let the Federal Union, under the operations of its own monstrous deeds, be brought into such palpable disgrace, in its own esteem, that it will have no alternative but to return to the original compact."

It would have been difficult to pack more unwisdom into the same number of words: but the letter represented the kind of advice which might have been expected to appeal to a dethroned leader. It, furthermore, found Davis smarting under what seemed to him a deliberate affront. A negro named Revels, had recently been chosen to occupy the seat in the United States Senate, which he had himself occupied; and the announcement of that fact had caused the curious to pack the visitors' gallery to see him take his seat, an incident which Sumner characterized as "an historic event, marking the triumph of a great cause." A few Senators had vigorously protested, but when the vote had been taken, forty-eight had voted yea, and only eight nay. Senator Wilson, after some remarks about the swan-song of slavery, and God's hand in affairs of state, had conducted Revels to the bar, to take the prescribed oath; and the Republican Senators had, as a resentful Southerner wrote, fallen "over each other to shake Revels' hand and congratulate him. Poor Mississippi! And Revels is not even a native. General Ames of Maine is her other Senator. Poor Mississippi!"

Giving no countenance to Mann's mad project, Davis now dedicated his leisure with new determination to a search for material, not for a history, but for an elaborate brief, designed to refute the charge that the Confederacy had been but a grim conspiracy for the perpetuation of slavery; and that his fellow-Confederates had been rebels and traitors to their country. Soon his mail was filled with letters from Southern leaders and Southern writers, offering assistance and, more valuable still, documents and other concrete evidence. On April 1, 1870, R. R. Stevenson reported that he had himself compiled a small work upon Andersonville prison, composed chiefly from official documents "found in the hands of one of the alleged conspirators of Captain Henry Wirz"; which he was vainly trying to have published. He claimed that these documents proved "beyond the shadow of a doubt" that Wirz and his "alleged co-conspirators" were innocent of the crimes charged against them. He also reported that General Winder was having difficulty in procuring a publisher for his work on the same subject.

The business of reorganizing the insurance company and of planting new branches in the South, however, occupied Davis until summer, when he spent a few weeks at White Sulphur Springs, before starting to join his family in England. Of his visit a fellow-guest wrote, "I never heard Mr. Davis laugh, but I never heard [him] . . . utter a complaint, or even allude to the cruel treatment he had received. . . . He did, however, express contempt and disgust for the three or four prominent Southern generals and others who, when he was a prisoner, turned their poisoned pens against him." In commenting upon the complaint that he had failed to sell the South's cotton crop in Europe, made so often by

General Joseph E. Johnston, he said: "Many silly people talk of the 'mistake,'" and "General Johnston is not the only ignoramus who does not know that the crop of 1860-61 had mostly gone forward before the birth of the Confederacy—that it all belonged to individuals, and the Confederate Government had not money to buy it, nor ships to transport it. The next crop was imprisoned by the blockade, and much of it in the interior, closed by want of land or river transportation. . . . Every vainglorious empiric can announce something as proposed or possible, however empty it may be, and find people who will accept it."

On August 10th, Davis again sailed for England. The tedium of the voyage was broken by reading and by talks with chance acquaintances who could give him information regarding the course of the Franco-Prussian war then in progress. On August 20th, he wrote from the ship, to his brother Joseph: "The men of Yankee proclivities are for the Prussians and those of the South for the French. I need hardly tell you that I wish the arrogant, robbing Yankees of Europe to be soundly thrashed and the little states they have appropriated released from consolidation."

To a man of Davis' military knowledge, Europe was at this time a scene of absorbing interest; but, after a few weeks spent with his family, he reluctantly returned to Memphis to resume the routine of business. Upon landing he received news which deeply affected him. His brother had died at Vicksburg on September 18th, and General Robert E. Lee at Lexington, on October 12th. Both deaths caused him deep personal grief, as he had loved these two men as he had loved no others. "You who, better than any other, can sympathize with me in this sad bereavement," he wrote to his niece, "will appreciate how bitter are the waters in which I am overwhelmed."

A few days later he delivered at Richmond an address which sums up his estimate of Lee's character, and in which, he said, "His moral qualities rose to the height of his genius." "Hitherto men have been honoured when successful, but here is one who amid disaster went down to his grave, and those who were his companions in misfortune have assembled to do reverence to his memory. It is an honour to you who give as well as to him who receives, for, about the vulgar test, you show yourselves competent to judge between him who enjoys, and him who deserves, success. . . . He sleeps with the thousands who fought under the same flag; he sleeps in the soil to him and to them most dear. That flag was furled when there was no one to bear it; and we, a remnant of the living, are here to do homage to his peerless greatness, and there is an army of skeleton sentinels to keep watch over his grave."

Davis' reappearance upon the public platform was followed by a flood of invitations from organizations eager to capitalize his publicity value, and by a flood of letters urging upon him the duty of hastening the completion of the book which was to defend the Lost Cause. His energies were, however, fully engaged in the effort to support his family, and he stuck stubbornly to the problems of his business. But soon there came another and more imperative call for a division of his energies, resulting from his brother's death. During the latter part of his life Joseph Davis had succeeded in regaining his plantation, "Hurricane," and with it Davis' estate of "Brierfield," whose title deeds had never been formally transferred to Davis. Both estates had been employed, while in Federal hands, as "a depot for captured and fugitive negroes," and when they had been regained, Joseph had attempted to put both again into cultivation; but the condition of labour in the South had rendered success impossible. He had therefore made his home at Vicksburg until his death.

When his will was read, it was found that Jefferson Davis had been made one of its executors, a post of extreme difficulty, as he felt it his duty to his family to claim "Brierfield" as his own.

Joseph Davis had been a lawyer, and could not have been ignorant of the fact that the ancient law of trusts estops one from accepting the duties of trustee under a will, and then himself setting up a claim to part of the estate provided for in the will, and it is fair to assume that his failure to declare his brother's full ownership of "Brierfield" was due to a desire to protect it from danger of confiscation by the Federal Government. The fact that Joseph's heirs had been brought up to look upon "Brierfield" as Jefferson Davis' property may well have appeared a guarantee against any effort on their part to deprive him of its possession. However, both plantations had been restored by the Government to Joseph, and his heirs now claimed both as part of their inheritance. Davis was therefore faced with the alternative of losing his estate or facing a suit which would again drag into the limelight every detail of his life, and give his enemies a new opportunity of misrepresentation and slander. Knowing, however, that the plantation to which he had brought his first wife, in the days of his youth, had been a gift and not merely a loan from his devoted elder brother, he attempted to convince the heirs of the justice of his claim, but failed. He then, reluctantly, instructed his lawyers to prepare the evidence and be ready for a trial of the case. The lawyers took depositions from every person, white or black, who was known to have any first-hand knowledge of the affairs of the two plantations. The manuscripts are still preserved, n their original form, in the historical collection at Jackson, and throw a flood of light upon that period of Davis' life.

In spite of the costs incidental to this litigation, and the diminishing returns from his business, Davis continued to offer hospitality to the throngs who flocked to Memphis, eager to ask concerning the progress of the suit, or learn his views concerning the exciting contest between Grant and Greeley, now contending for he Presidency. His frank preference for Greeley, whose earlier career had been one of bitter enmity towards the Confederates, deeply stirred many of his most loyal friends. On June 19, 1872,

James Lyons, one of his Southern bondsmen, wrote: "In the paper of last evening, I read a statement that you are in favour of Greeley. I regret that it is so, if it is, but I know that it proceeds from that noble trait of grateful fidelity to a friend which is so marked a trait of your character." Lyons, as he had before declared, found Grant less abhorrent than Greeley, who had laboured twenty years to get up the war, and then stayed at home "to fan the flame."

Davis, however, was weary of arguing. The hopelessness of his position, the evident impossibility of making clear his own honesty of purpose, oppressed him. Say what he might, his preference for Greeley was attributed to "fidelity to a friend" for a personal service. Again and again, he had protested his belief that Greeley had signed his bond, not out of friendship for him, but out of devotion to the cause of justice. Always, he was faced with the fact that the political mind thinks in less lofty terms. Greeley "had intervened to rescue him from prison and judgment, therefore support Greeley," ran inevitably the interpretation of his action. And he could not turn the tide. On August 6, 1872, he wrote to James Phelan: "Life has not been to me of the dramatic kind. . . . [but] a long tour of fatigue, marked by a succession of unjust reports. . . ."

Such moments of depression were, however, rare. In general his courage was as high as his prospects were discouraging, but as the campaign progressed, he refrained from written comment, and even to intimate friends spoke guardedly and with conscious self-restraint.

After Greeley's tragic collapse and Grant's triumphant election to the Presidency, however, he wrote to his British friend, Beresford Hope, of his wish that he were again in England, as America's true character had been destroyed by the supremacy of the catchword, "the will of the majority is the law of the land, than which nothing could be less like the theory of the compact of

Union, or a wider departure from the idea of security under a written constitution. Universal suffrage has brought in its train endless evils. Ignorance and depravity are making us the byword of nations." To his mind America was fulfilling his own prophecy of April 23, 1865, in which he had pictured "the long night of oppression which will follow the return of our people to the Union." "It is a common occurrence," he assured Hope, "to hear reflecting men say that the separation of these Colonies from the mother country has proved a misfortune to us. A few years ago the expression of such an opinion was never heard." Such a view, if made accessible to his enemies, would have called forth bitter comment; but he knew that his confidence was in safe hands, and it was doubtless a relief to be able to speak freely.

Generous as was the aid given him in his task of collecting documents for his book, some of it was most distasteful to him. He was inundated with worthless material sent by men eager to be immortalized, by ghastly stories of old wounds that would not heal, and tedious descriptions of personal prowess which had not been duly praised. All these required careful perusal, however, in the hope that there might be found some grains amid the chaff.

In the many public addresses, now demanded of him he once or twice fell into indiscreet utterances. In August, 1873, in an address before the Southern Historical Convention at White Sulphur Springs, he declared: "We were cheated rather than conquered," and urged that the children of the South should cherish and maintain the principles for which their fathers fought: words which were interpreted by his enemies as an attempt to incite sedition, certainly far from his intention, ill-chosen though they were. His friends, General Early among others, sought to answer the criticisms, and the discussions which followed fired the heart of at least one Southern sympathizer who certainly cherished visions of renewed slaughter.

"New York.
*"August 18, 1873.*

"SOUTHERN GENTLEMEN OF THE HISTORICAL SOCIETY, AND VERY HONOURABLE PRESIDENT, MR. JUBAL A. EARLY, GENERAL AND ESQUIRE:

"Dear Sir:

"It is my first occasion to announce to you and all those gentlemen which suffered for the Southern cause a kind of a consolidary relief!

"You and all may give up the Southern cause as a lost cause—I do not and will not give up the idea that the South and West must and will have their independenzy from the hungrey, corrupt, fiendish brute yankee rule!

"And I have the great remedy for it!

"I am the inventor of a perfect flying-machine for to navigate the current; with that flying-machine every aeronaut may bombard cities like New York, Boston, Philadelphia, and every Yankee city, and burn it to ashes. If we use it as artillery in the air, if other civil war breaks out, and it will come again, mark my words gentlemen, I will dedicate my so important invention for the Southern cause and her independenz, and keep it secret. That side of a government wish (which) has employed my flying machine must be victorious! Because with my flying-machine every aeronaut is able to destroy man-of-war fortifications of every description and troops on the battle-field, or on marsh or encampments. I am a american citizen, but for the South, more better as for the North. I am born in Germany, and hate the swindling magots of humbuging Yankees like a good Christian must hate the Devil.

"Bismark's motto is Blood and Iron! and my motto is Blood and Fire! . . ."

General Early gave this letter to the Press, with the following, whimsical explanation: "As our recent Historical Convention . . . has kicked up a great muss among our 'loyal' brethren of the

North, and all sorts of queer notions, I hasten to lay before the public the following letter, this morning received from the 'Return Letter Office,' Washington City. It seems that the officer having charge of that business has, after opening and reading it, deemed the letter of such value as to cause him instantly to subject the Government to the payment of six cents in official stamps, and myself to six cents in ordinary stamps, in order that I might receive the valuable communication (on which the postage was not paid) before there was time for it to cool."

As the strain of life was again telling heavily upon Davis, his physician, late in 1873, insisted upon a period of rest, urging another trip abroad. Reluctantly he yielded to necessity, and made an eight months' visit to England and France; but there remains scant information with reference to the journey. He returned early in the summer of 1874, much improved in health, but was immediately confronted with the disturbing news that the Carolina Life Insurance Company was in process of liquidation, which meant the total loss of the $15,000 which Davis had invested in it, as well as the loss of the salary upon which his livelihood depended. The demands of the suit for "Brierfield" continued, and his financial outlook was little short of disastrous.

On January 18, 1875, he wrote to Marcus Wright, who was attempting to find employment for him: ". . . Poverty compels me to seek for whatever employment may serve my needs, and nothing offers to me here. Therefore . . . I cannot give you a permanent address." In the narrow, circumscribed area now his he was finding, as Grant was finding in the White House, that the capacity for leadership in one line of life does not, of necessity, prove equal capacity for success in other lines. As a general in the field, Grant had shown himself a lion: but as President he was proving himself dangerously near zero. As President of the Confederacy, as even his severest critics admitted, Davis had been an able and brilliant leader, but his business ventures were discouraging, due in part, no doubt, to his overwhelming handicap of status.

On April 26, 1875, Davis wrote to W. T. Walthall, who had offered to help with the history: "The desire you express in regard to the vindication of the principles for which our battles were fought is the first object of importance with me. But poverty does not permit me to make it first in the order of things to be attempted. The transfer of the 'Carolina Life Insurance Company' to the 'Southern Life,' while I was absent and in disregard of my opinion, cost me $15,000, that being the amount of my stock, and note since paid; and that loss from my small means has kept me from that time to this in anxiety, and thus far unsuccessful efforts, to provide for the future wants of my family.

"Your kind offer to aid me by fragmentary labour may excuse me for saying that in the proposed work, I should if possessed of sufficient means to offer you a salary, have requested your assistance. Perhaps my fortunes may improve. From the wreck made by the war, I may get something, but confidentially I will tell you that those who should have been first to regard my interests are as eager to appropriate the wreck as the Yankees were to make it. . . . If the courts can be expected to view *my case* without prejudice, there is reason to hope for improvement in my condition and for leisure and rest for work on the history. . . ." His citizenship was gone, his business was gone, his property was in litigation, but still his chief interest in life was the hope that he might yet gain time to defend in writing the cause which had cost him so much and given him so little.

During the spring of 1875, the managers of the Agricultural Fair of Columbus, Indiana, conscious of a widespread interest in the man who had led the Confederate Government, invited Mr. Davis to open the fair with an address. The announcement that the invitation had been sent raised intense excitement, and threats were made against his life. These threats emanated from "warriors . . . who hired substitutes or had to go out as 'hundred days' men," commented one journal, friendly to Mr. Davis. "Not many of them," it added, "ever saw a rebel unless they guarded some captured by soldiers . . . none . . . ever killed one. So they announced that they would set themselves right on that charge by killing Jeff Davis, 'the biggest old rebel of all. . . .' " The officials, despite this clamour, repeated the invitation, but Mr. Davis wisely declined upon the ground of unwillingness to produce friction within the community, or censure or injury to the enterprise which they represented.

Before this decision had been announced, came a letter from H. P. Kimball, Secretary of the Winnebago County Agricultural Society, of Illinois, offering him "$400 to give us one hour's talk on Sept. 16th." Davis had not replied, however, when a second letter arrived from the same hand, promising "a grand ovation of 40,000 hearers, and a compensation of $500." Both invitations were answered in one reply, which ran, "I accept your offer on the terms proposed." Again his enemies raised a clamour, and the *Chicago Tribune* staged a scene, picturing the haggling by which the high rate of $500 had been fixed: "Mr. Davis demanded $500. The directors begged him to knock off something for the sake of the cause, and to seal the era of reconciliation for $400. He refused. Then they offered $450. Still he refused. He stood by his original stipulation, and, as the board was particularly zealous in the matter, all the members but one being Democrats or Independents, the $500 basis was finally agreed upon."

Indignant at so barefaced a misrepresentation, Kimball wrote to the editor of the *Tribune*, explaining that the sum of $400 had been set by the board of directors before the invitation was sent, and increased to $500 before a word had been received from Mr. Davis. But the matter had passed beyond a mere controversy concerning details. The Grand Army members, numerous in Illinois, had taken up the question, and their remonstrances and threats grew so bitter that the association felt it necessary to withdraw the invitation. Therefore, on August 11, 1875, Kimball wrote Mr. Davis, advising him to "decline in a statesmanlike manner, regretting that unexpected change in your business affairs have compelled you to decline. . . ." Such courteous indirection, however, was not Mr. Davis' method. He sent his declination, as requested, but explained that his object in accepting the invitation had been a desire to be of service. "Yesterday," he added, "I received a printed paper, being the protest of a number of your fellow-committeemen against the action of your board in their invitation to me. . . . Thereupon I sent you the telegram withdrawing mv acceptance . . . under the conviction that it would not be useful or agreeable to participate in the meeting. . . . My only regret is the loss of opportunity to promote a public interest. . . ."

Meanwhile, a gleam of hope had come in the shape of an offer from the Mississippi Valley Association, an English company, but most uncharacteristically English, as its scope was gigantic, its methods of financing obscure, and its management centred in one person, apparently unknown to Davis. It had in view two vast projects, the one to induce European immigration into Mississippi, by liberal grants of wild lands, the other to collect from London capitalists £1,500,000, "on the condition that we of the Mississippi Valley will subscribe £500,000, to make a capital of £2,000,000 with which to establish" a line of ships each large enough to carry 10,000 bales of cotton, and so built as to be able to cross the bar at the mouth of the Mississippi.

Desperate men dare desperate measures, and as we read the particulars of the post, it seems clear that Davis' financial difficulties had rendered him, if not desperate, at least strangely unlike the man who had presided so ably over the War Department of the United States, and husbanded so carefully the failing credit of the Confederate States of America. Without sufficient investigation of the risks he was running, he accepted, conditionally. "I have replied," he wrote to Mann, on August 6, 1875, "that if the London members would make the needful arrangements for compensation &c. &c., I would assume the duties."

These assurances given, Davis closed the contract, and on November 14th, wrote from a Mississippi River liner, to convey the good news to Walthall: "The position of president of the American branches of the London Society for the development of the Mississippi Valley has been tendered to me and accepted. The arrangements have not, however, been completed. If there is no slip it will cause me to reside in New Orleans. The Society is *non-trading*, but designed to encourage direct trade and investments of English capital in our section."

The uneasy sense that there might yet be a slip, however, caused him to remain on the alert for other openings, and to receive with interest the following letter from William M. Gwin, once United States Senator from California: "The manager and one of the principal owners of the Southern Pacific Railroad of California was and is in negotiation with the H. & T. Central road to fill the gap between the Colorado River and Austin, the former to build the road to El Paso, and the latter thence to Austin. It is of vital importance to get a charter from Texas to continue the road from Austin to El Paso; in fact the whole scheme fails unless the charter is obtained. So certain was I of their jumping at the chance of getting your aid, which made success certain, that I did not contemplate the possibility of their hesitating. Yet they so hesitate. . . . If they fail to employ you the whole scheme will fail, as I stated very decidedly today to those who have their hearts set upon making this the trunk line of the Southern Pacific Railroad. I hope by tomorrow night to have it all arranged. If exerting all my power will mean success, it is as good as achieved."

On December 2nd, Gwin wrote again to Davis: "My dear Friend: "The Houston and Texas Central Railroad Company have not yet decided to apply to Texas for a charter to extend their road from Austin to El Paso. They are slow and cautious and General Huntington, who acts for the Southern Pacific . . . fears to urge them to a decision for fear they may draw back. Their co-operation with him is of vital importance and he has no doubt he will secure it by giving them time. They see no necessity of an immediate application to Texas, as the legislature does not meet until January. He advises me to wait upon them until they agree to his proposition, which is to connect with them at El Paso, before I withdraw the proposition to send you at once to Texas. . . . What a fatality it is that money and brains do not go together." Nine days later Gwin added: ". . . I do not wish you to turn aside from any purpose you have in mind expecting anything from these parties. At the same time I believe they will ask for your services at an early date. Whether you can engage in the business or not will depend upon yourself. If they cannot command your services it is their fault. . . ."

Such a situation would have had unusual attractions for Davis, who as Secretary of War had made important surveys and had carefully studied the problem of Western development through railway building. But it came to nothing. Moreover, he must have been conscious that the Mississippi Valley project was as great a gamble as the Columbia Life Insurance Company had proved. However, for the present, he seemed certain at least of a salary, which in those Reconstruction days was not the lot of every Southerner.

From certain indications, Davis was now beginning to hope that the bitterness of which he had so long been the centre and target was passing at last. President Grant had pressed upon Congress a plan for universal amnesty, and the House, in accepting it, had rejected Blaine's demand that Davis be excluded from its benefits. It is true that the Senate had refused to concur in the bill, but there seemed hope that with changing public opinion it might in time agree to remove all disabilities imposed by the Fourteenth Amendment, including Davis'.

The centennial year 1876 opened with Reconstruction still unfinished; a fierce Presidential contest between the Republicans and the Democrats, now beginning to hope for their first Presidential victory since 1854, and Davis, scornful of both parties. "There is now a better prospect for the success of the Democrats than at any time since the war," he had written to Dudley Mann, on August 6, 1875, "but it is not that triumph of truth which we hoped for. It is rather the thrift that follows fawning, at least compounding with murderers of the Constitution as our fathers made it. . . . I am glad that you cannot witness the general decadence among the people you knew in their earlier and better days."

Since then the "better prospect" for the Democrats had become better still: but Davis' position was now rendered worse by proceedings in Congress, again led by James G. Blaine, the object this time being again to lay upon him the responsibility for the sufferings of the Federal prisoners at Andersonville. Blaine had been a member of the House Committee on Rules which had reported the general amnesty, whose defeat in the Senate had left unsettled a question which President Grant greatly desired to have settled. Therefore, on December 15th, Randall had reintroduced it, with the hope that the recent elections had altered the Senate's attitude. "At the last session of Congress," he said, "upon the motion of the gentleman from Tennessee, Mr. Maynard, the House . . . passed this bill." Then turning towards Blaine and Garfield, who were raising objections to its being again considered, he added, "I did not suppose that, in consequence of the change of political character which the House has undergone, there would be any objection from that side. But it is enough for me to know that the gentlemen desire to discuss it, and desire delay." He then left for future discussion his motion, which declared simply "that all disabilities imposed and remaining upon any person by virtue of the third section of the fourteenth article of the amendments of the Constitution of the United States be, and the same are hereby removed, and each and every person is hereby for ever relieved therefrom."

When the hour for its discussion came, as such a bill would of course have restored Mr. Davis' lost citizenship and rendered him once more eligible to federal as well as state office, it was challenged by Blaine with the words: "I desire . . . to have printed an amendment in the nature of a substitute which I propose to offer." The substitute contained the words: "with the exception of Jefferson Davis."

After this announcement of a desire to leave upon Davis alone the disabilities imposed by the Fourteenth Amendment, the matter was left till the following Monday, so far as Congress was concerned.

The news of Blaine's proposal, however, aroused immediate protest in the Southern and Border states. John Preston of Trimble County, Kentucky, presented to his legislature a resolution, "that Kentucky will not participate in the said Centennial until there shall be *universal* amnesty . . ." the local press supporting him with enthusiasm. "The proposition of Mr. Blaine to exclude Mr. Davis from the terms of a general amnesty," said the *Kentucky Yeoman*, of January 10th, "is an insult to those who are sought to be liberated from political bondage. The idea of making him the vicarious sufferer for acts for which he is no more amenable than thousands of his followers is one which every honourable Southern man will resent. It would be more grateful to remand them all to the original proscription under which they were placed by the Fourteenth Amendment than to ask them to consent to see such unmerited obloquy heaped upon their chief. . . ." These sentiments found a widespread echo throughout the South, but the protests failed to alter Blaine's purpose.

On Monday, January 10th, when Randall moved the consideration of his universal amnesty bill, Blaine pressed his substitute; Randall protested: "I do not know what has come over the gentleman from Maine. I do not understand why he should want to change the bill . . . as passed a year ago when he was Speaker and had in part control of the majority of the House."

Blaine's reply at least had the merit of frankness: "The gentleman is obstructing amnesty; he is withholding it from every man in the South now under disabilities because he will not even allow a vote on the proposition to except Jefferson Davis." James G. Blaine craved an opportunity to turn his famous eloquence and his much-feared vindictiveness upon the scapegoat who had led the South. Master of the rules of the House as he was, he knew that desire could not be thwarted, and when his hour came he boldly claimed for his party a "record of liberality, and large-mindedness, and magnanimity, and mercy far beyond any that has ever been shown before in the world's history by conqueror to conquered." He expressed himself ready to grant full amnesty to every Southern man, save one, and declared him excepted "on this ground: that he was the author, knowingly, deliberately, guiltily, and wilfully, of the gigantic murders and crimes of Andersonville prison, in comparison with which I here before God, measuring my words, knowing their full extent and import, declare that neither the deeds of the Duke of Alva in the Low Countries, nor the massacre of Saint Bartholomew, nor the thumb-screws and engines of torture of the Spanish Inquisition begin to compare in atrocity." He charged that Davis had sent Winder to Andersonville "with full knowledge of his previous atrocities" and "against the protests of others in the Confederacy, to construct that den of horrors." Blaine then quoted one of the most heart-rending descriptions ever penned, from a report, concurred in by Democratic investigators as well as Republican to prove, what needed no proof, the horror of a prison camp with 35,000 prisoners, at a time when the Confederacy was scarcely able to feed and clothe the soldiers in her armies. But his assertion that Davis, "by the wink of his eye, by a wave of his hand, by a nod of his head, . . . could have stopped that atrocity," was entirely without justification, as was his further declaration that Wirz had been Davis' tool. Hanging Wirz, he said, was "like skipping over the president, superintendent, and board of directors in the case of a great railway accident, and hanging the brakeman of the rear car." He admitted that the time for punishing Davis "has gone by," but demanded that Congress should not declare him "worthy to fill the highest offices in the United States." "Against . . . crowning with the honours of full American citizenship the man who organized that murder, I here protest."

This powerful and bitter arraignment was well calculated to persuade the two-thirds of each house needed to remove disabilities, to stop short of Jefferson Davis. But it was unfair inference, not proof, by which Blaine sought to make Davis responsible for the unavoidable conditions at Andersonville. During the trial of Wirz, which had lasted three months, over 160 witnesses had been examined, and not one unrefuted sentence had been found to connect Davis with a single atrocity, or to prove any connexion, other than that of commander-in-chief and subordinate, between him and the unhappy Wirz, as Benjamin H. Hill reminded Blaine during the debate. On the contrary, Hill continued, "when offered life and liberty upon the one condition that he implicate Davis in the crime of which he stood accused, he had gallantly replied, 'I would not become a traitor against him, or anybody else, even to save my life.'" And Hill quoted, effectively, Wirz's solemn assertion, made to his confessor, Father Boyle, just before his execution, "'I do not know anything about Jefferson Davis.'"

The horrors of Andersonville, Hill traced to General Grant's refusal to countenance the exchange of prisoners which the two Governments had agreed upon, his reasons being that a captive no less than a soldier in battle should be willing to die for his country, and to the refusal of the masters of the sea to allow even medicines to reach Southern prisons. He charged Blaine also with deliberately garbling the evidence which he had cited, and of speaking as a prosecutor rather than as a lawmaker seeking truth.

During Blaine's speech, S. S. Cox had intervened to inject the remark that "the persecuting spirit of England toward Scotland had caused Rob Roy McGregor to be executed," and had added,

"The gentleman from Maine has picked out his Rob Roy McGregor."

On January 12th James A. Garfield came to Blaine's rescue in a brilliant and impassioned speech, in which he said: "I do not believe in vicarious atonement in politics. Jefferson Davis was no more guilty for taking up arms, than any other man who went into the Rebellion with equal intelligence." His own desire that Davis alone be excepted from the proposed amnesty, he said, rested, as did Blaine's, on the ground that he was "the author, the conscious author, through his own appointed instrument, of the terrible work at Andersonville, for which the American people still hold him unfit to be admitted among the legislators of this nation." "Wipe out the charge," he added, "and I will be the first man here to vote to relieve him of his disabilities . . . but do not ask us to restore the right to hold power to that man who was the cause of their suffering—that man still unshriven, unforgiven, undefended."

The major attention of the South was, of course centred upon Blaine, who had led this movement to brand Davis as guilty of monstrous and inhuman cruelty. On January 12th, James Lyons wrote: "I am so goaded by rage, disgust, and mortification at Blaine's vile attack upon you . . . that I cannot rest or be still. I know your contempt and dispication for the foul-mouthed coward and all like him, but I beg you to suppress those feelings now and give your own statement about Andersonville. All the world will believe you, even the Blaine rascals, but if they don't, no matter, address it to the Speaker; but if you won't do this, then let me or some other friend. I beg you to do it. . . ."

Two days later, being, as he said, "cool today," Lyons wrote again, "in order that you may not suppose that my letter of yesterday was merely the effect of feeling. . . . He has assailed you before not the nation only, but the world, with accusations which I am sure he knew to be utterly false. . . . He has made them for a price, with the design to stain and blur the history of the

South and the war, and thus to draw off the attention . . . of posterity as well as the present voter from the truth. You alone can give such a reply as the whole world will listen to. . . . He has not merely slandered you, but the entire South, which sustained you. Do not permit him to escape unwhipt of justice. . . ."

Before Mr. Davis could reply came Lyons' third epistle: ". . . His is not the ordinary accusation of an unprincipled demagogue; for, although he is a demagogue . . . he has for years filled the high office of Speaker of the House of Representatives . . . and aspires to the Presidency . . . and before that House . . . he has dared to make his defamatory accusations, and thus secured for himself the world for an audience, and the nations as spectators of his reckless folly and injustice. Thomas, the dynamite destroyer . . . will not be more notorious hereafter than Blaine, the attempted assassin of the good name and reputation of one-half of the people of his own Country. . . ."

Davis' anxiety also was for the South; and on January 22nd he wrote to J. Proctor Knott, chairman of the Committee on Amnesty, urging that the passage of the General Amnesty bill should not be allowed to be endangered on account of "objection to including me in its provisions." "It may be proper to state," he added, "that I have no claim to pardon, not having in any wise repented, or changed the convictions on which my political course was founded, as well before, as during, and since the war between the states." This letter, among many, justifies the statement later made by James Redpath, after close personal contact with the man who had led the cause which Redpath himself had bitterly opposed from first to last: "He was true, all his life long, to the creed in which he has been reared, and hence it was impossible for him to 'repent or recant.' He could not repent of being honest, or recant what he believed to be the truth."

Knott replied to Davis, on January 27, 1876: "Such an exhibition of a chivalrous self-abnegation on your part . . . has . . . very greatly increased my reluctance to consent to the passage of any measure of amnesty from the benefits of which you are to be made the solitary exception. . . . Every intelligent mind in the country understands perfectly well that the objection to embracing you in the provisions of the bill . . . was intended merely to pander to the meanest passions of the rabble, and to furnish materials for the miserable scoundrelly demagogues in ensuing campaigns for the Presidency. . . . I think the bill will finally pass *including yourself*. . . ." In this, however, he was mistaken.

May, 1876, found Davis in New Orleans attending to business, but longing for leisure to work on his book. Such time as his business allowed him was largely devoted to furnishing information to other Southern leaders fortunate enough to be free to write their memoirs, or to prepare monographs upon various subjects which interested them. His board of directors had scheduled a meeting for May 29th, but before the day arrived he received word that it would take place in London. He therefore engaged passage upon the first available boat, for himself and his family. But even their presence, and the prospect of again seeing England and his loyal English friends, could not console him for the loss of time which might have been devoted to his book. And, on August 3rd, he wrote from London to Walthall, who was now associated with him in its preparation: "It would not be well for you to wait for my return before sending your correction, for several reasons, one of which is that the slow progress made in the business on which I came here, renders it doubtful how long it may be needful to remain in this country."

October found him still in London, but the end of the business which had brought him to England came soon after, and with it the end of the Company's hope of collecting millions to equip its fleets. He therefore prepared for his return, leaving his family in England to await his success in finding new employment.

What had happened is perhaps best told in a letter which he sent back to its president after reaching America, in which he wrote: ". . . When you invited me to accept the Presidency of the American Dept. [of the Mississippi Valley Society], and proposed a fixed salary with contingent emoluments, I could not have supposed that the parent society (in London) was without an assured revenue. . . . Had you earlier informed me that it had devolved on you, personally, to furnish funds for the current expenses of the society, and that pecuniary losses had rendered you unable to fulfil your undertaking, I should have ceased to hope for anything from the society and been better prepared to meet the disappointment which has been encountered."

## CHAPTER XXXI

# "BEAUVOIR" AND PEACE, AND CONFLICT

AT THIS point the proverb "The darkest hour is just before dawn" proved true. A childhood friend, Mrs. Sarah A. Dorsey, offered Mr. Davis the hospitality of her home at Biloxi, Mississippi. Always an ardent lover of the South, Mrs. Dorsey had been and remained an equally ardent follower of Mr. Davis; and, as a writer on a modest scale she was eager to help in his work of vindicating the South. She therefore volunteered to serve, in Mrs. Davis' absence, as his amanuensis and suggested that he invite to "Beauvoir" for conferences such of his friends and co-workers as were needed for the gathering of material.

Close upon this good fortune came news of another. The suit for "Brierfield" had been decided by the Chancery Court of Warren County, Mississippi, and the plantation awarded to Jefferson Davis. Upon examination of the mass of material which his lawyers had gathered, the court was convinced that since his first marriage, in 1835, the plantation had been almost universally regarded as his property. Joseph's direct heirs had taken an appeal to the Supreme Court of Mississippi, which had confirmed the verdict of the lower court, a triumph of justice, as a review of the evidence clearly shows. Even the hostile *Chicago Tribune*, although interpreting the case as another example of "Davis' base ingratitude," admitted that "the courts were compelled to decide in favour of Jefferson Davis because the law was plainly on his side."

Upon taking over "Brierfield," as undisputed master, Davis

found that it was still occupied by men, women, and children who had once acknowledged themselves his property, and who now as freedmen welcomed him as their ideal of a Southern gentleman whom, though free, they were still content to call master. His old relation with them had established an affection which neither civil war nor reconstruction had altered, and he heard with indignation their stories of rough treatment from Federal soldiers, many imaginary, no doubt, but fitting well into his own experience.

After arranging for the cultivation of the plantation through overseers and hired freedmen, as an absentee owner, Davis returned to "Beauvoir" determined to keep his book his first duty.

Another sign of the coming of better days was the news that, on April 3, 1877, President Hayes, counted, not elected, President, as the Democrats sullenly insisted, had withdrawn the Federal troops from South Carolina, and, a couple of weeks later from Louisiana, which meant that at last Reconstruction was over and the white man restored to his Constitutional rights. By a myriad of mistakes it had been proved again that the only sound government is government resting upon the consent of the governed. But in providing that, the radical Republicans had made the "Solid South." Democratic in overwhelming predominance, it was far more: it was a psychology, anti-Republican and bitterly anti-Republican, and it so remains to this day.

Soon Mrs. Dorsey's modest home became the Mecca to which flocked Confederate memorial societies, composed of white men again with votes; delegations from Lee memorial societies, Jackson bands, gallant Foresters, and Davis clubs, eager to pay their respects to their old chief. Their visits interfered with the progress of *The Rise and Fall of the Confederate Government*, but all were made welcome.

As the weeks passed, however, Davis, fearing that his strength would not prove equal to the magnitude of his task, planned for greater speed, and urged upon Walthall the need of more frequent and longer conferences. He sadly missed Mrs. Davis, who understood his needs and his methods of work better than Walthall or Mrs. Dorsey could ever understand them; but illness had long prevented her return from England, and her letters promised small chance of an early recovery.

In addition to this handicap, his work was constantly delayed by the continued attacks of his enemies, which had to be answered, and floods of documents rained in upon him from eager helpers. Benjamin sent from England copies of the original instructions which he had prepared for the delegates to the Hampton Roads conference, and the delegates themselves, Alexander H. Stephens, R. M. T. Hunter, and J. A. Campbell, prepared for him their personal recollections of what had occurred at the meeting with Lincoln and Seward. General J. A. Early reported "a letter from Governor Carroll, of Maryland . . . in which he says that shortly after the war, General Lee told him that if Longstreet had obeyed his orders and attacked, early instead of late, we should have gained the victory at Gettysburg."

The friends of General Joseph E. Johnston, seeking to deepen the impression which the latter's *Personal Narrative* had made, filled the Press with partisan praise, and their articles were sent to Davis by his followers, many of whom urged him to expose Johnston's fallacies, and "put him in his place," which, to their minds, could never be too low. Wiser friends urged him to steer clear of mere personal controversy, and to write as the voice of the South. "I trust you will not think me impertinent," wrote General Early, on September 22, 1877, "if I remind you that you are the representative of our cause, and caution you against the danger of entering into a mere personal controversy with General Johnston about the questions he has raised. . . . I know that your provocation is great, but a calm and lucid statement of facts, with dignified comment on the difficulties attending all the questions you were called upon to deal with, will have far greater weight . . . than bitter and sharp strictures on the querulousness of a subordinate who always seemed to think more of his own rank and position than of the public cause. . . ." And he sent, as his contribution, a memorandum of his own recollections, covering twenty large printed pages, which he had prepared for General Johnston, and which admirably followed the rules so ardently urged upon Mr. Davis.

General Johnston's book had declared that the failure of the Confederacy was traceable to the failure of Mr. Davis' Government to ship abroad the accumulated cotton of the South before the Northern blockade made shipment impossible. "The sum raised in that way," he argued, "would have enabled the War Department to procure at once arms enough for 500,000 men, and after that the Confederate Treasury would have been much richer than the United States." Davis and Walthall used every available witness in preparing an answer to this accusation, which they regarded as insincere and malicious. Among these witnesses was C. G. Memminger, Confederate Secretary of the Treasury from 1861 to 1864, who wrote on September 25, 1877, to explain that the reason why the Confederate Government had not bought up cotton at the opening of the war and exchanged it for arms before the ports were closed by blockade, was the fact that "we had no money to pay for arms, much less to buy cotton. . . . We had not in the Confederacy a sheet of Bank Note paper, and but one Bank Note engraver; and had first to establish a paper-mill at Richmond before we could even issue Bonds to raise money; and . . . such was the general opinion that there would be no war, that the first issue . . . was limited to one million of interest-bearing notes and the first loan to 15 millions, of which only two could be placed." This and other evidence establishes Davis' contention that his Government had gone as far in the direction of such a policy as reason could justify, or the resources of the Confederacy rendered possible.

Even criticisms, coming in the guise of material for the book, elicited rejoinders, often surprisingly patient. To E. L. Drake, who had suggested that he should have shown to the Confederate Congress the instructions given to the Hampton Roads delegates, he wrote: "One cognizant of the relations of the House of Representatives to the treaty-making power would justly be astonished if the Executive were to communicate to the House . . . the instructions given to commissioners." And he added, in reply to the criticism that the words "the two countries" had made negotiation with Lincoln impossible, that negotiation upon any basis but that of two countries would have been shameful surrender before conquest. "In shame and mortification," he added, "I would have resigned and left the office to be filled by some one fit for such service," rather than open negotiations on any basis but that of the recognition of two countries.

As the mass of material relating to any one subject reached what seemed adequate proof of the justice of the Southern position, Davis dictated his account to Mrs. Dorsey who in turn sent it on to Walthall for criticism, and the result was later considered at a joint conference.

Towards the end of November there arrived a substantial proof of the appreciation of those to whose defence Davis was devoting his energies. The Governor of Georgia wrote: "When some of your friends heard that in your business you had not been favoured with good fortune, they regarded it as affording them a cherished opportunity to repay to you some measure of that debt which they, in common with all of our Southern countrymen, owe you, and which, whatever they may be allowed to do, can never be adequately discharged. . . . Others beg the same privilege and it may be my pleasure to transmit to you further evidence, of a similar character, of the grateful affection in which you are held by your devoted countrymen of the South. . . ." Enclosed was a cheque for $1,000. Davis accepted this gift as a contribution to the cost of producing the book, but upon the Governor's letter, before it was filed, he wrote the words: "Would have asked to have it checked, as I did on former occasions, if I had known of the movement . . . requested that the further remittance mentioned should not be made. Approval of my countrymen the all-sufficient compensation for anything I have done and suffered. . . ."

The sincerity of this statement will hardly be questioned in view of his attitude towards another movement, then in progress, by which his friends hoped to relieve his necessities without offence to his pride. A bill was pending in Congress to grant Federal pensions to the veterans of the Mexican War, and as it stood it would, if passed, have included Davis. Realizing this fact, his enemies denounced the bill and threatened to defeat it. Therefore, on February 17th, Davis dispatched the following letter to one of its champions, the Hon. O. R. Singleton:

"My Dear Friend:

"In the published proceedings of the 14th inst. I observe that a member of the House (Mr. Powers, of Maine) is reported to have used the following language—He 'is also opposed to opening the door for the pensioning of all, including Jeff Davis, who had been in the Mexican War, but had afterwards participated in the Rebellion.'

"As this portends opposition to any measure granting pensions to soldiers in the war with Mexico, which should include me, I wish, in the event of the fate of the bill depending upon my exclusion from its benefits, that you, or one of your colleagues, if you should be absent, would request the friends of the measure silently to allow the malignants to impose upon it the condition of my exclusion from the benefit of its provisions. For this purpose I will write a more formal letter appended to this, to be used in the contingency described above. If Mrs. Singleton or either of your children is with you, please present them my kindest remembrance and believe me to be yours faithfully,

"JEFFERSON DAVIS.

"Hon. O. R. Singleton.

"P. S. It was said the 'Mexican veterans are mostly in the prime of life yet.' Add 30 years to mature manhood and you have the average age; but many, myself included, are on the verge of the limit allotted to man. As to 'the Rebellion' I left the Ho. of Reps. at the call of Mississippi and joined the Regt. which had elected me, when it was engaged in Mexico; at the expiration of their term of service I returned, on crutches, with them. At a later period, I left the Senate, at the call of Mississippi. In the one case as in the other, I served my sovereign and perilled my life, in obedience to her mandate. If sovereigns can rebel, then I may have 'participated in' a 'Rebellion.'

"J. D."

When the bill came to its final reading, a year later, it contained the clause, added upon motion of Mr. Hoar of Massachusetts: "Provided further, that no pension shall ever be paid under this act to Jefferson Davis, the late President of the so-called Confederacy." After a fierce debate, in which the returned Southerners gallantly defended Davis, while Blaine and others bitterly attacked him, the vote was taken. Hoar's exclusion passed, but only by one vote, 23 to 22. Public opinion was evidently changing so far as Davis was concerned.

Mrs. Davis, meanwhile, having recovered her health, had crossed the ocean, only to find herself compelled to remain at Memphis. On January 6, 1878, she wrote to Walthall: "My daughter's health is so precarious that I do not feel it quite safe to leave her here alone, so I cannot say at what time I will join my husband. . . . The separation from him is a sad disappointment. . . ." To Mr. Davis it was equally disappointing, for Mrs. Davis combined in a rare degree the qualities of sympathetic companion and efficient aid; and he felt increasingly the need of both, as documents multiplied on his hands and he struggled, day by day, to organize them and work them into his narrative.

"Mrs. Davis is now in Memphis," he wrote to Wright on April 18th, in answer to a request for information concerning the details of his capture, "and I have not the advantage of availing myself of her recollection of events. So . . . I can only give you at this time my own recollections, to be filled out as soon as may be with what I may learn from her."

The bitter attacks which Blaine and Garfield had made upon Davis in the Congressional debates over amnesty had caused many speeches and articles to be written in his defence, and many of these were sent to him for approval and praise. He gladly returned both, when the author seemed to him fair upon the main issues of the contest; but the slightest concession to the enemy called forth instant rebuke. On May 21, 1878, for example, he wrote to Congressman Chalmers: "You could not mean that Confederates had committed treason, or that any comparison could be drawn between your brave comrades, dead and living, and the knaves who robbed the people of the fruits of their election [of Tilden, in 1876] . . . Mr. Hayes continues to shield and to reward the knaves who secured for him an office to which he was not chosen. . . . Mr. Lincoln attempted to rob the people of the South of property which the Constitution guaranteed, and which he by his oath of office was bound to protect. . . ." He showed also that his views upon the effects of emancipation had not changed, by virtue of observations upon the state of free negroes. "You term it [emancipation] an act of humanity to the blacks. Would it not have been better to treat it as it was, an act of cruelty to the blacks, of robbery of the whites, in violation of his duty, for the purpose of enslaving men who were born free and who had proved themselves fit to govern? I write to you with the freedom born of cordial love and respect, and from a desire to see you shun the way which has always led ambitious Southerners to the husks of empty applause by those who receive demonstrations of fraternity on our part with such joy as the trapper feels when he finds the trail of the beaver is towards his trap. If the victorious North wish peace and forgetfulness, let them so speak and act; it better becomes the strong than the weak, the conqueror than the conquered, to promise peace and brotherly love. . . ."

Davis had been accused at the time of his inauguration of being a "reconstructionist"; but this letter, like many others, shows him still unreconstructed. Mistakes he admitted, frankly and often, but never crime: for to him still the cause which he had led was sacred. He often lamented the sad condition of the freedmen, also; but there appears no sentence expressing regret for the loss of what he had so long defended as slave property.

It was this steadfastness which caused many Southerners, who had opposed him as leader, or who had followed afar off, to rally to him now, and brought from his consistently loyal friends renewed expressions of affection. Congressman Chalmers' reply to Davis' rebuke was this: "I feel great pride in your interest . . . and recognize your right to speak freely to me of my faults." F. Stringfellow wrote, "So far as the love of your own people is concerned, you are more beloved today than if you had carried our victorious banners through every Northern state." But none reached the height which Walthall had attained in a letter to General Early: "If one hundred Southern men would unite with me, I would rob my family and defraud my creditors to a sufficient extent to remove his embarrassments and supply his needs—at least for the time—and my conscience would vindicate it as an eminently pious fraud."

In May, 1878, Mrs. Davis arrived at "Beauvoir," her daughter's recovery making it possible at last for her to take part in the work which absorbed her husband, Walthall and Mrs. Dorsey so completely. On the 28th she wrote to Miss Mason, a friend in Paris: "We may be, I suppose, considered settled here for a long time to come, as Mr. Davis has his material here for his work, and the climate agrees with him. We board with her [Mrs. Dorsey], and there is no one else in the house. She has a charming temper and makes us very comfortable, and she thus secures companionship when otherwise she would be alone. I am very fond of her but do not like the climate. . . . We have won back 'Brierfield,' but no money with it."

Mrs. Davis took over the heavy work of amanuensis to Mr. Davis, but Mrs. Dorsey continued her interest, and sympathy, and Walthall his invaluable aid. One story which was now run to earth was to the effect that L. Q. Lamar, whom Davis had sent on a secret mission to Russia in 1862, had later written a memorandum declaring that the Confederacy would have been recognized by European powers but for the fact that its President belonged to the repudiating state of Mississippi. To Walthall, who wrote to ask him about this document, Lamar replied, on June 29, 1878: "Nothing has ever fallen from my lips or pen which, either directly or indirectly, charged ex-President Davis with participation in what is popularly known as the repudiation acts of Mississippi, nor have I ever, either publicly or privately, attributed to him any act or thought that was not great and heroic."

Almost all of the records and documents which remain from these early days at "Beauvoir" relate to the work upon his book. Only very occasionally did Davis allow himself to be diverted for a visit or an address: and such addresses always stressed the right of secession, and the justice of the Confederate cause, while at times referring disparagingly to the Federal Government. On July 10, 1878, for example, in addressing the Army of Tennessee, whose members had presented him with a badge of membership, he declared that, while rejoicing that the Federal troops had at last been withdrawn from the South, he could not praise the man who had removed them. He regarded President Hayes as "an usurper, never lawfully chosen President. . . ." Such utterances he considered as within his rights as an American, even though an American without recognized citizenship, and indignantly repudiated the accusation that he was "seeking to disturb such peace as we have, or to avoid the logic of events."

The autumn of 1878 found Mr. Davis' health far from satisfactory; but his application to his task was not lessened, although it was made more difficult by the fact that an epidemic of yellow fever had called Walthall to Memphis, where he devoted himself heroically to the work of nursing. Towards the end of September the fever invaded Mississippi City: but still the work went on. On September 29th Mr. Davis wrote to his bishop—W. M. Green: "We are surrounded here by the dread scourge, which has this season desolated our land. Our children near Memphis are in like condition; but a merciful Providence has thus far spared us. We ask your prayers for further safety"; and a week later to J. C. Derby: "The noble generosity of the Northern people in this day of our extreme affliction has been felt with deep gratitude and has done more for the fraternization of which many idly prate, than would many volumes of rhetorical assurance." The latter letter deals, however, chiefly with the search for records, and, for the remainder of the year, his correspondence concerns almost exclusively the same.

Walthall returned early in October and was soon sent to Washington in the hope that he might be allowed to study the Confederate records there. At first he met with discouraging delays but, on December 3rd, reported that he had gained "admission to the archives for examination of such papers as I may wish to see." Incidentally, he reported that "the Government of the United States has purchased Col. W. P. Johnston's papers for $10,000, and is now treating with Mrs. Bragg and Dr. Polk (through W. P. J.) for the papers of Generals Bragg and Polk, respectively. Yours," he added, "are far more valuable than all the others together . . . but I hope you will not sacrifice any part of the full and perpetual control of them. . . ." But he knew, as he wrote, that there was no danger that gold would ever tempt Davis to part with any of the records in his possession.

The opening of 1879, his seventieth year, found Davis still at "Beauvoir," working, but with a heavy heart. His last surviving son, Jefferson Davis, Jr., had recently died of yellow fever, and the elder of his two daughters was ill in Memphis. On January 19th he wrote to Northrop: "Truly, as you write, our troubles thicken as the end approaches."

Davis' friends had long urged him to request pardon as Lee had done, but he had refused. On March 8, 1878, James Lyons wrote an account of his own experiences, meant to show Davis how easily pardon could be obtained: "When I went to Washington to receive my pardon . . . President Johnson . . . said, 'Well, Mr. Lyons, what have you done which requires a pardon?' 'Nothing, sir,' I replied. 'I was a Secessionist, but I do not regret it, and have no apology to offer.' 'Is that all?' he said, and signed the pardon. And when talking with Chief Justice Chase in my house in relation to your trial I said to him, 'The evidence upon which I shall rely for defence of Mr. Davis—for his justification—will be your message to the legislature of Ohio . . . declaring that if the Government of the United States attempted to coerce Ohio you would bring into the field to meet her the whole military force of the state." Lyons' meaning was clearly that Mr. Davis, who had made so many sacrifices for the South, should make one more; for he hoped, in common with many other Southerners, that Davis would regain his lost citizenship and return to national politics. "We want him in the Senate," he told Walthall, on March 28, 1879, "where he cannot be slandered by cowardly liars, and we through him." Once there, he added, "he would even treat Zac Chandler as a gentleman, or treat Hayes as if he was an honest and lawful President." But Davis indulged no such visions. Done with politics, his only anxiety was to finish his book, and prove that he had kept the faith.

Mrs. Davis, with a devotion to the cause almost as great as his own, had become his literary other self. Walthall still gathered documents for him, but Mrs. Dorsey, by reason of failing health, was now compelled to confine her efforts to encouragement. Her enthusiasm, however, had not failed and, as we now know, she had already formed, in secret, a plan to make easy and certain the completion of the task.

General Early, in one of the letters recently purchased by the Library of Congress, describes a visit to "Beauvoir" made during the Christmas holidays of 1877: "I had a very full conversation with Mrs. Dorsey about Mr. Davis' condition, when she informed me of her intention to leave her estate to Mr. Davis. When I commenced speaking to her on the subject of Mr. Davis' condition, it was on her front porch, and she asked me to walk out on the beach where we could talk without being overheard by Mr. Davis, as she said he would not allow anything to be done for him if it came to his knowledge. There was much conversation between us, all going to rebut the idea that Mr. Davis was attempting to influence her in any way. This was less than ten days before the date of her will, and she asked General Joe Davis, in my presence, if by the laws of Louisiana an autograph will require witnesses—which showed that she understood the importance of the step she contemplated."

There is good reason for the opinion which Walthall expressed to Early, soon after this conversation, that Mrs. Dorsey deserved to be remembered by the South as one of the heroines of the Lost Cause; for she knew that scandalous tongues had already placed cruel interpretations upon her kindness to Davis, and that the announcement of her bequest, when made, would be cited to confirm the slanders. But she never faltered, nor did the faintest hint of her intention reach Davis until after her death on July 4, 1879. And the letter in which he conveyed the news to Walthall is sufficient to confute all scandalmongers, and should have shamed into silence the equally unfair critics who, when the will was read, whispered of undue influence.

"New Orleans
*4th July, 1879.*

"MAJ. W. T. WALTHALL.

"My dear Friend:

"The dreaded event has occurred. Mrs. Dorsey ceased to breathe about 4 o'clock A.M. She was known to be dying early in the night. With laboured breathing but otherwise painlessly she passed the night. She had been for some days expecting death, was resigned, calm, and hopeful. She said she was at peace with the world, and feared not to meet her God. She took the communion and hopefully looked beyond this life to a better state. She was pleased to receive your message and sent loving remembrance to your family and [your]self.

"After she was unable to converse, her mind remained entirely clear and composed. In repeating to her the beatitude, 'Blessed are the pure in heart, for they shall see God,' she responded by repeated motion of the head.

"You know more than most others how self-sacrificing she was, how noble in sentiment, how grand in intellect, but you cannot know how deeply grateful I am to her for years of unvarying kindness and service, and therefore cannot realize how sorrowfully I feel her loss.

"We leave tomorrow evening on the packet for Natchez; after the interment I shall return without delay.

"You will, I know, regard it as a labour of love, and it will also be a favour to me, if you will write an obituary notice for the *Sea Shore Gazette* and for any other papers you may choose.

"Please give my cordial regards to each of your household and believe me

"Faithfully
"JEFFERSON DAVIS."

The words of her will, when it was read to him, must have been as the words of a benediction, not on account of its bequest, but because it breathed complete confidence in him, and love for the cause which he had led: "I owe no obligation of any sort whatever to any relative of my own. I have done all I could for them. . . . I therefore give and bequeath all my property, real, personal, and mixed, wherever located and situated, wholly and entirely, without hindrance or qualification, to my most honoured and esteemed friend, Jefferson Davis, ex-President of the Confederate States, for his own sole use and benefit, in fee simple, for ever; and I hereby constitute him my sole heir, executor, and administrator. If Jefferson Davis should not survive me, I give all that I have bequeathed him to his youngest daughter, Varina. I do not intend to share in the ingratitude of my country towards the man who is in my eyes the highest and noblest in existence."

There was an outcry from certain expectant relatives, none of them very close, who had hoped to inherit Mrs. Dorsey's estate: but others, knowing of the childhood friendship renewed in age, were content; and one of the latter generously offered to take up the work to which her cousin had been so devoted. The following letter is Davis' reply:

"Beauvoir P. O. Miss.
*5th Sept. 1879.*

"My dear Mrs. Ferguson,

"Please accept my sincere thanks for your kind and very welcome letter. In your generous wishes and self-sacrificing desire to serve others, I see the traits that characterized your noble cousin, whose recent death is to me an unending sorrow. You will I am sure be gratified to learn some of the particulars of her last illness. Too stoical to complain, too brave to fear death, she suffered more pain than could be known to those round, save by the expression of her face and the wasting of her form. Her mind remained clear and the near approach of death was calmly confronted. She received the communion with a few devoted friends, and to the last seemed more anxious for those who loved her, than for herself. After she was unable to speak, she would indicate her approval of, or dissent from, what was said to her by signs, e.g., when all hope was lost of recovery, I repeated to her the beatitude 'Blessed are the pure in heart, for they shall see God.' She nodded her head several times, to mark her hope and consolation from the promise. In the constellation of your gifted family, your cousin Sarah is entitled to rank as a star of the first magnitude; but her earnest desire to benefit her race, her noble soul in which there was neither hatred nor malice, her devotion to truth, and sublime patience under injury, were the brightest jewels in her crown. Her friends, her fellow-beings, have lost much, but I rest assured that to her, 'to die was gain,' that He who knows the hearts of men will give her a reward, which this world could not bestow. Intellectual triumphs & domestic bereavement checkered her career with light and shadow, but over the whole shone the halo of a life spent in efforts to do good. . . .

"The expenses of Mrs. Dorsey's last illness were a heavy draft on her small revenue, and my own means are not large; but from such resources as I have, it is my purpose to repair and beautify the home she loved, and it will be a pleasure to me to show you the improvements made and contemplated when you next visit the sea shore. . . .

"Many thanks for your kind willingness to aid me in writing, as your dear cousin did; I readily appreciate the difference in circumstance, and entirely concur with you in placing the obligation of a Wife and Mother supreme in the list of her duties. . . . Present my affectionate regards and best wishes to your Husband and children and believe me most respectfully and cordially yours,

"Jefferson Davis."

On November 1st he wrote to Northrop, "The oranges are shining on the trees, and our pine-knot fires soar in the chimneys; in their light I try to bury my unhappiness."

On December 20th Northrop wrote: "I was sorry to see in the paper yesterday a statement that Mrs. Dorsey's will is to be assailed. I thought the statement of Mr. Farrar conclusive. You were bound to maintain that will. I hope it will not worry or occupy you too much." After a bitter contest, the Court of first instance, the Circuit Court of the United States for the District of Louisiana, dismissed the bill on demurrer, and the Supreme Court, upon appeal, sustained the earlier verdict, leaving Davis in full possession of the benefits bequeathed him, which amounted, including the house, to about $10,000. The final decision was made public in the following announcement:

"In the Supreme Court today the case of Stephen Percy Ellis and others, Appellants, against Jefferson Davis, came up on appeal from the Circuit Court of the United States for the District of Louisiana. This was a suit in equity brought by the next of kin and collateral heirs of the late Sarah Ann Dorsey, of Mississippi, for the purpose of having set aside as void and of no effect a will whereby the said Sarah Ann Dorsey bequeathed all her real and personal property to her agent and confidential adviser, Jefferson Davis. It is maintained by the complainants that the relief sought should be granted for the reasons that the testatrix at the time the will was drawn and signed was not of sound mind, and that she was unduly influenced.

"In the court below the bill of complaint was dismissed on demurrer. This Court holds that the action of the Circuit Court in dismissing the bill was right, for the reason that the claim of Mrs. Dorsey's collateral heirs was properly the subject of an action of revendication, which furnishes a plain, adequate and complete remedy at law, and therefore constituted a bar to proceedings in equity. The decree of the Circuit Court is affirmed, with costs."

"Beauvoir," the chief item in this unexpected inheritance, was described by a visiting journalist of the time, as: "Pleasantly situated on the beach in the midst of a grove of magnolia, live oak, beech, cypress, cedar, pine and other native trees . . . its wide halls, spacious verandas and elevation above the ground show it to be a true type of Southern plantation residence. . . . Nothing costly and grand met our eye, but the neatness, cleanness, taste, and good housekeeping were apparent in every room and department." Here Davis with his two remaining assistants, Walthall and Mrs. Davis, continued for several months longer to work on *The Rise and Fall of the Confederate Government*, the completion of which Mrs. Davis thus describes: "After three years from the commencement of the book, it was finished. . . . Mr. Davis dictated, 'In asserting the right of secession it has not been my wish to incite to its exercise. I recognize the fact that the war showed it to be impracticable, but this did not prove it to be wrong.'" After writing what he had dictated, Mrs. Davis "looked up . . . to remind him that he had forgotten to continue." With a smile he answered, "I think I am done."

Davis' book would have been a more valuable contribution had he followed the advice which General Lee had given to Early when the latter contemplated the preparation of a Memoir: "I would recommend . . . that, while giving the facts which you think necessary for your own vindication, you omit all epithets or remarks calculated to excite bitterness or animosity between the different sections of the country." *The Rise and Fall of the Confederate Government* is far removed from such an ideal, for, as Davis himself frankly declared at New Orleans, about a year after its publication, its aim was defence, not history: "The other side has written and is writing their statement of the case. We wish to present ours also, that the future historian by considering both may deduce the unbiased statement which no contemporary could make. . . . I would distrust the man who served the Confederate cause and was capable of giving a disinterested account of it. If he had any heart it must be on his own side. I would not give two pence for a man whose heart was so cold that he could be quite impartial. You remember the fable of the lion who, seeing a statue which represented a lion prostrate, and a man victorious, bending over him, said that if a lion had made the statue, the figures would have been reversed. We want our side of the war so fully and exactly stated, that the men who come after us may compare and do justice in the case."

Much the same may be said of Nicolay and Hay, who were, at the same time, gathering material for their monumental *Life of Abraham Lincoln*; for it too is less history than a case of special pleading. Upon the surface, these two gifted authors appeared, as Davis never sought to appear, to preserve that detachment and ruthless impartiality which the word history connotes; but in their conversations and correspondence with one another they made no pretence of impartiality. "We are Lincoln men all through," wrote Hay to Nicolay on August 10, 1885. And a little later: "If you can see your way to soften your tone towards Old Jeff—though I don't suppose you can—it would be politic. Let the facts make him as despicable as he is—*we* do not want to appear to hate and despise him." Lincoln, as Rhodes says, they made "a saint," a rôle which, had he lived to see it played, would certainly have called forth droll comments. Lucian had in mind the temptations to which they yielded when he wrote: "A writer of history ought in his *writings* to be a foreigner, without country, living under his own law only, subject to no king, nor caring what any man will like or dislike, but laying out the matter as it is."

There still persists in the firm of Appleton, which published Davis' two volumes, a tradition that they were "ghost written": but this is not true if by the term is meant written by one man and signed by another. Davis gathered his material from hundreds of men and thousands of documents, but when gathered, interpreted it in a book distinctly his own creation. His are its virtues, his its faults.

When *The Rise and Fall of the Confederate Government* was at last in the hands of the reviewers, Mr. Davis waited to learn by experience the meaning of Job's words: "O! . . . that mine adversary had written a book." He expected controversy from the North, had indeed invited it: but the first reports from friends in what he still considered the enemy country proved disappointing. On September 6, 1881, W. N. Pendleton wrote: "In *Appleton's Review*, I have noticed extracts from some English publications justly and highly commending your great contribution to reliable history, but rarely has been published, so far as I know, any mention of your work, even in professedly Democratic papers at the North." On December 1st, C. J. Wright reported from Chicago, "I hear little of it here."

From the South came much uncritical approval, but this was of only passing interest. He had not written to please the South, but to convince the world of the justice of her cause, and apparently his proofs were being passed over in contemptuous silence. But when the leading Eastern periodicals began to arrive they contained criticism enough to satisfy the most exacting author. The *Nation* complained of the lack of light upon the inner history of what it called the conspiracy for precipitating the rebellion, and was dissatisfied because Davis had not recognized that success had proved that "the prima facia rights" were with his opponents. It was outraged at the discovery that he still insisted that slavery, with him a political, not a moral, question, had been injected into the contest, and that "absolute centralization" had been the real issue. The *Atlantic Monthly* pronounced the work well done, from the standpoint of a mind that remembers nothing and learns nothing, the type that refuses to recognize the fact that secession is not a Constitutional term. In its opinion, the author had but proved that responsibility for the "rebellion" rested upon the leaders, of whom he himself was chief.

Such general comments, and they now came in a deluge, seemed to Davis poor answers to his carefully documented argument.

But a new kind of controversy was on the way. On the 18th, the *Philadelphia Press* published what purported to be an interview with General Joseph E. Johnston, furnished by Frank A. Burr, charging Davis with having failed to account for some two and a half million dollars in gold belonging to the Confederacy. Whatever the justification which Johnston had given Burr, the interview, when seen in cold print, with its monstrous insinuation, caused the former, on December 20th, to send the editor the following guarded repudiation:

"To the Editor of the Philadelphia Press.

"Dear Sir:

"I was greatly annoyed by reading the article in your paper of the 18th inst. headed 'General Johnston's Narrative' and signed 'F. A. B.' This article is evidently based on a conversation which I did not take to be an interview. In that conversation, therefore, a good deal was said which nothing could induce me to say for publication, notably what relates to Confederate treasure at Greensboro. Beside this, the narrative is inaccurate, so much so that I will not undertake to correct it, and it contains letters which not only did not come from me, but which have not been in my possession for years. So I beg you to publish this to relieve me of responsibility for the narrative.

"Most respectfully yours,

"J. E. JOHNSTON.

"Washington, December 20, 1881."

The *Press* published this disclaimer, not of the accusation, but of the intention to give it out as a newspaper interview. But Mr. Davis' friends had no idea of allowing such a quibble to pass. "Joe Johnston has been the first of your bitter opponents who has dared to couple theft with your honest name," wrote Thomas F. Drayton on December 22nd, "and I can account for the bitterness of this attack upon you in no other way than by assuming that Joe has gone mad in his old age. One word, more, Jeff; don't forget that you are the most conspicuous figure of our Lost

Cause who survives; so be careful not to indulge in harsh recrimination in any reply that you may feel called upon to lay before your friends and countrymen; for in doing so, you will be treading in the footprints of your denouncer, whose crazy attack upon *you* must not be repeated upon *him*!!! Our Lord, when he was reviled, reviled not again."

M. H. Clark, who, as Confederate Treasurer, was thoroughly informed upon the subject, wrote on December 23rd, "You have no doubt had sent you from various quarters newspapers containing an account of an interview . . . with General J. E. Johnston, in which the latter gives utterance to slanderous insinuations in regard to your connexion with the Confederate Treasury matters. As, while you were in Europe, I was asked to nail the Yankee lie to the counter, I have taken the liberty to enclose you the article copied from the *Nashville American*.

"As I was the last Confederate Treasurer and disbursed the specie assets of the Treasury, taking receipts from all, I felt authorized to speak, for I alone can now speak with authority upon that subject, giving exact facts, and should you find it necessary to notice the attack, your last Treasurer can give his report." To this letter Davis sent an affectionate answer and waited to see whether it would become necessary to reply to his enemy. But he did not have to reply, as the testimony of officers who had taken part in the final distribution of the Confederate funds soon made it evident that Johnston's equivocal denial had served him not at all. The facts as they emerged caused Mr. Davis' friends and many who had been enemies to re-echo the words of J. Stoddard Johnston, that General Johnston has been "willing to smirch you without having it authoritatively reported." "Poor Johnston has ruined himself at last," wrote Benj. H. Hill, on December 27th, "unless he can save his character by a retreat. If he can do anything at all, he can retreat, though I think even that oft-practiced habit will fail him this time. . . . The whole Southern people are your defenders, and the calumny has only served to show once more how devotedly they love you. . . ."

Hill's confident prediction, that Johnston would find no possible avenue of retreat, was based upon a letter received from Burr, who had published the interview in dispute: "I am, of course, more than pleased that the effort to impeach the accuracy of my work and to charge a breach of faith on my part has utterly failed. . . . My letter was a very temperate review of what passed between General Johnston and myself. I spent the greater part of two afternoons with him in his room, and dictated, immediately after each talk, the notes of it to my stenographer, and no man living knew better than General Johnston that they were to be given to the public."

On April 25, 1882, Davis appeared at the French Opera House in New Orleans to plead for public support for the Southern Historical Society. There, despite past suffering and present financial difficulties, he boldly declared: "Our cause was so just, so sacred, that had I known all that has come to pass, had I known what was to be inflicted upon me, all that my country was to suffer, all that our posterity was to endure, I would do it over again."

While the discussion over Johnston's attack was still raging, Davis accepted an invitation to speak at Lexington, Virginia, at the laying of the corner-stone of one of the many monuments to Lee; but when informed that Johnston would also speak, he declared, "That fact . . . causes me . . . to withdraw my consent." And, despite much pressure brought to bear upon him, he persisted in his refusal. John W. Daniel was therefore asked to make the chief address, and at the casual mention of Davis' name there followed a "spontaneous and seemingly irresistible" outburst of applause.

Davis' financial problems had been simplified, but by no means solved, by the restoration of "Brierfield," and the confirmation of Mrs. Dorsey's generous, but not large, bequest. "He is not dependent," wrote William Preston Johnston, on October 11, 1883, "but he has not the means, I think, to live with any display or abounding hospitality." The latter, however, was difficult to avoid, as his friends flocked to him, each with some valid claim to the best that he could offer. But he economized in such ways as he considered consistent with dignity and the tradition of open house which has always characterized the South. To the owner of a fine collie which he very much desired, he wrote: "My preference is for pure black-and-tan. The principal objection, however, is to the price, which seems to me, my plantation being threatened by overflow, to be like the river, too high for me."

He was also often called upon to make gifts to namesakes, who were numerous, or to write letters to the children of admirers, as they reached critical periods of life. In one of the best of the latter class, written on December 8, 1883, he expressed his whole philosophy of life:

"My dear young friend,

"You are entering on life's troubles while our country is in a transition state. Providence, for some inscrutable end, has permitted the overthrow of an old civilization and devolved upon the rising generation the task of developing a new system. Virtue will sooner or later overcome vice, and intelligence gain the mastery over ignorance. Get wisdom, let all your aims be moral, and your guide be God's laws as revealed in His holy word, so shall your life be useful and honourable, and however the world may ill-treat you, an approving conscience will sustain you here, and a reward be yours in the life eternal, compared to which the world's honours are but dust in the balance.

"Faithfully,
"JEFFERSON DAVIS."

Early in the following November General Sherman announced that he had seen a letter, written during the war, in which Davis had threatened to turn Lee's army against any Confederate State which might attempt to secede. As this touched the very essence of Davis' political theory, and made him deny state sovereignty, his indignation was great and just, and his answer unequivocal:

"Beauvoir, Mississippi, *November 6, 1884.*

"EDITOR St. Louis Republican:

"Dear Sir—I have tonight received the enclosed published account of remarks made by General W. T. Sherman, and ask the use of your columns to notice only so much as particularly refers to myself, and which is to be found in the following extracts:

"The following is taken from the *St. Louis Republican*:

" 'Frank P. Blair Post G.A.R. opened their new hall, corner Seventeenth and Olive Streets, last night.

" 'General Sherman addressed the assemblage. He had read letters which he believed had never been published, and which very few people had seen. These letters showed the rebellion to be more than a secession—it was a conspiracy most dire. Letters which had passed between Jeff Davis and a man whose name it would not do to mention, as he is now a member of the United States Senate, had been seen by the speaker and showed Davis' position. He was not a secessionist. His object in starting the rebellion was not merely for the secession of the South, but to have this section of the country so that he could use it as a fulcrum from which to fire out his shot at the other sections of the country and compel the people to do as he would have them. Jeff Davis would have turned his hand against any state that would secede from the South after the South had seceded from the North. Had the rebellion succeeded, General Sherman said, the people of the North would have all been slaves.'

"The following is from the *Globe Democrat's* report:

" 'Referring to the late war, he [Sherman] said it was not, as was generally understood, a war of secession from the United States, but a conspiracy. "I have been behind the curtain," said he, "and I have seen letters that few others have seen, and I have heard conversations that cannot be repeated, and I tell you that Jeff Davis never was a secessionist. He was a conspirator. He did not care for separation from the United States. His object was to get a fulcrum from which to operate against the United States, and if he had succeeded he would today be the master spirit of the continent and you would be slaves. I have seen a letter from Jefferson Davis to a man whose name I cannot mention, because he is a United States Senator. I know Davis' writing and saw his signature, and in that letter he said he would turn Lee's army against any state that might attempt to secede from the Southern Confederacy." '

"This public assault, under the covert plea that it be based upon evidence which regard for a United States Senator does not permit him to present, will, to honourable minds, suggest the idea of irresponsible slander.

"It thus devolves upon me to say that the allegation of my ever having written such a letter as is described is unqualifiedly false, and the assertion that I had any purpose or wish to destroy the liberty and equal rights of any State, either North or South, is a reckless, shameless falsehood, especially because it was generally known that for many years before, as well as during the war between the States, I was an earnest advocate of the strict construction State-rights theory of Mr. Jefferson. What motive other than personal malignity can be conceived for so gross a libel?

"If General Sherman has access to any letters purporting to have been written by me which will sustain his accusations, let him produce them, or wear the brand of a base slanderer.

"Yours respectfully,

"JEFFERSON DAVIS."

Sherman replied through the Press: "This is an affair between two gentlemen. . . . We will settle it between us. . . . My reply to Mr. Davis will not be through the newspapers. They are not

Jefferson Davis at Seventy-five

Portrait furnished by Dr. Dunbar Rowland, of Jackson, Mississippi

the . . . go-betweens for any dispute. I have nothing more to say." He did, however, say a great deal more, but he never said where he had seen the letter. "His reiterations, even a thousand times," said Davis, "will fail to convince any reasonable man that he had seen any letter in which I threatened to use the army against any state of the Confederacy."

The affair had now reached a point at which an interested public eagerly watched to see what Sherman would do, and on December 10, 1884, Davis received from H. C. Michie, of Charlottesville, Virginia, the following offer: "I would consider it the greatest honour to be permitted to act for you, in any capacity you may name, if he, the great incendiary of the late war, attempts to execute his contemptible threat." Fortunately, the matter got no farther; but Davis filed away Michie's letter, with the memorandum, "H. C. Michie of Va. offers to act as my second *vs.* Sherman."

Davis' denials, however, had not stopped the slander. Senator John Sherman reiterated his brother's charge on the floor of the Senate, to which Davis replied in a letter of September 23, 1886: "The epithets which Senator Sherman in debate applied to myself are his mode of retaliation for my denunciation of his brother. I have been compelled to prove General Sherman to be a falsifier and a slanderer in order to protect my character and reputation from his wilful and unscrupulous mendacity. If his brother, the Senator, felt the sting of that exposure, and his epithets are any relief, I am content that he shall go on the record as denouncing me as a 'traitor' because I have proved his brother to be a liar. As the Republican party renounced the issue of treason when it abandoned my trial in 1867, not at my instance, but in face of my defiance, its leaders of the present day but stultify themselves in the cry of traitor which they raise at the mention of my name."

So far as General Sherman was concerned, Davis dismissed him with the words, "He stands pilloried before the public and all future history as an imbecile scold, or an infamous slanderer—as either he is harmless."

Northrop later told Davis that he had shown his wife one of these replies to the Sherman slander, and that she had read it with the remark, "What a terrible letter, and he has such a sweet face."

## CHAPTER XXXII

# "BY REASON OF STRENGTH"

BEFORE the bitterness of his conflict with Sherman had subsided, Davis learned that General Grant, who had long been ill, would soon join the great majority. He recalled the fact that as a man Grant had shown great consideration, both for Mrs. Davis and for himself; and that, while ruthless as a general in the field, had as President displayed a desire for fair treatment to the conquered South. When, therefore, the Boston *Globe* sent a reporter to "Beauvoir" to ask for an interview on the subject of Grant's career, Davis refused upon the following grounds:

"1. General Grant is dying.

"2. Though he invaded our country ruthlessly, it was with open hand, and, as far as I know, he abetted neither arson nor pillage, and has, since the war, I believe, shown no malignity to Confederates, either in the military or civil service.

"Therefore, instead of seeking to disturb the quiet of his closing hours, I would, if it were in my power, contribute to the peace of his mind and the comfort of his body."

The editor hastened to explain that he had no idea of any criticism of Grant, or of "publishing your view of him while he is lying in his present condition, agreeing fully with you, that it would be unkind and ungenerous." His aim, he said, was only to prepare an article to be used after Grant's death. Davis, however, still refused to contribute.

Grant's illness caused many Southern editors to search their files for material relating to the passing soldier and statesman, and on April 3, 1885, Charles Herbst enclosed to Davis an editorial clipped from the *Telegraph and Messenger* of Macon, Georgia, and written by the editor, Albert Lamar, which ran as follows: "As these lines are written, General Grant may be dead. . . . A life emblazoned with great enterprises has no blur upon its escutcheon. Jefferson Davis . . . must soon follow. It will not be forgotten that Jefferson Davis, as Secretary of War, saved Grant, a sub-lieutenant, from lasting disgrace by permitting him to resign in the face of a court martial. If the North expects the South to weep for Grant, may not the South expect the North to dismiss its malignity at the side of an open grave and treat Jefferson Davis, the United States officer, the United States Senator, and once the Secretary of War, with becoming respect?" This also failed to draw from Davis any comment upon his great antagonist.

On July 23, after an heroic and successful struggle to finish his *Memoirs*, and thus furnish a source of revenue for his wife, who was ill-provided for, Grant died on Mount McGregor, and, six weeks later, George H. Coursen wrote to secure from Davis a confirmation, or denial, of the story that he had saved Grant from disgrace. "About a year ago," he said, "I read what purported to be an interview with you, in which you were reported to have said that while you were Secretary of War, and on a visit to the Pacific coast, Grant was brought before you charged with drunken, disorderly conduct; that you gave him the choice of resigning and leaving the army, or court martial; that he chose the former." To this also Davis refused all comment.

A pleasing picture of Davis was drawn, at about this time, by a New York *World* reporter sent to observe his condition and mode of life: "His manner is genial and very kindly, with the charming courtesy characteristic of the high-bred Southern gentleman. Seventy-seven years of age, Mr. Davis has yet a fresh and vigorous look. His hair, moustache, and whiskers are white in part, but his eye is bright and cheerful. His face in repose is almost severely intellectual, but the smile which lights up his mouth, and his quietly cheerful laugh, dispel the first impression of coldness. Few of our public men have the quiet fascination of manner, the old-fashioned grace, and the charming conversational powers of Jefferson Davis. His memory is capacious and retentive. One might with a facile phonographic pen collect great stores of reminiscences from his lips. He loves to talk of the Confederacy, and his eyes flash with their old fire when he indignantly defends his administration of the Southern cause from the slanders of its enemies. A patriotic regard for the public safety imposed silence upon Mr. Davis while the war continued, and a magnanimity which they have neither deserved nor appreciated, coupled with a proper sense of personal dignity, have impelled him since to refrain from the refutation of many misstatements by his enemies, utterly scandalous and inexcusable.

"He is a man of studious habits, a consistent Christian, the truest of husbands, the most affectionate of fathers, the best of neighbours, and one of the kindest of masters. He rises about nine o'clock in the morning, reads his mail and answers it, then devotes the remainder of the day to receiving visitors, riding over his estate, or studying in various fields of literature and philosophy. He is a skilful euchre player, and nearly every evening enjoys a social game with his family or visiting friends."

Davis was growing old, almost gently, and even the ever-present consciousness of blighted hopes could not destroy his zest for life. "I am suffering from acute rheumatism in my foot, the one broken at Buena Vista," he wrote to Northrop, "but I do not find consolation for physical ills, as you do, in the prospect that they may soon come to an end. My downs have been so many, and the feeling of injustice so great, that I wish to hold on and see whether the better day may not come, and mine eyes behold retributive justice upon the knaves now flourishing 'as a green bay tree,'" an ending which proves the "almost." He could be gentle with a Grant, but, as the Sherman contest was showing, was as ready as ever to defend the justice of his cause and the honesty of his motives and conduct.

In the spring of 1886, Alabama unveiled a monument to the Confederate dead, on the spot to the right of the old Capitol building in Montgomery, where the Confederate States of America had organized its short-lived government, and where Davis had taken the oath as Provisional President. An invitation was sent him to be present as the guest of honour, and he accepted. He was to reach Montgomery on April 24th; to attend various functions on April 28th, and speak at the laying of the corner-stone. The announcement of his acceptance caused a flood of invitations from other Southern states and, in spite of age and infirmities, he allowed himself to be scheduled for a number of visits, with the understanding that only brief addresses should be expected of him. Atlanta begged him to attend the unveiling of a statue to the late Senator Benjamin Harvey Hill, the date to be set by him. "The committee would meet you in Montgomery with a special car," wrote H. W. Grady, ". . . You would then have rest and seclusion, which we would guarantee, and on the next day come out to the unveiling. . . . An address of perhaps ten minutes will then be made, blending allusions to Mr. Hill and an introduction of you . . . and ten minutes, five minutes, whatever you wish, is all that will be expected of you, unless your strength permitted you to speak longer." Savannah clamoured for a personal appearance, urging a few words at the unveiling of a monument to General Nathanael Greene, Rhode Island's famous Revolutionary general, who had spent his closing years in Georgia: and Governor Henry D. McDaniel of Georgia, asked that you "give our people an opportunity to pay their respects to you . . . at the Executive mansion, at such hour . . . as may suit your convenience. . . ."

These and many more invitations enticed him, and so it came about that when he left "Beauvoir" for Montgomery, he faced a tour of sufficient extent to daunt a younger man.

He was not, however, prepared for the ovations which awaited him. "This section seems to have gone wild with excitement," wrote the reporter sent to cover the Montgomery meeting for the *New York World*, in describing Davis' arrival: "More than fifteen thousand citizens stood in the muddy streets in a drizzling rain to welcome Jefferson Davis to the capital of Alabama. He reached here about eight o'clock in a special car taken to 'Beauvoir' for his use, by the mayor and a delegation of prominent citizens. Wherever the train stopped there were crowds of people, who brought enthusiasm and flowers for their old chief. Half a carload of floral offerings were showered upon him during his trip, and thousands of other tokens of love. . . . When he and General Gordon were finally seated in the barouche and the four white horses began to draw it up the street, there was such a sight as I never witnessed in many years of writing of events of this character. . . .

"When the hotel was reached, the crowd had swelled in volume until the streets and squares . . . were a sea of faces. As the driver drew up in front of the entrance, a motto, 'Our Hero,' caught his glance. . . . Mr. Davis seemed overwhelmed with the heartiness of his reception . . . and . . . kept constantly bowing his head with an evident show of emotion. When he reached the top of the stairs . . . crowds of ladies awaited his coming. Some of them lost their self-possession in the excitement of the moment and literally threw their arms about his neck. . . . As he entered his room they threw flowers in his way, and his apartment, floor, bed, and furniture, was so strewn with roses that it may truthfully be said that he walked . . . on a bank of flowers. . . ."

The crowd outside clamoured for immediate recognition, and Mr. Davis consented to appear upon the balcony, to address to them a few words of thanks. As he appeared, the band struck up "Dixie" and its appeal was so great that he could utter only the simple words, "With a heart full of emotion I greet you." He then retired, while cheering crowds and sounding brass continued to express enthusiasm.

The preparations for the ceremonies represented a definite attempt to wipe out all distinctions between the sections. The decorations were in the hands of a wounded Yankee soldier and member of the Grand Army of the Republic, Frank Foster, of Ohio, who wore his badge of honourable service while hanging out "bunting by the ton to honour the President" of the late Confederacy. The electric illuminations also were in charge of a Northern man. The Exchange Hotel, where Davis lodged, was now run by a Bostonian, "a Yankee who makes both Davis and General Gordon comfortable with the best in the land," commented the *World* reporter, and "Room 101, which he occupied in 1861, is again his home. The corridor leading to it is an arch of Union flags; over the door is hung the picture of Robert E. Lee, and round it are two American flags falling carelessly on either side. . . . The bed is covered with a quilt, sent here expressly for the occasion, which covered Lafayette during his visit."

That night Mr. Davis' dreams must have dwelt upon the distressing history of the twenty-five years since he had slept in that room, awaiting his inauguration as President of what he fondly hoped would prove a new nation, and the astounding fact that his welcome was now wilder, deeper, and more heartfelt than had been his welcome then.

The enthusiasm of the next day was a redoubled replica of that which had greeted his arrival. The Press displayed headlines meant to emphasize, not only love of Davis, but love of the reunited nation. "We honour the furled under the unfurled flag," said the *Dispatch*. In reviewing the scene, without a too scrupulous regard for facts, the *New York World* declared: "Not a member of the Confederate Congress that elected him was there to welcome him. . . . None of his old Cabinet, although most of them were younger men than he, stood ready to grasp the hand of their old chief. They are all dead. So also is every other man of prominence who was part of the great melodrama of twenty years ago."

When the moment arrived for his address, Davis responded to the note of reconciliation, though yielding nothing of his love for the cause that was lost. Warned by long experience that extempore speaking was dangerous, he read from a carefully prepared manuscript, designed to avoid all chance of feeding the fires of sectional hate, on the one hand, and on the other to show that "we do not seek to avoid whatever responsibility attached to the belief in the righteousness of our cause and the virtue of those who risked their lives to defend it." The monument he declared would commemorate "the deeds of Alabama's sons who died that you and your descendants should have what your fathers in the War for Independence left you."

In his brief summary of the events which led to the war, "not revolution . . . as sovereigns never rebel," he set forth the doctrine of state sovereignty, as boldly as he had proclaimed it upon his retirement from the United States Senate in 1861. Twenty-five years of suffering, defeat, and disappointment had not weakened his faith in the principles of the cause. In closing, he declared that while "our glorious past must ever be dear to us, duty points to the present and the future. Alabama having resumed her place in the Union, be it ours to fulfil all the obligations devolving upon all good citizens, seeking to restore the general Government to its pristine purity, and, as best you may, to promote the welfare and happiness of your common country." Excluded from the benefits of amnesty, he could not say "our common country"; for he remained to the end "a man without a country."

That he had avoided any remark, inflammatory in character was evidenced by the fact that the *World* reporter, after hearing his speech, wrote in his dispatch, "the Old World will pause for a moment to wonder at free America, and wish that forgiveness and forgetfulness and charity had a home amid them too." That he avoided also any word which might be construed as an apology for his course and that of his fellow-Confederates is also evident from the praise bestowed by the *Porcupine*, edited by Major Horace Bell, an ex-Federal officer: "One thing we honour Jefferson Davis for. He refused to bend the pregnant hinges of his knee and eat at the feet of the Government which so outraged him [by putting him in irons] and through him the people whom he represented."

That night Frank A. Burr, who had reported Sherman's attack, telegraphed to his paper: "The address . . . found approval in the applause of the people who heard it. After this effort, Mr. Davis held a reception in the Governor's chamber . . . then went out to help his hosts decorate the graves of their fallen comrades. . . . The committee from Atlanta reached here tonight with three special cars, and Mr. Davis will leave for that place early in the morning. All along the route great preparations have been made to do him honour. . . . All the South is aflame, and where this triumphant march is to stop I cannot predict. There is, however, a broad chance that what was only intended for a visit to this, the first capital of the Confederacy, may extend to Richmond. Now that Mr. Davis has consented to go to Savannah, Charleston is clamouring for his presence. Macon, Georgia, where he was first taken a prisoner after his capture by Wilson's cavalry, demands that he shall stop there. If Mr. Davis goes to Charleston . . . the pressure for him to continue the journey to Richmond will be too great for him to resist. The danger is that he may break down."

But Davis did not break down. The demonstrations of affection which he met everywhere acted upon him like a tonic, and, as he scanned the papers, purchased as his train approached Atlanta, he saw that there too boundless enthusiasm awaited him. "At no period in his previous history," declared the *Atlanta Constitution*, "has Atlanta had within her borders such a host. From every section of the state; from Florida, Alabama, Mississippi, Tennessee, Kentucky, Virginia, North Carolina and South Carolina;

from a score of other states, including those of the far North, the people come to do honour to . . . the revered Davis." Mr. Grady, in introducing him, when the hour for his speech arrived, declared that "never king inhabited more splendid palace than the millions of brave hearts in which your dear name and fame are for ever enshrined."

The contrast between this reception and the sufferings of his prison days might well have drawn from him some biting comment. But again the theme of his discourse was reconciliation: "The friend whose memory we have met to honour taught us the lesson of peace as well as resistance. He taught us that it was through peaceful methods we were to regain our rights. We have trodden the thorny path and passed over our worst part of the road. Let us still remember fealty to every promise we have given, but still let us love Georgia and her rights, and may her rights of freedom and independence, such as your fathers gave you, be yours and your children's for ever."

The *Atlanta Constitution* summed up the spirit of the speech and of the ceremony in the words: "Ten years ago the Republicans looked forward to the time when the dead of both sides . . . would be honoured together. . . . The time is at hand. Ours is one country; all that has been done in it to the credit of the American character is the heritage of the whole country, not solely of one section. . . . In the tribute to Mr. Davis . . . there is no quarrelling with results, and those who gave their old leader unmistakable evidences of their devotion have as strong a love for the Union as it is, and as it will be, as can be found in any section of the country."

On May 6, 1886, the two scenes, Montgomery and Atlanta, were re-enacted at Savannah, where "two occasions . . . the Chatham Artillery centennial and honouring . . . the memory of General Nathanael Greene—were most happily blended." This dual program required two brief speeches, in the first of which Davis advanced a favourite theme: "In 1776 the Colonies acquired state sovereignty. They revolted from the mother country in a desperate struggle. That was the cause for which they fought. Is it a lost cause now? Never! Has Georgia lost the state sovereignty which, with Rhode Island, she won in 1776? No, a thousand times, no! Truth crushed to earth will rise again . . . in its might, clothed in all the majesty and power that God gave it, and so the independence of these states, the Constitution, liberty, state sovereignty, which they won in 1776, and which Nathanael Greene, son of Rhode Island, helped to win for Georgia, as well as for Rhode Island, can never die. . . ."

This was the nearest approach to inflammatory utterance made during his speech: and at its close "there was a mighty surge in the crowd, and the next moment the stage was filled by veterans eager to grasp the hand of the old statesman. So great was the rush that there was some danger of Mr. Davis' being crushed. A lane was cleared, however, and he was escorted to the carriage."

That evening, at a banquet given in his honour by Governor McDaniel, Davis deliberately sought to correct an impression which he had not desired to make. "There are some," he said, "who take it for granted that when I allude to state sovereignty I want to bring on another war. I am too old to fight again, and God knows I don't want you to have the necessity of fighting again. However," he added, after deliberation, "if that necessity should arise, I know you will meet it as you always have discharged every duty you felt called upon to perform." Thus ended his tour of glory, which would have made a better impression had it stopped earlier. He had long kept off the dangerous subject, but in the end had toyed with high explosives, and invited violent criticism, which came in abundance. Slanders bloomed again in the pages of the hostile Press. One paper declared that he had said: "I have often prayed to live to see the day when both Lincoln and Grant were dead and in hell, and as my prayers have been granted, I am ready to die." This was pure invention, which merited no denial: but Davis furiously denied it. His words, however, had no effect upon ingenious inventors; and imaginary pictures of the violence of the "Great Rebel" continued to flood the Press and to deceive the more credulous. On June 8, 1886, the Rev. Edward Bailey, who had read some of these slanders, and who had also misunderstood some of Davis' remarks, wrote, urging that Davis should cultivate the spirit of repentance, and offering the service of his prayers. Davis' reply merits a careful reading, even though it repeats many things which he had often said before:

"Beauvoir, Miss., *15th June 1886.*

"Revd. Edwd. Bailey,

"Dear Sir,

"I have this evening received your letter of the 8th inst. and the Christian spirit in which you write leads me to reply hoping that I may remove what I think is a misconception of my position. I certainly did not mean that the war was not to me a cause of regret. I laboured before its inception with all the power I possessed, as my speeches in the U. S. Senate and my action on a select committee in Jan., 1861, clearly prove, to avert, if practicable, the catastrophe of war. I believed then, and do now, that the states possessed sovereignty and therefore had a right to withdraw from any league into which any of them had entered. My opinion was that secession would, but should not, produce war. When Mississippi passed her ordinance of secession I felt I no longer had any right to remain in the Senate as her representative and therefore withdrew. As a citizen of Miss. I owed her my allegiance and went home to serve the State as her needs might require. When the General Government, in violation of the Constitution, attempted to coerce the State, I served her as best I might. On her part it was a war of defence, the only kind of war which I believed justified by man's duty to his Fellow and to his God.

"Now my dear Sir, with this introduction you will need no

argument to show you that with my convictions unchanged, I could not repent, for all I had done or attempted to do for the maintenance of the Constitution and natural rights of the State, to whom my first duty was due, under the limitations of man's obligation to his Maker.

"If I had desired war, had provoked war, had not endeavoured, after the Confederacy was organized, by a commission to find a peaceful solution of all pending issues, then I should have much cause to repent of sins of commission and omission, but your reading has no doubt taught you that the facts are otherwise. In my book, entitled *The Rise and Fall of the Confederate Government*, I have more fully than it would be possible to do in a letter, presented my view of the whole subject. If suffering for the cause I espoused could produce repentance, I have surely borne enough for that end, but martyrs have gloried in their faith when yielding up their lives for its assertion and if I mistake not your character, you would scorn the man who recanted and called it repentance. You seem impressed by my assertion in this connexion that if it were to do over again I would do as I have done. Surely Sir, believing myself to have been right, you would not have me to say or to feel otherwise. Looking beyond the prejudice and malice of men, I trust my case to Him who knoweth the hearts of men and 'doeth all things well.'

"Accept my thanks for your prayers, for I am not self-righteous enough to believe I do not need them, and believe me, Sir,

"Very respectfully yours,

"JEFFERSON DAVIS."

After Mr. Davis' tour, the claims of hospitality and the cost of entertaining visitors, greatly increased at "Beauvoir," and as a result his financial position became ever more difficult. The Library of Congress contains a letter to President Cleveland, sent without Mr. Davis' knowledge, and in defiance of his known wishes, by a friend, asking that something be done by the Federal Government to lessen his financial worries. There is no record of any comment by the President, but in July, 1886, Davis was told that the latter had expressed hostility towards him and his family. At once a protest was dispatched to L. Q. C. Lamar, a loyal Confederate and member of Mr. Cleveland's Cabinet, whose reply was immediate: "It gives me great pleasure to say that, so far as my knowledge goes, the President has never expressed any sentiment of hostility to your family." And he added, "No man has, either in public or private, assailed your name or made a slighting allusion to your fame and character in my presence without receiving a prompt and indignant rebuke from me."

History has pictured "Stonewall" Jackson as a religious fanatic, and Lee as the ideal Christian soldier; but propaganda has placed Jefferson Davis in a different class. No one, however, can study the mass of evidence regarding him, without admitting that his religious life was as deep and sincere as was theirs, and his religion, moreover, like that of Lee, was broadly tolerant, even to the point of religious cosmopolitanism, at every period of his life. He was also ready, at all times, to urge the consolations of religion upon friends in distress. When the gallant Christian knight, James Ewell Brown Stuart, universally known as "Jeb Stuart," lay wounded and dying, after turning Sheridan from the Richmond Road at Yellow Tavern, President Davis prayed with the fallen hero's wife, that this "precious life might be spared to our needy country." While President of the Confederacy, he was confirmed in the Episcopal Church, thus drawing from cynical old Edmund Ruffin the remark: "It would have been better . . . if he had . . . completed his individual and private duty before he began his Presidency." While in prison at Fortress Monroe, he eagerly read devotional books, of whatever creed, and conversed upon religious subjects with Dr. Craven, Dr. Minnigerode, and many other visitors. When the Pope sent him his likeness, bearing the words, "Come unto me, all ye who are weary and heavy laden, and I will give you rest," he accepted it with an appreciation learned in his childhood from the fathers who had taken part in his education. Upon receiving news of General Gorgas' death in 1883, he wrote to Mrs. Gorgas: "Together we three knelt before the altar to receive confirmation. In the order of our nature, I, the oldest, should have been first called away; but it pleased Him who doeth all things well that my friend should go before. If, as I believe, we shall know each other in the future state, it will, I pray, be permitted me to join him in the blessed abode vouchsafed to him by the pure and faithful use of the 'talents' committed to his care." And his letters concerning Mrs. Dorsey's last illness and death, already quoted, are of the same character.

With full knowledge of his interest in religion, some of the inhabitants of his birthplace suggested that he donate the home of his birth to the Fairview Baptist Congregation, to be used as the site for a new church building. In reply Davis wrote to M. H. Clark, a friend living in the neighbourhood of Fairview, explaining that he did not have the means "to buy the lot, costing about $1,000," much as he would like to aid the project. Therefore, wrote Clark to Dean Fleming, in giving his recollections of the incident, "Captain Lewis R. Clark and myself subscribed most of the money, and he [Davis] made the deed to the church."

In 1886, Davis made the long journey to Kentucky, to take part in the ceremony of dedication, but upon the condition that he should not be expected to speak. In response to insistent demand, however, when the regular speakers had finished, he spoke, quite simply, of his faith in a God who knows not sectarianism. "It has been asked," he said, "why I, who am not a Baptist, give this lot to the Baptist Church. I am not a Baptist, but my father, who was a better man than I, was a Baptist. . . . When I see this beautiful church, it fills my heart with thanks. It shows the love you bear your Creator; it shows your capacity for building to your God. The pioneers of this country were men of plain, simple habits, full of energy and imbued with religious principles.

They lived in a day before the dawn of sectarian disturbances and sectional strifes. In their surroundings, it is no wonder they learned that God was love. . . . May the God of Heaven bless this community for ever, and may the Saviour of the world preserve this church to His worship for all time to come." He then shook hands with the congregation and departed, never again to see his birthplace. Twenty-three years later, in June, 1909, six thousand Americans met at the same spot to dedicate the Davis Memorial Park.

After his return from Fairview, Davis continued his practice of refusing interviews to the Press, and sought also to avoid controversial subjects, as he was weary of strife; but in 1887, when the state of Texas was engaged in a contest over prohibition, he felt called upon to issue a protest against that method of seeking a solution for the evil of intemperance. He therefore wrote to ex-Governor Lubbock, who had shared his flight and his capture, a strong letter, declaring that: "To destroy individual liberty and moral responsibility would be to eradicate one evil by the substitution of another, which . . . would be more fatal than that for which it was offered as a remedy. . . . Action should clearly be directed against the abuse rather than the use. If drunkenness be the cause of disorder and crime, why not pronounce drunkenness itself to be a crime, and attach to it proper and adequate penalties? If it be objected that the penalties could not be enforced, that is an admission that popular opinion would be opposed to the law; but if it be true that juries could not be empanelled who would convict so degraded a criminal as a drunkard, it necessarily follows that a statutory prohibition against the sale . . . of intoxicants would be a dead letter. . . . You have already provision for local prohibition," he added. "If this has proved the wooden horse in which a disguised enemy to state sovereignty as the guardian of individual liberty was introduced, let it be a warning that the progressive march would probably be from village to state and from state to United States." His solution of the liquor evil, which he did not underestimate, was simple; leave it to be solved, as it has begun to be solved, by "the refining influence of education and Christianity."

His words were "emblazoned on banners and transparencies at anti-prohibition meetings, and repeated glibly by saloon men all over Texas," which grieved and offended many of Davis' friends among the Texas prohibitionists and their sympathizers throughout the country. Among these was Bishop Charles B. Galloway, D.D., of the Methodist Episcopal Church, South, who in a public address lamented: "How sad that the last words of a soldier, sage, and Christian should become the shibboleth of the saloons!" To this criticism Davis replied, reiterating his former statements, that prohibition would work evil not good, and defending his opinion by arguments the meaning of which has of late been illustrated to the conviction of the majority of American citizens. "If," he said, ". . . there should be [enacted] Federal laws to enforce the prohibition policy, your recollection of the war and Reconstruction days should enable you to anticipate . . . the moral decay which would inevitably result from such a condition. . . . To me it seems the plain duty of every citizen who loves the liberties our sires bequeathed to us to check this scheme before it acquires dangerous proportions. . . .There are surely better remedies for offences against the peace and good order of society than such a departure from our principles of Constitutional government and community independence as would be Federal legislation to enforce a sumptuary policy. . . . Why not trust to religion and education, to refinement and science, aided by the laws which have the sanction of experience, to prevent the formation of habits of intemperance, rather than at the sacrifice of personal liberty and moral responsibility to undertake, by coercive means, the reformation of the drunkards? The former may be practicable; the latter, by such methods, is hopeless." "Not by coercion, but by instruction and persuasion and religious influence," according to his view, was the evil of intemperance to be abated.

Before the end of the debate, Davis saw his letters erected into flaming campaign documents, and his name cheered by inebriates wherever two or three were gathered together. And in the end Galloway was able to point out that while Jefferson Davis was questioning the right of the sovereign people "to determine the manufacture and sale of intoxicating liquors in their midst, the Supreme Court of the United States renders a decision sustaining the constitutionality of prohibition, *and on his paramount doctrine of state rights.*" "The decision," commented the *Central Law Journal*, "leaves no legal foothold upon which an opponent of prohibition could make a stand." But Davis had already taken his stand, and history has since emphasized its wisdom. It served also to influence the decision of the Texas electorate; for Lubbock later assured him that his letters against prohibition had served as a great force towards the 100,000 majority which his ticket received in Texas. It "gained us a large vote from the best citizens of the state," he wrote on August 6, 1887, "because you enunciated good and honest democratic truths." "The local-option counties," he added, "went almost unanimously against the amendment."

This contest, so much more bitter and extended than he had expected, deepened Davis' reluctance to make public statements of any kind. "Public discussion," he said, "is now to me objectionable." But he still expressed personal opinions with vigour, when situations developed which seemed to demand a word from the leader of the South, as he knew himself still to be. In the summer of 1887, for example, President Cleveland made a well-meaning attempt to restore the Confederate battle flags to the states from which they had been captured. At once he was denounced as a skulker who had purchased exemption from the dangers of the war, and now presumed to decide the fate of banners taken in battles of which he could only guess the meaning. Governor Foraker of Ohio announced, "No rebel flags will be surrendered while I am Governor"; and General Sherman, who should have known that the war was over, complained that a President who had never fought could not "think of the blood and torture of battle," nor "understand what it means to a veteran" to capture a standard. Mr. Cleveland, however, was not attempting to think of "blood and torture," but of emphasizing that the past was forgotten, the Union restored.

On July 21st, Davis wrote to C. W. Frazer: "I consider the whole attempt to create an excitement about President Cleveland's order, . . . political. . . . According to the theory of the North, it [the war] was only a rebellion, or insurrection . . . and if they are right, property could not be acquired by capture as in foreign war. . . ." He was clearly of the opinion that the President had only recognized this fact, and arranged for the return of property to its proper owners. In the end, however, Mr. Cleveland took a different view, and decided that the flags by capture had become the property of the nation, to be alienated only with the consent of Congress.

During his eightieth year, Davis made a brief address at Mississippi City, which opened with the customary formula, "Mr. Chairman and fellow-citizens." At this point there came to him a flood of recollections of amnesty bills which had not included him, of the general amnesty controversy of 1876 in which Blaine and Garfield had tried to persuade Congress to single him out and make him the only exception, and of the failure of that bill in its final stage because he was not excepted. Sadly he corrected himself, with the words: "Ah! pardon me. The laws of the United States no longer permit me to designate you as fellow-citizens, but I am thankful that I may address you as my friends. I feel no regret that I stand before you . . . a man without a country, for my ambition lies buried in the grave of the Confederacy. There, has been consigned not only ambition, but the dogmas upon which that Government was based. The faces I see before me are those of young men; had I not known this I would not have appeared before you, men in whose hands the destinies of our Southland lie. For love of her I break my silence, to speak to you a few words of respectful admonition! The past is dead; let it bury its dead, its hopes, and its aspirations; before you lies the future—a future full of golden promise, a future of expanding national glory, before which all the world shall stand amazed. Let me beseech you to lay aside rancour, all bitter sectional feelings, and to take your places in the ranks of those who will bring about a consummation devoutly to be wished—a reunited country."

This was a noble utterance for an old and disappointed leader, and its realization in a new spirit of a new South has made it prophecy.

At the age of eighty most men are free from the importunities of publishers desiring copy, but the spectacular charges of Blaine and Garfield, making Davis responsible for what they termed "the crime of Andersonville" had never been so fully met as to satisfy the public, and James Redpath, managing editor of the *North American Review*, decided to go in person to "Beauvoir" and persuade Davis to write an article in reply. It was the summer of 1888, a season not likely to attach a Northerner to a gulf town; and Redpath's views were such that an intimate friendship with Davis seemed among the remotest of possibilities. Born a Scot, at Berwick-on-Tweed, Redpath had come in youth to America, and had early identified himself with the Abolitionists. He had served as a reporter in Bleeding Kansas, and his reports had not been calculated to endear him to Davis who, as Pierce's Secretary of War, was considered in large measure responsible for the Administration's policy. During the Civil War, Redpath had followed the armies of Sherman and Thomas, as a war-correspondent; and when he appeared at "Beauvoir," he awakened memories which Davis detested. But he brought also a Scottish persistence, hard to resist. He had come for an article on Andersonville, and settled down to a siege, when Davis refused it.

During their conversations, which grew ever more friendly and confidential, Davis referred to a plan which he had long entertained, of having some competent student of American history write a Short History of the United States which "would do justice to our people and their ancestors," to quote his own words. From time to time friends had urged him to undertake such a book himself, but he had been too busy with life, and with *The Rise and Fall of the Confederate Government*, seriously to consider it. Redpath tactfully dropped for the moment the question of Andersonville, and urged the preparation of the Short History of the United States, which Davis was disposed to undertake, and an article upon Robert E. Lee, which he gladly promised. With the Andersonville article held for a later attack, and satisfied to have committed Davis to so much, Redpath now prepared to return to New York. During his visit, he had met many "Beauvoir" visitors, and had formed a friendship with Mrs. Davis. Towards the end of his visit, he had been ill, and, after his departure, Mrs. Davis wrote, with characteristic lightness of touch:

"Beauvoir House
*"6th Sept., 1888.*

"My dear Mr. Redpath:

"Your kind letter has been gladly received and I am so glad you did not elope. I am so glad you thought of our anxiety about you and wanted to write, and I am sorry for the girl that she did not get you, and sorry you have gone back to the eternal grind. Perhaps you were wise not to go on that long river trip. There is a good deal of malaria liberated at night from these immense swamps that lie on each side of our splendid, lawless river. Firmly believing as I do that you are going to get well, and that a relapse might be brought on by any disordering cause, I am glad you did not try the river. We had a faint hope that you would come back this way, and Bettie promised you many little attentions, among which ice water figured conspicuously. . . .

"We are about as usual here, but we missed you greatly after your departure. We left so much unsaid and unheard that sometime we must finish our talk facing the Mississippi sound, with the sunshine filtering through the trees. . . .

" 'Gen. Lee' is done! I insisted upon popularizing the article as much as possible, for I thought it was not a military critique you wanted, but to see the heart of the man through the eyes of one who knew and loved him. Fortunately, my husband agreed with me, and has left out everything which could suggest controversy, —Genl. Longstreet's lateness, etc. Instead he has written all his sunny memories of our great hero, and I think the world will hear him with eager sympathy.

"We go to the plantation Saturday, and if we come back alive, the prefatory article [for the Short History] will be sent very soon thereafter. Mr. Davis' belief is so firm in the principles he advocates that the motive causes of the war will be easily and quickly, excuse my vanity if I say, worthily and fitly told. Your love was reverently delivered to him, and warmly welcomed. Please accept our affectionate acknowledgments, and reciprocation to you.

"If you do not like the articles, just preserve the graceful silence that you did when we disagreed about your horrid 'puritan saint,' and I shall know how you feel without a pronouncement, but I am very pleased with the Lee article. . . ."

From time to time similar letters were exchanged between the abolitionist, Redpath, and the wife of Jefferson Davis, who reported slow progress towards a promise of the Andersonville article. On October 1st, 1888, she wrote, in appreciation of an interview highly complimentary to Davis which he had sent:

"My dear Mr. Redpath:

"Just a line to say that I hope Mr. Davis will accept the invitation to write of Andersonville, but you know the Indian saying, 'White man mighty uncertain.' I . . . am heartily glad you like the Lee article. I was pleased with it in the main; and do hope Mr. Rice [the editor] may publish the prefatory article in the *Review* for the sake of the book which is forthcoming, and for the sake of the audience it will have in the *Review*.

". . . I am so much a part of everything Mr. Davis does, being his hand, and in Aesop's sense one of his members, and also in the Mosaic sense, that there is only one part of his writings I do not in some sense share, and that is their composition. He was a little doubtful at times as to whether his very plain expression of opinion was, well, whether you had not 'bought a pig in a poke,' in the prefatory, but I thought a prefatory article to the characterization of Southern heroes should set forth our convictions as though none other had triumphed, and if Mr. Davis reserves his opinion, the dignity and force of his reasoning are lost. He is a man who sees but one side because he is so firmly persuaded in his own mind that he cannot understand everyone not accepting dogmas which he sees so plainly demonstrable and irrefutable. I envy him his strength of mind and steadfastness of purpose.

"Just now I am inconsolable at seeing that Longfellow and John Bunyan were plagiarists. I could stand the former, but the latter was the love of my childhood, and the holy prisoner of my latter days, and I would that 'Mr. Worldly Wiseman' had left Mrs. 'Pliable' alone in her ignorance and childish faith.

"While the 'heathen do furiously rage together' over the Presidential election, time flows on here without troubling us much with the drift. We went to the plantation, found nothing right; the negroes thievish and sunk in a slough of immorality you could not dream of without seeing it—predatory and migratory like a flock of blackbirds; the only civilization that which we imparted in brighter if not better days. . . . It was 'most unpleasant' and heart-wearing. Bettie longed to come home and so did I. . . .

"Many thanks for the tender way in which your approval of Mr. Davis was spoken in your interview. He deserves all you said but 'apples of gold in pictures of silver' are rare nowadays. People are busy now with such fine words that the setting excels the jewel, and there are some common words which are the 'red rag to the bull' to me. I feel like fighting when people 'correlate' or 'formulate' or have an 'outcome,' and so on. Thanks for your kind opinion of me. I *do not* deserve it, but glory in your errors on this score.

"With kindest regards to Mrs. Redpath,

"Affectionately your friend,

"VARINA HOWELL DAVIS."

On January 21, 1889, she wrote again to Redpath, "Mr. Davis has gone to New Orleans to a reunion of our old soldiers, our G. A. R., and I hope has gone home before this hour to rest and dream of happier things than our sad-eyed, poverty-stricken veterans and tattered banners suggest; and yet their fragments of 'songs that nobody sings' are the dearest memories of earth to me, and I suppose some of these will be sung tonight and wish I could be invisible and hear them lilted with the old ring."

At length, early in 1889, the Andersonville article was dispatched to the *North American Review*, and Rice sent the author a cheque for $250, the price agreed upon. It was a polemic, undisguised, and dealt so frankly with facts and persons that Rice decided to postpone its publication. He, however, published in May the first of three articles contributed by General Viscount Wolseley, K. P., Adjutant-General of the British army, which was based upon "information supplied by the *Century's* history of the Civil War." It ventured, with this scant knowledge, to call into question Davis' fitness for the post of President of the Confederate States, and declared that Davis, now "a man weighed down with years, with misfortunes, and, above all, with sad memories of a lost cause, and, I presume, the conviction that he was a failure, appeals to our pity rather than invites our censure." "That he was a third-rate man, and a most unfortunate selection for the office of President," he added, "I cannot conceal from myself."

Foreseeing the interest which such an attack would arouse, Rice authorized Redpath to offer Davis $250 for a reply, which was gladly furnished, and with little of the character of the writing of a man "weighed down with years," and the "conviction" of failure. Frankly declaring, "I have no excuses to make and no apology to offer," and adding that he had fought but to defend the Constitution "as framed by its founders and as expounded by them," he paid an old man's tribute to a young man in these words: "I might well be ashamed of my public career if I could feel that the opinion of any European stripling, without an earned record of ability either in civil or military life, could affect my reputation in America, and therefore I pass unnoticed his personal depreciation." Of the remainder of the indictment he said: "Each and every allegation . . . is either false in direct statement or false by inference," and proceeded to specifications, answering each criticism in detail.

Shortly after this article was finished, but before it was published, news came that Redpath had resigned his connexion with the *North American Review*, and Mr. and Mrs. Davis feared that his resignation had been due to his steadfast friendship for them and his defence of their interests. "We have been worried 'out of our propriety' for fear you had given up your connexion with Mr. Rice because of the Andersonville prison article, in some way," wrote the latter on February 23, 1889. "It has not been published and we feared your friendly consideration for Mr. Davis might have led you to urge its being made public too strongly. Now do not suffer anything in our behalf. As our old nurse used to say, 'burnt brandy would not save us.' We are in the trough of the sea and the waves will drown us, but we will die game. So there will be no moans made. Yet we both affectionately thank you for your efforts to save us."

Redpath, however, had no idea of allowing them to suffer be-

JEFFERSON DAVIS AT EIGHTY-ONE

cause of the policy of the *North American Review*. He easily formed another business connexion, this time with Robert Belford, publisher and magazine editor, and when, on April 24th, Davis asked his advice concerning the Andersonville article, which was still unpublished, he consulted his new chief. Belford suggested that Redpath make another visit to "Beauvoir," and help Davis to complete his *Short History of the Confederate States*, and to arrange for its publication by the Belford Company. When the suggestion was conveyed to him, Davis replied, "The sooner you come and the longer you stay the better it will please us."

The result was a visit of several months during which Redpath, the Abolitionist, not only helped with the preparation of the *Short History*, and with the *Autobiography*, which was never finished, but strengthened his conception of Davis' character which he later embodied in his own book, *Neither Traitor nor Rebel*, perhaps as fair a picture as has ever been penned:

"Lest any foreigner should read this article let me say for his benefit that there are two Jefferson Davises in American history —one is a conspirator, a rebel, a traitor, and the 'fiend of Andersonville'—he is a myth evolved from the hell smoke of cruel war—as purely imaginary a personage as Mephistopheles or the Hebrew devil; the other was a statesman with clean hands and pure heart, who served his people faithfully from budding manhood to hoary age, without thought of self, with unbending integrity and to the best of his great ability: he was a man of whom all his countrymen who knew him personally, without distinction of creed political, are proud, and proud that he *was* their countryman." "I never met any public man," he added, "who reverenced the Constitution as Mr. Davis reverenced it. . . . If the Constitution had been lost, I think Mr. Davis could have rendered it from memory." But the qualities which Redpath most emphasizes were "goodness" and "intellectual integrity," and these had left their imprint in his face; for Redpath continues: "I never saw an old man whose face bore more, or more emphatic, evidences of a gentle, refined and benignant character. He seemed to me the ideal embodiment of 'sweetness and light.' "

Meanwhile, Rice had died, and in September, 1889, Lloyd Stephens Bryce became editor of the *North American Review*. Davis' Andersonville article and the reply to Lord Wolseley he found still unpublished; and one of his first acts was to send a cheque for $100, in payment of the reply to Lord Wolseley, at the same time asking permission to "omit two or three paragraphs." In reply, Davis referred to his agreement with the former editor, and Bryce at once forwarded the additional amount which had been offered, though explaining that he could not publish the article on Andersonville, as it stood, because of its reference to General Miles as a "heartless vulgarian." Davis answered that unless he was prepared to publish it without alteration, he should return the manuscript and receive back his cheque which had not been cashed. In the meantime, the reply to Wolseley had been published, but with alterations which displeased Davis, who, on November 3, wrote that the Andersonville article must be produced exactly as written, or promptly returned. The same day he wrote to Redpath, giving him authority to claim the manuscript of Andersonville in the event of refusal. "I would rather," he said, "not appear as a correspondent of the *North American Review*, as it puts me in company I do not care to keep."

The manuscript of the Andersonville article was accordingly turned over to Redpath, who arranged that it should be published in *Belford's Magazine* exactly as Davis had prepared it. Mr. Belford returned to the *North American Review* the sum of $250, which had been paid to Davis, and Redpath reported to him that the matter was finally adjusted, and that in due time his article would appear.

How much such a cheque meant to Davis at that moment is evident from the fact that General Early had, on May 15, 1889, presented him with a new suit of clothes, costing $20, and, upon the plea of old friendship, persuaded him to accept it. But when other offers of help came, his reply was that any funds which could be raised should be devoted to the relief of widows and orphans, or disabled veterans. His friends, however, continued their efforts to devise methods of relieving his embarrassment without offending his pride, and finally D. R. Porter, Assistant Secretary of the State of Mississippi, suggested a plan to which he believed Davis would offer no objections. Knowing that he owned a large tract of land in Arkansas, unproductive, but potential, if properly developed, Porter formed a corporation called the Davis Land Company, and issued the following announcement of its plans: (Undated.)

"It is known that the Hon. Jefferson Davis owes more than $40,000, and that his actual income, over and above the requirement of interest on this debt, does not amount to $200, thus necessitating an annual increase of his enormous debt. It is also known that a forced sale of all he has would leave no margin after payment of this debt, and that his present condition arises in great measure from the boundless hospitality made necessary by his exalted position.

"He owns about 5700 acres of land in the richest regions of Arkansas, . . . with a clear title and all taxes paid to date. Our company is organized to buy this land as an investment and, on a business basis, for development and profit, and to this we may add the satisfaction of thus enabling him to pay his debt, thereby relieving him, in his advanced years and bodily infirmities, of the mental harassment and physical exertion of finding purchasers and negotiating sales. Our company is duly incorporated, the shares are $10 each. Our Treasurer is S. S. Carter, President of the

First National Bank of Jackson, Miss. All remittances to him will be responded to by stock."

This well-meant movement for Mr. Davis' relief came too late, however. In the vain hope of bringing order out of chaos at "Brierfield," Mr. Davis was already preparing for his last visit. On November 6, 1889, three days after authorizing Redpath to withdraw the Andersonville article from the *North American Review*, he embarked on the steamer, *Laura Lee,* from New Orleans, to visit his plantation. "I had generally gone to our plantation with him, but the presence of guests prevented," Mrs. Davis later explained. He therefore travelled alone, although suspecting that an attack of grippe was coming on. As "Brierfield" was on an island, visited by night boats only, he wisely decided to go on to Vicksburg and return to the plantation the next day. It was, however, night again before he landed and started on the drive of several miles, through an atmosphere of malaria, to his plantation. Upon his arrival, his condition grew worse, and he was compelled to take to his bed.

News of his condition was telegraphed to Mrs. Davis on November 11th, but before she could arrive Mr. Davis had decided to start home, alone. Just before his departure, little Alice Desmaris, niece of his agent at "Brierfield," presented her album, with the request that he write in it. The words which he wrote seem to have been his last written words: "May all your paths be peaceful and pleasant, charged with the best fruit, the doing good to others. 'Brierfield,' 13th Nov. 1889."

When his wife boarded his boat in the midst of the great "Father of Waters," "He was asleep . . . but waked very soon and seemed better for meeting me. Two physicians whom we consulted at Bayou Sara declared that he had acute bronchitis, complicated with grave malarial trouble."

They reached New Orleans in a cold rain, with Mr. Davis' condition growing rapidly worse. Mr. J. U. Payne, his commission merchant and close personal friend, accompanied by his son-in-law, Justice Fenner, and Dr. Chaillé, met the party, and persuaded them to abandon their plan of proceeding at once to "Beauvoir." An ambulance was summoned, and Mr. Davis was taken to the Payne residence. There, surrounded by alternate fear and hope on the part of his wife and friends, he lay helpless, but still with a will to live. "It may seem strange to you," he said to his physician, "that a man of my age should desire to live; but I do. . . . There are still some things that I have to do in this world."

At this point, in ignorance of Mr. Davis' illness, the editor of *Belford's Magazine* wrote that he was preparing the Andersonville article for early publication, and suggested that Mr. Davis write an introductory note, stating his views upon the treatment which he had suffered in connexion with the article. Mrs. Davis replied to Redpath on November 28th in a pitiful pencil scrawl: "Mr. Davis can do absolutely nothing. We sit up with him every night and he is a very ill man. He could not write his name, still less read a proof. . . . He is weeks, it may be months, it may be for ever, from being 'out.' I do not want the household told, but am miserably anxious."

At this point, Davis' friends in Congress quietly conducted a canvass to discover whether, in view of his approaching death, a motion to remove his disabilities could be carried, but soon decided that it would be best to let the matter drop. The politicians were not yet ready to sanction such a step, although, according to the *Baltimore Sun*, of December 5, 1889, a similar canvass among Union soldiers had revealed an almost unanimous approval of such removal.

The day after this statement appeared, Davis' doctors reported a sudden rally, and Dr. C. J. Bickham, who attended with Dr. Chaillé, announced that he was free of fever and able to take nourishment, and Mrs. Davis wrote to a friend: "The doctors here [give] every hope of his recovery, but it must be nearly two weeks, if not more under the most favourable circumstances before we can come home."

Mr. Davis, however, did not share in this optimism. His interpretation of the outlook had been given early that morning when he remarked to his wife: "I want to tell you I am not afraid to die." At six o'clock that evening he was seized with a congestive chill, and began sinking slowly. At seven, Mrs. Davis urged him to take his medicine. He took part, and then said courteously, "Pray excuse me. I cannot take it." "In three hours," says Mrs. Davis' *Memoir*, "his brave, true heart had ceased to beat." The "Scapegoat" had gone home at last.

# THE SOURCES

## A CRITICAL BIBLIOGRAPHY

STUDENTS in process of training are accustomed to the exhortation, "exhaust your sources"; but the investigator, when studying a subject such as the life of Jefferson Davis, is soon conscious that the sources can never be exhausted. Indeed, they can never be fully catalogued, for they include all records, public and private, which interpret any phase of the cause which he led, and the productions of all the pens of all the nations which watched its rise and fall. And, in addition, they include all similar records concerning the events with which he was prominently associated, in the course of a life that covered every administration from Jefferson to the second Harrison.

It is necessary, however, to catalogue the manuscript material, and the printed documents which have proved most valuable in the preparation of the present biography, and to list the books of chief value for the student of Jefferson Davis, whether biographies dealing with him as the primary subject, or memoirs, biographies, and histories throwing important if incidental light upon his character and career. This is the more important because it has been decided not to print footnotes, which would be of little interest to the general reader.

For the convenience of special students who wish to know more about the sources relied upon for particular statements the full text, with footnotes attached, has been deposited in the New York Public Library.

### A. MSS. COLLECTIONS, AND FUGITIVE MSS.

#### I. In the Confederate Memorial Hall, New Orleans

On January 24, 1866, Jefferson Davis wrote to his wife: "I never sought to make up my own record, intent on the discharge of my duties in the various public positions I have held. If the question had occurred to me, how will this be told hereafter, I would have preferred to leave that task to others." And yet, he must be classed with that rare type of man who collects and preserves the records of his own life.

Early in his student days Davis began the practice of filing letters and other personal records, and the habit grew as the complications of life increased. Indeed, the chief interest of his later life was the search for material bearing upon his own public career. Holograph letters of Mr. Davis are, however, rather rare, partly because so many were lost or destroyed during and immediately after the Civil War; partly because, during the latter part of his life his eyesight was bad, and most of his letters were written from dictation by Mrs. Davis, who so perfectly imitated his handwriting and his signature that he was himself puzzled at times when called upon to identify his own signature or his own script. It is probably true that many letters written by Mrs. Davis have fetched high prices upon the supposition that Davis himself wrote them.

Davis' earlier papers, securely packed, were carried to Danville after the abandonment of Richmond, together with the later records of his life, and the Archives of the Executive Office which he had filled, and which he hoped to continue to fill. As his retirement merged into flight, however, he naturally lost sight of these boxes; and when, after his release from Fortress Monroe, he sought for them, intending to use them in the preparation of a systematic defence of the Southern Confederacy, he found them scattered. Much of the material had been captured by Federal troops and placed in the custody of the War Department at Washington; some had been preserved by his faithful private secretary, Colonel Burton N. Harrison; some was lost, and Davis at once set himself the task of finding it, but the task proved difficult.

Towards the end of the 'seventies, when he took up his residence at "Beauvoir," in Mississippi, he settled down to a systematic effort to repair his losses by calling upon his chief associates in the government, and in the army, to send him their personal recollections of important events, and such documents as they might be able to gather in their respective communities. These, together with such other material as he had preserved or recovered, he stored in a little detached "office" which he used as a study. There he produced his *Rise and Fall of the Confederate Government*, his *Short History of the Confederate States*; and the numerous critical articles hereinafter listed.

After Mr. Davis' death, in 1889, Mrs. Davis transferred these "Beauvoir" manuscripts to the Louisiana Historical Association at New Orleans, where they are still safely lodged in a fire-proof building which Mr. Harry T. Howard had presented to the association some years before Mr. Davis' death. Mrs. Davis' wish, that the papers should not be opened to students until five years after her own death, was of course respected; and, as a result, it was 1911 before the Memorial Hall Collection was accessible. Dunbar Rowland was then allowed to make the copies which appear in his, *Jefferson Davis, Constitutionalist* (described under V, on p. 702). Before his death, Mr. Davis had allowed his letters dealing with military history to be transcribed for the "Official Records of the Union and Confederate Armies," but most of those relating to other subjects were published for the first time in Rowland's ten volumes.

### II. In the Confederate Museum, Richmond

A detailed account of this rich collection, containing, among other Davis' material, a mass of manuscripts preserved by Mr. Davis' elder daughter, Mrs. Margaret Davis Hayes, will be found in Douglas Southall Freeman's "Calendar of Confederate Papers" (Described on p. 748, and listed on p. 751), which contains brief abstracts of all the manuscripts deposited in the Confederate Museum prior to 1907, and forms, incidentally, a valuable source of information bearing upon Davis' career.

The collection, and the documents deposited since 1907, were carefully studied during the preparation of the present biography, together with small but important collections in the Virginia State Library and in the Virginia Historical Association Library, also in Richmond.

### III. In Mss. Division of the Library of Congress, the War Department, etc., Washington, D. C.

While no division devoted specifically to Jefferson Davis manuscripts has been established in Washington, the Government's unique manuscript collections furnish material of the greatest value to the student of Davis' life. No detailed comment is necessary in view of the elaborate guides and bibliographies which are available; but a recent purchase, the papers of General "Jubel" (J. A.) Early, is of especial interest, in view of the general's long intimacy with Davis: and a long letter from Mrs. Davis to Francis P. Blair, describing the history of her husband's capture, has recently been added.

In a letter to Walter L. Fleming, dated November 11, 1908, the chief of the Division of Prints, Library of Congress, lists eleven engraved portraits of Davis, and five biographies containing his likeness. He also mentions fifteen issues of *Harper's Weekly*, and the following list of other magazines, foreign and domestic, which contain his picture: *United States Magazine*, May, 1855; *Illustrated London News*, March 16, 1861, p. 207; *L'Illustration*, March 23, 1861, p. 181; *Leslie's Weekly*, four issues, April 21, 1860, March 9, 1861, July 9, 1881, and November 1, 1862; *Ueber Land und Meer*, April 7, 1861, p. 440; *Frank Leslie's Illustrated Magazine*, August 28, 1888, and *Peterson's Magazine*, August, 1896, p. 787.

### IV. In the Mississippi Department of Archives and History, State House, Jackson

A rich collection of manuscripts, pamphlets, books, and press cuttings, much of which bears directly upon Mr. Davis' career. New items are systematically added as they become available, by either gift or purchase. Notable among these are depositions taken during the suit for Brierfield, bound in one enormous volume, which reveal the minutest details of Davis' plantation days, his relations with his slaves, and his success as a planter.

### V. Special Collections, Chiefly Copies, Made Available to the Present Author

#### *1. The Dunbar-Rowland Collection*

From the four collections already described, and by some twenty-odd years of painstaking research in other directions, Dr. Dunbar-Rowland compiled his monumental *Jefferson Davis, Constitutionalist, His Letters, Papers and Speeches—Jackson, Miss., 1923, Printed for the Mississippi Department of Archives and History—10 vols.* (Listed on p. 729, with Rowland's other contributors.) It is, to quote Dr. Rowland's own words: "In no sense the publication of selected letters, papers, and speeches. . . . No effort has been spared to collect and publish in continuity and in chronological order every bit of historical material which serves in any way to throw light on the causes of the War of Southern Independence and on the motives and principles which moved its leaders. Every letter appears as it is, without editing and without explanation. Every speech is published as it was reported at the time of its delivery. Every report is given as it was made. No matter from what repository the material came, if it was real, genuine, and duly authenticated, it was used."

At the end of his *Introduction*, Dr. Rowland wrote: "I hope in the due course of time to follow up this publication with a 'Life of Jefferson Davis.' " As the years passed, however, he decided that it would be wise to place the responsibility for that work in other hands, because, he said, "Long study of Davis' papers have made me a hero-worshiper, and no hero-worshiper should attempt the biography of his hero." In 1931, he generously offered his entire collection of mss., published and unpublished, books, pamphlets, and press cuttings, to the present author, without condition, save that he should write Davis' biography according to his own conception of its meaning.

#### *2. The Fleming Collection*

For many years the late Walter L. Fleming, Dean of Vanderbilt University, gathered, from the above collections, from extensive personal solicitations, and from standard and fugitive literature, all available items which seemed to him likely to be of value in the preparation of a definitive biography of Jefferson Davis, which he planned writing. During the course of these researches, he published a number of enlightening pamphlets and articles upon special phases of Davis' life, which are listed in the present bibliography, on p. 721, but he died before he had addressed himself to the major task of writing the biography itself. His entire collection was generously placed at the disposal of the present writer by Mrs. Fleming, with permission to deposit it in the New York Public Library when the present biography should have been completed. It has been so deposited, and with it have gone also, by Mrs. Fleming's generosity, Dean Fleming's collections dealing with the Ku Klux Klan, and Reconstruction, upon which subjects he had won recognition as an authority.

Scattered throughout Dean Fleming's entire collection are carefully prepared comments, in his own handwriting, which have been of great value to the present writer, enabling him to check conclusions formed upon the evidence available before the Fleming material came into his possession.

In the manuscript department where the Fleming Collection is preserved, the New York Public Library has also a large body of documents bearing indirectly upon Mr. Davis' life, notably the Horace Greeley papers, and a valuable memorandum on the Fort Sumter Expedition (ms. of 22 pages), which explains Lincoln's attitude towards that expedition as a member of his Cabinet, Gideon Wells, understood it. The department possesses also the John Bigelow papers, which give the evidence of France's complicity in plans to build vessels for the Confederate navy. They contain transcripts of correspondence relating to the activities of agents of the Confederate government operating in France, or with France, including letters from J. M. Mason, J. Slidell, J. P. Benjamin, William Preston, and others—1861-1864. Some of these documents were used by Bigelow in writing his *France and the Confederate Navy* (New York, 1888). (Listed on p. 749.) The collection contains also the *Opinion Book of the Confederate Government*, with ms. opinions upon various important subjects covering April 1, 1861, to March 24, 1865. The law required the Confederate Attorney-General to give "his advice and opinion on questions of law" when requested by the Heads of Departments (p. 137).

## VI. Incidental Contemporary Material Gathered from Other Sources

The Boston Public Library, the Widener Library, at Harvard, and the Massachusetts Historical Society, while having no large collections of Davis mss., contain many documents which throw light upon his life.

The Boston Public Library's collection of CARTOONS AND BROADSIDES concerning Davis is unique. The following are examples:

(1) "The Way to Fix 'Em"; representing Jefferson Davis roasting chestnuts over the fire at Fort Sumter. By "Michel Angelo Woolf." New York, 1861.

(2) "Jeff. Davis on His Own Platform, or The Last 'Act of Secession.'" New York, Currier & Ives, 1861.

(3) "Jeff's Last Shift." Capture of Jeff. Davis, May 10, 1865, at Irwinsville, Ga. By Joseph E. Baker. Boston, Bufford, 1865.

It presents Davis in a bonnet with strings and a loose woman's dress, with a dagger in his hand. Three Federal soldiers and officers are taking him, while Mrs. Davis stands by, saying, "The men had better not provoke the President as he might hurt some of 'em."

(4) "Oh, What a Fall Was There!" relates to the capture of Jefferson Davis. Boston, Anon., 1865.

(5) "The Capture of Jeff. Davis." New York, Giles, John Lawrence & Co., 1865.

(6) "The Capture of an Unprotected Female, or The Close of the Rebellion." New York, Currier & Ives, 1865.

(7) "The Confederacy in Petticoats." Anon., New York, 1865.

It shows Davis leaping a fence, with hoopskirts caught, and a woman's bonnet hanging by its strings. Two Federal soldiers only are near, but many in the background. Mrs. Davis stands stiffly by, with her inevitable words, "Don't irritate the 'President,' he might hurt somebody."

(8) "The Last Ditch of the Cavalry, or a President in Petticoats." New York, Currier & Ives, 1865.

Davis in woman's hat and long dress is running, saying as he runs: "Let me alone, you bloodthirsty villains. I thought your government more magnanimous than to hunt down women and children." Four soldiers on foot are near him, with a crowd following. Mrs. Davis stands near, shouting, "Lookout you vile Yankees. If you make him mad he will hurt some of you."

(9) "The Head of the Confederacy on a New Base." New York, Hilton, & Co., 1865.

It shows Davis in hoopskirts and bonnet. He has let fall the pail in falling. Five Federal soldiers are beside him and his wife stands by, saying, "Don't provoke the President, or some of you may get hurt."

(10) "Jeff's Last Skedaddle. Off to the Last Ditch: How 'Jeff' in His Extremity Put His Naval Affairs and Ramparts under Petticoat Protection." By F. Welcher, New York, 1865.

It represents Davis with bonnet tied under his chin and dressed in a woman's dress, carrying bucket and Bowie knife, in flight from six soldiers on horseback. Mrs. Davis stands by, saying: "Please, gentlemen, don't disturb the privacy of ladies before they have time to dress."

(11) "The House That Jeff Built." Anon., New York, Amer. News Co., 1868.

A badly rhymed satirical poem built on the lines of "The House That Jack Built." Interesting as an example of the partisan methods of war days.

(12) "Jeff. Davis' Confession! A Singular Document Found on the Dead Body of a Rebel!" Philadelphia, Alexander & Co., 1861. A broadside 16½ x 11 inches.

A very clumsy attempt to place upon Davis the onus of vaulting ambition to become the Emperor of America. It is obviously a fraud, and not even a skillful one. It purports to be an address to the American people, issued from Richmond, 1861, and is endorsed, "This document was securely sealed and endorsed 'to be opened after my death.' Jefferson Davis." It is printed on a two-column broadside published by Alexander & Co., 619 Jayne Street, Philadelphia. Its confession of criminal ambition is inconsistent with all known authentic utterances and with the accepted character of Mr. Davis. It declares the object of his life, "the destruction of the Union—upon the ruins of which my intended throne was to have its foundation."

With these documents is a photograph of the clothes in which Davis was captured, and which are still preserved in the Confederate Museum in Richmond. With it is a clipping from the Richmond *Times Dispatch* of October 5, 1924, entitled, "Boston halts calumny against Jefferson Davis."

The Widener Library has recently acquired, through the activities of Professor Samuel Eliot Morison, of Harvard, the papers of J. A. Quitman which furnish convincing evidence of Davis' assertion, "I was slandered in relation to the Cuban Expedition." Mrs. Davis, in her *Memoir*, admits that Lopez once offered her husband "$100,000 down, and another $100,000 in event of success," if he would lead the ill-fated expedition to Cuba; but declares that he rejected the offer, as demanding action inconsistent with his sense of honour. Davis, however, never hesitated to defend Lopez's attempt to free Cuba from unbearable Spanish tyranny. See text, vol. II, p. 143.

In the Massachusetts Historical Society is a "Life of Jefferson Davis in Five Explosive Tableaux," a brutal little cartoon depicting Mr. Davis in various positions on his way to be hanged.

## B. NEWSPAPERS, MAGAZINES AND PRINTED SOURCES

The chief collections of Davis' papers, described under A of the present Bibliography, contain masses of newspaper and magazine cuttings of great value. The Jackson Mississippi Historical Collection has a *Scrap Book*, 5 volumes and almost 1,000 pages, devoted entirely to clippings taken immediately after Mr. Davis' death. These are all rapidly disintegrating on account of the quality of the paper used.

In addition, the present author has studied the files of many important magazines and reviews, both of Europe and of America. In them he has found much Davis material not elsewhere preserved, and interpretations which throw light upon the wider aspects of his career. The Queen's College, Oxford, has an almost complete file of leading British reviews covering the entire period of Davis' life. The Southern Historical Society papers contain a wealth of material relating to Davis, not elsewhere obtainable. They were published at Richmond in 47 volumes, 1876-1930. Mrs. Kate

Pleasants Minor has published a general index through Vol. 38; Nos. July-October, 1913, of Virginia State Library Bulletin, now out of print.

Careful search has been made also in the American daily press for articles concerning special incidents, such as Davis' first political activities in Mississippi, his New England tour of 1858, his "tour of glory" towards the end of his life, etc., etc., and his life during his Richmond days.

During this search for new material, the text here presented has nine times crossed the Atlantic, and has been carried by car through the chief European countries, Russia and Spain not included.

## C. JEFFERSON DAVIS' OWN PUBLICATIONS: AND BOOKS AND PAMPHLETS PREPARED UNDER HIS SUPERVISION

DAVIS, JEFFERSON:

Speeches delivered in the Senate, 1848-61. Washington, etc., 1848-61. Seven pamphlets bound in one volume. Widener Library.

Speech on the Oregon bill, Senate, July 12, 1848. Pamphlet, pp. 2-16: no publisher's imprint. Widener Library.

Speech on the Coast Survey of the United States, Senate, February 19, 1849. Pamphlet, pp. 2-40: no publisher's imprint. Widener Library.

"A Defence of Mississippi." An article contributed to the Washington *Daily Union*, of May 25, 1849. Text in Robert J. Walker's *Jefferson Davis and Repudiation*. (Listed on p. 739.) It does not appear in Rowland's "Jefferson Davis, Constitutionalist." It discusses the Mississippi Repudiation. The London *Times* answered it in its money article of July 13, 1849.

Speech on the measures of Compromise. Senate, June 28, 1850. Pamphlet, pp. 1-16: Washington, 1850: no publisher's imprint. Widener Library.

Speech "On the Exercise of Civil Power and Authority by Military Officers." Senate, Monday, Aug. 5, 1850. Pamphlet, pp. 1-16: no publisher's imprint. Widener Library.

Report of the Secretary of War, communicating, in compliance with a resolution of the Senate of February 2, 1857, information respecting the purchase of camels for the purposes of military transportation. Pamphlet, Washington, A. O. P. Nicholson, printer, 1857. Virginia State Library.

Speeches delivered during the summer of 1858. Pamphlet, pp. 3-56: Baltimore, J. Murphy & Co., 1859.

In dedicating the little volume to the people of Mississippi, Davis wrote:

"I have been induced by the persistent misrepresentations of popular addresses made by me at the North and at Sea during the year 1858, to collect them, and with extracts from speeches made by me in the Senate in 1850, to present the whole in this connected form; to the end that the case may be fairly before those by whose judgment I am willing to stand or fall." Widener Library.

Speech upon his resolutions recently presented to the Senate. Senate, May 7, 1860. Pamphlet, pp. 1-15: Baltimore, J. Murphy & Co., 1860.

Important in connexion with the division of the Democratic party. Widener Library.

Speech in reply to Douglas' speech on "Non-Intervention by Congress with Slavery in the Territories." Senate, May 16 and 17, 1860. Pamphlet, pp. 1-16: Baltimore, J. Murphy & Co., 1860. Widener Library.

Report of the Commissioners on the Military Academy of West Point. Issued by U. S. 36th Cong., 2nd Sess., Senate, 1860. Widener Library.

Speech upon the Message of the President of the United States on the condition of things in South Carolina. Senate, January 10, 1861. Pamphlet, pp. 2-16: Baltimore, J. Murphy & Co., 1861. Widener Library.

Correspondence between the President and the Governor of Georgia, relative to the law usually known as the Conscription law. Pamphlet, pp. 1-20. Richmond, Ritchie & Dunnavant, 1862.

Governor Brown also published this correspondence under title:

"Correspondence between Governor Brown and President Davis on the Constitutionality of the Conscription Act." Pamphlet, pp. 1-52: Atlanta, Ga. Atlanta *Intelligencer* print, 1862.

It contains simply the texts of letters beginning with Brown's letter of April 22, 1862, and ending with one from the same, on July 22, 1862. Brown argued that the Conscription Act would make it possible to conscript the members of the Georgia Legislature, between the ages of eighteen and thirty-five, and threatens "all the remaining military force of the state in defence of a coördinate Constitutional branch of the government." It would also take all the judges, and officials, as well as slave overseers of the designated age, thus leaving thousands of slaves without overseers. He also complained "this act does not leave to the states the appointment of a single officer to command the militia." It "enables him [Davis] at his pleasure to cripple and destroy the civil government of each state." Widener Library.

An address to the people of the free states, Richmond, Jan. 5, 1863. Reprinted in *Magazine of Hist.* Extra numbers, no. 113, p. 67. Tarrytown, N. Y., 1925.

An examination of this strange document will be found on pp. 364-367, vol. II, of the present biography. Massachusetts Society, *E.* 171.

Two addresses to the soldiers of the Confederacy, issued respectively on August 1, 1863, and February 2, 1864. In Southern Hist. Soc. Publications, xiv, pp. 466-470.

They do not appear in Rowland, but are worth preserving as indicating the situation at those important dates.

In the second of these addresses Davis declared:

"By your will (for you and the people are but one) I have been placed in a position which debars me from sharing your dangers, your sufferings, and your privations in the field." And he added this promise: "Assured success awaits us in our holy struggle for liberty and independence, and for the preservation of all that renders life desirable to honourable men."

Reply to Mr. [R. M. T.] Hunter, dated Mississippi City, March 27, 1878, and addressed to Rev. J. W. Jones, secretary of the Southern Historical Society. In Southern Hist. Soc. Papers, v, pp. 222-227: not in Rowland.

It deals with Hunter's criticisms of Davis, and denies that his movement from Richmond to Danville was "a flight."

*The Rise and Fall of the Confederate Government.* 2 vols., New York, Appleton & Co., 1881.

This is Davis' *magnum opus*, not "ghost written," as is sometimes asserted, but prepared by Davis himself, with the assistance of Walthall, Mrs. Davis, and, for a time, Mrs. Dorsey. The details of its preparation will be found in vol. II, pp. 642-660, of the present Biography. It is disappointing chiefly because it deals so extensively with controversies which have largely lost their interest, and throws so little light upon the writer's own way of life and of thought concerning things not matters of military or political controversy. Throughout the two ponderous volumes the author's evident purpose is to justify himself, with the honest conviction that by so doing he would justify the South. In this, as in all Davis' writings, one misses the wide sweep of human sympathy which gilds every page of Lincoln's writings. Davis quarrelled with Johnston, and many others, and his book is filled with endless details and innuendoes about their misunderstandings and differences—Lincoln quarrelled with no one, but endured in silence and humorous good temper the most brutal insults even from Cabinet officials, and the active commander of his armies.

"The Indian Policy of the United States." In *North American Review*, July-December, 1886. Copy with Fleming mss., folder xiv.

It is a defence of the intentions of the American Government in its dealings with the Indians, but an arraignment of its methods. It pleads for reforms which would insure justice to the Indian.

The story of his capture. An account written by himself. Newspaper clipping from St. Louis *Globe Democrat*, December 7, 1889.

It contains a deposition by Andrew Bee, one of his captors, which is very interesting and convincing, and a statement by Col. Johnston of Charlotte, N. C., about Davis' reception of the news of Lincoln's assassination. Massachusetts Historical Society.

"Life and Character of John C. Calhoun." In *North American Review*, vol. cxlv, pp. 246-260.

It is more than an eulogium: it is an interpretation, and a strong defence of his old friend from all charges of having been, ever, a disunionist. It declares it "absurdly strange that currency could have been obtained for a report that he desired to destroy a confederation to which his life had been devoted." Even his nullification theory, says Davis, who did not accept it, "was intended to conserve, not to destroy, the Union." Transcript in Fleming mss., folder xiv.

"Lord Wolseley's Mistakes," an essay in reply to certain criticisms of Davis by the distinguished British general, Lord Wolseley. Ms. copy in form of transcript, but without printed source indicated, in Fleming mss. xiv.

The article itself shows that it was written for the *North American Review*, in answer to a second attack made "in the *North American Review* for May" by Wolseley, whom he describes as an "European stripling without an earned record of ability either in civil or military life." Davis declares, "Each and every allegation in Lord Wolseley's indictment above quoted . . . either false in direct statement or false by inference," and he quotes the texts of official documents in support of his declaration.

For history of the manuscript in the office of *North American Review*, see vol. II, pp. 688-697, of the present Biography.

*Messages and Papers:*

Every message, letter, and dispatch, public or confidential, which has escaped destruction, and was available at the time, is contained in the Official Records of the War of the Rebellion. Davis' Executive papers are easily accessible also in James D. Richardson's Standard Edition, "Messages and Papers of the Confederacy," 2 vols. Nashville, 1905.

"Robert E. Lee." Pamphlet, pp. 1-12. New York, 1890, taken from Southern Historical Society Papers, xvii, pp. 362-372. It appeared also in the *North American Review*, January, 1890, pp. 55-56.

It preserves personal incidents of permanent interest in view of the long intimacy of the two leaders, never broken while both lived. Widener Library.

Andersonville and other War Prisons. Posthumous, *Belford's Magazine*, New York, January, 1890. Reprint in *Confederate Veteran*, March-April, 1907. Copy in Fleming mss. xiv.

Its confessed purpose was "to vindicate the conduct of the Confederacy," and it was prepared at the request of "some eminent citizens of the North, who were farthest removed from the class known as 'Southern Sympathizers' . . . who desire to know the whole truth." It is a convincing testimony to the good intentions and humanity of the Confederate Government, though marred at times by a too evident desire to direct similar charges of intentional cruelty at the Federal authorities, especially Stanton. One difficulty in the continued exchange of prisoners, he mentions, but minimizes: the South was not ready to recognize Negro troops as entitled to the privilege of exchange. From the larger point of view, the North was certainly justified in rejecting all exchanges with that limitation involved. To Davis this "pretence served General Grant as an excuse to decline negotiations, and for 'putting the matter offensively for the purpose of preventing an exchange,' as he recommended General Butler, his Commissioner of Exchange, to do."

It is interesting to compare Davis' account of Andersonville with:

(1) "An account of conditions in Andersonville Prison, as reported by an escaped officer." *New York Day Book,* January 13, 1866.

(2) "Escape of a Confederate Officer from Prison, with what he saw at Andersonville." Pamphlet, pp. 1-72: Norfolk, The Landmark Publishing Co., 1892.

The anonymous writer was captured, sentenced to death, and saved by the intervention of President Lincoln. The pamphlet abounds in thrilling personal details, and contains valuable evidence concerning conditions at Andersonville, which he was able to compare with Federal prisons.—Confederate Museum.

*A Short History of the Confederate States of America.* 1 vol., pp. xii-505: Belford Co., 1890.

Redpath, the historian, spent some months helping Davis prepare it. It has little value for the biographer, and offers the historian little not to be found elsewhere.

"The Doctrine of State Rights." In *North American Review*, Jan.-June, 1890.

A brief summary of the historical arguments in favour of the right of a state to "resume" its sovereignty. At the end of the argument, Davis confesses his abiding faith in the principles of the lost cause, and among these he does not include slavery.

Davis vs. Bowmar (Joseph H. D.) and Smith (Joseph D.): being the lawsuit for ownership of the "Brierfield" plantation:

I. Argument of Pittman and Pittman, for the complainant (Jefferson Davis), in the Chancery Court of Warren County, in Jefferson Davis' suit for "Brierfield Place." Pamphlet, pp. 1-62: Vicksburg *Herald*, without date. Fleming Collection, New York Public Library.

It gives the evidence of Davis' ownership of "Brierfield," and throws valuable light upon Davis' plantation days.

II. Argument on appeal from the Chancery Court of Warren County, by Harris and George, solicitors, before the Supreme Court of Mississippi, April Term, 1877. Pamphlet, pp. 1-39: Jackson, Miss., Charles Winkley, 1877. Fleming Collection, New York Public Library.

It reviews the history of Davis' life as a planter, in so far as it was thought to affect his claim to the estate of "Brierfield."

The decisions were in favour of Jefferson Davis, the complainant.

*Davis, Jefferson and Davidson:*

A chapter of War History Concerning Torpedoes. It is a correspondence between President Davis and Captain Davidson in relation to the latter's services. In Southern Hist. Soc. Papers, vol. 24, pp. 284-291.

Of interest chiefly to those seeking details of torpedo warfare in Civil War days.

Davis, Jefferson, and Galloway, Chas. B.:

Open letters on prohibition: a controversy between Hon. Jefferson Davis and Bishop Chas. B. Galloway." Pamphlet, Nashville, 1893.

A debate of especial interest in view of America's recent experiment in prohibition. Jackson, Mississippi Historical Collection.

DAVIS, VARINA HOWELL (MRS. JEFFERSON DAVIS):

*Jefferson Davis, Ex-President of the Confederate States of America, a Memoir by His Wife.* 2 vols. Bedford Co., 1890.

On page 2 Mrs. Davis thus explains her purpose, "I shall endeavour . . . to make the book an autobiography—to tell the story of my husband's life in his own words; to complete the task he left unfinished." In view of this declaration, Mrs. Davis' *Memoir* has been taken as authoritative upon Davis' early life. In so far as Davis himself knew the facts of family history, pp. 3-12 of Vol. I is authoritative, for it was, according to Mrs. Davis, dictated by him shortly before his death, and incorporated without "verbal or other changes." But on December 31, 1900, in a letter to Mrs. Green, Mrs. Davis says: "I am perfectly aware that my account of my husband's ancestry was very vague, but it was not so much so as his own and that of his sisters, who evidently knew but little. The 'Plantation at Augusta' was what my sister-in-law, Mrs. Bradford, an old lady of eighty-eight, wrote Mr. Davis. None of the family attached any importance to genealogy, and so their history has fallen silent and can only be resurrected out of the old records. . . . Mr. Davis . . . had no time to think of the dead, contending as he was with the living, and attached no importance to any ancestor except his father, whose Revolutionary services he knew." (Text: Fleming mss. xviii.) This confirms the statement, made on pp. 143-144, Vol. I, of Mrs. Davis' *Memoir*, that this part of her *Memoir* is a compilation, based upon other books and such stories as she could recall. These sections are inaccurate and often confusing, but her personal knowledge concerning events which followed her own marriage to him is very detailed, and in the main accurate, as she was Mr. Davis' most trusted counsellor. Her bias is, however, apparent throughout the two volumes. Her manifest purpose was to defend a cause and justify a person, not to write impartial history. And to the end of her life, Mrs. Davis continued to "defend the cause," in frequent articles, often very bitter in their attacks upon those whom she considered his enemies.

Harrison, Burton N.:

"The Capture of Jefferson Davis." *Century Magazine,* 1883.

Harrison was President Davis' confidential secretary, and his companion in the arrest. He writes, therefore, as an eye-witness. His proofs were sent to Davis, who made notes of suggestions, most of which were accepted. His account almost certainly was reviewed by Mrs. Davis, also an eye-witness.

It is included in *The Harrisons of Skimino,* edited by Fairfax Harrison from material collected by Francis Burton Harrison, and privately printed for them in 1910. Pp. 1-413.

Some unpublished letters of ——. In Massachusetts Historical Society Publication, viii, pp. 81-85.

The letters treating of the imprisonment of Davis are of unusual interest, showing that Thaddeus Stevens volunteered to defend Davis.

The reasons for Stevens' offer are interpreted in no friendly light in *The Harrisons of Skimino,* p. 201. The statement is that "the wily old rascal has a purpose of his own to accomplish. His doctrine is that there is no treason in war after it has once been set on foot, that the opposing enemies represented independent belligerent governments, and that the Southern communities are not now states with rights under the Constitution, but merely conquered territories. . . . In order to get that doctrine established, he wants Mr. Davis tried for treason and acquitted." Boston Public Library.

Harrison, Mrs. Burton:

*Recollections, Grave and Gay.* 1 vol., New York: Charles Scribner's Sons, 1916.

This volume contains a considerable amount of first-hand information about Mr. Davis, derived chiefly from the author's husband, who was Mr. Davis' confidential secretary and friend.

Johnson, Bradley T. [Editor]:

Reports of cases decided by Chief-Justice Chase in the Circuit Court of the United States, for the Fourth Circuit, during the years 1865 to 1869, both inclusive. 1 vol., New York, Diossy & Co., 1876.

The volume was revised and corrected by the Chief Justice himself, and contains, on pp. 1-124, the "Case of Jefferson Davis," with:

(1) The Statement of the Case, pp. 1-85, signed Charles O'Conor, William B. Reed, Robert Ould, James Lyons.
(2) The Argument for the Defence, pp. 86-91.
(3) The Argument for the United States, pp. 91-106.
(4) The rest of the Argument for the Defence, pp. 106-122.
(5) The Certificate of Division: and the Chief Justice's opinion "that the indictment should be quashed, and all further proceedings barred by the effect of the Fourteenth Amendment to the Constitution of the United States."

It is the most valuable source for the trial of Jefferson Davis. Charles O'Conor, who was Mr. Davis' chief attorney, wrote of it, on September 3, 1877, to Mr. Davis, then preparing to write his *Rise and Fall of the Confederate Government*: "Hon. Bradley T. Johnson . . . is the author of a lawbook in 1 vol., being reports of cases decided by Chief-Justice Chase in the circuit including Virginia. The first article in it is a somewhat graphic statement of the proceedings had against you. I should not know how to present a more distinct and intelligible exhibit of the matters to which you refer than is to be found between pp. 11 and 18 and pp. 106 and 122. . . . Nothing in my possession could be more useful to you than this. . . ."

O'Conor apparently did not know that Mr. Davis had been consulted by Bradley T. Johnson during the preparation of his book. "I would like to consult your wishes," he wrote, "as to how far . . . to preserve some of those details—for instance an order of General Miles that no officer should escort Mrs. Davis to or from your quarters. Be pleased to give me a sketch of such a statement as will do for the opening of my report—I shall follow it by an exposure of Mr. Johnson's complicity in the indictment at Norfolk, May 10, 1866—of the surrender to civil authority and bail 1867 and the motion to quash, etc., etc., giving the official papers as the cause progressed—Mr. O'Conor is revising the argument for me—Ould will do the same—Dana has sent his and I hope to preserve this record of perfidy for posterity—a record of honor for you and for us—How it affects the other side,—let history decide. . . ." This shows that his report is not history, but a brief though an extremely able one. Va. State Library.

In a note on page 439 of his Confederate Calendar, Douglas Freeman says "General Bradley T. Johnson prepared an elaborate *Report* of Davis' trial, "which is, unfortunately, very rare." If it is a report not included in "the Reports of cases decided by Chief-Justice Chase," I have failed to find it.

Walthall, W. T.:

"The True Story of the Capture of Jefferson Davis."

In Southern Hist. Soc. Papers, v. 5, 1878, pp. 97-126.

It is a detailed and documented reply to the interpretation of Davis' flight and capture which Major-General James H. Wilson had published in the Philadelphia *Weekly Times* of July 7, 1877. (See Section D, *seq.*) Walthall inserts a letter from Col. William Preston Johnston, late aide to President Davis, dated Lexington, Va., July 14, 1877; a letter from Raphael Semmes, dated August 13, 1877; a letter from ex-Governor Lubbock of Texas, late aide to President Davis, dated Galveston, August 2, 1877, and a letter from Hon. George Davis, late Attorney-General of the Confederate States, dated Wilmington, N. C., September 4, 1877, in refutation of the Wilson story.

It is a convincing, critical survey of the details of Mr. Davis' arrest. *Athenaeum,* Boston.

Jefferson Davis, a sketch of the life and character of the President of the Confederate States: Pamphlet, pp. 1-53; *Times Democrat,* 1908.

It first appeared in the *Times Democrat* of December 6, 1889; was published in pamphlet form as "the most faithful and accurate appreciation of Mr. Davis yet written." It had been submitted to Mr. Davis for his personal criticism by its author who was his chief assistant in the compilation of *The Rise and Fall of the Confederate Government.* Virginia State Library.

## D. DAVIS BIOGRAPHIES, OR ITEMS OF BIOGRAPHY, BY AUTHORS, ALPHABETICALLY ARRANGED

Abrams, A. S.:

President Davis and his administration: Being a *review* of the *Rival Administrations,* lately published in Richmond and written by E. A. Pollard. Atlanta, Ga., published for the author, 1864.

An extreme answer to extreme views, as much partisan on the side of Davis as Pollard was against him. Widener Library.

Alfriend, Frank H.:

*The Life of Jefferson Davis.* Cincinnati, Caxton Pub. House; Philadelphia, National Publishing Co., 1868, pp. 1-645.

A general sketch up to Davis' capture with a few words on later events up to the date of publication. The author is a frank partisan rather than an historian, writing under the excitement of Davis' pending trial which never came. His account of Mr. Davis' capture, given largely in the words of Mr. Mallory, Secretary of the Confederate Navy, is fairly accurate; Walthall declares it "measurably" so. (Southern Hist. Soc. Papers, v. 107). Davis himself is more critical: "The accounts in Alfriend of the siege of Monterey and the battle of Buena Vista," he wrote to Walthall, on October 13, 1877, "are imperfect and inaccurate in many particulars, too many to be enumerated in a note." Text: Rowland VIII, 33. Widener Library.

ANON.:

Life of Jefferson Davis. From authentic sources. By "A South Carolinian." London: G. W. Bacon (1865). 1 vol., pp. 1-123.

A brief sketch, made up chiefly of excerpts from Davis' speeches and public papers. Appendix contains the text of Davis' letter to Lincoln, July 6, 1861, threatening retaliation if the men taken from the *Savannah* are executed. Boston Public Library.

*Life and Imprisonment of Jefferson Davis, Together with the Life and Military Career of Stonewall Jackson.* From authentic sources, with portraits of Jefferson Davis, Stonewall Jackson, and General R. E. Lee. New York, M. Doubleday, publisher, 1866. 1 vol., pp. 1-300.

Only 97 pages are devoted to Davis, and they cover his career from birth to the date of publication. It is made up chiefly of brief quotations from known letters and speeches of Mr. Davis, from Dr. Craven's Journal and other well-known sources.

The most interesting documents are those in the Appendix, showing how evidence against Davis was secured by bribery, notably the letter of the Judge Advocate-General, J. Holt, dated August 7, 1866, pp. 141-146, and J. Holt to S. Conover, March 17, 1866. Boston Public Library.

It appears also with the publishers' imprint, Philadelphia, J. E. Potter & Co., 1866. Widener Library.

"A Sketch of the Life of Jefferson Davis," *Times Democrat* of New Orleans, December 6 and 10, 1889.

It was reprinted as a pamphlet, on June 3, 1908, the Centennial of Davis' birth, by the *Times Democrat*, and copies were presented to the school children of Louisiana and Mississippi. The pamphlet bears title, "Jefferson Davis, a sketch of the Life and Character of the President of the Confederate States." Widener Library.

"Jefferson Davis, and His Complicity in the Assassination of Abraham Lincoln . . . and Where the Traitor Shall Be Tried for Treason." Philadelphia, Sherman & Co., printers, 1866, pp. 1-16.

A bitter plea: (1) for the trial of Davis for treason, of which, he says, "All agree that he was guilty," a statement which in itself condemns the pamphlet as unreasonably partisan; (2) for the conviction of Davis for complicity in the assassination of Lincoln, with what he calls evidence of that complicity. From such trivial items as he presents he declares, "The conclusion is inevitable of the complicity of Jefferson Davis in the assassination of Abraham Lincoln." Interesting only as one of the surviving pamphlets from a list which was doubtless very long in the days of Davis' pending trial. Widener Library and Boston Public Library.

"Why Jefferson Davis Was Never Tried." In Southern Hist. Soc. Papers, vol. 38, pp. 347-349. From Richmond, Va., *Times-Dispatch* of February 19, 1911.

A brief summary of the history of the famous case. Boston Public Library.

"A Statement of the Facts Concerning the Imprisonment and Treatment of Jefferson Davis While a Military Prisoner at Fortress Monroe, Va., in 1865 and 1866." Washington, D. C., Gibson Bros., 1904, pp. 1-12.

It is a brief collection of interesting letters and reports, in chronological order. *Athenæum,* Boston: Boston Public Library.

"Jefferson Davis," in *Eminent Persons,* v. 4, 1893. Articles reprinted from the *Times.* London, Macmillan & Co., 1893.

Pages 181-195 are devoted to Jefferson Davis, being (1) his obituary notice of Saturday, December 7, 1889; (2) leading article, Saturday,

December 7, 1889. They are rather ill-informed articles, of interest chiefly as showing the reactions of the *Times. Athenæum,* Boston.

Arnold, George:

"Life and Adventures of Jefferson Davis. By (Pseud. "McArone.") New York, J. C. Heney & Co., 1865.

A burlesque life, with insulting pictures beginning with a frontispiece of Davis escaping in woman's clothes, and ending with him hanging from a gibbet. An interesting lampoon. Widener Library.

Bacon, G. W. (of North Carolina):

*Life of Jefferson Davis from Authentic Sources.* London, 1871: a sketch of little value.

Bancroft, A. C. (editor):

*The Life and Death of Jefferson Davis.* New York, J. S. Ogilvie, 1889, 1 vol., pp. 1-256.

A very poor compilation, made up chiefly of extracts from newspapers and documents, heterogeneously arranged. A large part of the volume is given up to minute details of his funeral, etc. Va. State Library.

Blackburn, Benjamin M.:

"Life and Character of Jefferson Davis."

Address delivered in the Georgia House of Representatives, June 3, 1905. Pamphlet, pp. 1-22. Atlanta, 1905. It gives little of distinctive value.

Blackford, C. M.:

"The Trials and Trial of Jefferson Davis"; a paper read before the twelfth annual meeting of the Virginia State Bar Association, held at Old Point Comfort, Va., July 17, 18, 19, 1900. In Virginia State Bar Association Papers, Richmond, 1900. Reprinted by John T. West, Richmond, 1900, and at Lynchburg, J. P. Bell Co., 1901.

A valuable summary of details of Davis' flight and capture, with a detailed and sympathetic sketch of his prison life at Fortress Monroe. The latter half is devoted to the details of the trial that never came, in which the author exhibits a strong pro-Davis bias. It is invaluable for a study of Davis' indictment, and why it was quashed. Mass. Hist. Soc.; Southern Hist. Soc. Papers, vol. 29, pp. 45-81; *Athenæum,* Boston.

Bledsoe, Albert Taylor:

(1) Is Davis a Traitor; or Was Secession a Constitutional Right Previous to the War of 1861? Innes & Co., Baltimore, 1866. 1 vol., pp. 1-263.

The object of the book is stated: "to appeal from the mad forum of passion to the calm tribunal of reason." But so detached a course regarding secession was impossible in 1866; and this book is really a Confederate brief for the right of secession. It is, however, an informed brief. Bledsoe had gone to Europe in 1863 to collect material for a defence of secession, and his views are brilliantly condensed into this little volume which, he hoped, might influence public opinion while Davis' trial was pending.

"The whole Southern people," he wrote, "the dead as well as the living, is about to be tried in the person of our illustrious chief." Mass. Hist. Soc.

(2) "Jefferson Davis and Robert E. Lee." *Southern Review,* vol. ii, pp. 231-242. Bledsoe had served as Acting Assistant Secretary of War in the Confederacy, and therefore writes of military problems with authority.

Boutwell, George S.:

"The Assassination of Lincoln," a report upon the evidence implicating Jefferson Davis and others in the assassination of President Lincoln. Pamphlet, pp. 1-41, Washington, 1866, being Report No. 104, 39th Cong. 1st Sess. A convenient form of Boutwell's report for the Committee on the Judiciary. Boston Public Library.

Brown, John Wilcox:

"Why Jefferson Davis Was Never Tried." In Southern Historical Society Papers, vol. 38, pp. 347-349.

A brief account of a conference between Davis' counsel the night before he was brought before Mr. Justice Chase, in which it was agreed by Davis' counsel that they would accept the Government's proposal of a *nolle prosequi* which later followed. Virginia State Library.

Bruce, George Alexander:

"President Davis." In Military Hist. Soc. of Mass. Papers. Vol. 13, 1913, pp. 347-389.

A very compact and able sketch of Davis' entire career. *Athenæum*, Boston.

Campbell, Hon. J. A. P.:

Address upon the life and character of Jefferson Davis, delivered before the Legislature of the State of Mississippi, in Joint Memorial Session, January 22, 1890, Jackson, Miss., R. H. Henry, State Printer, 1890, pp. 1-19.

The author was the last surviving member of the Confederate Congress. The speech is the usual type of eulogium, and contains a brief sketch of Mr. Davis' career. Jackson, Miss. Collection.

Clark, Micajah H.:

"Retreat of the Cabinet from Richmond." In Southern Hist. Soc. Papers, 26, pp. 96-101.

As the last Confederate Treasurer, the author's comments upon the so-called "Confederate treasure" have especial interest.

Cox, Hon. Samuel S.:

Speech on amnesty and Jefferson Davis amendment. Washington, January 10, 1876.

A plea for the larger justice which is mercy. Mass. Hist. Society.

Craven, John J.:

*The Prison Life of Jefferson Davis*. New York, Carleton, 1866. 1 vol. pp. 11-377.

Embracing details and incidents of his captivity, particulars concerning his health and habits, together with many conversations on topics of great public interest. The best account of Davis' prison life, described by his physician, with sympathy and skill.

Another copy with an autograph letter from Jefferson Davis to Mr. Henry S. Howe, dated March 11, 1889, and another note, also in his hand, inserted. Eight editions have appeared. Widener Library.

A French translation, La vie de prison de Jefferson Davis . . . au Fort Monroë. Scènes tirées du Journal rédigé par le Dr. Craven.

Traduites de l'anglais par Wallace S. Jones. Paris, France. Pamphlet. Achille Faure, 1866, pp. 1-32. Boston Public Library.

Cutting, Elisabeth:

"Jefferson Davis Political Soldier." New York, Dodd, Mead & Co., 1930, pp. 1-361.

One of the most satisfactory biographies of Mr. Davis, and of unusual literary merit. Its author was associate editor of the *North American Review* from 1910 to 1921. Widener Library.

Dana, Richard Henry:

"The Reasons for Not Prosecuting Jefferson Davis." In Mass. Hist. Soc. Proceedings. Vol. 64, April, 1931.

A brief statement of the facts that led to the abandonment of prosecution, by a son of one of the counsel for the prosecution. The father would probably have taken the principal part in the trial had it proceeded. Dana quotes a letter from his father to William M. Evarts, asking, "Why should the United States voluntarily assume the risk of failure, by putting the question of the treason of Jefferson Davis to a petit jury of the rebel vicinage?" (p. 203), and one from Mr. Evarts expressing the view that the pending impeachment of the President would be brief and result in removal (p. 204), an interesting confession for Johnson's chief counsel.

Daniel, John Warwick:

Oration on the life, services, and character of Jefferson Davis, delivered under the auspices of the General Assembly of Virginia, January 25, 1890. Pamphlet, pp. 1-51. Richmond, J. H. O'Bannon, 1890.

A brilliant, highly rhetorical and suggestive oration, not always reliable in matters of detail; as, for example, when the orator says: "Colonel Davis won the battle of Buena Vista, and Buena Vista made General Taylor President," p. 17. Copy in Southern Historical Papers, vol. 17, pp. 113-159.

Davis, George:

"The capture of Jefferson Davis." In Southern Hist. Soc. Papers, vol. 5, pp. 124-126.

A letter to Major W. T. Walthall, dated Wilmington, N. C., September 4, 1877, pointing out the absurdity of General Wilson's statement that Davis had made arrangements to escape to the *Shenandoah* many weeks before the fall of Richmond, and bearing the testimony of an eyewitness to his high courage and his patience. Virginia State Library.

Davis, Harry Alexander:

*The Davis Family (Davies and David) in Wales and America. Genealogy of Morgan David of Pennsylvania.*

Compiled and published by H. A. Davis, Washington, D. C., 1927. 1 vol., pp. 1-445, with Index.

A page, following the Preface, gives a coat of arms, in red and black, marked "Davis," [Davies] [David], with the inscription,

Heb DHUW Heb DDYM
DAUW A DIGON

Jackson, Miss., Historical Collection.

Davis, Varina Anne:

"Jefferson Davis in Private Life." An intimate, personal sketch by Mr. Davis' daughter. In New York *Herald*, August 11, 1895, a five-column article.

De Leon, Thomas Cooper:

"The Real Jefferson Davis in Private and Public Life." In Southern Historical Society Papers, vol. 36, pp. 74-85.

It deals chiefly with Davis' genealogy, and contains little of value. Virginia State Library.

Denison, Claude B.:

Address delivered before the State Chapter, U.D.C., Raleigh, N. C., October 10, 1900. Pamphlet, pp. 1-20. Of little value.

Dickinson, Julian G.:

"The Capture of Jefferson Davis." Pamphlet, pp. 1-15, Detroit, Ostler Printing Company, 1888.

In Military Order of the Loyal Legion of the United States, Michigan Commandery; War Papers, No. 10.

The author was adjutant of the 4th Michigan Cavalry which captured Davis. His story of Davis' disguise is capable of various interpretations, and quite consistent with the story told by Davis and confirmed by his wife. Boston Public Library.

Dinkins, James:

Address on Jefferson Davis, delivered at the presentation of crosses of honour, by Stonewall Jackson Chapter No. 1135, U.D.C. at Memorial Hall, June 3, 1910. Pamphlet, pp. 1-6. New Orleans, Picayune Job Print., 1910.

The character of the address is illustrated by the statement, "Mr. Davis was a very demigod in war."

Dixon, Thomas:

"The Victim; a Romance of the Real Jefferson Davis." New York and London, D. Appleton & Co., 1914.

Although professedly fiction, it gives much of the atmosphere and many of the details needed for a comprehensive view of Davis' career. Virginia State Library.

Dodd, William Edward:

(1) "Jefferson Davis." In the "American Crisis Biographies," edited by E. P. Oberholtzer, 1 vol., pp. 1-396. Philadelphia, George W. Jacobs & Co., 1907.

An excellent outline biography. The author, a well-known historian, is ambassador to Germany.

(2) "Statesmen of the Old South; or, From Radicalism to Conservative Revolt." 1 vol., pp. 1-242. New York, Macmillan, 1911; reissued January, 1926. Contents: Thomas Jefferson, John C. Calhoun and Jefferson Davis. Widener Library.

(3) "Robert J. Walker." In the *Bulletin* of Randolph-Macon Woman's College, vol. i, no. 2, Jan., 1915.

It presents a searching analysis of Walker's attempt to connect Davis with Mississippi repudiation and vindicates Davis.

Eckenrode, Hamilton James:

"Jefferson Davis, President of the South." New York, Macmillan Co., 1923, 1 vol., pp. 1-371.

A politico-military history of the Confederacy, based upon a study of the official records and Confederate correspondence, with memoirs of participants. It is "an effort to apply" anthropology to American history. The design is to follow the path blazed by Madison Grant's *The Passing of the Great Race*, and to apply Grant's "'Nordic instinct for mastery" to the interpretation of Davis' life. Eckenrode paints the South as Walter-Scott-land, filled with idealism and romance by the perusal of the Waverley Novels. He feels that "It was the outdoor romanticism of the South and the practicality of the North which, primarily, brought about the antagonism that ended in secession and war" (p. 12). He laments that in life "Commonplaceness is always defeating imagination" (p. 12). The Southerner he feels, "was beginning to be tropical, while remaining, in large part, Nordic" (p. 12). The border South he considers only in part Nordic, with conscience pricked by the evil of slavery. The Nordics of the far South had no such scruples. There the Nordic boldly towered over inferiors, worked them as chattels, beat them, killed them. To him slavery was a right and proper relationship between the Nordic master race and the slave (p. 13). The far Southerner is "the one real creation of America."

A London edition appeared in 1924, George Allen and Unwin, 1 vol., pp. 1-371.

Ford, Worthington C.:

A review of H. J. Eckenrode's "Jefferson Davis."

In *Atlantic Monthly*, February, 1924. Ford declares, "the book is worthy of study and offers novel views on men and measures." Mass. Hist. Soc.

Fleming, Walter L.:

The following articles, preserved as pamphlets in Fleming Collection, New York Public Library, represent patient research and are invaluable contributions to obscure periods of Davis' life:

(1) "The Early Life of Jefferson Davis." In Mississippi Valley Hist. Ass'n Proceedings, April, 1917, vol. ix, pp. 151-176. It was reprinted, pamphlet, pp. 151-176, from University Bulletin, Louisiana State University, vii, no. 6.

(2) "Jefferson Davis at West Point." Pamphlet, from the Publications of the Miss. Hist. Soc., vol. x, pp. 247-267. Louisiana State Univ., 1910.

A very valuable contribution to our knowledge of this obscure period of Mr. Davis' life.

(3) "Jefferson Davis' First Marriage." Pamphlet, from Miss. Hist. Soc. Publications, vol. 12, pp. 21-36. Univ. Miss., 1912.

A detailed and fully documented story of this incident in Davis' career, settling many points of long controversy.

(4) "Jefferson Davis, the Negroes and the Negro Problem." Pamphlet, from the *Sewanee Review*, Oct., 1908, pp. 1-23. Louisiana State University, Baton Rouge, Louisiana, 1908.

An article of unusual interest and value, in its interpretation of the character as well as of the views of Jefferson Davis.

(5) "Jefferson Davis' Camel Experiment." Pamphlet, from *Popular Science Monthly*, Feb., 1909, pp. 142-152.

A detailed history of the experiment, with footnote references to sources and a Bibliography: reprinted in University Bulletin, Louisiana State Univ., vii, no. 1, par. 2. Baton Rouge, 1909.

(6) The religious life of Jefferson Davis. Pamphlet from University Bulletin, Louisiana State University, vol. i, no. 5, pp. 325-342. Baton Rouge, 1910.

It does justice to the sincerity of Davis' religious convictions.

(7) "Jefferson Davis and Andersonville." Pamphlet from Southern Hist. Soc. Papers, vol. 36, pp. 8-12.

Mr. Fleming here prints for the first time two letters of Mr. Davis which escaped Mr. Dunbar Rowland. They show conclusively that Mr. Davis did not see the report made on the condition of Andersonville Prison by Col. Z. T. Chandler in August, 1864, and that the censure of such orators as Blaine and Garfield were quite unjustified. Virginia State Library.

(8) "Life of Jefferson Davis," published in the *Methodist Review* of April, 1910.

A brief but suggestive sketch.

Freeman, C. E.:

Address delivered, October 10, 1909, before the Unity Club of Wisconsin, entitled "Two Local Questions." In the *Dun County News,* Menomonie, Wis., Oct. 14, 1909. Copy in Fleming mss., xxi.

It gives evidence to prove that Jefferson Davis "once cut timber on the Red Cedar River," and contains valuable items upon other disputed points of Davis' frontier days.

Freeman, Douglas Southall (editor):

*Lee's Confidential Dispatches to Davis, 1862-1865.* New York: G. P. Putnam's Sons, 1915. 1 vol., pp. 1-400, with an introduction of xxxviii pages by the editor.

The collection, the editor explains, was taken from "a file kept for his own reference by President Davis himself." Most of the letters are addressed to Mr. Davis and "show no evidence of having passed through the hands of other persons." They were bought "of a well-known Southern writer by their present owner, Mr. W. J. DeRenne, of Wormsloe, Chatham County, Georgia, an historian and collector to whose patient and discriminating labor the South owes a debt not yet fully appreciated."

Mr. Freeman thinks that Davis took these documents with him when he left Richmond. His volume contains only about one-third of the DeRenne collection, those which, for the most part, are not printed elsewhere.

For Freeman's other works relating to Davis, see pp. 701, 742, 748, 751.

Galloway (Bishop Chas. B.) and Davis (Jefferson):

Open Letters on Prohibition; a controversy between ———. Pamphlet, pp. 1-47. Nashville, Tenn. Publishing House of the Methodist Episcopal Church, South, 1893.

Of especial interest in view of America's recent experiment.

Galloway, Charles Betts:

Jefferson Davis, a judicial estimate; an address delivered at the University of Mississippi, June 3, 1908. Pamphlet, from Bulletin of Univ. of Miss., series 6, no. 3, pp. 1-48, Aug., 1908.

Bishop Galloway fails to produce a "judicial estimate," which was hardly possible for a writer of his generation, but gives an excellent outline summary of Davis' entire life. His point of view is, of course, Southern, as the following quotation shows: "It was by surrendering the constitutional argument and resorting to what was denominated 'the higher law' of political conduct and conscience that the North found apology or defence for its attitude toward the inalienable rights of the Southern States."

Gilbert, C. E.:

Two Presidents, Abraham Lincoln, and Jefferson Davis. Univ. of Va. Library.

Gordon, Armistead Churchill:

Jefferson Davis. New York, Scribner, 1918, 1 vol., pp. 1-329.

A comprehensive sketch of the Civil War, with Davis as a prominent figure, rather than a biography of Davis.

Grasset, E.:

"Jefferson Davis," in author's *La Guerre de sécession*. Paris, Librairie Militaire de L. Baudoin et Cie. 1887. 2 vols., pp. 314-334, for Davis. *Athenæum,* Boston.

Greeley, Horace:

"What Horace Greeley knows about the rise and fall, the arrest and imprisonment, the trial and release on bail, of Jefferson Davis."

A series of quotations purporting to show what Greeley thought of Davis at various stages from 1854 to 1870. These are evidently meant to answer the question: Why did Greeley join with Cornelius Vanderbilt, Gerrit Smith, John M. Botts, and others in liberating Davis on bail? Widener Library.

Green, B. W.:

Speech on Jefferson Davis, delivered at Richmond, June, 1915. Pamphlet, privately printed, pp. 1-24. It is devoted chiefly to Davis' life after 1861, and quotes Alexander H. Stephens' words: "I was not very friendly and in no ways chummy with Mr. Davis, but I wish to say he was the bravest and most courageous man I ever knew" (p. 22). Jackson, Mississippi, Collection.

Greeno, Charles L.:

"The capture of Jefferson Davis and what I know of it." Paper read before the Ohio Commandery of the Loyal Legion, Oct. 4, 1911. Pamphlet, pp. 1-11, privately printed, Cincinnati, 1911.

A very brief sketch with little of special interest. Boston Public Library; Widener Library.

Hampton, Wade:

"An effort to rescue Jefferson Davis." In Southern Historical Papers, vol. 27, pp. 132-136.

Hampton's account was elicited by an article in the *Century* of May, 1898, and furnishes a few details of Davis' movements, not elsewhere attainable. Va. State Library.

Harnden, Henry:

"The capture of Jefferson Davis." Pamphlet, from Military Order of the Loyal Legion of the U. S. Wisconsin Commandery, War Papers, vol. 3, pp. 102-121, Milwaukee, 1903, reprinted from State His. Society in Wisconsin Collections, vol. 14, pp. 516-532, Madison, 1898.

It throws light upon the question of the relative importance of the services of the Michigan and the Wisconsin troops in the capture of Davis. Boston Public Library.

Hepworth, George Hughes:

"The Criminal, the Crime, the Penalty." A pamphlet reproducing a sermon on the text, Job iv: 8, "They that plough iniquity, and sow wickedness, reap the same." Boston, Walker, Fuller & Co., 1865, pp. 1-31.

An absurd arraignment of Davis as an arch-criminal: a plea that he be tried for treason and executed. Its only historical value is as a specimen of the unbounded bitterness of the period. New York Public Library.

Hill, B. H.:

Address on Jefferson Davis, delivered before the Georgia Branch of the Southern Historical Society, at Atlanta, Ga., Feb. 18, 1874. Pamphlet from Southern Historical Society Papers, 14, pp. 484-505.

It is a hymn of praise to Lee and Davis, but is highly critical of the conduct of the South in many particulars. "The truth is," Hill boldly declares, "we failed because too many of our own people were not determined to win. Malcontents at home and in high places took more men from Lee's army than did Grant's guns. . . . We failed to win independence because our sacrifices ceased, our purpose faltered."

Mr. Davis was greatly pleased with the speech. On April 24, 1874, he wrote to Dr. McKay, from London: "B. H. Hill, who was in the Confederate army, has lately made a speech which contains many facts which I think will interest you, and which it might be useful for the British public to learn. If you think thus after reading it, will you have it republished? I send you the paper containing the speech."

Hope, A. J. Beresford:

(1) "A Political View of the American Civil War." Pamphlet, pp. 1-26. London, James Ridgway, 1861.

A lecture delivered at Kilndown Library on Nov. 13th and 20th. Hope ridicules the newly-elected President Lincoln. "I dare say," he writes, "nobody in this country (England), clever as he might be at rail-splitting, at navigating a barge, or at an attorney's desk, would, with no other qualifications, ever become Prime Minister." He then compares the choice with that of the South: "Without relying too much on physiognomy, I appeal to the cartes de visites of both Lincoln and Davis, and I think all who see them will agree that Jefferson Davis bears out one's idea of what an able administrator and a calm statesman should look like better than Abraham Lincoln, great as he may be as rail-splitter, bargee, and country attorney. There is no doubt that Mr. Davis is an able man, a good orator, and thoroughly versed in military affairs." In Lincoln he saw "an incapable pretender"; in Davis "a bold, a daring, yet politic statesman."

(2) "England, the North, and the South." Pamphlet, pp. 1-78. London, James Ridgway, 1862. Hope's Kilndown lecture, enlarged and reprinted.

(3) The Social and Political Bearings of the American Dispute. Pamphlet, pp. 1-42. London, Wm. Ridgway, 1863.

A strongly pro-Southern argument, the essence of which is found in these words: "The cause of the Confederates is the cause of freedom, the cause of true English feeling, the cause of those principles of constitutional government which we desire to see prevailing all over the world" (p. 5). The author admits that "there were a few Englishmen who sympathized with the South before the battle of Bull's Run; there were many whose sympathies sprouted up after that action" (p. 4). It was his opinion that "by the side of Cavour will blaze with equal splendour on the historic page the name of Jefferson Davis, the man of British descent, the man with the British name, who speaks and writes and acts so nobly the language of British independence" (p. 6).

Hope unhesitatingly labels Lincoln "a man all whose blunders are crimes, and all whose crimes are blunders." He declared that Lincoln had only "stuttered, muttered, and mouthed" in his debates with Douglas in 1858, and that "the writers and reporters set to work and fabricated a telling speech in his name," after each encounter, "which was duly circulated as his throughout the whole country." He insists that this story came directly from the lips of Douglas, who declared "that Mr. Lincoln had not delivered any of the speeches that were attributed to him."

On the whole, it is an interesting partisan defence of the South, and of her "peculiar institution," and a plea for England's recognition of a nation that has "passed the Red Sea."

With three such publications over Hope's signature, it was natural for Davis to make contact with him when he visited England after being released from prison.

Hope wrote also:

(1) "Results of the American Disruption," 1862.

(2) "The American Church in Disruption," 1863.

Johnson, Byron Berkeley:

Abraham Lincoln and Boston Corbett, with personal recollections of each; John Wilkes Booth, and Jefferson Davis, a trio story of their capture. Pamphlet, pp. 13-71. Waltham, Mass., B. B. Johnson; Boston, The Lincoln & Smith Press, 1914.

The Davis section is pp. 56-71, and gives several important documents relating to his capture. It seeks to prove what all now admit, that the story of Davis' attempt to escape in woman's clothes was untrue. Widener Library: *Athenæum,* Boston.

Johnston, John L.:

Address on Jefferson Davis, delivered at Winchester, Tenn., Dec. 11, 1889. Pamphlet, pp. 1-15, Turney Bivouac, no. 13.

A funeral oration by the president of Mary Sharp College, with the faults common to such utterances. Johnston was wise enough to put Lincoln next to Washington, but foolish enough to place Davis before both. Confederate Museum.

Johnston, Joseph E.:

"Jefferson Davis and the Mississippi Campaign." *North American Review,* vol. 143, Dec., 1886. Listed in the *Writings of graduates (of West Point) 1802-1902*, p. 231. (This volume lists thirty-two items under the name of Jefferson Davis.)

Johnston's article was reprinted in Johnson, R. U. and Buel, C. C., *Battles and Leaders of the Civil War,* The Century Co., 1884-1888, vol. iii, pp. 472-482. Its purpose is to place upon Davis responsibility for certain actions for which Johnston had been criticized. *Athenæum,* Boston.

Johnston, William Preston:

"The True Story of the Capture of Jefferson Davis." In Southern Historical Society Papers, v. 5, pp. 118-121.

An accurate account, by one of Davis' intimate friends, and a companion in the days of the flight and the arrest. Virginia State Library.

Jones, Charles Colcock, Jr.:

Funeral oration in honour of President Jefferson Davis, delivered at Augusta, Ga., Dec. 11, 1889. Pamphlet, pp. 1-18. Chronicle Printing Establishment, 1889.

It is the usual sketch of his life, with the unmeasured eulogium common to such occasions. Widener Library.

Jones, George Wallace:

*A Tribute from a Class-Mate.* Jones had been a fellow-student with Davis at Transylvania, Class of 1824; had served in the Black Hawk War, on General Henry Dodge's staff, and later as United States Senator from Iowa (1848-1859). He touches with his own memory very early incidents in Davis' life, for which we have few documents.

Jones, John William:

(1) *The Davis Memorial Volume, or Our Dead President, Jefferson Davis, and the World's Tribute to His Memory.* Richmond, B. F. Johnson & Co., 1889; reprint, 1890; pp. 1-672.

The material was collected and the volume entrain, when the author learned that Mrs. Davis was preparing to publish a memoir which Mr. Davis had started and which she had completed, after his death. He, therefore, gave up his own plan, until Mrs. Davis herself approved it, and consented to accept "a royalty on every copy." It was then completed and published. While not professing to be "a full biography," it is a valuable contribution to the study of Mr. Davis' career. It is made up largely of selected documents, or extracts from pamphlets, speeches, newspaper articles, etc., woven together into something like a connected narrative and is, therefore, a mine of what is really "source material." Widener Library.

(2) "A visit to Beauvoir, in the summer of 1886." In Southern Historical Society Papers, vol. 14, pp. 447-454. A simple narrative of a brief visit, reporting some striking comments by Mr. Davis, e.g. "A Sovereign cannot rebel." Va. State Library.

(3) "A Review of the Rise and Fall of the Confederate Government by Jefferson Davis." In Southern Historical Society Papers, ix, pp. 285-288.

Jordan, Thomas:

"Jefferson Davis." In *Harper's New Monthly Magazine*, vol. 31, New York, 1865, pp. 610-620.

Jordan was chief of staff to General Beauregard from June, 1861, to May, 1864, and writes as a bitter critic of Davis; indeed, he lays most of the ills of the South to what he considers Davis' inadequacy. But he admits (p. 611) that "his course, both as Secretary of War, and Senator . . . must acquit him of any tendency to extreme sectional sentiment," and that he had, when the secession movement became imminent, "higher and better founded hopes of Federal preferment than any other Southern statesman." Boston Public Library.

Julian, George Washington:

Speech on the punishment of rebel leaders, delivered in the House of Representatives, April 30, 1866, in support of a resolution demanding "the speedy trial of Jefferson Davis." In select speeches, Cincinnati, 1867, pp. 51-56.

It is a fierce and unbalanced denunciation. Boston Public Library.

Kirke, Edward (*nom de plume* under which J. R. Gilmore wrote):

"Our visit to Richmond."

On Jan. 28, 1888, in reply to a question about the visit of James F. Jaquess and J. R. Gilmore to Richmond, L. Q. Washington wrote to Davis (text Rowland x, 32-35) that he had just read an article in the *Atlantic Monthly* of Sept., 1864, describing the Gilmore-Jaquess visit to Richmond, and written by Gilmore under the *nom de plume*, "Edward Kirke." Washington also refers to a second article by "Kirke" in the *Atlantic* of April, 1887, entitled "A Suppressed Chapter of History." Washington adds, "I think . . . Gilmore has written other articles on this subject, but it is needless to hunt them up, as the two cited probably cover the whole story that Mr. Gilmore tells and deserves to be credited as history."

The two articles above cited appear to be "Kirke's" only published contribution to the history of a very interesting incident in Davis' life. L. Q. Washington pronounced both "pure fiction." But Davis evidently held a different view, for, in his *Rise and Fall of the Confederate Government*, ii, 610, he agrees in general with "Kirke's" account of the visit of Gilmore and Jaquess; but he dismisses the subject with a single page. He spells the latter's name Jacques, instead of Jaquess as Gilmore spells it. Nicolay and Hay (ix, 209-211) also follow "Kirke's" version of the visit. They record this statement from Davis as of the interview: "We seceded to rid ourselves of the rule of the majority."

Kirke's *Atlantic Monthly* article of Sept., 1864, records this remark of Davis': "You have already emancipated nearly two millions of our slaves, and if you will take care of them, you may emancipate the rest . . . but we will be free. We will govern ourselves" (p. 382). Copy in Fleming Mss., Folder xi.

The visit of Jaquess and Gilmore is discussed in detail on pp. 410-414, vol. II, of this biography. The notes, not published but attached to the Ms. now in the New York Public Library, give references and additional details.

That Jaquess' mission was not without some connexion with Lincoln is evident from a letter from Lincoln to Rosecrans, dated May 21, 1863 (text: Nicolay and Hay, *Speeches, Letters and State Papers of Lincoln,* ii, 339), which says: "For certain reasons it is thought best for Rev. Dr. Jaquess not to come here. Present my respects to him, and ask him to write me fully on the subject he has in contemplation." On May 28, 1863, Lincoln again wrote to Rosecrans (Nicolay and Hay, ix, 203) of Jaquess, "I know him very well by character." The fact that he consented to his visit to Richmond and gave him a passport (*Ibid.,* ix, 20, note 1) seems to show that he considered Jaquess' character good.

See also, 42nd Congress, 2nd Sess., Report 64, in Fleming Mss. xi, for details of this problem.

Knight, Landon:

"The Real Jefferson Davis." Pamphlet, pp. 9-203. The Pilgrim Magazine Co., Battle Creek, Mich., 1904. A very light sketch. Widener Library.

Larrick, Herbert S.:

"The True Jefferson Davis." An address delivered at Winchester, Va., March 9, 1903. Pamphlet, privately printed, pp. 1-14.

A general sketch, with no new material. Confederate Museum.

Lee, Stephen D.:

Oration at the laying of the corner stone of the monument of President Davis, in Monroe Park, Richmond, Va., July 2, 1896. In the Southern Historical Society Papers, 24, pp. 366-380.

An interesting summary of the principles for which Davis stood, rather than a narrative of the events of his life.

Long, Daniel A.:

"Jefferson Davis," an address delivered at Concord, North Carolina, June 3, 1921. University of Va. Library.

Louthan, Henry T.:

"A proposed abduction of Lincoln." In the *Confederate Veteran*, April, 1903, vol. ii, no. 4, pp. 157-158. A very interesting incident, based upon an account by Col. Wm. Preston Johnston, an eye-witness of the interview in which Major Walker Taylor, a cousin of President Davis' first wife, proposed to Davis a plan to abduct Lincoln, and was refused on the ground that it might result in killing Lincoln. Facsimile letters confirming the story were sent by Mr. Louthan to the present author in 1932, and were given by him to the Confederate Museum.

Lubbock, Francis Richard:

"The capture of Jefferson Davis." In Southern Historical Society Papers, vol. 5, pp. 122-124.

A reply to General Wilson's *Philadelphia Times* article (see Wilson, on p. 740) by a companion of Davis at the time of his capture. Va. State Library. "McArone" (a pseudonym for George Arnold): See Arnold, *Ante,* D.

MacBride, Dorothy:

"Lieutenant Jefferson Davis." The Palimpsest, vol. iv, no. 10, Oct., 1923.

A brief sketch, interesting as it (p. 353) furnishes evidence that Davis did not enlist Lincoln for service in the Black Hawk War. Massachusetts Historical Society.

Mallory, Stephen R.:

"The Last Days of the Confederate Government." *McClure's Magazine,* Dec., 1900.

It was written in Fort Lafayette Prison in 1865, and gives a first-hand interpretation of the last days of Davis' career as President.

Mason, Capt. Frank H.:

"General Stoneman's Last Campaign, and the Pursuit of Jefferson Davis." In Military Order of the Loyal Legion of the U. S., Com. of Ohio, *Sketches of War Hist.,* v. 3, 1890.

A story of a chase, ending with the discovery that the object had been "captured by another command." *Athenæum,* Boston.

Maurice, Sir Frederick Barton (Major-General, K.C.M.G., C.B.):

"Jefferson Davis and J. E. Johnston—Jefferson Davis and Lee." In Maurice's *Governments and War, a Study of the Conduct of War.* London: Wm. Heinemann, 1926, pp. 1-171. The sketch of Jefferson Davis is pp. 13-65.

The book is the Knowles' Lectures for 1925-26, at Trinity College, Cambridge. The chapters are: I. Jefferson Davis and J. E. Johnston. II. Jefferson Davis and Lee. III. Abraham Lincoln and McClellan. IV. Abraham Lincoln and Grant. V. A System for the Conduct of War.

In the brief preface Sir Frederick explains that a conversation with Lord

Kitchener in 1915 had given him the idea of the book. "I had long been dissatisfied that the judgments of Lord Wolseley and of Colonel F. R. Henderson upon Lincoln's conduct of the war, written by the former on incomplete information, and by the latter on a study of one part only of the American Civil War, should stand as the British military criticism of a great statesman." *Athenæum,* Boston.

An American edition, under title, *Statesmen and Soldiers of the Civil War; a Study of the Conduct of the War.* Boston, Little, Brown & Co., 1926. Va. State Library.

Minnigerode, Rev. Charles:

A memorial address delivered in St. Paul's Church, Richmond, Va., Dec. 11, 1889. Pamphlet, pp. 1-20. Baughman Brothers, Richmond, 1890.

It is an interesting comment on Davis' religious life—speaking of his imprisonment as he saw it, the rector says: "The imprisonment itself was better than those who ordered it. . . . The officers were all polite and sympathetic and the common soldiers . . . spoke of him in a subdued and kindly tone as 'Mr. Davis.' " Confederate Museum.

Murray, John Ogden:

(1) "Jefferson Davis Not a Traitor." Pamphlet, pp. 1-15. Winchester, Va., The Geo. F. Norton Pub. Co., 1904.

A condensed argument for the constitutional position of the South, with highly laudatory comment upon Davis. Boston Public Library.

(2) "Jefferson Davis and the Southern people were not traitors, nor rebels. They were patriots who loved the Constitution and obeyed the laws made for the protection of all American citizens. . . . A short story of the Confederate soldier, the ideal soldier of the world." Pamphlet, pp. 1-48. Manassas, Manassas Democratic Press, 1911. A mere eulogium. Widener Library.

(3) Three stories in one: "The Statesman"; "The Confederate Soldier, the Ideal Soldier of the World"; "The South's Peerless Women of the World." Pamphlet, privately printed, pp. 1-65, 1915.

"The Statesman" is a brief sketch of Jefferson Davis, which Mrs. Davis described as an "eloquent outpouring of enthusiastic esteem and confidence." Va. State Library.

Nichols, Ray F.:

"United States vs. Jefferson Davis." In the *Amer. Hist. Review,* vol. 31, no. 2, Jan., 1926, pp. 266-284.

An elaborate study which deserves careful attention from students of the question, Why was Davis never tried? Massachusetts Historical Society.

Oglesby, T. K.:

"Captor and Captive; the Shackler and the Shackled." Atlantic, 1899.

Parker, James Henry:

"The Capture of Mr. Jefferson Davis." In the Southern Historical Society Papers, v. 4, pp. 91-92.

A brief letter, in reply to General Wilson's *Philadelphia Times* article (see Wilson, on p. 740), by a Federal soldier who was present when Mr. Davis was taken. He declares, "I defy any person to find a single officer or soldier who was present at the capture of Jefferson Davis who will say upon honour that he was disguised in woman's clothes." He says that he knew the reporter who "fabricated the story." Va. State Library.

Perry, Leslie J.:

"Davis and Johnston." In Southern Historical Society Papers, vol. 20, pp. 95-108.

An explanation of how Lee came to be put over Johnston, and a detailed examination of the long and bitter controversy between Johnston and Davis that resulted. Va. State Library.

Pollard, Edward Albert:

*Life of Jefferson Davis, with a Secret History of the Southern Confederacy Gathered "Behind the Scenes" in Richmond.* 1 vol., pp. 1-536. Philadelphia, Chicago, etc. National Publishing Co., 1869.

It contains curious statements concerning the leading Southern characters in their connexions with President Davis, and in relation to various intrigues of his administration. Widener Library.

Pollard's other and numerous writings on the Civil War have little special interest for the Davis biographer. For list see pp. 755-756.

Quaife, Milo M.:

"The Northwestern Career of Jefferson Davis." In Transactions of the Illinois State Hist. Soc., p. 28. Same in Journals, vol. 16, nos. 1-2, pp. 1-19. July, 1923.

A well-documented and convincing study of the dark period of Davis' life; very valuable. It also appeared in *Fort Gibson Post*, Oct. 15, 1904. Copy in Fleming Mss. xxi.

Reagan, John Henninger:

Reagan's writings have especial value in view of the fact that he was Davis' Postmaster-General from 1861 to the end of the Confederacy, and the companion of his flight and his arrest.

(1) A letter to President Andrew Johnson, from Prison at Fort Warren in Boston Harbor, May 28, 1865. In Southern Hist. Association Publications, March, 1902, vol. vi, no. 2, pp. 132-143; no. 3, pp. 210-219.

A discussion of the great issues then before the country.

(2) Flight and Capture of Jefferson Davis:

Written by leading participants, North and South: in *Annals of the War*, Philadelphia, The Times Publishing Co., 1879.

Reagan's sketch of Davis' flight and capture is on pp. 147-159. It is an answer, by a companion of Davis' flight, to General James H. Wilson's letter to the *Philadelphia Weekly Times* (see Wilson, on p. 740) which Reagan pronounces "utterly void of truth." *Athenæum,* Boston.

(3) Reasons against the trial of Jefferson Davis.

A letter to Geo. W. White. In Southern Hist. Ass'n Publications, vol. vi, pp. 422-427. Washington, 1902.

An argued statement, by a member of Davis' Cabinet, of the reasons why the Federal Government should not try Davis. It is of negligible value. Boston Public Library.

(4) "Memoirs, with Special Reference to Secession and the Civil War."

Redpath, James:

"Neither Traitor nor Rebel." *The Commonwealth,* Jan., 1890, ii, no. 4, 385-392.

It expresses views formed by close contact at "Beauvoir" during nearly the entire summer of 1889, as guest in the house of Davis. "I was in his company from 6 to 10 hours every day."

The Denver Commonwealth Pub. Co. issued a reprint from the magazine, in 1890. Widener Library.

Robertson, Mrs. M. E.:

"The last meeting of President Davis with his officers and those of his Cabinet remaining with him, in the old State Bank Building at Washington, Ga." In Publications of the Southern Hist. Association, May, 1901, vol. v, no. iii, pp. 291-299.

An account by "an eye-witness and participator in these events." It is, however, of little interest or value. Boston Public Library.

Robinson, Mrs. J. Enders (editor):

"The restoration of the name of Jefferson Davis to the Cabin John Bridge, Washington, D. C.; being the official correspondence leading to the restoration." Pamphlet, pp. 1-95, New Orleans, The Confederated Southern Memorial Association, 1909.

It deals exhaustively with a controversy of little lasting importance. Jackson, Miss., Collection.

Rose, U. M.:

"Jefferson Davis." In Rose's Addresses, Chicago, Geo. I. Jones, 1914, pp. 171-192.

A brilliant and basic essay which weighs Davis' political philosophy. The author was a lawyer of eminence, and a serious student of American political and constitutional history. *Athenæum,* Boston.

Rowland, Dunbar:

(1) "Jefferson Davis' Place in History as Revealed in His Letters, Papers and Speeches." Pamphlet, pp. 1-25. Jackson, Miss., 1923.

(2) Speech of acceptance upon the presentation of a portrait of Jefferson

Davis to the State of Mississippi by the Daughters of the Confederacy, Miss. Division. Pamphlet, pp. 1-8, Nashville, 1905.

(3) "Private and Official Papers of Jefferson Davis," *Harper's Magazine,* December, 1911, vol. 124, pp. 97-104.

(4) "Life in Mississippi before the War." Pubs. of Miss. Hist. Soc., vol. iii. Of value in connexion with Davis' plantation days.

(5) Editor, *Mississippi, an Encyclopedic History.* Rowland's own articles on "Repudiation," and Walthall's on Jefferson Davis, are of especial interest.

(6) "Jefferson Davis, Constitutionalist," described on p. 702.

Rowland, Eron (Mrs. Dunbar Rowland):

Varina Howell, Wife of Jefferson Davis. 2 vols. New York, Macmillan, 1927 and 1931.

Mr. Davis and his wife were inseparables, and Mrs. Rowland in presenting one life of necessity presents the other also. An able and readable book, with, of course, clear Southern sympathies.

Russell, Wm. Hepburn:

"Jefferson Davis." An address delivered Jan. 26, 1903. Pamphlet, privately printed, pp. 1-9.

A very brief and not very suggestive sketch of Davis' life and theory of government. The author should not be confused with William Howard Russell, famous correspondent of the London *Times* during the American Civil War. Massachusetts Historical Society.

Rutherford, Mildred Lewis:

(1) Contrasted lives of Jefferson Davis and Abraham Lincoln. In Miss Rutherford's "Hist. Notes (formerly a Scrap Book)," vol. 1, nos. 1-3, Mildred Lewis Rutherford, editor and publisher. Athens, Ga., 1927, pp. 1-40.

An unwisely bitter attempt to revise history in the interest of a fairer view of the Southern cause, and to stop "this glorification of Abraham Lincoln," while adding glory to Jefferson Davis. Confederate Museum: *Athenæum,* Boston.

(2) "Wrongs of History Righted." Pamphlet, pp. 1-36. Savannah, Ga., 1914.

A clever balancing of the relative value of certain factors, slavery, coercion, etc., in the causes of the war between the states. Confederate Museum.

Sanderson, Joseph Warner:

"Guarding Jefferson Davis at Fortress Monroe." In Military Order of the Loyal Legion, of the U. S., Wisconsin Commandery, War Papers, vol. 3, pp. 122-124. Milwaukee, 1903.

A perfunctory sketch of little value. Boston Public Library.

Savage, John:

"Jefferson Davis." In Savage's *Our Living Representative Men,* 1 vol., Philadelphia, Childs and Peterson, 1860.

Interesting as showing the high place held in the nation in 1860 by

Jefferson Davis, whose life is sketched on pp. 168-180. *Athenæum,* Boston.

Schaff, Morris:

*Jefferson Davis, His Life and Personality,* 1 vol., pp. 1-277. Boston, John W. Luce & Co., 1922.

A protest against historians' unfair treatment of Davis, by a West Point graduate who fought in the Union armies.

Scheibert, Justus (a major in the Prussian Army):

"Jefferson Davis, President of the Late Confederate States." In Southern Historical Society Papers, vol. 19, pp. 406-416.

It is largely a condensation of Hon. John W. Daniel's oration before the General Assembly of Virginia, on Jan. 25, 1890 (*ante*), and was first printed in the Annual Register of the German Army and Navy of Dec., 1891. The tone is sympathetic to the South. Va. State Library.

Schurz, Carl:

"The South After the War." *McClure's,* April, 1908, vol. xxx, no. 6, 651-657.

An article attacking Davis as deliberately fomenting "a sullen animosity against the Union." It shows, however, that Schurz pleaded with Johnson not to allow Davis to be tried, as "the immediate accomplices of Booth were tried by a military court." It also admits that "the evidence of Jefferson Davis' complicity in the assassination of Lincoln, which the President had in his possession when he issued his proclamation offering a reward for Davis' capture, subsequently turned out to be absolutely worthless."

Scott, Winfield:

Documents relating to his contest with Davis, Secretary of War. Senate Ex. Doc. 34, 34th Cong., 3rd Sess.

These documents were sent to the Senate on January 30, 1857, in compliance with a resolution of the Senate, passed Dec. 23, 1856, requesting information relating to pay and emoluments of Lieutenant-General Scott.

Scott, W. W.:

*Some Reminiscences of Famous Men*—Part III, "Jefferson Davis." The *Southern Magazine*, Sept., 1894.

This title was changed to *Mid-Continent Magazine*—some time after 1875.

Shea, George:

"Jefferson Davis: a statement concerning the imputed special causes of his long imprisonment by the Government of the United States, and of his tardy release by due process of law." Pamphlet, pp. 1-20. London, Edward Stanford, 1877. Reprinted from the New York *Tribune* of Jan. 24, 1876.

It is a straightforward statement of the way in which the author was led by a careful investigation of the facts to become counsel for Davis, a man whom he had come, reluctantly, to regard as a victim of unreasoning persecution. Invaluable as a source for a study of Davis' trial. A reprint appears in Southern Historical Society Papers, vol. 37, pp. 244-252.

This pamphlet should be studied in connexion with the papers of George Shea, deposited by his heirs in the Confederate Museum in Richmond. A calendar of them is published in Douglas Southall Freeman's Calendar of Confederate Papers, pp. 439-478. Jackson, Miss., Collection.

Skelton, W. O.:

Answer to (Carl) Schurz's attack on Davis (see Schurz, *ante*). The *Times-Dispatch* of Richmond, Va., April 19, 1908. Clipping in Miss K. M. Rowland's Collection, Confederate Museum. (See K. M. Rowland, *seq*. F.)

Smith, Ernest A.:

*The History of the Confederate Treasury.* In Publications of the Southern Hist. Association, Jan., 1901, vol. v, no. i, pp. 1-34; no. ii, pp. 95-150; no. iii, pp. 188-227. Bibliog., 226-7.

A detailed account of how Davis and his government managed finances.

Smith, Geo. G.:

"Davis' Ancestry." In *Atlantic Monthly*, June-February, 1905. It throws little light upon the more puzzling questions concerning Davis' genealogy.

Smith, Gerrit:

(1) "No Treason in Civil War." Speech at Cooper Institute, New York, June 8, 1865. Pamphlet, pp. 1-25, New York, The American News Company, 1865.

An able argument to prove the folly of attempting to try Jefferson Davis for treason. Jackson, Miss., Collection.

(2) "The Bailing of Jefferson Davis." Pamphlet. Peterboro, 1867.

An article defending the action of the signers of Davis' bond from the attack made upon them. Like all of Smith's writings, it is strong, logical, and convincing. Jackson, Miss., Collection.

Smith, Hampden Harrison:

"Jefferson Davis. A Character Sketch." Pamphlet, pp. 1-40. Richmond, Va., Williams Printing Co., 1926.

A mere summary of Davis' life, but interestingly written. Va. State Library.

Smolnikar, Andreas Bernardus:

The great encyclic epistle, divided into two parts; the first of which was occasioned by the death of President Abraham Lincoln, and the second by the capture of Jefferson Davis: both being preparatory to a work with the title, "The heavenly mission to all governments and all nations for the introduction of Christ's peaceable reign on earth." Pamphlet, pp. 1-32. Baltimore, printed by S. S. Mills & Co., 1865. Widener Library.

Stanton, Edward M.:

"The Capture of Jefferson Davis," a letter from the Secretary of War, transmitting all information on file in that department relative to the capture of Jefferson Davis. Washington, Government Printing Office, 1868. 40th Cong., 2nd Sess., House Ex. Doc. No. 115. Va. State Library.

Stanton says: "No other information on this subject can be given, except what is in Executive Document No. 90, 39th Congress, 1st Sess., House of Reps., containing a report of the Adjutant-General and Judge-Advocate-General to which reference is made." See under "Various," 2, *seq.*, for description of this document.

Stephenson, N. W.:

"A Theory of Jefferson Davis." *American Historical Review,* Oct., 1915, pp. 73-90.

A very suggestive, though at certain points misleading, summary of Davis' career. It is, however, one of the most valuable of the briefer contributions to Davis' biography.

Stephenson insists that Davis "ignored the states' rights idea whenever it got in his way," a statement which could scarcely be made by one who had covered the Davis' papers with any degree of thoroughness. The states' rights idea was always in his way: but he continued to reverence it, always placing it first in the list of basic ideas of the Confederacy.

Stewart, William Henry:

"Prison Life of Jefferson Davis." In Southern Historical Society Papers, vol. 32, pp. 338-346.

A rather hysterical presentation of the details of Davis' imprisonment; far less convincing than Dr. Craven's *Prison Life of Jefferson Davis.* Va. State Library.

Sturges, Mrs. Hezekiah:

"Recollections of Jefferson Davis." In Register of Kentucky History, Frankfort, May, 1912.

Contains several interesting sidelights upon Davis' character.

Sutherland, George F.:

"Abraham Lincoln and Jefferson Davis as Commanders-in-Chief." In Military Order of the Loyal Legion, of the United States. Wisconsin, Commandery, War Papers. Vol. 2, pp. 110-136. Milwaukee, 1896.

A rather superficial comparison chiefly on the military side. Boston Public Library.

Tate, Allen:

Jefferson Davis, His Rise and Fall; a Biographical Narrative. 1 vol., pp. 1-311, New York, Minton, Balch & Co., 1929.

An unimportant sketch.

Taylor, Robert L.:

"Jefferson Davis." In the *Taylor-Trotwood Magazine* of June, 1907.

It has no special value.

Copy in Fleming mss., XVII.

Townsend, J. W.:

"Jefferson Davis at the University." In *The Transylvanian*, June, 1907, p. 435 *et seq.*

A brief sketch with details not elsewhere obtainable.

Trent, William Peterfield:

"Jefferson Davis, in Trent's *Southern Statesmen of the Old Régime,*" which represents a series of lectures delivered at the University of Wisconsin in 1896. New York, Thomas J. Crowell & Co., 1897.

Superficial and of little value. *Athenæum,* Boston.

Trexler, Harrison H.:

"Jefferson Davis and the Confederate Patronage." In *South Atlantic Quarterly*, vol. 28, Jan., 1929, pp. 45-58.

A sketch designed to show Davis' determination to appoint only good men to office. "The mildest term we can use in describing his dispensation of patronage," he says, in summing up, "is that he was impracticable in a land where politicians were far from dead."

Van Horne, John Douglass:

"Jefferson Davis and Repudiation in Mississippi." Pamphlet, pp. 1-14, privately printed, 1915.

A convincing reply to Theodore Roosevelt's charge that Jefferson Davis was one of the Mississippi repudiators of State bonds in the early 'forties. It gives a convenient list of references to other writers who had discussed the subject. Confederate Museum.

Various, United States:

(1) "The Pursuit and Capture of Jefferson Davis: May 1-10, 1865." In the War of the Rebellion Series, Series I, vol. XLIX, part I, pp. 515-556.
Reports of Bvt. Maj.-Gen. James H. Wilson.
Brig.-Gen. John T. Croxton.
Lieut.-Col. Henry Harnden.
Col. Robert H. G. Minty.
Col. Horace N. Howland.
Lieut.-Col. Benjamin D. Pritchard.
Capt. John C. Hathaway.
Maj.-Gen. George Stoneman.
Bvt. Brig.-Gen., William J. Palmer.

*Athenæum,* Boston.

(2) 39th Congress, 1st Sess., House Ex. Doc. No. 90. Government Printing Office, 1866.

It relates chiefly to the awards for the capture of Booth and others, but includes a report on rewards for the arrest of Lewis Payne, G. A. Alzerodt and Jefferson Davis.

Documents relating to Davis' camel experiment. Pamphlet, pp. 1-238,

Washington, A. O. P. Nicholson, 1857, from Senate Ex. Doc. No. 62, 34th Cong., 3rd Sess.

House Report No. 101, 43rd Cong., 2nd Sess., 1875, on Louisiana Affairs, especially "an old negro's testimony," at p. 121.

"Debate on Pensioning Jefferson Davis, Condensed from the Proceedings of the United States Senate, March 7, 1879." Pamphlet, pp. 1-8, Washington, 1879.

A convenient form of a savage debate. Boston Public Library.

Senate Ex. Doc. No. 36, 48th Cong., 2nd Sess., 1885, relating to Davis' connexions with Sherman and others.

Fleming mss. XVI.

*Various, Unofficial:*

"In Memoriam; a Tribute of Respect to the Memory of Jefferson Davis, Offered By the Citizens of Charleston, S. C." Pamphlet, pp. 1-79. Charleston, S. C., Walker, Evans & Cogswell Co., Publishers, 1890. *Athenæum,* Boston.

"Life and Reminiscences of Jefferson Davis. By Distinguished Men of His Time; with an Introduction by John Warwick Daniel, Senator from Virginia." 1 vol., Baltimore, Woodward & Co., 1890.

A badly organized body of personal sketches, followed by a series of chapters upon different episodes of Davis' life, written by men able to speak from personal experience. A somewhat forbidding volume, but well worth reading. Boston Public Library; Widener Library.

"The Jefferson Davis Memorial in the Vicksburg National Military Park." Pamphlet, pp. 1-28, Vicksburg, Miss., Printing Co., 1927.

Of little value. Boston Public Library.

"The Obsequies of Jefferson Davis, the Only President of the Confederate States of America; in the City of New Orleans, Wednesday, Dec. 11, 1889." Pamphlet, pp. 1-73. New Orleans, Brandao & Gill, 1890.

A volume filled with the minutest details of Davis' last illness, funeral, etc. Confederate Museum.

"A Memorial of the Sixth Annual Reunion, and the Laying of the Cornerstone of the Jefferson Davis Monument, Richmond, Va., June 30, July 1, 2, 1896." Pamphlet, Richmond, 1896.

A volume of little interest.

*Athenæum,* Boston:

"Unveiling of the Jefferson Davis Monument at Jefferson Davis Parkway, February 22, 1911, the Fiftieth Anniversary of the Inauguration of Mr. Davis as President of the Confederate States of America." Pamphlet, pp. 1-40. New Orleans, La., the Jefferson Davis Monument Association.

Vose, Caroline E.:

"Jefferson Davis in New England." In the *Virginia Quarterly Review*, Oct., 1926, pp. 557-568.

It adds nothing of unusual interest. Massachusetts Historical Society.

Walker, Robert J.:

"Jefferson Davis and Repudiation." Pamphlet, pp. 1-84. London, William Ridgway, 1863.

It contains the texts of Walker's three letters written to convince the British public that Davis was the author of Repudiation. Fleming Papers, New York Public Library, and Widener Library.

Compare William E. Dodd's "Robert J. Walker, Imperialist," in Bulletin of Randolph Macon Woman's College, January, 1915, where Walker himself is shown to have been far more the author of repudiation in Mississippi.

Washburn, W. B.:

"Capture of Jefferson Davis" (to accompanying bill H. R. No. 1277, 40th Cong., 2nd Sess., Report No. 60). Pamphlet, pp. 1-14, ordered printed, and recommended to the Committee of Claims, June 17, 1868.

It is a discussion, by the Committee of Claims, of the problem of distributing the reward offered by the President of the United States, in May, 1865, for the capture of Jefferson Davis. It contains invaluable information regarding the capture.

Watts, Thomas H.:

"Life and Character of Ex-President Jefferson Davis." An address delivered at Montgomery Theatre, December 19, 1889. Pamphlet, privately printed.

An eulogium, of little historical value. Confederate Museum.

Weddell, Elizabeth Wright:

*St. Paul's Church, Richmond, Virginia; Its Historic Years and Memorials.* Richmond, the William Byrd Press, Inc., 1931. 2 vols., pp. 1-285 and 289-638.

A valuable work with many documents bearing upon Davis' connexion with St. Paul's, as well as upon his public life. Confederate Museum.

Whitehead, Albert Carlton:

*Two Great Southerners, Jefferson Davis and Robert E. Lee.* New York, Cincinnati, and Chicago. American Book Company, 1912. 1 vol., pp. 1-190.

A textbook "to acquaint the children of the South with the goodness and grandeur of the lives of two of her noblest sons." A comprehensive though by no means critical sketch of Davis' career.

Whitsitt, William Heth:

(1) "Genealogy of Jefferson Davis"; address delivered Oct. 9, 1908, before Lee Camp, No. 1, Confederate Veterans. Pamphlet, pp. 1-16. Richmond, Everett Waddy Co., printers, 1908.

A brief summary by an authority. Widener Library.

(2) "Genealogy of Jefferson Davis and of Samuel Davies." Pamphlet, pp. 1-65. New York, the Neale Pub. Co., 1910.

An interesting review of the problems of Davis' family history, with a family tree. Fleming considered it "the most satisfactory of all the genealogies." ("Early Life of Jefferson Davis," p. 2.) *Athenæum*, Boston.

Wilson, Maj.-Gen. James H.:

Article on the capture of Jefferson Davis: *Philadelphia Weekly Times*, July 7, 1877.

Burton Harrison declared it "full of inaccuracies" (Rowland VIII, 588, 592). But Davis characterized it as "a tissue of reckless falsehoods" (Davis to Walthall, July 12, 1877. Text, Rowland VIII, 560). It, however, caused much discussion and called forth many replies, a number of which are listed in the present bibliography.

Winston, Robert Watson:

*High Stakes and Hair Triggers: the Life of Jefferson Davis,* with portraits and Bibliography. 1 vol., pp. 1-306. New York, Holt & Co., 1930.

A well-studied account of Davis' life, the title to which is misleading. Boston Public Library. *Athenæum,* Boston.

Wise, John Sergeant:

"Jefferson Davis." In Wise's *Recollections of Thirteen Presidents.* New York, Doubleday, Page & Co., 1906.

The sketch of Jefferson Davis is (pp. 67-97) made up of many light personal experiences, combined with sections of serious history. *Athenæum,* Boston.

Wolseley, Garnet, later Viscount Wolseley:

(1) "A month's visit to the Confederate Headquarters." *Blackwood's Edinburgh Magazine,* 93, No. 567, January, 1863.

Interesting in view of his later controversy with Davis in the *North American Review.*

(2) "An English View of the Civil War." *North American Review,* May, 1889: a scathing criticism of Jefferson Davis, upon grounds not always consistent with known facts.

In a letter to the *North American Review*, May 8, 1889, Mr. Davis answered the criticism, showing much bitterness, but also much better knowledge of the facts. (See C, *ante.*)

Zincke, F. Barham:

"Last Winter in the United States." London, John Murray, 1868. 1 vol., pp. 1-314.

It is the "table talk" of the vicar of Wherstead and chaplain in ordinary to the Queen, and records his observations and opinions after a tour through the Confederate States, etc. It revived in England the charge that Davis had been a leader in Mississippi's repudiation of debts, and aroused his bitter resentment, which he put into an article, designed for the British press, but never published. Rhodes Library, Oxford.

E. BIOGRAPHIES OF OTHER MEN WHICH THROW LIGHT UPON SEVERAL IMPORTANT INCIDENTS IN MR. DAVIS' CAREER

It is, of course, impossible to list all the Biographies, Memoirs, and Reminiscences which bear incidentally upon Mr. Davis' life. The following is a selected list of special value:

Adams, Henry:

"The Education of Henry Adams." Boston, 1918.

It shows the British reactions to certain acts of President Davis, during the author's service as secretary to his father, the American minister to the Court of St. James's, from 1861 to 1868. It is one of the classic autobiographies of American history.

Bixby, W. K. [Editor]:

*Letters of Zachary Taylor*. Rochester, 1908.

Contains many letters interpretive of Davis' career, by his associate in early Western days, the father of his first wife, and his commander in the Mexican War.

Butler, Pierce:

"Judah P. Benjamin, Philadelphia." George W. Jacobs & Co., 1907.

A good outline sketch of Davis' most intimate Cabinet adviser. A more detailed life of Benjamin is much needed.

Capers, Henry D.:

*The Life and Times of C. G. Mimminger*. Richmond, 1893.

Contains important financial history closely connected with Davis, as Mimminger was Secretary of Treasury in Davis' Cabinet.

Chestnut, Mary Boykin:

*A Diary from Dixie*. Edited by Isabella D. Martin and Myrta Lockett Avary. 1 vol., pp. 1-424. New York, D. Appleton & Co., 1906.

One of the most delightful and revealing of the contemporary accounts of the days of Civil War, by a lady whose position, as wife of James Chestnut, Jr., United States Senator from South Carolina from 1859 to 1861 and later aide to Jefferson Davis and a brigadier-general in the Confederate army, gave her access to many secrets.

Christian, W. Ashbury:

*Richmond, Her Past and Present*. 1 vol., pp. 1-618. Richmond, L. H. Jenkins, 1912.

A comprehensive history, with a wealth of material concerning affairs in Richmond while it was the seat of President Davis' government.

Clark, M. H.:

"The Last Days of the Confederate Treasury and What Became of Its Specie." Southern Hist. Soc. Papers, IX, 542 (1881).

It throws light on dark places.

Clay, Mrs. Clement C.

*A Belle of the Fifties.* New York, 1904.

A famous account of Southern society during Davis' residence in Richmond.

Dabney, R. L.:

*Life and Campaigns of Lieut.-Gen. Thomas J. Jackson.* New York, 1866.

This was the best life of Jackson until Henderson's was published. (See G. F. R. Henderson, *seq.*)

Day, Samuel P.:

*Down South, or an Englishman's Experience at the Seat of the American War.* London, 2 vols., 1862.

Its chief value lies in the fact that it reflects the English mind.

De Leon, Thomas Cooper:

(1) *Four Years in Rebel Capitals.* 1 vol., pp. 1-372. Mobile, Ala., The Gossip Publishing Co., 1890.

A volume of personal recollections which does not rise to the dignity of history, but which throws some light upon details of Davis' life in Richmond.

(2) "Belles, Beaux and Brains of the '60's."

A series of light articles on Confederate days and Confederate leaders. In *Town Topics*, no date.

It contains incidents relating to Davis not elsewhere obtainable. Confederate Museum in Richmond.

Dicey, Edward:

*Six Months in the Federal States.* 2 vols. London, 1863.

It records the observations of an English scholar of the first rank.

Edwards, Harry Stillwell:

"Memories of Winnie Davis." *Armstrong's Magazine,* Jan., 1899, vol. iv, no. 1.

A brief, very personal, very sentimental sketch, which condenses much of the pathos of later years of the Davis family. Confederate Museum.

Freeman, Douglas Southall:

(1) *Robert E. Lee, a Biography.* 4 vols. New York and London, Charles Scribner's Sons, 1934 and 1935.

The most comprehensive and scholarly life of Lee, and awarded the Pulitzer prize. The Select Critical Bibliography in vol. iv, pp. 543-569, is excellent, and the footnotes superabundant.

In view of the completeness of Freeman's bibliography, it is unnecessary to list distinctively Lee material, although most of it has important bearing upon Davis' life also.

(2) For Freeman's other works, see pp. 701, 722, 748, 751.

(3) For Lee's Confidential Dispatches to Davis, edited by Freeman, see Section D, *ante*.

Freemantle, Arthur James:

*Three Months in the Southern States: April-June, 1863*. Edinburgh and London, 1863.

An account of personal observations by a colonel of the Coldstream Guards as he followed Lee in the Pennsylvania campaign. Freemantle shows an abiding faith in the principles of the Lost Cause as he interpreted them, but references to Davis are incidental. It was republished in New York in 1864. Rhodes Library, Oxford.

Grant, Ulysses S.:

*Personal Memoirs*. 2 vols. New York, Webster, 1885-86.

The value of Grant's comments upon Davis are invaluable; his generosity to Davis was deeply appreciated both by Davis and by Mrs. Davis.

Hay, Thomas Robson:

"Braxton Bragg and the Southern Confederacy." The Georgia Hist. Quarterly, December, 1925, pp. 267-316.

An article concerned with military details centring on Bragg, but incidentally throwing some light upon Davis' many military conflicts. "We both bear," Davis wrote to Bragg, "the consciousness of faithful service, and . . . the sting of feeling that capacity for public good is diminished by the covert workings of malice and . . . falsehood."

The article is a review of Don C. Seitz's *Braxton Bragg,* The State Co., 1924, and repudiates the traditional view that there was a "long-continued and apparently unfailing and unthinking friendship of Davis for Bragg." Hay is confident that Davis selected Bragg "in the early months of the Confederacy, because he appeared to possess the qualifications requisite for high command," and continued to support him, "despite bitter and continued criticism because, in Davis' opinion, no competent and acceptable successor seemed to be available."

Henderson, G. F. R.:

*Stonewall Jackson*. 2 vols. London, 1898.

A book interpreting the war in a manner most friendly to the South. It has had a lasting influence on the English judgments concerning Davis and his cause. Henderson's criticisms of Lincoln and Davis for employing too freely their constitutional right to command army and navy are criticisms of the Constitution rather than of the men. Henderson's political opinions deserve much less consideration than do his military views.

Hughes, Robert M.:

"General Johnston." New York, 1912.

It is little more than a revamping of General Johnston's own, not very reliable, account as given in his personal narrative.

James, Alfred P.:

"General Joseph Eggleston Johnston, Storm Centre of the Confederate Army." In *Miss. Valley Hist. Review*, 14 June, 1927. March, 1928, pp. 342-359.

A brief but searching analysis of the conflict between Johnston and Davis, its origin and evil results. It is of value to the biographer, who feels it important to delve deeply into an ancient feud. It is judicial rather than partisan, and shows the alignment which involved many of the most important leaders of the Confederate army and of Confederate politics.

Johnson, Bradley T.:

A Memoir of the Life and Public Services of Joseph E. Johnston. Baltimore, 1891.

Contains little not previously published in Johnston's personal narrative.

Johnston, Gen. Joseph E.:

*Narrative of Military Operations during the Late War between the States.* New York, D. Appleton & Co., 1874.

It contains evidence upon the many controversies between the author and Davis and is a polemic rather than a military history. It fails to present the details of a movement, whether sponsored by Johnston or without his knowledge, to persuade Davis to resign the Presidency and have the Cabinet put Johnston into the office. In a letter, now in the possession of Mrs. Macon A. Leiper, of the Kentucky Library, Bowling Green, Ky., and never before published, Davis thus replies to Dr. Jno. D. Woods, of Frankfort, Ky., who had sent him a newspaper cutting upon the subject:

"Beauvoir, Missi.
24$^{\text{th}}$ April, '86

"Private

"Jno. D. Woods, Esq.

"My dear Sir:

"I have received your letter with the printed slip claiming to be a report of a conversation held with me. The Reporter and the Publisher of the story must have been vastly ignorant of our system of Gov$^{\text{t}}$. You can not have failed to perceive the absurdity of my tendering my resignation as President to my Cabinet provided they would put Gen$^{\text{l}}$ Johnston in my place. A school boy in the lowest form would be pronounced a dunce if he supposed the Cabinet could receive my resignation and appoint my successor as President of the Confederacy. I had the highest opinion of *Albert Sydney Johnston*, had known him long, intimately and under trying circumstances and may have expressed the opinion which I now entertain that he was better qualified for the office of President of our Gov. than myself, but I knew very well that that office did not go by appointment.

Respectfully and truly yours,
Jefferson Davis."

For Joseph E. Johnston's other works, see p. 723.

Jones, John Beauchamp:

*A Rebel War Clerk's Diary at the Confederate States Capital.* Philadelphia, 2 vols., 1866.

A book filled with interesting gossip of war days. The writer was a Southerner, but was engaged in literary work at the North when the war began. He took service in Davis' government, in the War Department, before the capital was moved to Richmond, with the understanding that he would write for the press. He presents much interesting material bearing upon the internal history of the Confederacy, and upon life in Richmond.

Kohler, Max J.:

"Judah P. Benjamin, Statesman and Jurist," in Publications of the American Jewish Society, No. 12.

Inadequate but of value.

Le Clair, Antoine (interpreter to the Saes and Foxes):

*Life of Mà-Kà-Tai-Me-She-Kia Kiak* (the Black Sparrow Hawk), dictated by himself to Le Clair. 1 vol. Boston, Odiorne & Metcalf, 1834. Edited by J. B. Patterson.

In transmitting extracts from this volume to Walker L. Fleming, Joseph H. Wilson, grandson of General Joseph M. Street, says: "My father knew Le Clair well, being quartermaster at Fort Armstrong, Rock Island, in 1834, and often spoke of his high character and integrity." Wilson's letter to Fleming, Fleming Mss., N. Y. Public Library, vol. XXI.

Le Clair's references to Davis' conduct as officer in charge of Black Hawk are of unusual interest.

Milton, George Fort:

(1) *The Age of Hate. Andrew Jackson and the Radicals.* New York, Coward-McCann, Inc., 1930.

The careers of Davis and Johnson crossed often, and any adequate history of the one must help to interpret the other. Mr. Milton records the fact that Benjamin Butler cast his vote for Davis in the Democratic National Convention throughout more than forty ballots, a fact little connected with Johnson; but he fails to detail the debate in which Jefferson Davis won Johnson's everlasting hatred, by a careless remark about tailors, for which he generously and publicly, but vainly, apologized. (See vol. I, pp. 70-71 of present biography.) His references to Davis before and during the war are scant and unimportant, only half a dozen in all. He deals more fully with his career while Johnson was President, and he holds the scales with an impartial hand: but in general the book has little which adds to our knowledge of Davis.

(2) *The Eve of Conflict. Stephen A. Douglas and the Needless War.* Boston and New York, Houghton Mifflin Co., 1934.

The career of Davis is treated with unusual fullness; but the treatment contains little that is new or distinctive. He says, however, that after the Committee of Thirteen failed to agree on Crittenden's Compromise proposals, Davis joined with other Senators in urging Lincoln to come at once to Washington, and promising that he would be received "with all the respect due to the President-elect," and that Buchanan would cordially unite with him "in the measures necessary to preserve the Union." If this is true, it has failed to leave any trace in Davis' papers.

Myers, William Star:

*General George Brinton McClellan.* 1 vol. New York, D. Appleton-Century Co., 1934.

The author, by careful investigation, has thrown light upon Davis' connexion with McClellan's earlier career.

Polk, W. M.:

*Leonidas Polk: Bishop and General.* 2 vols. New York, 1893.

Polk's friendship with Davis went back to West Point days, and these volumes contain many incidents which illustrate Davis' character.

Prentiss, George L.:

A memoir of Sergeant Smith Prentiss, edited by his brother. 2 vols. New York, Charles Scribner's Sons, 1855. New edition, 1870.

It gives details of Prentiss' connexions with Davis, and a history of Mississippi repudiation. Copy in Jackson, Mississippi, Collection.

Pryor, Mrs. Roger A.:

*Reminiscences of Peace and War.* New York and London, 1904.

A well-known book of recollections which reflects many incidents in Davis' life.

Russell, William H.:

(1) *My Diary North and South.* 1 vol. New York, Harper & Brothers, 1863.

It also appeared in London, in 1863; 2 vols., Bradbury and Evans.

(2) "Pictures of Southern Life, Social, Political and Military" (written for the London *Times*). New York, 1861.

(3) "Recollections of the Civil War." (*North American Review,* clxvi, 234, 362, 491, 618, 740, 1898.)

Russell was a clever Irishman sent to America in March, 1861, by the London *Times*, to report upon the war. Public opinion in the South, where he spent most of his time, accorded him almost the position of a special representative of England, and gave more weight to his opinions than his position or influence warranted. He gravely offended the Federals by his graphic description of the route of the Northern armies at the first battle of Bull Run, which he witnessed. His dispatches were so friendly to the South that he was virtually forced by Northern pressure to leave in April,

1862, although toward the end of his stay his sympathies veered toward the North. He later declared that, if he had been allowed to remain in America, he might have done something to turn the *Times* from its Southern sympathy.

Like Olmsted, but with less evidence presented in support of the view, Russell was emphatic about the ill effects of slavery. The Diary is, of course, of great interest to the student of Davis.

Semmes, Raphael:

(1) *The Cruise of the "Alabama."* New York, 1864.

(2) *Memoirs of Service Afloat during the War between the States.* Baltimore, 1869.

When Alabama seceded, on February 15, 1861, Semmes, then secretary of the Lighthouse Board at Washington, resigned his commission in the United States Navy and reported to President Davis at Montgomery. Davis sent him North to procure mechanics skilled in the manufacture of ordnances and rifle machinery, and to buy war material. His later services to the Confederate cause, as captain of the *Alabama*, which captured sixty-two American merchantmen, is a matter of history.

Smith, William Ernest:

*The Francis Preston Blair Family in Politics.* 2 vols. New York, The Macmillan Co., 1933.

It is of especial interest in connexion with the Hampton Roads Conference.

Street, Wm. B.:

A sketch of General Joseph M. Street, in *Annals of Iowa*, July-October, 1895.

Vol. ii, at p. 92, describes Davis taking the irons from Black Hawk's hands. Copy, Fleming Mss. xxi. Vol. iii, p. 74, of the same *Annals*, contains a letters from Wm. B. Street stating how Davis happened to be given charge of Black Hawk.

Turner, R. S.:

*Recollections of Secession Convention of Virginia.*

A manuscript (unpublished) preserved in the Virginia Historical Society at Richmond. It argues the case of States' rights vs. Coercion with skill and erudition. The account of Lee's confirmation as head of Virginia's forces is of particular interest.

White, Laura A.:

*Robert Barnwell Rhett: Father of Secession.* New York and London, The Century Co., 1931, pp. 1-264, with Bibliography and Index.

It throws some light upon Davis' relations with the secession extremist group, led by Rhett.

## F. BOOKS AND COLLECTIONS OF GENERAL CHARACTER WHICH THROW ESPECIAL LIGHT UPON MR. DAVIS' CAREER

It is, of course, impossible to list the vast accumulation of books relating to the cause which he led or even the biographies of its chief actors. It is sufficient to refer the student to the extensive bibliography of some Confederate publications in the Confederate Museum, published in Part Two of Douglas Southall Freeman's *Calendar of Confederate Papers* (see p. 701 and p. 751).

It gives:

I. "Official Publications of the Government of the Confederate States of America."
II. "Official publications of the Governments of the Southern States."
III. "Unofficial Publications Relating to War Organization."
IV. "Contemporary History and Biography."
V. "Literary Works."
VI. "Confederate Text Books."
VII. "Political Miscellany."
VIII. "Religious Publications."
IX. "Periodicals."
X. "Almanacs and Miscellaneous."

In the present section are listed only such sources as have been found of value with reference to Davis.

Adams, Ephraim Douglass:

"Great Britain and the American Civil War." 2 vols. New York, Longmans, Green & Co., 1925.

The most comprehensive and authoritative history of British-American Relations during Davis' Presidency. It unfortunately lacks a Bibliography, without which the numerous footnotes are of little practical value.

Anon. [Rutledge]:

"Mr. Douglas and the Doctrine of Coercion." A rare pamphlet known as Tract No. 2. Copy in Confederate Museum. Pp. 1-24. It is signed "Rutledge."

Anon. (Wm. T. Thompson written in under the title):

*A Voice from the South.* Pamphlet, pp. 1-72, Baltimore, Samuel E. Smith, 1848.

A controversial pamphlet discussing the issues between the North and the South in 1848. Despite the absurd form in which it is written, a series of nine letters from "Georgia" to "Sister Massachusetts," and two to the Southern states, its arguments are so similar to those later used by Davis as to lead to the supposition that he had studied it. Copy of 8th ed. in Jackson, Miss., Collection.

Anon.:

*Life in the South by a Blockaded British Subject.* 2 vols. London, Chapman and Hall, 1863.

It covers the years 1860-1862, and is an interesting comment upon events as they transpired.

Anon. (The Great Seal):

Sigillologia, being some account of the Great Seal of the Confederate States of America. Washington, 1873.

The history of the finding of the Great Seal appears on pp. 457-458, vol. II, of the present biography.

Anon.:

"The Expedition against the Sauk and Fox Indians, 1832. By An Officer Who Served with General Atkinson." New York, 1914. Pamphlet (reprinted from the *Military and Naval Magazine of the United States*, of August, 1833). Copy in Rhodes Library, Oxford, England.

Bernard, Montague:

"A Historical Account of the Neutrality of Great Britain during the American Civil War." 1 vol., pp. 1-506, with index, 507-511. London, Longmans, Green, Reader and Dyer, 1870.

A comprehensive treatment of questions touching the history of international law which arose during the Civil War. The author quotes chiefly from printed dispatches and state papers available in England when the book was written. It is of value as showing the point of view of an eminent English scholar, but has only incidental connection with Mr. Davis' life as such. Bernard had previously published *Two Lectures on the Present American War*, Oxford and London, Nov., 1861.

Bigelow, John:

*France and the Confederate Navy, 1862-1868.* 1 vol., pp. 1-274. New York, Harper & Brothers, 1888.

A diplomat's account of the building of Confederate war vessels in France, and of the efforts made by the author, then Minister of the United States in Paris, to prevent their delivery to Davis' Government.

Bingham, R.:

"The Misunderstandings between the Sections of Our Common Country." Pamphlet, pp. 1-20, Hackney and Moale Co., Asheville, N. C., about 1904.

A highly suggestive and valuable pamphlet, but marred by errors of fact, as, for example, that Lee and Davis were of the same class at West Point. It seeks to prove that from 1825 to 1840 the United States Government taught her West Point cadets, from Rawle's view of the Constitution, that the Union was dissolvable, and that, if dissolved, allegiance reverted to the states. It also seeks to prove that, on the whole, the South had been less dominated by race prejudice than the free states.

Blackman, E. L.:

"Our Relations with America," a pamphlet published for distribution by the Committee of the Manchester (England) Southern Club. Manchester, England, 1863.

It is a reply to Richard Cobden's speeches in the House of Commons regarding the supply of ammunition to the belligerents, and British interest in the Federal pretensions. It advocates "immediate recognition of the South as an established confederacy."

Blaine, James Gillespie:

(1) "Jefferson Davis—Amnesty." In the House of Representatives, Jan. 10, 11, 12, 13, and 14, 1876. (In "Speeches by James G. Blaine, Benjamin H. Hill, James A. Garfield, and others.") Washington, 1876.

A convenient series of extracts from the records of Congress. Boston Public Library.

(2) *Twenty Years in Congress.* 2 vols. Norwich, Conn., The Henry Bill Publishing Co., 1886.

This well-known work presents Blaine's mature views of Davis and the cause which he led.

Bradford, Gamaliel:

(1) *Lee and Davis.* In *Atlantic Monthly*, Jan., 1911, vol. 107, pp. 62-72.

(2) *Confederate Portraits.* Boston, 1914.

(3) *The First Lady of the Confederacy,* a portrait of Mrs. Jefferson Davis. In *Harper's Magazine* for Aug., 1925.

(4) *Wives: a Set of Biographical Sketches of Wives of Outstanding Figures of American History.* Chap. vi is devoted to Mrs. Jefferson Davis. 1 vol., pp. 1-298. New York, Harper & Brothers, 1925.

An easy and interesting sketch of Mrs. Davis, with a full set of source references, and abundance of light incidents meant to reveal character. Massachusetts Historical Society.

(5) *Lee, the American.*

It contains chapters on Lee and Davis. An excellent style and a good knowledge of the sources make Bradford's books of value.

Bullock, James D.:

The Secret Service of the Confederate States, and how the Confederate cruisers were equipped. 2 vols. London, 1883.

An authoritative history, by the naval representative of the Confederate States in Europe. John Bigelow, Minister of the United States in France, in his *France and the Confederate Navy*, p. 70, n. (see Section E, *ante*), declares it proven by documents in his possession that the French Emperor knew that Bullock and his associates were equipping vessels for the Confederacy in France.

Callahan, J. M.:
*Diplomatic Relations of the Confederate States with England, 1861-1865.* American Historical Association Report, 1898, p. 267.
An excellent study.
Cowell, John Welsford:
"Southern Secession: a Letter Addressed to Captain M. T. Maury, Confederate Navy, on his letter to Admiral Fitzray." Pamphlet, pp. 1-99. London, Robert Hardwicke, 1862.
The first thirty-five pages are a plea to the South to avoid allowing the protective tariff principle to gain a footing among the states. The rest of the pamphlet consists of the texts of letters and documents quoted in the plea itself. The pamphlet aims to prove that the sole cause of Southern secession was the protective tariff. "The noisy and odious contest about 'free soil and slave soil,'" he says (p. 92), "was not a contest about slavery itself, nor for the extension or contraction of this hateful condition, but it was throughout a struggle on the part of the South to defend itself against a direct spoliation, never amounting in any year to less than £8,000,000." It is the argument of an anti-slavery Englishman who insists that the English have a right to trade with the South.
Curry, J. L.:
*A Civil History of the Government of the Confederate States.* 1 vol. Richmond, B. F. Johnson Publishing Co., 1901.
It shows the Federal and the Confederate Constitutions, printed in parallel columns.
Fisher, Sydney G.:
"The Suspension of Habeas Corpus during the War of the Rebellion." *Political Science Quarterly,* iii, 454-88 (Sept., 1888).
A convenient summary of an important, critical question.
Freeman, Douglas Southall:
*A Calendar of Confederate Papers, with a Bibliography of Some Confederate Publications.* Preliminary report of the Southern Historical Manuscripts Commission. Prepared under the direction of the Confederate Memorial Literary Society. A limited edition of one thousand numbered copies. 1 vol. Richmond, The Confederate Museum, 1908. (Described on p. 748.)
Gildersleeve, Basil:
*The Creed of the Old South.* 1 vol., pp. 1-128. Baltimore, The Johns Hopkins Press, 1915.
It was a jubilee reprint of an article which had appeared in the *Atlantic Monthly* of Jan., 1892, "which attracted wider attention than anything I have ever written," says the author. With it is an article entitled "A Southerner in the Peloponnesian War," from the *Atlantic Monthly* of Sept., 1897.
Gildersleeve, later a famous Greek scholar and professor at the Johns Hopkins University, fought as a private in the First Virginia Cavalry. N. Y. Public Library.

Goddard, Samuel A.:

*Letters of the American Rebellion.* 1 vol. London, Simpkin, Marshall & Co., 1870.

A series of detached letters, all strongly, often violently, pro-Northern in tone, discussing the war at various stages from the beginning to its end. It is at times careless of fact, especially in its persistent contention that the war was from the first a fight for the destruction of slavery in America.

If read as a brief and not as history, it is of great value, as it is an index of the opinions of the British press and other formers of British opinion from the beginning of the Civil War to its close.

The fervid character of Goddard's defence of the North reminds one of Thomas Jefferson's early enthusiasm for the French Revolution. "Rather than not see this most wicked rebellion put down," he wrote, on July 1, 1861, "I would see the whole American people sunk into the bottom of the ocean and myself with them" (p. 43). Rhodes Memorial Library, Oxford. It does only justice to Lincoln, but is unfair to the character of Davis.

Goode, John, Jr.:

"Personal Recollections of Peace Conference in Hampton Roads, and last meeting of General R. E. Lee and President Davis." Delivered before R. E. Lee Camp, No. 1, C. V., Jan. 10, 1902. Pamphlet, pp. 1-19. Richmond, 1902.

As Goode was not himself present at the conference, his recollections are really gleanings. Massachusetts Historical Society.

Hay, Thomas Robson:

"The South and the Arming of the Slaves." *The Mississippi Valley Historical Review,* June, 1919.

A convenient summary of somewhat obscure history. Fleming Mss., N. Y. Public Library.

"The Campaign and Battle of Chickamauga." *The Georgia Historical Quarterly,* Sept., 1923, pp. 213-250.

A searching criticism from a purely military point of view, but with little special reference to Davis, except as showing how loyally he supported leaders whom he trusted.

"Davis, Bragg and Johnston in the Atlanta Campaign." *Ibid.,* March, 1924, pp. 38-48.

An article designed to correct what its author considered H. J. Eckenrode's "rather erroneous and inaccurate account of the mutual relations of President Davis and General Bragg, especially as they relate to the Confederate leadership in the Atlanta campaign of the summer of 1864." It is of interest to students of military controversies, but throws little light upon Davis' character or life.

"The Atlanta Campaign." *Ibid.,* March and June, 1923.

The development of the campaign, Davis' increasing distrust of Johnston and the details of Johnston's removal, to give place to Hood and new Confederate disasters, are clearly set forth in this continued article which, however, gives nothing of value not to be found in Davis' own papers and writings.

"Joseph Emerson Brown, Governor of Georgia, 1857-1865." *Ibid.*, June, 1929.

A brief but comprehensive sketch of the Georgia Governor whose bitter quarrels with Davis have been the theme of many studies. A list of the chief ones is given in footnote 25 on p. 9 of the article under discussion.

"The Davis-Hood-Johnston Controversy of 1864." *Ibid.*, March, 1923.

A study of Davis-Johnston conflicts from the date of Johnston's assignment to the command of the Confederate army of Tennessee in December, 1863, to Hood's appointment of July, 1864. It is, therefore, a study of only a section of the long contest between Davis and Johnston, which began in West Point days. It was a contest which helped to reveal Davis' character, but presents a wearisome succession of military details which have lost all interest for any save technical students of military history.

The foregoing articles are but the evidences of preparation for Hay's *Hood's Tennessee Campaign*. New York, Walter Neale, 1929. 1 vol., pp. 17-265.

A detailed study of the use made by Hood of the power given him when Davis sent him to supersede Joseph E. Johnston during the Atlanta campaign. The book throws frequent flashes of light upon Davis as President and commander-in-chief of the Confederate armies, but is of only incidental value in the study of Davis himself. In Chapter vii, "The Responsibility for the Tennessee Campaign," Davis' actions and opinions are subjected to sharp and discerning criticism. "His inclination was for the glory of the battlefield rather than for the theory and practice of politics" is a statement which Davis' papers fully justify. In view of the long criticism of Davis for too much interfering in military matters, it is refreshing to find this author criticizing him for not cancelling the order for Hood's movement.

On the whole Thomas Robson Hay's able articles and book belong to the military historian rather than to the biographer of Jefferson Davis, whose chief importance lay quite outside military manœuvrings.

Highway, Davis:

"The Jefferson Davis National Highway." In *United Daughters of the Confederacy, 1929.*

A pamphlet outlining the history of the movement for a Jefferson Davis highway from sea to sea, with a map showing its route. It contains also many items of interest in connexion with Davis' life story. Massachusetts Historical Society.

Hunter, R. M. T.:

"The Peace Commission of 1865." First published in the *Philadelphia Weekly Times* and republished in April, 1877, in the *Southern Historical Society Papers*, vol. iii, no. 4, pp. 168-176: given in full in Rowland, viii, 128-136, together with several letters which Mr. Davis uses to prove Hunter's contentions false.

Johnson (R. U.) and Buel (C. C.), editors:

*Battles and Leaders of the Civil War.* 4 vols. New York, 1887.

It contains much first-hand material contributed by leaders in the war, Northern and Southern. Davis was invited to contribute and to answer the criticisms which General Johnston and General Beauregard had made of him in the series; but, says Robert Underwood Johnson, one of the editors, "he found our conditions unsatisfactory and the article was not written."

Johnston, R. M.:

*Bull Run, Its Strategy and Tactics.* Boston, 1913.

A valuable contribution to a difficult problem involving Davis' actions as President.

Latta, James W.:

"Was Secession Taught at West Point?" A pamphlet printed by the Military Order of the Loyal Legion of the United States, Commandery of the State of Pennsylvania, 1909, pp. 1-40.

The author's well-sustained contention is that "Secession was not taught at West Point." N. Y. Public Library, Fleming Collection.

Lothian, Marquis of (Wm. Schomberg Robert Kerr):

*The Confederate Secession.* Edinburgh and London, Wm. Blackwood & Sons, 1864. A book highly approved by Davis, on account of its sympathy with the South. See Davis to A. J. Beresford Hope, May 15, 1873. Text Rowland, vii, 343-344.

It was republished in French, *Librairie Achille Faure,* Paris, 1865, with an Appendix of one hundred and twenty-eight pages, meant to show the condition of slaves in America.

Moore, Albert Burton:

*Conscription and Conflict in the Confederacy.* 1 vol., pp. 1-367. New York, The Macmillan Co., 1924.

A history of the military problems of the Confederacy behind the lines. The author is Professor of History in the University of Alabama. The book gives a rather detailed, at times tedious, history of conscription, exemptions, the movement to enlist negroes, etc. The lack of dates at times makes the narrative confusing, but the book has substantial merit.

Moreau, Henry:

*La politique française en Amérique, 1861-1864.* Paris, 1864.

Valuable as giving a Frenchman's interpretation of the Civil War.

O'Sullivan, John L.:

(1) "Union, Disunion and Reunion." A letter to General Franklin Pierce. Pamphlet, pp. 1-122. London, Richard Bentley, 1862.

The aim is stated, to show "the absolute necessity of now modifying our Confederate system, by moderating our great national parties, purifying our politics, and reducing the action of the central forces, in order to adapt it to its enlarged scale of application." The footnotes contain material of much interest, illustrative of the principles involved in the war.

(2) "Recognition; Its International Legality, Its Justice and Its Policy." A letter to Lord Palmerston. Pamphlet, pp. 1-30. London, Waterlow & Sons, printers, 1863.

A not very convincing plea for recognition of the Southern Confederacy by England.

(3) "Peace, the Sole Chance Now Left for Reunion." A letter to Professor S. F. B. Morse. Pamphlet, pp. 1-25. London. Printed by Wm. Brown & Co., 1863.

An argument for peace "with amicable separation." Its tone is extreme as indicated by the statement: "Every man old and young, every child male and female, every woman, mother, wife, or girl, has now come to hate the North, with an indignant abhorrence beyond all words" (p. 8); or by this statement: "As a trustee I would at this moment (1863) prefer to place trust funds for permanent investment in the Southern war debt, at par, rather than in the Northern at one-fourth of its face" (p. 20). Or this: "The position of the inferior race is no better at the North than at the South" (p. 23).

Olmsted, Frederick Law:

*Journey in the Seaboard Slave States.* New York, 1856 (new edition in 2 vols., 1904).

This standard work upon slavery in the South was later combined with the author's *Journey through Texas*, New York, 1857, and his *Journey in the Back Country*, New York, 1860, to form the series, "Our Slave States." The three combined are the bases of his *Journeys and Explorations in the Cotton Kingdom*, 2 vols., London and New York, 1861.

Charles Eliot Norton declared Olmsted's books "the most important contributions to an exact acquaintance with the conditions and results of slavery in this country that have ever been published." Norton to H. H. Clough, Sept. 24, 1860: *Life and Letters,* i, 211.

Pollard, Edward Albert:

Pollard's undisguised hostility to Davis impairs but does not destroy the value of his writings, from the point of view of Davis' biographer. The following are his chief works:

(1) *Life of Jefferson Davis.* (See Pollard, under D, *ante.*)

(2) *The Southern Spy. Letters on the Policy and Inauguration of the Lincoln War.* Richmond, 1861.

(3) *The First Year of the War.* New York and London, 1863.

(4) *The Second Year of the War.* New York, 1864.

(5) *The Third Year of the War.* New York, 1865.

(6) *The War in America, 1863-4.* London, 1865.

(7) *The Lost Cause.* New York, 1867.

(8) *The Lost Cause Regained.* New York, 1868.

(9) *The Confederate Congress.* (*The Galaxy,* vi, 749. Dec., 1868.)

Rawle, William:

*A View of the Constitution of the United States of America.* 1 vol. Philadelphia, H. C. Carey and I. Lea, 1825.

This famous work is wrongly cited as the basis of Davis' training in constitutional law at West Point. It declares when discussing the proceedings of the Convention of 1787 (p. 297): "It was known, though it was not avowed, that a state might withdraw itself."

Rowland, Kate Mason:

"The English Friends of the Southern Confederacy."

A paper read on the "Third Historical Evening, Richmond, Va., Nov. 9, 1911." Pamphlet, pp. 1-10. Privately printed.

A very brief index to some prominent English friends of the South. Confederate Museum.

Miss Rowland's collection in the Confederate Museum contains many clippings, largely from Southern papers, touching many of the most controversial points in the life of Mr. Davis, though made with reference to the period rather than the person. They contain also an interesting photograph of John Wilkes Booth, and much information about his strange mind and "madness."

Scharf, Thomas:

*History of the S. C. Navy,* New York, 1887.

E. C. Wharton wrote to Davis, April 14, 1888: "He has evidently been at great pains to present a complete and accurate narrative" (Rowland, x, 49-54). Scharf's book was quoted with approval by Davis on May 8, 1889. *Scrap Book,* i, 15.

Schwab, John Christopher:

*The Confederate States of America, 1861-1865.* New Haven, Yale Univ. Press, mcmxiii.

A sketch of the financial and industrial history of the South during the Civil War, with a bibliography in which are listed many foreign publications regarding the fiscal history of the Confederacy.

Smith, Goldwin:

(1) *England and the War of Secession. Atlantic Monthly,* lxxxix, 303 (1902).

(2) *Does the Bible Sanction American Slavery?* London, 1863.

(3) *On the Morality of the Emancipation Proclamation.* London, 1863.

(4) *The Civil War in America,* 1866.

The author was an active and effective champion of the Federal Government during the American Civil War, when he was Regius Professor of Modern History at Oxford.

Spence, James M. P.:

(1) *The American Union; Its Effect on National Character and Policy,* with an *Inquiry into Secession as a Constitutional Right, and the Causes of the Disruption.* 1 vol., pp. 1-366. London, Richard Bentley, 1861.

A book by an Englishman highly sympathetic with the South. The closing sentence gives the gist: "We express earnestly . . . the clear conviction that nothing is more essential to the real welfare of the American people than a termination of the American Union." N. Y. Public Library.

(2) "On the Recognition of the Southern Confederation." Pamphlet, pp. 1-48. London, Richard Bentley, 1862.

A brief but not very convincing argument in favour of British recognition.

Stephens, Alexander H.:

*A Constitutional View of the Late War between the States.* 2 vols., 1867.

Generally considered the ablest book produced on the Southern side: written by the Vice-President of the Confederate States. As Stephens and Davis differed upon many points of public policy, the volumes contain invaluable material bearing upon the latter's life and public services. On October 13, 1877, Davis wrote Walthall: "In looking over Stephen's book I find it very valuable for dates and quotations, but his egotism causes many obliquities and more than improbable statements." (Rowland's *Jefferson Davis, Constitutionalist,* viii, 33).

A comparison of the quotations given by Stephens and those which later appeared in Davis' *Rise and Fall of the Confederate Government* will convince any fair-minded reader that Davis greatly profited by Stephens' labours.

Townsend, Hon. John:

"The Doom of Slavery in the Union: Its Safety Out of It." Pamphlet, pp. 1-39. Charleston, S. C., Evans and Cogswell, 1860.

It predicted that Lincoln would be elected and would proceed to attack slavery in the states.

Tyler, John, Jr.:

"Our Confederate States, Foreign and Domestic," *De Bow's Review,* July and August, 1864.

An article, largely speculative, about the attitude of foreign countries toward the Confederacy. Confederate Museum.

Wallis (S. Teackle) and Sherman (John):

Correspondence between. Pamphlet, pp. 1-31. Baltimore, Kelly, Hedian & Piet, 1863.

Its contents concern the arrest of the members of the Maryland Legislature, and the Mayor and Police Commissioner of Baltimore in 1861.

It throws valuable light upon these interesting items in Civil War history, which caused Davis so much thought and anxiety.

## DESIDERATA

The following works, referred to in Davis' papers, have not been found by the present author:

Davis, Creed T.: *The Davis Family.*

Mrs. Davis, writing to "Mrs. T. M. Green," on Dec. 31, 1900, from New York City, says: "There is a gentleman in Richmond, Mr. Creed T. Davis . . . who has written a book of the Davis' family which is now, he informs me, going through the press." (Text: Fleming Mss., xviii.)

Writing to Mrs. T. M. Green, from Richmond, Feb. 23, 1901, Creed T. Davis says of his book: "It is very comprehensive, and is made up almost entirely from the county records of Virginia." Writing again to Mrs. Green, on Jan. 17, 1902, he says: "Untoward circumstances have prevented the appearance of my book."

The present location of the manuscript is unknown to the present author.

Davis, Jefferson: *Unalterable Opposition to Repudiation.*

A pamphlet said by Davis' daughter, Margaret H. Jefferson Davis Hayes (text, Rowland's Clippings, dated Jan. 19, 1905), to have been prepared and circulated at his own expense during his race for Congressman-at-large, in 1843. The present author has not succeeded in finding a copy.

Drake, Benjamin:

*The Life and Adventures of Black Hawk.* Fleming Mss. XXI, quotes extracts from it. The present author has not found a copy.

Stevenson, R. R.:

*The Southern Side, or Andersonville Prison,* by one of the surgeons of the prison. Baltimore, 1876.

On Oct. 13, 1877, Davis wrote to Crafts J. Wright (text: Rowland viii, 35-36), "I presume you have . . . the book by Dr. R. R. Stevenson, one ol the surgeons at Andersonville. It contains a list of those who died and the diseases and treatment, etc."

And in his article, "Andersonville and Other War Prisons" (*Belford's Magazine,* Jan., 1890, p. 162), Davis says, "for a full description illustrated by a map, reference is made to the exhaustive work entitled, *The Southern Side; or Andersonville Prison,* by R. R. Stevenson, M.D., surgeon of Military Prison Hospital, etc."

The present author has not succeeded in finding a copy.

Williams, Benjamin:

"Davis' Career and Secession."

L. B. Northrop to Davis, Minor Orcus, Va., Sept. 8, 1886, says: "Have you read a piece by Mr. Benjamin Williams, of Mississippi, on your career and secession? It is the very best paper published since the war, a complete condensation of all that you wrote and did in your United States and Confederate career. . . . No Southern writer can approach him" (text; Rowland IX, 469-470). The present author has failed to find a copy.

# INDEX OF NAMES

# INDEX OF SUBJECTS